The consequences of economic rhetoric

The consequences of economic rhetoric

Edited by

ARJO KLAMER
University of Iowa

DONALD N. McCLOSKEY
University of Iowa

ROBERT M. SOLOW
Massachusetts Institute of Technology

The right of the
University of Cambridge
to print and sell
all manner of books
was granted by
Henry VIII in 1534.
The University has printed
and published continuously
since 1584.

CAMBRIDGE UNIVERSITY PRESS

Cambridge
New York   New Rochelle   Melbourne   Sydney

Published by the Press Syndicate of the University of Cambridge
The Pitt Building, Trumpington Street, Cambridge C2 1RP
32 East 57th Street, New York, NY 10022, USA
10 Stamford Road, Oakleigh, Melbourne 3166, Australia

© Cambridge University Press 1988

First published 1988

Printed in the United States of America

Library of Congress Cataloging-in-Publication Data

The consequences of economic rhetoric / edited by Arjo Klamer, Donald
McCloskey, Robert M. Solow.

  p.   cm.

Includes index.

ISBN 0-521-34286-4

1. Economics–Congresses.   2. Rhetoric–Congresses.   I. Klamer,
Arjo.   II. McCloskey, Donald N.   III. Solow, Robert M.
HB71.C65   1988
330–dc19   88–15095
                    CIP

British Library Cataloging-in-Publication applied for.

Contents

Preface

In the early spring of 1986 about thirty economists, economic journalists, rhetoricians, philosophers, a political scientist, and a literary theorist gathered at Wellesley College for a conference on the Rhetoric of Economics. The composition of the group seemed unusual. Economists and humanists, after all, live in two different cultures and usually do not take each other's scholarly activities seriously. The conference could be an indication that times are changing.

The change is the emergence of a new "conversation" *about* economics that aspires to displace the dominant, positivistic view. The time is ripe, since positivism is losing its grip on the collective consciousness of economists and others as well. Its claim that "logic" and "facts" are the sole standards for the appraisal of economic theories does not appear to do justice to the complex reality in which economists operate. The new conversation attempts to alter our understanding of the reality by calling attention to the discursive aspects of economics, more particularly to its rhetorical forms.

The editors of the volume called the conference to explore the consequences of and to understand the resistance to this new point of view. We considered the participation of philosophers, rhetoricians, and literary theorists alongside economic practitioners to be critical. After all, now that we economists are becoming interested in our language and in our rhetorical devices, we would do well to pay attention to those scholars who have spent their professional lives thinking, writing, and talking about these subjects.

We should make clear that we are not in full agreement on the importance of the new "conversation." In the first paper of the volume Arjo Klamer and Donald McCloskey express their unmitigated support, laying out the main characteristics of this new "conversation" and meeting the main arguments that have been leveled against it. In fact, the conference was very much a response to their earlier work, notably McCloskey's *Rhetoric of Economics* (1986), which expands on his 1983 *Journal of Economic Literature* article of the same title, and Klamer's *Conversations with Economists* (1983). Robert Solow, in the second paper, endorses the project, though expressing some reservations.

In recognition of the importance of authority and context, we briefly introduce the contributors and the context in which their papers should be placed.

Stanley Fish (English and Law, Duke University) represents the profession of literary theorists. His book *Is There a Text in This Class? The Authority of Interpretive Communities* (1980) stresses, among other issues, the constraints that an audience, or interpretive community, imposes on the reading of a text. We were informed that his talks are highly literary – perhaps too literary for an audience made up mostly of economists – and can be surprising. We are glad we invited him. The title of this book is a direct response to the challenge he posed.

Robert L. Heilbroner's authority does not need introduction. His *Worldly Philosophers* (first edition 1953) is still widely read, and he recently completed a book entitled *The Nature and Logic of Capitalism*. He did not formally present his essay at the conference, but expressed his criticism in the discussions. His criticism is an important one and we are therefore pleased that we could include his essay, which originally appeared as a review of McCloskey's book in the *New York Review of Books*.

Stephen Resnick and Richard Wolff (Economics, University of Massachusetts) are Marxist economists who have articulated in previous writings on epistemological issues a position that has remarkable similarities to the rhetorical position as developed by McCloskey and Klamer. We hoped to discover how far the similarities extended.

A. W. Coats (Economics, University of Nottingham, emeritus, Duke University) is one of the few economists who have written about the social and professional context of economics as a discipline. With Bruce Caldwell (an economic methodologist) he wrote a criticism of McCloskey's *Journal of Economic Literature* article on the rhetoric of economics (Caldwell and Coats, 1984). We asked him to elaborate on his criticisms and especially to explore the differences between the sociological and rhetorical approaches.

Robert W. Clower, former editor of the *American Economic Review* and currently at the University of South Carolina, presented a paper entitled ''Keynes and the Classicals Revisited.'' During the discussions he told us that more than ten years ago he had written about the rhetoric of economics, although without calling it so. We decided to reproduce his paper, which he originally gave as an address, because of its historical relevance and because it makes an important contribution to the discussion.

Cristina Bicchieri (Philosophy of Science, University of Notre Dame) has written on various subjects in the philosophy of science, in particular on the foundations of game theory. Since she is also interested in the role of metaphors and analogies in the development of scientific theories, we asked her to develop a philosophical perspective on the role of metaphors in scientific discourse.

Philip Mirowski (Economics, Tufts University) has written several articles in the vein of the new conversation. His participation offered an opportunity to explore the significance of the connections. In his contribution to this volume he argues that neoclassical economics started on the wrong analogical foot by taking nineteenth-century physics as its exemplar. (The essay has also appeared in *Economics and Philosophy*, 3 [April 1987]: 67–96).

E. Roy Weintraub resides in the bastion of history of economic thought, Duke University. He has written extensively on the recent history of equilibrium analysis. Until the year prior to the conference, his writing had applied the ideas of Lakatos, a philosopher whom McCloskey and Klamer would locate as being part of the old conversation. But Weintraub expressed interest in the possibilities of a rhetorical analysis. His paper in this volume is his first application of such an analysis.

Frank T. Denton (Economics, McMaster University) had already joined Ed Leamer, Zvi Griliches, and Donald McCloskey in the exploration of the rhetoric of econometrics. In view of the impressive status that econometrics currently enjoys, we considered the representation of this line of research critical.

Heidi Hartmann (in 1986 at the National Academy of Sciences) has written much on women's work and comparable worth, among other subjects. Nancy Folbre (Economics, University of Massachusetts) has written a variety of articles on the political economy of the family. The writings of both Hartmann and Folbre develop a critical view of neoclassical economics from the feminist perspective. We were interested to know whether the focus on language and metaphor could be of significance to their critical writings.

Craufurd D. Goodwin is the editor of the journal *History of Political Economy* and, like Weintraub, is at Duke University. As in Weintraub's case, the philosopher Imre Lakatos features dominantly in Goodwin's writing; his presidential address to the History of Economic Thought Society is an evalution of Lakatos's ideas (*HOPE* 12[4] 1980:610–19). At the conference Goodwin was willing to explore the territory beyond the one outlined by Lakatos and study the rhetorics of the interactions between economists and the people of the foundations who support economic research.

James K. Galbraith (Lyndon B. Johnson School of Public Affairs, University of Texas) served as executive director of the Joint Economic Committee. After his departure from active political life he began to write on the making of economic policy. He seemed the obvious person to ask for reflections on the effectiveness of economic rhetoric in the political arena.

Robert O. Keohane (Political Science, Harvard University) was invited as a political scientist to comment on the rhetoric of economics. In his field he is known as one of a small but growing group of political scientists who are interested in the applications of neoclassical economic theory.

David Warsh (Boston Globe) was invited along with other economic journalists to comment on the rhetoric of economists from a journalistic perspective. We expected that the rhetorical aspects would be especially clear to those who make a living deciphering and translating economics lingo. Warsh's paper is the only written, but representative, account of their contributions.

We recognize the financial support of the National Endowment for the Humanities, the Ford Foundation, and the National Science Foundation and appreciate the hospitality of Wellesley College. We also acknowledge the Wellesley students in the seminar on Economics as an Art of Persuasion for their active and critical participation in the conference. Stacia Quimby has been very helpful in the editing of this volume.

Arjo Klamer
Donald N. McCloskey
Robert M. Solow

The consequences of economic rhetoric

PART I

Economic rhetoric:
Introduction and comments

CHAPTER 1

Economics in the human conversation

Arjo Klamer and Donald N. McCloskey

Exordium

"As civilized human beings," wrote Michael Oakeshott in 1933, "we are the inheritors, neither of an inquiry about ourselves and the world, nor of an accumulating body of information, but of a conversation begun in the primeval forest and extended and made more articulate in the course of centuries." In economics a few years ago a conversation about the conversation began.

Why it began is not clear. It might be interpreted as just carrying on an old conversation about how economists know (if they do), a methodological conversation started a century and more ago by John Stuart Mill. The new remark in the early 1980s was simply that economists use arguments beyond syllogism and measurement. The point of making it was not to undercut the mathematics in economics, as nonmathematicians sometimes wish they could. The point was merely to note that all economists, mathematical or not, use analogies, appeals to authority, and other rhetorical devices, using them as thoroughly as poets and preachers, though with less understanding of why they do so. So the recent conversation about conversation can be interpreted as more of the old stuff, an inward and philosophical affair (Klant 1985).

The new conversation might also be interpreted as arising from the battle of schools. This would be additional looking inward. Disagreements among economists are commonly exaggerated, even by economists themselves, yet it is true that the field had become by 1980 more warlike than fifteen years before. Everyone knows about the battle between Keynesians and monetarists (the tags mean something different now to politicians than they once meant to economists). The other battles – Marxist versus neoclassical, classical versus Bayesian, Austrian versus statist, Chicago versus the rest of the world – have been more academic though no less vicious. By 1980 no economist could announce with a straight face that the business cycle was dead, science regnant, justice done. His pinstripe was ripped in the struggle, his tie blood spattered. The gore makes him wonder: What's going on here? The new conversation about the conversation noted merely that the weapons wielded were figures of speech, not strict logics alone; it noted that the older alliance had required stories to keep it together and that other alliances would require stories of their own.

These interpretations are fine. They go some way towards explaining why economists have begun a conversation about their conversation.

Narratio

But another interpretation is that they have started overhearing other conversations, becoming at last aware of the din outside. After a long and useful isolation, economists have begun to recivilize themselves.

Outsiders are surprised at how far economics has wandered away, since the 1940s, from the human conversation. The main, neoclassical conversation will listen to what is said among a few statisticians and a few electrical engineers; it listens intently to mathematicians, when it can catch their drift, hoping to achieve the Parisian accents of Bourbaki; it listens to the blare of the newspapers, or at least to the financial page. But beyond these there is not much listening going on. Economists are deaf on the job to history or philosophy; most of them yawn at talk of geography or psychology; they do not take seriously the incantations of anthropology or sociology; although they want to speak to law and political science, they do not want to listen. They ignore remoter conversations, as well as their own past. The suggestion that the study of literature or communication or even the nonliterary arts might speak to them would be regarded by many economists as absurd.

This deaf isolation is a shame. Economics is such a sweet discipline, such a beautiful model for social thinking, that it is a shame that most thoughtful people, irritated by the cultural barbarism of its practitioners, write it off as nonsense. They lose a chance to think clearly about economic growth or social justice. Yet it is also true that the conversations outside economics are so varied, so close to life as lived, that an economist who writes them off as emotion or nonscience or pictures at an exhibition irrelevant to the real thinking at hand will lose a lot, too. He will lose in fact the same thing the outsiders lose: a chance to think clearly about economic growth or social justice. A lot can be gained on both sides from breaking the isolation.

The conversation about conversation has helped break it. Economists have begun to see that their talk is rhetorical – in the ancient sense of honest argument directed at an audience. Realizing at last that economics uses arguments besides axiom-and-theorem and data-and-regress, they have begun to listen more intently to arguments elsewhere.

Reasons to participate in the new conversation are varied. We recognize some of them in the ruminations of the following characters.

FRUSTRATED SCIENTIST: I came to economics thinking it would be a science, like my high school chemistry. My teachers said it would be. I always liked chemistry – so much more conclusive than the discussions in history or English. As I moved beyond textbook verities in economics, though, I grew discouraged. Seldom is a result replicated (Dewald et al. 1985). The classical statistical procedures are violated daily (Tullock 1959; Griliches 1976; Denton 1985; McCloskey 1985). Empirical tests in economics are indecisive, predictions uncertain. I find now that economic seminars have as much inconclusive discussion as history or English ever did. Controversies in economics seem never to be decided; they just stop, at mutual exhaustion, or move on to some new fashion: rational expectations this year, game theory next. What, then, is the economic conversation really about? What sort of "knowledge" does it produce? It doesn't look a bit like the science I signed up for (Mayer, 1980).

POST-POSITIVIST PHILOSOPHER: My interest in economics is mainly philosophical. I expected it to be a fulfillment for the social sciences of the positivist program: objective, operational, quantitative, hypothetico-deductive, a chapter in a scientific philosophy, an entry in the international encyclopedia of unified science. This expectation, formed in graduate school, has been painfully disappointed. I share in part the disappointments of my friend here, Frustrated Scientist. But after late Popper, Toulmin, Kuhn, Lakatos, and Feyerabend (not to speak of Rorty and the wild French and Germans) I'm less sure that the science/nonscience dichotomy is worth much. The search for a demarcation criterion seems to have run out steam. I grow cynical: adherence to "knowledge" in economics, then, must be a matter of sheer taste or sheer power, right? Or are there other ways of reestablishing standards, once the old rules, which did not provide standards, go by the board?

POLITICAL ECONOMIST: All of you miss the point, which is not to understand history but to change it. In this, too, there's something wrong with the conversation. It seemed to me in my youth that economics was a tool for social engineering and social betterment. I came to Washington in 1968 filled with enthusiasm for cost-benefit analysis in the department of defense and fine tuning in the Federal Reserve System; but I left ten years later depressed. I saw the social engineers propose a dozen different designs for the same bridge. After a while there was a finished bridge, but it didn't go where it was supposed to go. At last the whole thing fell to pieces in a light wind out of Saudi Arabia. I get no credit here for quick insight, by now at least I know what the question is: Why doesn't social policy work? Sure, sure: The politicians and bureaucrats don't carry it out. But there's something wrong, too, with our conversation as economist that we can't advise them – and each other – in more persuasive ways.

SOPHISTICATED ACADEMIC RESEARCHER: Don't give yourself airs. I myself know, roughly, how to write a paper that will persuade my academic colleagues on a certain point of logic or fact. That's all you know. You've been listening to social and scientific visionaries. What is important is the change in the way economists argue. I see changes coming in statistical procedures, for example, that will alter the conversation radically. Microcomputers have made simulations possible for the masses. The cheapening of computation has made algorithms more respectable relative to existence theorems. The academic philosophy or public policy never did matter: What matters is the next turn in the argument. The old, Hilbertian way of arguing will have to move over.

ECONOMIC JOURNALIST: The Ivory Tower speaks. And no one listens. Look, what matters to most people is what comes down from the tower as newsworthy ideas. I once viewed economists either as social weather forecasters or as spokespeople for special interests. So my stories had one of two lines: either this is Herr Doctor Professor delivering the genuine scientific Word or this is just another lobbyist. But I have become uneasily aware that such categories are not good ways to get the story. Like everybody else, economists try to manipulate the press, but to what end is seldom clear (Solow 1981: 17). Economists seem to be passionately attached to ideas that can't predict, that can't be proved, that they can't be made understandable, and that don't always serve their self-interests. What is the talk among economists for? Is it just "communicating results," as the rhetoric of science would imply? I ask again the journalist's question: What's going on here?

There are plenty of others: Sophomore Student, a wise fool ("Why does economics have to be so far from common sense?"), Worried Forecaster ("A noncommonsensical science should be able to predict better"), Rational Expector ("It's common sense that economic science *can't* predict the future"), Irritated Eleemosynary Executive ("If this stuff isn't predictive science, beyond common sense, what am I giving all this dough for?"). All of these have contributed to the unease, or have constituted it. It is the unease that comes before people change the subject of conversation.

Explicatio

The knowledge these unhappy people seek presents certain puzzles, which account for their unhappiness.

Presumably economic knowledge is manufactured in the 10,000 or so articles catalogued annually in the *Index of Economics Articles*. Economics is a field of articles rather than one of books, although less so than physics, its model beloved from afar. Most of the articles present a fact or two, advise the prince, suggest an easy tool. Probably most of the articles, as is said to be the case in the physical and biological sciences, are wrong or irrelevant. Only a few have influence.

The articles pose the puzzle of what constitutes economic knowledge, the puzzle of publication. Even the most influential articles are puzzling. Consider Robert Lucas's famous article, "Some International Evidence on Output-Inflation Trade-offs" (1973), or Gary Becker's even more famous article, "A Theory of the Allocation of Time" (1965). Is their knowledge a set of hypotheses, exactly? What is the hypothesis in either case? Or is it a method of analysis, perhaps a way of talking? Or a pleasing story?

In Becker's article the knowledge is presented in the rhetoric of the hypothetico-deductive model of science ("little systematic testing of the theory has been attempted. . . . The theory has many interesting . . . implications about, empirical phenomena. . . ."), but it looks more like a charming metaphor, an analogy between budgets of income and budgets of hours. In Lucas's article the knowledge is presented in the rhetoric of the empirical finding, but looks more like a reading of history, one of many possible readings permitted by the data. One wonders whether economists could agree on what constituted the remarkableness of these remarks in the scientific conversation. And for more routine articles the puzzle is more puzzling. T. F. Cooley and S. F. LeRoy (1981) have showed that prior convictions about monetarism as against Keynesian have large effects on the *econometric* results of the normal science they studied. What would be the point of publishing one's prior convictions dressed up as "findings"?

Or consider another literature of economics, the textbook, and another forum, the classroom. These pose the puzzle of teaching. The textbooks are usually written in the same fiercely scientific rhetoric as the articles. But the professor facing the class must compromise with human speech. An economist cannot teach successfully with axiom and finding. Those who try receive low ratings, except from the math majors, who miss the main point anyway. And the students do not learn how to reason economically.

But if axiom and finding constitute economic knowledge, why is it so disastrously dull and ineffective to use them in the classroom? Real knowledge is interesting. What then is to be taught in a class beyond the number of Federal Reserve Banks and the definition of elasticity of demand? Something more than unconnected bits of fact and logic must be involved. The puzzle is that the bigger bits of analogy and attitude are not mentioned in the texts. Such is the puzzle of teaching.

Or consider what happens in academic seminars or in the hallway, away from the students: the puzzle of scientific doubt. Economists will often express doubt that a properly scientific finding in economics is true: "Sure, his *t*-statistics are fine, but I just don't believe it." Such doubt plays a role in other sciences, too. It is not scandalously unscientific, though economists think so, and mope around the faculty club depressed by the unscientific character of their field. Economists have no rhetoric beyond the grunt of disbelief for articulating most doubts. The rhetorical situation is demoralizing. An economist asked why he goes on writing such dubious stuff will say with lame cynicism, "I don't really *believe* it: I do it just for fun."

There is an opposite puzzle to that of doubt: It is the puzzle of scientific dogma. Economists march to and fro under different banners, raising huzzahs for different candidates for the Nobel Prize. Party loyalty provides a career. The young upwardly mobile economist always votes at his party's call. And never thinks of thinking for himself at all. Yet the existence of schools fits poorly with the received theory of science. The theory most economists espouse (although unlike their physicist heroes, they seldom carry it out) says that "findings" will falsify the "hypothesis," and then of course everyone will change his mind. But nobody changes his mind.

Partitio

Economists, we would suggest, may be looking in the wrong direction altogether, or to put it better, listening to the wrong words. The notion of knowledge has long been influenced by a metaphor of seeing. Since Descartes and the New Scientists of the seventeenth century we have spoken habitually of the known as "seen" (Rorty 1979): "I see what you mean"; "Seeing is believing." Scientific reflection is to be a mirror of nature, as Bacon wrote in 1620: ". . . the minds of men are strangely possessed and beset, so that there is no true or even surface left to reflect the genuine ray of things" (Bacon 1965; 317).

This seeing or reflecting, however, is a lonely, pallid sort of event, and does not look especially promising as a foundation for thought. The seeing metaphor is specific to a culture and language, not written in the heavens. Contrast the "seeing" = "knowing" = "loving" in the Hebrew of the Bible. The lonely and antisocial character of "seeing" is apparent in the Greek grammatical distinction between verbs of seeing (or honest-to-goodness, dignified, God-given knowing) and verbs of saying (or mere social, human, temporary believing). The grammatical distinction in Greek between the mind's eye and the society's ear has blindly and silently influenced later thinking.

A student can by himself *see* with his mind's eye the proof of the irrationality of the square root of two. But if another person is to believe, there must be communication, saying. There must be a sender/encoder sending a message to a receiver/decoder. It is not enough to point wordlessly at the sheer message, mirrored from nature. The positivist model of scholarship cuts out the sender and the receiver as irrelevant to knowledge. Knowledge without human speech is merely an ideal type in the mind of God, or of the godlike mathematician inarticulate at his desk. Science entails communication. And the better metaphors for communication are speaking and listening, not seeing.

The way things are communicated matters in economics. The mere idea that people are paid "what they are worth," for example, can be uttered in various languages, resulting in different economics. Uttered in the language of historical relations and moral indignation it is a statement in classical Marxism. Uttered in the language of evolution and competition it is a statement in social Darwinism, a comfort to the country club. Uttered in the language of continuous mathematics it becomes the "marginal productivity" of economics since 1900, carrying with it a rich set of images about "production functions" and "amounts" of labor. Uttered again in the language of discrete mathematics it becomes a branch of a new Marxist economics in the 1960s, or the linear programming of an oil refinery. These all contain, one might say, "the same basic idea" (all ideas are "basic" when this point is being made). And so it may be "the same," crudely speaking. But the way of speaking modifies the idea, reversing, for instance, its political uses. "Marginal productivity" can justify a stony laissez-faire; "to each according to his need" can justify a revolutionary slaughter.

A disorder in communication, we are suggesting, explains the unhappy mood of economics. The analogy of "sender" and "receiver," however, which is what springs to mind when people start talking about "communication problems," oversimplifies the situation, making it sound like a job for the repairman. In most communication the message is not a preformed slug, a mere telephone number to be read out by a computer at Directory Inquiries (once named "Information"). Commonly the demands of the communication – which is to say, the presence and character of the audience, the attitudes of audience and speaker to each other, the language spoken in common, the history of earlier talk, the practical purpose to be achieved from the communication – change the message. They do not "distort" it always (the metaphor of distortion assumes again that the preformed slug sits there ready to be found); the demands of communication merely change the message. Commonly, in other words, there is no "it" to be communicated without communication.

The issue is the rhetoric of economics. This is not its "rhetoric" in a merely ornamental sense. The sender–receiver metaphor, though an improvement on the metaphor of merely "seeing" the message without transmission, suggests that anything aside from the message slug is noise. But the use of a certain kind of mathematical language in expressing, say, the reward for labor sends along its own substantive message. What is sent is not mere prettiness (although prettiness has its place, too). Rhetoric is not ornament added on after the substance has been written. It is not rhetoric in the sense usual nowadays, the "mere rhetoric" we all wish to avoid. On the contrary, it is the whole art and science of argument, the honest persuasion that is good conversation.

The point of talking about "rhetoric" is to make available to economists again another river of our civilization, running as most do down from the mountains of Greece. It is the river of discourse, the thought sprung from the sophist Protagoras of Abdera concerning orations, persuasion, poetry, symbolism, storytelling, and literature in general. It is the thinking of literary intellectuals and of lawyers.

If economists were to consider the matter they would probably view themselves as paddlers on the rivers sprung from the mathematician Pythagoras or the philosopher Plato or the scientist Aristotle (although while we are on the subject, it might be noted that they are in fact more deeply immersed than they realize in the history of Thucydides). The task is get them to listen to more Greeks. Greek and Latin resound again in the halls of the intellectuals (Keynes and Edgeworth and Mill among economic intellectuals had the advantage that they could read the classical languages with ease). The tags invented by Plato and refined by Descartes, Kant, and Russell were once dominant in the conversation but have recently seemed unpersuasive, to be replaced by rhetorical appeals from Aristotle, Cicero, and Quintilian. The new rhetoric has been attended to by an audience of philosophers (Toulmin 1958; Rosen 1980; Rorty 1983; Walton 1985), rhetoricians (Scott 1967; Lyne and McGee 1987), lawyers (Perelman and Olbrechts-Tyteca 1958; White 1984, Ch. 9; White 1985), anthropologists (Geertz 1988; Rosaldo 1987), theologians (Ball 1985; Klemm 1987), literary critics (Fish 1980; Booth 1974; Burke 1950; Richards 1925), political scientists (Nelson 1983), psychologists (Carlston 1987), historians (White 1973; Megill and McCloskey 1987), and even mathematicians (Davis and Hersh 1981). These people have noticed in their works on philosophy or anthropology or mathematics that they use analogies, tell stories, adopt a persona. Economists should join the crowd.

The new conversation replaces the logic of inquiry with a rhetoric of inquiry. "Replaces" is perhaps too strong a word: Rhetoric, the art of argument, already includes what is presently called "logic" as a part. The logic is usually a routine and minor part, even in regions of the conversation supposedly dominated by it. A. E. Housman noted of textual criticism that "accuracy is a duty, not a virtue"; in mathematics, too, logic is a duty, not a virtue. The mathematical idea is the virtue. But anyway the old talk about the logic of appraisal, the criteria for truth, the logic of explanation, and the rational reconstruction of research programs is to be expanded into talk about genres, arguments, metaphors, implied authors, and domains of discourse. The point is to figure out why some arguments work in economics and others don't. Figuring it out in literary ways will resolve some of the puzzles.

Amplificatio

When economists look at a phenomenon like "child care" they think of markets. "Child care" – which to other people looks like a piece of social control or a set of buildings or a problem in social work – looks to economists like a stock certificate traded on the New York exchange. By this choice of metaphor they are driven to identify a demand curve, a supply curve, and a price. If the economists are of the regular, neoclassical kind, they will see "rational" behavior in such a market; if they are Marxists or institutionalists or Austrians, they will see somewhat different things. But in any case the seeing will seem to them to make ordinary sense, to be the way things really truly are.

A rhetorician notes that the "market" is "just" a figure of speech. It is a commonplace, a *locus communis, a topos* – a place where economists hunt for their game. In the way of talking here the metaphor of a "conversation" is a *topos* for the language game of economics.

The conversational figure of speech implies the Similarity Argument: that the economic conversation shares many features with other conversations, so differently placed. The economic conversation has much in common with, say, poetic conversation, as is demonstrable in a detail beyond rational patience. Solomon Marcus (1974) listed fully fifty-two alleged differences between scientific and poetic communication (rational versus emotional, explicable versus ineffable, and so forth), and after much thought rejected the majority as crudities. He notes that there is as much variation within scientific and poetic communication as between them.

Logic, for example, is not the preserve of economists and calculators. The Metaphysical poets were addicted to logical forms, forms viewed as figures of speech by writers still educated in rhetoric. John Donne's "Song" begins with a *reductio ad absurdum* ("Go and catch a falling star,/ Get with child a mandrake's root/ . . . And find/ What wind/ Serves to advance an honest mind"), turns then to an inferential argument ("Ride ten thousand days and nights . . . And swear/ No where/ Lives a woman true and fair"), and finishes with what an economist would call an assessment of a low prior probability ("If thou find'st one, let me know;/ . . . Yet do not; I would not go,/ Though at next door we might meet./ . . . Yet she/ Will be/ False, ere I come, to two or three'').

Marvell's ''To His Coy Mistress'' is the type of an argumentative poem. The argument is, of course, economic: Had we but world enough and time I could court you, Lady, as your value warrants, to satiation, but time is scarce, and life especially so; the rate of time discount is therefore positive, and the optimal consumption plan is therefore *carpe diem*. Marvell makes his appeal relentlessly but smirkingly: He plays with a convention and mocks it, as language games have a tendency to do. The economist plays no less within a convention when drawing on inference (N = ten thousand days and nights) or time discount (t = Deserts of vast Eternity), or when making little jokes about islands in the labor market or how the data have been massaged. The flatfooted among economists and poets lack this sense of irony about arguments. They pen lines like ''The coefficient is significant at the 0.00000001 level'' or ''I think that I shall never see/ A poem lovely as a tree.'' But Keynes or Yeats, Stigler or Stevens sing on.

Similarity is not identity. Economics may be *like* poetry, but it is plainly not the same, unhappily. The likenesses between stocks and child care will allow the *topos* of the Market to work, but there are differences, too, that will figure sometimes. Academic poets have different conversations sometimes from greeting card poets, and different in other ways from economists, however poetic the economists may be.

It is illuminating therefore to look at more obviously similar conversations, such as economic journalism. It is sometimes written by journalists with no academic pretensions, but it is also written at times by academic economists gifted in this way, such as Milton Friedman, J. K. Galbraith, and Lester Thurow. The audience commonly thinks that such writings are academic economics ''translated'' into plain English. Without prejudice, they are not (Which is not to say that economic journalism is easy, or inferior to seminar talk: Anyone who can replicate Adam Smith would be justly rich; few academic economists are rich.)

The journalistic conversation runs on a particular psychology, depending on individuality, evil, and suspense. In the talk that market people use to dignify their work a market is ''excited'' or ''depressed,'' overrun with bulls or bears, slit with cutthroat competition. Entrepreneurs are portrayed as pioneers whose courage and creativity extends the frontiers of what is economically possible, or they are portrayed in a story from Lincoln Steffens or Ralph Nader as the devils who oppress the powerless and drive up prices. The ''story'' is just that: a piece in a newspaper. The black hat appears in it as a foreign country underselling ''our'' products or ''beating us'' in productivity. Us/ them is the order of day, expressed in pervasive sporting and military metaphors. Personalizing images are common, as in the talk of the street.

A masterful example is Lester Thurow's recent book, *The Zero-Sum Solution* (1985). The book is sporting. "To play a competitive game is not to be a winner – every competitive game has its losers – it is only to be given a chance to win. . . . Free market battles can be lost as well as won, and the United States is losing them on world markets" (p. 59). One chapter is entitled "Constructing an Efficient Team." Throughout there is talk about America "competing" and "beating" the rest of the world with a "world-class economy." Thurow complains that many people do not appreciate his favorite metaphor and calls it a "reality": "For a society which loves team sports . . . it is surprising that Americans won't recognize the same reality in the far more important international economic game" (p. 107). In more aggressive moods he slips into a military uniform: "American firms will occasionally be defeated at home and will have no compensating foreign victories" (p. 105). Foreign trade is viewed as the economic equivalent of war.

Three metaphors govern Thurow's story: (1) the metaphor of the international zero-sum game, (2) a metaphor of the domestic "problem," and (3) a metaphor of "we." *We* have a domestic *problem* of productivity that leads to a *loss* in the international *game*. Thurow has spent a long time interpreting the world with these linked metaphors.

The metaphors are not the usual ones in economics. The metaphor of exchange as a zero-sum game, in fact, has been the favorite of antieconomics since the eighteenth century. The subject in Thurow as (on the other side) in Adam Smith the Elder is the exchange of goods and services. If exchange is a game, it might be seen as one in which everyone wins, like aerobic dancing. Trade in this view is *not* zero sum. To be sure, from the factory floor it looks like zero sum, which gives Thurow's metaphor an air of common sense. To a business person "fighting" Japanese competition in making automobiles, her loss is indeed Toyota's gain. But the competitive metaphor looks at only one side of the trade, the selling side. Economists more usually claim to see around and underneath the economy. Underneath it all (as the economists say, in their favorite metaphor) Jim Bourbon of Iowa trades with Tatsuro Saki of Tokyo. A Toyota sold pays for 2,000 tons of soybeans bought. The economic metaphor suggests a different attitude towards trade than that of Friedrich List, the German theorist of the *zollverein,* or Henry Carey, the American theorist of protection in the nineteenth century, or Lester Thurow.

Talking in such a rhetorically self-conscious way about a piece of economic journalism is not just a rhetorical trick for attacking it. The point is that all conversations are rhetorical, that none can claim to be the Archimedean point from which others can be levered. The neoclassical economists use metaphors, too, of humans as calculating machines and rational choosers. The human situation is said to be a situation of rational choice, the maximization of an objective function subject to environmental constraints. The metaphor is less warm than one that portrays economics as a struggle between good and evil or as the final rounds of the NBA playoffs, but it is no less metaphorical on that count.

The rational-choice model is the master metaphor, enticing one to think "as if" people really made decisions in this way. The metaphor has disciplined the conversation among neoclassical economists – the discipline is: If you do not use it, out you go – and has produced much good. To it we owe insights into subjects ranging from the consumption function in the twentieth century to the enclosure movement in the eighteenth. Yet, to repeat, it is a metaphor.

Neoclassicals are very fond of it, and regard it as the fundament of their being, the part on which the body of their knowledge rests. What is problematical is the "positive" and "objective" status they ascribe to it. It was not always so. Ambiguity and contention surrounded the triumph of choice logic as the definition of economics, and it was by no means always regarded as an innocent analytic technique. Jevons found it persuasive on the nonmodern grounds that it fitted with Bentham's calculus of pleasure and pain; Pareto, too, credited it with psychological significance. Like most of the inventors of economics, Pareto was no isolated talker: a sociologist as much as an economist, he declared, "Clearly, psychology is fundamental to political economy and all the social sciences in general" (1971; 129), a suggestion that has only recently been revived.

Nor was J. M. Keynes, our blessed inventor of macroeconomics, isolated in Gordon Square from the wider human conversation. Keynes probably did not get much support from Virginia or Lytton for using the logic of choice as a metaphor of human behavior, and G. E. Moore up in Cambridge surely would not have approved. Whatever little there is of it in *The General Theory of Employment, Interest and Money* is subordinated to talk of "animal spirits," "psychological laws," waves of optimism, crises of confidence, and other notions in business psychology.

But later modernists disciplined this expansive spirit of Keynes, rereading him as a Keynesian. Hicks and Hansen reduced him to a page and a diagram; Tobin, Modigliani, and their heirs fitted him into the corsets of choice theory. By such rhetorical moves the text was permanently transformed. Economists have known for some time how the book should be read (Leijonhufvud 1968) but do not want the old meanings back. They have made up their own text, and now the graduate student need not read the original. The conversationalists have forgotten what they were saying. As Axel Leijonhufvud said: "The impression of Keynes that one gains from [his interpreters] is that of a Delphic oracle . . . mouthing earth-shattering profundities whilst in a senseless trance – an oracle revered for his powers, to be sure, but not worthy of the same respect as that accorded the High Priests whose function it is to interpret the revelations. If this be how Economics develops – where will it all end?'' (1968: 35). All the founders of modern economics have been reread this way, though an end may be near: Pareto's sociology was for a long time ignored, Marshall's economic history forgotten, Walras's similarity to linguistics overlooked, and Frank Knight's philosophy, matured in Iowa, has been rewritten as a step in the neoclassical synthesis circa 1960.

The neoclassical conversation about the logic of choice, despite the centripetal force of a mathematics teachable to all, has itself tended to break into smaller groups. The new classical macroeconomists have enchanted many young people with their fervor. The neo-Keynesians, once themselves fervent, hold back (Klamer 1983), finding solace in tales of Akerlof and sayings of Sen. The other heirs of David Ricardo diverge more sharply from the faith. Even when educated in neoclassical economics the Marxists object to its reduction of the social to the individual; the Austrians object to the aggregation of the individual in the social. The Marxists prefer a conversation about the class basis of work, the Austrians a conversation about the ineffable individuality of the entrepreneur. The mutual overlap of these conversations is large – you can get any economist to talk to you about the entry of new firms into ecological niches, for example, or the adequacies of a monetary theory of inflation – but the lack of overlap is large, too.

To speak of conversations being more or less similar yet having different notions of how to persuade makes a monist angry. Such speech is in fact a good monist-detection device. Say ''Truth is plural'' and watch the color of his nose. The device should be more widely applied. The monists have had their way for too long in the modern world, traveling about from conversation to conversation instructing people in the Monist Law. ''Intelligence,'' they say, ''must be measured in a single number and be used for social policy.'' ''The writing of history is chiefly a matter of gathering preexisting facts from archives.'' ''Economics must not use questionnaires, because any behaviorist knows that these might be falsely answered.'' ''Economics will only be a real science when it uses experiments like those a withered branch of psychology once depended on.''

The new pluralist and pragmatic and rhetorical conversation about the conversation ''weaves a web of significance,'' in Clifford Geertz's phrase, around the talk of economists. The new conversation in economics is only imitating what the economists themselves actually do with their stories and metaphors when they talk about the Federal Reserve.

Economics, then, should step down from the pedestal on which, like the women of the 1950s, it fondly imagines it stands. A conversation in modern economics differs from economic journalism but is similar, differs from poetry but is similar, differs from mathematics but is similar. There is no hierarchy here, no monist philosopher king reaching into conversations to spoil their tone. We recommend a rhetorically sophisticated culture for economists, following Richard Rorty (1982), "in which neither the priests nor the physicists nor the poets nor the Party were thought of as more 'rational,' or more 'scientific' or 'deeper' than one another. No particular portion of culture would be singled out as exemplifying (or signally failing to exemplify) the condition to which the rest aspired" (p. xxxviii). The present attitude, at least among those who have not yet felt the doubts of the Frustrated Scientist and the others, is ignorance about the variety of economics and of similar conversations, an ignorance breeding contempt. Economic scholars should oppose ignorance and contempt.

Being a good conversationalist asks for more than does following some method. Alarmingly, it asks for goodness. Cato the Elder said that an orator was no mere hired gun, ready with pen or computer to advise whatever power offered the most satisfactory career. He (in Rome not "she") was *"vir bonus dicendi peritus,"* the *good* man skilled at speaking. Plato, who detested a rhetoric without moral purpose, has Socrates announce towards the end of the *Gorgias* that "rhetoric is to be used for this one purpose always, of pointing to what is just, and so is every other activity" [527 C]. These Romans and Greeks were much inclined to moral talk.

Talking about goodness in this connection embarrasses modern sensibilities, like announcing loudly to a dinner party that one has been born again in Jesus Christ. But it is hard to see a relevant epistemology other than a moral one (and the usual epistemology is merely moral argument that does not recognize itself). It is not good method that makes an economist good or bad, but goodness, in the usual scout handbook sense: honesty, bravery, tolerance, consideration. Mere intelligence is not enough to sustain the conversation.

Refutatio

Such conversation about the conversation usually evokes affirmative nods. The main reaction is "Well, yes, I see what you mean, and, of course, it's true: We economists do employ a wider range of argument than we imagine. Perhaps we *had* better think through what sort of conversation we are having. And as for goodness, I've always favored that." But the philosophically committed – few in economics, it should be noted – will sometimes shake their heads vigorously, "No." They need here to be refuted; or, more considerately, reassured.

The Chaos Argument: "If we abandon all standards and deny the existence of any criterion of truth, anything goes. And everything will." For most important questions there is of course no universal, timeless, culture- and value-free standard of what a worthwhile coefficient in a regression is or what a serious divergence from competition is. But that does not mean that real conversations take place without standards. The conversations of a scholarly community such as that of economics are disciplined. We have argued that they are disciplined by a wider and more difficult set of standards than are provided by Marxism or Positive Economics. One learns to speak in the conversations by internalizing the standards. The least informative remarks are those that take their standards from a philosophy rather than from a practice of speech.

The Hitler-and-Other-Irrationalists Argument: "According to the rhetorical approach, everything is relative, so Hitler would be irrefutable." No, he would not: he was no *vir bonus,* however much a *dicendi peritus.* He was refutable by appeal to rhetorical standards and was indeed so refuted. He was *not* refutable by a *wertfrei* economics. It is sometimes claimed, as Terence Hutchison put it in 1938, that Hitler and all our woe came precisely from "psuedo-science," and that testability of the usual simpleminded sort is "the only principle or distinction practically adoptable which will keep science separate from pseudo-science" (p. 11). This is unpersuasive. Victorian – and even British and statistical and scientific – theories of race were testable and tested. They passed the tests, at least to the satisfaction of scientists in the grip of positivist metaphors of objectivity and measurement (Gould 1981). Probably the successes or failures of science had little to do with the rise of Hitler. But if anything, it is a narrow, amoral economics that leads to slave labor camps.

The Fallacy Argument: "These rhetorical methods are mere fallacies beside the certainty of syllogism and measurement." To repeat, what we assert is that there are no timeless claims for or against a particular discursive practice. We take no pleasure in reporting from the 2,500-year-old discussion of the matter that there are no foundations, but there you are: One must learn to live with it. Syllogism and measurement are fine but represent merely one among many rhetorical turns. The twenty-first century may revive the argument from design or begin again to make philosophical arguments in Latin hexameters. Now we use the arguments we find persuasive.

Such cultural relativism does not commit us to nihilism. No one could attack an economic argument nowadays by asserting that its advocates have red hair. The rhetorical approach makes it possible to understand why such an argument would fail in our speech community. The methodological approach, on the other hand, dumps the red-hair argument into a big box labeled "Fallacy." The dumping ignores the great relevance in some cases of the argument *ad hominem:* It would not be irrelevant that the advocates of an empirical finding were notoriously sloppy at econometrics or were employed by Hitler.

The Reactionary-Plot Argument: "Rhetoric is merely another justification of neoclassical economics." No, it is not. Radical and Austrian economists have in fact seen it as a way to criticize neoclassical economics. They have also seen it as a way to criticize each other. Fine. Let a hundred flowers blossom.

Peroratio

The Antieconomics Argument: "Rhetoric is an attack on economics, undermining the claims of economics to be a scientific discipline." No, no. Economics is too successful to be undermined by mere self-consciousness. The archaic attachment to scientism is the real danger, narrowing the conversation and raising false hopes of certainty. Like doctors, sociologists, and others in love with scientific status but uncertain whether they are actually scientific, economists now seek to overawe the world, and overawe each other. As actually practiced, though, economics is more down-to-earth than this, but more complicated, too. It uses many arguments, difficult to devise – the good story as much as the good theorem, the good analogy as much as the good regression equation. A rhetoric of economics examines all the arguments, and encourages admirable goodness in argument all round.

References

Bacon, Francis. 1965. *The Great Instauration [Instauratio Magna]*. In *Francis Bacon: A Selection of His Works*, edited by S. Warhaft. Indianapolis: Bobbs-Merrill.

Ball, Milner S. 1985. *Lying Down Together: Law, Metaphor, and Theology*. Series on the Rhetoric of the Human Sciences. Madison: University of Wisconsin Press.

Becker, Gary S. "A Theory of the Allocation of Time." *Economic Journal* 75 (September): 493–517.

Booth, Wayne C. 1974. *Modern Dogma and the Rhetoric of Assent*. Chicago: University of Chicago Press.

Burke, Kenneth. 1950. *A Rhetoric of Motives*. Berkeley: University of California Press, reprinted 1969.

Carlston, Donal E. 1987. "Turning Psychology on Itself: The Rhetoric of Psychology and the Psychology of Rhetoric." In *The Rhetoric of the Human Sciences*, edited by J. Nelson, A. Megill, and D. N. McCloskey. Madison: University of Wisconsin.

Cooley, T. F., and S. F. LeRoy. 1981. "Identification and Estimation of Money Demand." *American Economic Review* 71 (December): 825–44.

Davis, Philip J., and Reuben Hersh. 1981. *The Mathematical Experience*. Boston: Houghton Mifflin.

Denton, Frank. 1985. "Econometric Data Mining as an Industry." *Review of Economics and Statistics* (February): 124–7.

Dewald, William G., Jerry G. Thursby, and Richard G. Anderson. 1985. "Replication and Scientific Standards in Empirical Economics: Evidence from the *JMCB* Project." Unpublished, Ohio State University.

Fish, Stanley. 1980. *Is There a Text in This Class? The Authority of Interpretive Communities.* Cambridge: Harvard University Press.

Geertz, Clifford. 1988. *Works and Lives: The Anthropologist as Author.* Stanford: Stanford University Press.

Gould, Stephen Jay. 1981. *The Mismeasure of Man.* New York: Norton.

Griliches, Zvi. 1976. "Automobile Prices Revisited: Extensions of the Hedonic Hypothesis." In *Household Production and Consumption.* Studies in Income and Wealth, vol. 40, edited by N. E. Terleckyj. New York: National Bureau of Economics Research.

Hutchison, T. W. 1938. *The Significance and Basic Postulates of Economic Theory.* London: Macmillan.

Klamer, Arjo. 1983. *Conversations with Economists: New Classical Economists and Opponents Speak Out on the Current Controversy.* Totowa, N.J.: Rowman and Allanheld.

Klant, J. J. 1985. *The Rules of the Game.* Cambridge: Cambridge University Press.

Klemm, David. 1987. "The Rhetoric of Theological Argument." In *The Rhetoric of the Human Sciences,* edited by J. Nelson, A. Megill, and D. N. McCloskey. Madison: University of Wisconsin Press.

Leijonhufvud, Axel. 1968. *On Keynesian Economics and the Economics of Keynes: A Study in Monetary Theory.* New York: Oxford University Press.

Lucas, Robert E., Jr. 1973. "Some International Evidence on Output-Inflation Trade-offs." *American Economic Review* 63 (June): 326–34.

Lyne, John, and Michael McGee. 1987. "What Are Nice Guys Like You Doing in a Place Like This? Thoughts from Communication Studies." In *The Rhetoric of the Human Sciences,* edited by J. Nelson, A. Megill, and D. N. McCloskey. Madison: University of Wisconsin Press.

Marcus, Solomon. 1974. "Fifty-two Oppositions Between Scientific and Poetic Communication." In *Pragmatic Aspects of Human Communication,* edited by C. Cherry, 83–96. Dordrecht, Holland: Reidel.

Mayer, Thomas. 1980. "Economics as a Hard Science: Realistic Goal or Wishful Thinking?" *Economic Inquiry* 18 (April): 165–78.

McCloskey, D. N. 1985. "The Loss Function Has Been Mislaid: The Rhetoric of Significance Tests," *AER* 75 (May): 201–5.

———. 1985. *The Rhetoric of Economics.* Series in the Rhetoric of the Human Sciences. Madison: University of Wisconsin Press.

McCloskey, D. N., and Allan Megill. 1987. "The Rhetoric of History." In *The Rhetoric of the Human Sciences,* edited by J. Nelson, A. Megill, and D. N. McCloskey. Madison: University of Wisconsin Press.

Nelson, John. 1983. "Models, Statistics, and Other Tropes of Politics; or, Whatever Happened to Argument in Political Science?" In *Argument in Transition: Proceedings of the Third Summer Conference on Argumentation,* edited by D. Zarefsky, M. O. Sillars, and J. Rhodes. Annandale, Va.: Speech Communication Association.

Pareto, Vilfredo. 1927. *Manual of Political Economy*. Translated by Anne S. Schwier. Clifton, N.J.: Augustus M. Kelley, 1971.

Perelman, Chaim, and L. Olbrechts-Tyteca. 1958. *The New Rhetoric: A Treatise on Argumentation*. Translated by John Wilkinson and Purcell Weaver. Notre Dame: University of Notre Dame Press, 1969.

Plato. 1925. *Lysis, Symposium, Gorgias*. Translated by W. R. M. Lamb. Cambridge, Mass.: Harvard University Press.

Richards, I. A. 1925. *Principles of Literary Criticism*. New York: Harcourt Brace Jovanovich.

Rorty, Amelie Oksenberg. 1983. "Experiments in Philosophic Genres: Descartes' *Meditations*." *Critical Inquiry* 9 (March): 545–65.

Rorty, Richard. 1979. *Philosophy and the Mirror of Nature*. Princeton: Princeton University Press.

———. 1982. *The Consequences of Pragmatism*. Minneapolis: University of Minnesota Press.

Rosen, Stanley. 1980. *The Limits of Analysis*. New York: Basic Books.

Rosaldo, Renato. 1987. "Where Objectivity Lies: The Rhetoric of Anthropology." In *The Rhetoric of the Human Sciences,* edited by J. Nelson, A. Megill, and D. N. McCloskey. Madison: University of Wisconsin Press.

Scott, Robert. 1967. "On Viewing Rhetoric as Epistemic." *Central States Speech Journal* 18 (February): 9–17.

Solow, Robert. 1981. "Does Economics Make Progress?" *Bulletin of the American Academy of Arts and Sciences* 36 (December).

Thurow, Lester. 1985. *The Zero-Sum Solution: Building a World-Class American Economy*. New York: Simon and Schuster.

Toulmin, Stephen. 1958. *The Uses of Argument*. Cambridge: Cambridge University Press.

Tullock, Gordon. 1959. "Publication Decisions and Tests of Significance: A Comment." *JASA* 54:593.

Walton, Douglas N. 1985. *Arguer's Position: A Pragmatic Study of* Ad Hominem *Attack, Criticism, Refutation, and Fallacy*. Westport, Conn.: Greenwood Press.

White, James Boyd. 1984. *When Words Lose Their Meaning: Constitutions and Reconstitutions of Language, Character, and Community*. Chicago: University of Chicago Press.

——— 1985. *Heracles' Bow: Essays on the Rhetoric and Poetics of the Law*. Series in the Rhetoric of the Human Sciences. Madison: University of Wisconsin Press.

White, Hayden. 1973. *Metahistory: The Historical Imagination in Nineteenth-Century Europe*. Baltimore: Johns Hopkins University Press.

CHAPTER 2

Comments from outside economics

Stanley Fish

In terms of the larger institution of the academy, as opposed to the smaller institution of any one of our disciplines, something remarkable has happened in the past twenty-five years. For one thing, I am now a professor of law, and that is itself a remarkable fact since, if the truth were told, my qualifications are much smaller than I'd like them to be. Moreover, if twenty-five years ago you had asked a bunch of law professors which of the other disciplines was most likely to provide help for their work and their thinking, I dare say that literary criticism would have been *extremely* low on the list. In fact, if you had put that question to almost any other discipline *but* literary criticism, literary criticism would have been extremely low on anyone's list. It is now *very* high. Now this is a marketplace consideration, a political and sociological phenomenon from which I draw certain kinds of sustenance: moral, professional, and monetary. So I don't want to exactly sneer at it, but I *do* want to comment on it for a moment.

Because of the influence of the work of some of the people whose names have been bandied about here, because of the impact of essays like Clifford Geertz's "Blurred Genres" in *The American Scholar* (1980), there's been a tendency for disciplines to begin to think of themselves as components in a cultural inquiry rather than as isolated units. For reasons that would take too long to explore, this has had the effect of a great many disciplines suddenly finding in literary theory and in literary study (of all places) ways of talking and ways of thinking. As recently as ten to fifteen years ago, students of literature routinely looked elsewhere for models more firmly based than the ones they knew. The situation has been reversed, and we find philosophy, anthropology, sociology, and now even economics – my God! – turning to literary studies. The turn to literary studies in law is well advanced and truly frightening. In fact, you cannot now pick up an issue of the *Stanford Law Review* or the *USC Law Review* or the *Yale Law Review* without thinking that you've mistakenly picked up *Diacritics* or *Critical Inquiry:* The essays are concerned with the same issues, and they use the now familiar terms from "advanced" literary theory.

Now this is, as I've already indicated, extremely heartening from a number

This chapter is based on a speech given at the first session of the conference on the Rhetoric of Economics.

of perspectives, but I think it holds at least two dangers. One is that you tend to get a valorized, idealized, and therefore idolized, picture of the literary. What we should now be realizing is that "the literary" is a game like any other. It is not the place in which all the values driven out by modernism now reside; it is not our last best "hope." It is just a practice, and therefore it is not a good idea to follow Klamer's recommendation that the speech of economics should be the same as the speech of poetry. Think of this situation: A judge decides at the end of a case to do a literary analysis of the plaintiff's and the defendant's presentations. He finds himself very much taken by the metaphors employed by the defense attorney and equally taken by the sense of sequence and transition in the presentation of the prosecuter. He then declares himself unable to decide on the merits of the two arguments because they are so stylistically impressive and says, "Let's have lunch." He will not be a judge very long – and for *very* good reasons. So I would say, do not, *do not* take into your discourse, if it's working fairly well, anything from literary studies. That's recommendation number one.

Don McCloskey also said that the rhetorical approach sensitizes. I want to say something more about that in a few moments but just as a preliminary, I will say that *everything* sensitizes. Not all the time, not every time, but in the context of some contingent, unpredictable set of circumstances, something could or may or is even likely to sensitize – though I don't want to lean too heavily on *likely*. Nothing, however, sensitizes by right. Nothing. Rhetoric, mathematics, psychoanalysis, you name it, nothing sensitizes by right! Nothing has the particular property in contrast to other ways of discourse, or ways of talking, of sensitizing.

Now it might be the case that you have a discipline so fed up with the conversation – a word I detest but will continue to use – that things have become stultified, uninteresting, even boring, and what you really want to do is shake it up. So you start doing things in an effort to "goose" the tired intellects of your fellows, and then you say you've sensitized them. In critical legal studies, which is the left-wing movement more or less parallel to the rhetoric of economics movement in law, sensitizing takes the place of writing paragraphs that begin – and I'm thinking of a recent (1984) essay in the *Stanford Law Review* by Professor Mark Kelman – with a sober analysis of some legal problem in relation to legal education and then ends by declaring "It's all a fucking oppression." That *does* something. It is at least open to question whether the something it does is sensitize.

It was also said that it matters what metaphor one uses. I agree that it does matter what metaphor one uses; one way of reformulating the rhetorical or antifoundational insight has it that ways of talking – rather than of simply existing in a relationship of verisimilitude (or failure of verisimilitude) to fixed, independent objects – constitutes the objects, to which we can then point. So it's always the case, given the rhetorical point of view, that ways of talking, metaphorical and others, matter but the way they matter is not itself a matter of choice or rational analysis, so while it is true that it matters what metaphor one uses, this truth will not help you do anything in the world. Nothing whatsoever. More of that later.

The statement was made that the isolation of economics is bad. I take the word of an economist. I don't know; it's possible. But these, again, are contingent historical matters. At the end of the past century and the beginning of this one, there was a deliberate move in philosophy (at least in the Anglo-American community) to narrow the range of questions a philosopher could ask and answer. That is to say, there was a decision on the part of that discipline to become, in some sense, more isolated, a decision that was made, I think, for good, professional reasons. Those reasons led to a certain kind of success and also to a certain set of problems that now beset many a philosophy department in this country. If the isolation of economics is bad, it has to be, not because isolation is bad in and of itself, but because the present state of isolation isn't good for economics, by which I mean people aren't listening to you, your students aren't getting jobs, or there aren't enough consultation fees out there. If in fact you can "do isolation" and have the rest of it very well in hand, my advice is, continue isolation.

The big point in Klamer's presentations* came when he complained that, in the context of his seminar, there came a moment when argument meant war, and victory meant slaying the opponent. I'm here to tell you, that's right! Argument means war. There's no other way. And I don't care whether you have classrooms in a circle or hang by your toes from the ceiling or take No-Doze – or rather, Let's-Doze – every ten minutes to make sure that your blood pressure doesn't get up too high: Argument *is* war! There are lots of ways to wage war. One of the most exasperating – passive aggressives have it down pat! (I'm an aggressive aggressive myself) – is to *not* appear to be waging war and to rebuke your opponent for waging war. It's a good move, gets *me* every time! But the idea that it's not war is crazy.

I think I'll pass by the old Emerson Hall problem because it is such an old problem that I can't think that anyone could ever, any longer, find it interesting. However, the point that some methods of persuasion are better than others is certainly interesting, to the point, and true. Some methods of persuasion *are* better than others but you cannot name in advance what they are. That is, some methods of persuasion are better than others, and it depends – and this is, of course, a commonplace – on the context: It depends on the job you want to get done, it depends, as Richard Rorty would say, on what you want.

*In the oral presentation of Chapter 1. – Ed.

And when you know what you want or, as we're now told, when you know your desires, then you also know which arguments are better than others, but it is not a philosophical or theoretical question (there are no philosophical or theoretical questions); it is an empirical question.

To the statement that all arguments have to be weighed up, I say no. All arguments are always weighing *in,* and that's quite different. Every argument that is made already carries its weight since being recognized *as* an argument is a significant (and weighty) achievement. Arguments are already weighing in when you're talking about them. The weighing is not a rational act after the fact; the weighing *is* the content of the so-called conversation itself. That's the preliminary.

Now we start with the real thing. There has been a lot of talk already and will continue to be a lot of talk for the next two or three days about the rhetorical view or critique or neopragmatism, and so forth. So I thought it would be good to read a paragraph so that we all knew what it was that we were talking about. I've selected a paragraph from Rorty's work largely because he is so accessible, something that both delights and infuriates people – sometimes the same people. The paragraph is from *The Consequences of Pragmatism* (1982), from the essay "Pragmatism, Relativism and Rationalism," and he's speaking here of "the general pragmatist doctrine," or what is known around my house as "the position." "It is the doctrine," says Rorty, "that there are no constraints on inquiry save conversational ones" (for which we might read: cultural, conventional, institutional, and so on, social) "no wholesale constraints derived from the nature of the objects or of the mind or of language" (he's just ticked off about 2,500 years of philosophy) "but only those retail constraints provided by the remarks of our fellow inquirers." That is, what seems to be a fact for us, what seems to be an urgent issue, what seems to be probable, is always a function of the conversation in which we are imbedded, and everything you've seen and talked about at this seminar depends on the institutional conversation and not on a perspective that stands outside it. The pragmatist, Rorty says, will tell us that "it is useless to hope that objects will constrain us to believe the truth about them, if only they are approached with an unclouded mental eye or a rigorous method, or a perspicuous language. He wants us to give up the notion that God or evolution or some other underwriter of our present world picture has programmed us as machines for accurate verbal picturing and that philosophy brings self knowledge by letting us read our own program. The only sense in which we are constrained to truth is that we can make no sense of the notion that any view which can survive all objections might be false." That's the Rorty paragraph, and seems to me to be a very good one. He makes only one mistake, and that is when he suggests that if we give up the notion that "God or evolution or some other underwriter of our present world picture has programmed us,'' important things will follow, and I'm going to argue, as I always do, that nothing will follow.

A sentence from Klamer and McCloskey, which I call quotation 1, might be considered the Ur text for the rhetorical line: ''The point is that all conversations are rhetorical, that none can claim to be the Archimedian point from which all others can be levered.'' That's the point. My question is what follows the point? My answer is going to be: Nothing follows from the point.

But before I give that answer, I have to at least acknowledge another kind of objection – or not so much an objection as another kind of response to the point that Klamer and McCloskey make. Quotation 2 is a footnote in the paper by Professor Coats: ''As Arthur Collins notes . . ., Rorty inevitably encounters the problem facing all relativists: he necessarily argues that his own relative position is objectively correct and that that of his opponents is objectively wrong.''* Now this is *the* objection most often heard to the rhetorical or deconstructive or neopragmatist view. If *the* claim is that any assertion has traction only within a set of social and political and historical assumptions and can never be absolute, how is it that you can so absolutely make that very claim? The answer is (and this is, as you will all recall, the last line of Mickey Spillane's *I the Jury*), it's easy. It's extraordinarily easy because the objection makes a very simple mistake. The mistake is to think that when someone says, as all the rhetorically minded among us in the world now say, that a challenge has been made to some assertion or other, that all assertions are challengeable. But to say that all assertions are challengeable or that all arguments have force only in context is only to say about any argument, including itself, the following: Insofar as conviction can be secured (and conviction certainly can be secured), it is always a matter of making arguments in local, particular contexts in relation to actual objections and counterobjections. So that there is no form of argument, no rhetoric, no point of view, no perspective that would in and of itself compel – and here I use a phrase we've heard before – any reasonable person. (I don't think there is any such thing as *the* reasonable person because what is and is not a reasonable person is itself a matter of dispute and argument and therefore the ''reasonable person'' cannot be referred to or invoked as a way of judging between arguments.) Although the following is not a hard point, it is a point a lot of people find difficult: ''Whatever convinces does so from within some set of assumptions or presuppositions that are social in origin and therefore challengeable, *but* that assertion does not, in and of itself, constitute a challenge to anything, including itself, because by the very thesis, challenges are issued and met, if they are met, only within particular circumstances, objections, and so on. All the po-

---

*Editors' note: Coats's chapter in this volume is a revised version of the paper he presented at the conference and does not contain this footnote.

sition says is that everything must earn its way by argument and that includes this position. It certainly does not bar anyone from asserting anything with conviction; it's just an account of the source of conviction when and if it occurs.''

Now, of course, what this means from a negative point of view is that the assertion (as we find it in Klamer and McCloskey) that all conversations are rhetorical, while true, doesn't tell you anything about any particular assertion (including itself) until it is tested against the objections and counterobjections that occur to those who hear it. This means that the rhetorical insight, at least in this particular context, has no relevance to anything except the kinds of epistemological arguments and debates in which it is asserted. And I am going to go further and say it has no relevance at all. Let's start again with the ''Ur'' quotation: ''. . . none can claim to be the Archimedian point from which others can be levered.'' Certainly, none can make that claim on grounds that are not already presupposed by the rhetoric in whose name it is made. If that's what is meant, it's a true statement. But you can (and do) make that claim whenever you are convinced of something, whenever you've heard everything that has been brought against it, and you still believe it. I make absolute (Archimedian) claims all the time, and in this spirit: I have disputed with many about it, I have convinced them, I continue to convince myself, and until someone or something convinces me otherwise, I will take what I am claiming to be absolutely true. Now, of course, the evidence that produces my conviction is itself rhetorical in the sense of being evidence only within assumptions that are not *now* under debate but could be. Another way of putting this is to say a rhetorical claim can only have a rhetorical success. But it is the thesis of the rhetorical view that rhetorical successes are the only ones you could possibly have, and since it's the only one you could have, it is more than good enough. What other kind of success could you imagine? Success by an argument that no one imbedded in any rhetorical situation could recognize? That does not make any sense.

The first point, then, is that absolute claims are always rhetorical, but that this in no way denies that they can be made; it just specifies the conditions both for making them and for making them ''good.'' The second (the really important one) is that absolute claims – the claim to an Archemedian position – cannot be avoided. You cannot help believing – and this is going to sound tautological and commonplace – that what you take to be the case is true. No fancy epistemological work is ever going to shake your convictions about what you take to be true. It would only be possible to avoid claiming superiority for your own point of view if you could somehow get to that side of that point of view; it would only be possible if you could have either outside or within you something called critical self-consciousness or self-awareness or self-reflexivity, which you could consult as a qualification of, or a caution on, your beliefs. But, of course, it is the very thesis of the rhetorical point of view, or antifoundationalism, that there is no such corrective or qualification available. Therefore, the point of view you hold or, to be more precise, the point of view that holds you will always be for you – appear to you – the right one. Moreover, your point of view, your rhetoric, is not something you can hold at arm's length with a view toward rejecting it or confirming it. Nor can you hold it tentatively or with a certain reserve. This is a mistake made by Stephen Toulmin in "The Construal of Reality" (1982) and also in *Human Understanding* (1972). Toulmin has bought the antifoundationalists' rhetorical line wholesale. That means that he now says things like "there are no unmediated facts," "all activity is irremediably interpretive," "there is no such thing as a neutral observation language," "there is no escaping politics," "all descriptions are from a perspective." The question is, does it go any further than that? In the case of Toulmin, it doesn't go any further than that, because immediately after having said all these things, he says the following: What we have learned is that it is impossible to get outside our biases and prejudices, and therefore when we come to any serious intellectual piece of work, what we must do is discount our biases and prejudice so that we can get on with the job in a more responsible way. I will dot the *i*'s and cross the *t*'s and point out that there could not possibly be any content to the verb *discount* if Toulmin were taking the first part of his argument seriously. It could not be the case that after having admitted the inescapability and pervasiveness of interpretation, belief, and culture, he can then think that our realization of this pervasiveness can be a means of insulating ourselves against it. That is the most common mistake made by everyone who has ever been enamored of the rhetorical or deconstructive or neopragmatic line: to think that because we now know that we are in a situation, imbedded, constituted socially, we can use that knowledge to escape the implications of what we now know. I call that error antifoundationalist theory hope. I love antifoundationalist theory hope because I see everyone committing it. And that puts me in possession of something that all scholars aspire to: a position that no one else holds, and in relation to which everyone else can be said to be mistaken.

Let me say a little bit about antifoundationalist theory hope. I believe that all convictions about the way things are, about what is or is not the case, have their source not in independent objects or facts, nor in a neutral observation language, but in the historically instituted conditions within which perception occurs and in relation to which objects, facts, events and meanings emerge and become available. In other words, I have bought and am in the process of retailing, selling, and pushing the antifoundationalist-rhetorical epistemology. I am fully committed to it and have so testified on many an occasion.

However, I also believe certain things – let us say, about *Paradise Lost*. When I teach *Paradise Lost* and come to the line that says Satan "gently raised'' the spirit of his fainting troops, I do a number on the phrase ''gently raised''; it goes on for about three hours, in the short version. I am absolutely committed to my response to that line. I think my response is the truth. I have performed a historical analysis in which I ask and answer the question; how is it that I so firmly see what I so firmly see when I open *Paradise Lost?* The result was an essay entitled ''Transmuting the Lump: *Paradise Lost, 1942–1982,''* which purports to show how what we now take to be the facts of *Paradise Lost* came to be the facts of *Paradise Lost.* I examined the history of criticism and rejected from the outset the assumption that the facts of *Paradise Lost* are available independent of interpretation. In my role as a historian of institutions I can give an analysis of the sources of my convictions, beliefs, and perceptions, *but* – and this is the important part – my ability to give that analysis in no way alters my convictions, beliefs, perceptions, and so forth. And no matter what I decide about where these notions that now possess me came from, the next time I open that long poem, I am going to be just as possessed as I was before. Another way to say this is that what we now have as a result of the rhetorical, postmodern, deconstructive, poststructuralist, neopragmatist revolution is a new account of our epistemology, that is, a new belief about where our beliefs come from. The mistake is to think that by adding this new belief, our other beliefs about things other than epistemology will be altered. That is, when I am in an argument about epistemology with theorists or philosophers or literary types – or legal academics – then I'm arguing epistemological view rather than some other, because that is what the discussion is all about. But when I start talking about who is or is not the hero of *Paradise Lost,* my epistemology, which I was rehearsing so blithely and liberally to the theoreticians on Monday, is irrelevant to what I see and say about the poem on Tuesday. To think otherwise is to buy, as many have, the scam that philosophy as a discipline has been selling us for so long. The scam is the claim that the questions philosophy asks and the answers it gives are finally and deeply relevant to everything we do as human beings, even when we are not doing philosophy, as most of us are not. This, of course, has given the philosophers the opportunity to say to all of us, ''Yes, you kind of have an idea of what you're doing, but if you were as well-trained philosophically as we are, you'd have a much better idea.'' This seems to me to be bizarre. Philosophy is not the name of a natural kind, it's the name of an institutional discipline that has, in a variety of ways, become narrower and narrower in the twentieth century. The idea that its questions and answers would have any necessary relevance to any other arena of human activity seems to me to be totally unfounded. When I am a philosopher or, less grandly, someone who is trying to get epistemology straight, I'm doing one kind of task. When I'm trying to get straight what is going on in *Paradise Lost,* I'm doing another kind of task. And the two tasks don't have anything to do with one another. Here I invoke a happy phrase from one of Rorty's recent essays: "Time will tell, but epistemology won't," which means simply that with respect to any particular task, problem, or decision you're engaged in, there are going to be resources at your disposal, obstacles to your success, antici- pated and unanticipated objections, and whether you can work through the obstacles and take advantage of the resources and build a little here and tear down a little there – time will tell, but epistemology won't.

What I'm saying, therefore, is that bringing economists into a conversation that has been going on for some time in other disciplines is certainly going to do something, but there are some things it's not going to do. What it *is* going to do is give economists new kinds of work, and anything that produces more work for academics, I'm for. If a discipline is getting tired, if its routines are no longer appealing, if the students aren't coming, if the classes are getting smaller, if the administrators don't look you in the face when they pass you in the corridors, then it's time to do something else. This (i.e., a rhetoric of economics), at least if I can believe these gentlemen in the world of econom- ics, is the "something else." Terrific! We'll have some conferences, we'll hear some papers, we'll write some nice historical essays that explore the conditions under which certain economic metaphors emerge and become powerful.

But there are two things that bringing the economists into the conversation won't do. One is the thing feared by the antirhetoricians, the other is the thing hoped for by the prorhetoricians. The first thing a "rhetoric of economics" won't do is disable us by taking from us our confidence in the arguments we make, the assertions we put forward, the facts we point to. That's the great fear felt by those who are horrified when they hear a Kuhn, or a Rorty, or a McCloskey talk, the fear that if lots of people get persuaded by that talk, no one will any longer have standards, norms, procedures, and so forth. That fear, I think, is unfounded and it is unfounded because, given the anitfoun- dationalist insight that there's nothing outside your beliefs that can be invoked as a critique or qualification of your beliefs, you could never get a distance on the norms and standards that your beliefs subtend. Normative thinking comes with the territory, the territory of being not a machine but a situated human being. Correctly seen then, the thesis that we can never get outside of our beliefs, rather than loosing us from our moorings, tells us that we can*not* be loosed from our moorings. That, of course, is what the people on the other side, the Klamer and McCloskey side, don't like to hear because they *want* to be loosed from their moorings. They think that now that we have discov- ered that our perceptions, our sense of what is and is not a fact or a possible course of action, have not been given to us by God or Aristotle or Kant or Chomsky, but rather have been socially and politically produced, we can now use that knowledge somehow to – how shall I say? – "soften" the way in which we go about asserting and believing. That is antifoundationalist theory hope. It is the mistake of making antifoundationalism into a foundation, of thinking of it as a lever with which we can pry ourselves away from the world delivered to us by our beliefs.

We fear that our hold on standards, norms, and facts will be relaxed and we will loose our moorings if we listen to the likes of Klamer and McCloskey. That's antifoundationalist theory fear. But then there's the *hope* that our hold on standards, norms, and facts can be relaxed so that we will be able to break free of our moorings. That's antifoundationalist theory hope. One fears to be free; the other hopes to be free. *Neither* the fear nor the hope is cashable. You can neither be deprived of nor achieve a distance from the norms, criteria, distinctions, and so on that constitute your consciousness.

References

Geertz, Clifford. 1980. "Blurred Genres." *The American Scholar* (Spring 1980): 165–79

Kelman, Mark. 1984. "Trashing." *Stanford Law Review* (January): 293–348

Rorty, Richard. 1982. *Consequences of Pragmatism*. Minneapolis: University of Minnesota Press.

Toulmin, Stephen. 1972. *Human Understanding*. Princeton N.J.: Princeton University Press.

———. 1982. "The Construal of Reality." *Construal Inquiry* (September): 93–111.

CHAPTER 3

Comments from inside economics

Robert M. Solow

I must be a person of no particular character. As Klamer and Mc-Closkey described each of their five types of economists a voice kept saying, "That's me; no, *that*'s me; no, no, *that*'s me." It must have been my own voice: Anyone else would have said, "That is I." What I am is a hopeless eclectic.

Most of you probably think that we eclectics have an easy time of it. No principles to preserve, no purity to protect: The wind bloweth where it listeth and the hopeless eclectic – like me – sayeth whatever he damn pleaseth. You have it all wrong. The life of a conscientious eclectic is hard. He or she must decide every issue on its presumed merits. There are no automatic answers. It's decisions, decisions, decisions. The eclectic has to be alert all the time because you cannot trust true believers. They always tend to *go too far*. In the army, guard duty used to be two hours on and four hours off; no conscientious eclectic has it so good.

It is that tendency to go too far that causes all the trouble. Let me give you an example not taken from economics but nevertheless not wholly irrelevant to the theme of this conference. In a recent *New York Review of Books,* Jerome Bruner and Carol Fleisher Feldman (1986) review a recent book by the philosopher Nelson Goodman. As it happens, I admire both the author and the reviewers. Goodman – also one of Don McCloskey's favorites – advocates a view he calls "constructivism." It starts from the observation – with which I agree – that what we call "perception" always incorporates a lot of interpretation. Our empirical statements have a lot of theory built into them before they start. In that sense, says Goodman, Mr. Justice Bruner concurring, we construct our own world. It's a metaphor disguised as a down-home sentence, but it will have the desired effect of causing naive empiricists to pay attention.

But then Goodman goes too far and, as far as I can tell, Bruner goes with him. Since we each construct our world, it is more accurate to say that we construct our several worlds. They are the only worlds we have. None is to be preferred to any other. You might naturally tend to prefer the ones that are closest to the "real," "objective" world. But every world was built by some-

This chapter is based on a speech given at the first session of the conference on the Rhetoric of Economics.

one. There is no real world at all. Or so, at least, Goodman's words appear to say. Presumably he means it. Similar things are being said here.

The eclectic digs in his heels. Bruner and Feldman begin their review by recalling the old days at Harvard University, when both the Philosophy and Psychology departments had their offices in Emerson Hall, and they look forward with favor to the day when the two departments will be back together again. I am tempted to say to them, "Try an experiment. Take an entering class at Harvard College, freshly arrived in Cambridge and strangers to one another. Ask them one by one to stand facing the foot of the Widener Library steps, look to the left, and construct a world. About 999 out of every thousand will construct Emerson Hall. Maybe one in a thousand will construct the St. Louis railroad station, and one in a million may construct the Taj Mahal. The rest will construct Emerson Hall. Of course they will *interpret* it differently. Some will see it as a prison, some as a dull academic building, and some as a veritable temple of learning. Nevertheless, it is recognizably dear old Emerson Hall, time after time. Why is that?" (It is a pity to have to make this commonplace point. But how else can one deal with this sort of foolishness?)

Now let me turn to Klamer and McCloskey. I want to emphasize that I am on their side. They are right to deflate the pompous methodology of economics as science. They are right, in the first place, because the practice differs so much and so openly from the prescribed method. They are right, in the second place, because it is a damn lucky thing that the practice differs so much from the prescribed method. Given the poverty and precariousness of the raw material, and the complexity of the problems, economists would never get anywhere if they stuck literally to their textbook canons of scientific method. Opportunism is the only hope. We need all the help we can get and on the whole we take it wherever we get it. So much for the normative side of the McCloskey–Klamer position.

One can also pursue the rhetoric of economics as a kind of natural history or descriptive science of the way the species behaves. I don't see how anything but good can come from studying how trained economists actually go about persuading one another. We will learn something about the strategy and tactics of their arguments. Self-knowledge might help to make the arguments better, or at least honest if they are not so. (I am slightly less interested in how economists persuade outsiders, but that might be amusing, too.)

Nevertheless I have to report a certain discomfort, a vague itch. It feels like my eclecticism warning me that Klamer and McCloskey are in grave danger of Going Too Far. To be specific, I worry that their version of the occupational disease is to drift into the belief that one mode of argument is as good as another. In this instance I side with Orwell's pigs: All arguments are equal but some are more equal than others. For that reason I mistrust Mc-

Closkey's favorite image – borrowed from Rorty – of economics, or science generally, as an ongoing conversation. It seems *too* permissive.

During my lifetime I have participated in dozens of conversations about one of the difficult questions that profoundly concerned young men of my time and place: Was Peewee Reese or Phil Rizzuto the better all-round short-stop? To tell you the truth, those conversations were on the whole more disciplined, more precise in definition, more respectful of fact, more subtle in analysis, more careful in inference than many of the other dozens of conversations I have participated in on that other deep question: Is the monetarist model or the Keynesian model a better representation of macroeconomic life? McCloskey might say that I have made his point. Yes, I meant to. But I also want to emphasize – as he does not – the judgmental character of what I just said. Some modes of argument lend themselves to sloppiness. Some modes of argument tend to give the impression that they have proved a point when they have not proved anything and it is not even clear that there is a point. Some methods of persuasion are more worthy than others. That is what I fear the analogy to conversation tends to bury. I would prefer the image of the ongoing seminar, say, to suggest a group of knowledgeable and critical old pros. I hope that no one who knows me could possibly think that I am here defending mere solemnity. I am more often in hot water for just the opposite sin.

Methodological prescriptions are intended to address just this problem, by restricting the range of permissible modes of argument. The problem is real. The trouble, of course, is that methodological scolds also tend to Go Too Far.

Let me see if I can give some examples of Wholesome Eclectic methodological prescription. I choose unpopular ones, deliberately. On the whole, I would say, logical or mathematical deduction from explicitly stated assumptions is better than reasoning by assertion, allusion, suggestion, or rough analogy, mainly because, in the former case, what you see is what you get. It goes without saying that mathematics can be erroneous or misleading or tendentious just as analogy can be irrelevant or misleading or tendentious. I only mean that *ceteris paribus,* to coin a phrase, chains of reasoning ought to be *exposed* as possible, and mathematics does that. It will not transform bad assumptions into good conclusions, I fear I need to say. But mathematics makes it a little easier to know when you're being had. (It also lends itself to browbeating, I admit.)

I would argue that, on the whole, formal statistical evidence – qualitative or quantitative – is better than anecdote. The reasons are rather different this time. In nonexperimental subjects formal statistical testing can easily turn into a snow job. What you think you see can be much more than what you get. Much econometrics is no doubt formal-mechanical, inappropriately grounded because out of touch with real economic beliefs. Still, I think the chances of detecting unrepresentativeness and bias are enhanced by the rules of statistical inference, whereas anecdotal evidence is more likely – not infinitely more likely – to carry more or less conviction than it ought, depending on the narrative skill of the teller of the tale. Mind you, I have no wish to rule anecdote or analogy out of court. There may be nothing better available, and they may be pretty good. I am only trying to illustrate the proposal that some modes of argument are better than others.

It would be easy to produce other such judgments, but these will illustrate the two general points I want to make. First, you have no doubt observed how aggressively commonplace these methodological precepts are. Naturally, your wholesome eclectic is not likely to come up with exotic methodological ideas, nor does he regret that. (I do have some more controversial ideas about the right way to do economics; but they do not so routinely come with the eclectic's territory. So this is not the place to promote them.)

Second, I do not regard these remarks as being in basic opposition to the Klamer–McCloskey line, but rather as an important second-order correction. God knows I have no objection at all to a good anecdote or analogy, either as a literary device or as a way to clinch an argument. In the end, however, all the arguments for and against a proposition have to be weighed up somehow, and "one argument, one vote" does not strike me as the best system.

I have the feeling that too many of the papers at this conference stop at the "look, Ma, a metaphor" stage. Yes, the practice of economics is full of metaphors; so is the practice of mathematics. Now that we have reminded ourselves that they are there, the more important question is, How do they work? What distinguishes a good metaphor from a bad one? Don McCloskey often writes as if a metaphor is a purely literary device for the economist, a way of expressing what he or she already knows. But I think a good metaphor is rather a way of finding things out. A metaphor in science is not good or bad, it is more or less *productive*. If Professor R. Burns's love is like a red, red rose, OK, well said, know what you mean, but I can't see that the thought is going to help me get on with anything, especially if my love doesn't happen to be like a red, red rose. But if someone tells me that a complex number is a point in the plane, that is the beginning of something *big*. It suggests questions and it actually tells me how to find answers. I am almost afraid to suggest that there are interesting studies to be done along these lines. I know my customers: I expect a series of papers on intertemporally optimal choice of metaphors under rational expectation. The Walrasian auctioneer is an example of a metaphor that once was productive but has outlived its usefulness.

While I am on this subject, I think it is misleading to hint that the mathematical (or even economic) use of metaphor is the same sort of thing as the literary or poetic metaphor, even apart from the functional aspect I have just been emphasizing. The arguments adduced to support the metaphor are very different in kind, and the permissible responses are altogether different. If I say to you, "You are my sunshine, my only sunshine," you are at liberty to say, "The hell I am." We can discuss the question and if, in the end, we disagree, even after I have told you that you make me happy when skies are gray, there's not much more to be said. If you tell me that an everywhere convergent power series is an analytic function, I can reply "The hell it is." Our discussion will take an altogether different form; and if I end up unconvinced, I have revealed myself to be dumb or incompetent. That is a nontrivial difference, and it suggests we may be stretching the concept or using "metaphor" in a metaphorical way.

It occurs to me that Klamer and McCloskey have been operating under the unexamined premise that the practice of rhetorical analysis is neutral with respect to the substance of what is believed by economists and therefore passes for economic knowledge. I think that I have assumed that up to this moment. On reflection, however, one sees that there is no warrant for that presumption. The practice of rhetorical analysis could easily be biased with respect to substance. Even if one could make some sort of case for "long-run" neutrality, there is no reason why in any particular decade there should not be a definite bias.

How about a general speculation: In any period the dominant school of thought is likely, consciously or unconsciously, to impose on professional discussion rhetorical conventions that favor the case it has to make. The dominant school then has the advantage of being able to rule some of its opponents' ideas out of court on methodological grounds. This certainly economizes on argument. But then rhetorical analysis – "unbiased" rhetorical analysis, said he dubiously – is likely to be subversive, in much the way that the Society to Encourage Children to Watch Royal Parades might be subversive of the Guild of Swindling Tailors.

That, by itself, is not very interesting. Much more so would be to analyze the connection between particular lines of economic analysis and particular rhetorical conventions. A moment ago I spoke mildly in favor of mathematical model building and formal statistics as better ways of doing business than analogy and anecdote. Suppose I carried the day: What substantive things would economists be more likely to believe than they would if formal methods were *infra dig* and anecdote and analogy were the favored modes of argument? For instance, I think I could make a case that formalism favors the habit of drawing substantive conclusions from models of perfect competition. And so on.

I think that Klamer and McCloskey sometimes mix up rhetoric and method. I mean, they attribute the discomfort many economists feel with their own science to the restrictions the tradition has placed on the permitted rhetoric.

In some of the cases they describe I would be more willing to blame the excessive ambitions and resulting self-deception of economics. Perhaps all I mean is that those things drive the rhetoric rather than the other way around.

I am particularly interested in the way that theoretical commitments of economists constrain or control their empirical judgments. That is partly a rhetorical matter and partly a methodological one. One important example – practically important, I mean – is the concept known as "the natural rate of unemployment." God knows that form of words is evocative enough for anyone; it is bathed in normative overtones. If the unemployment rate in the United States nowadays seems to fluctuate around 7 percent of the labor force, say 2 percent higher than it used to do, economists all over the country, of (almost) all persuasions, ask themselves whether the "natural rate" has risen by 2 percent or whether unemployment just tends now to be higher than it used to be, relative to an unchanged "natural rate." They usually opt for the first alternative. Given the phrase, they almost have to. There is much talk and some action about measuring the natural rate.

The term was coined by Milton Friedman in 1968. He gave a definition in terms of an "equilibrium" unemployment rate given the ruling level of real wages. He was rather casual about specifying the model relative to which this equilibrium occurs, but there is a famous phrase about the unemployment rate "ground out by the Walrasian equations," given the current structure of the labor market, its imperfections, search mechanisms, information flows, and so forth.

Since then, however, the concept itself has been transformed both in measurement and in application. In practice the "natural rate" is associated with the location of a vertical long-run Phillips curve. It is the unemployment rate, tacitly assumed to be unique, with the property that an economy whose unemployment rate is kept indefinitely below (or above) its natural rate will experience indefinitely accelerating inflation (or deflation). It is estimated from data by procedures that depend wholly on this idea and have essentially no connection with the "Walrasian equations."

What is more, my own reading of the empirical experiments is that there is only the flimsiest evidence that any "natural rate" exists by either definition. The data are equally compatible with the contrary hypothesis that there is no equilibrium unemployment rate, or rather that any unemployment rate within reason could be an equilibrium unemployment rate if it persisted long enough. We have been conned by analogy and by the rhetoric of econometrics and by authority and by much else.

References

Bruner, Jerome, and Carol Fleisher Feldman. 1986. "Under Construction: Review of *Of Mind and Other Matters* by Nelson Goodman." *New York Review of Books* (March 27): 46.

Friedman, Milton. 1968. "The Role of Monetary Policy." *American Economic Review* (March): 1–17.

CHAPTER 4

Rhetoric and ideology

Robert L. Heilbroner

> Men always endevour to persuade others to be of their opinion even when
> the matter is of no consequence to them. If one advances anything concern-
> ing China or the more distant moon which contradicts what you imagine to
> be true, you immediately try to persuade him to alter his opinion. And in
> this manner every one is practicing oratory on others thro the whole of his
> life.[1]

This is Adam Smith speaking – literally speaking, because the words
come from the transcript of his "Lectures on Jurisprudence." Smith is discussing the "principle in the human mind" on which is based the famous
disposition to "truck, barter, and exchange," the cornerstone on which the
equally famous division of labor is based. For the division of labor could not
take place unless people wanted to exchange their wares. Evidently, to Smith
this exchange did not take place because of the direct appeal of self-interest.
It required an exercise of persuasion to convince the buyer that he would be
better off exchanging whatever he had for what the seller offered. "The offering of a shilling, which to us appears to have so plain and simple a meaning," says Smith, "is in reality offering an argument to persuade one to do
so and so for it is in his interest."

Thus, in the opinion of the first, and to many still the greatest, economist,
the basis for economic relationships lies not in a disinterested calculation of
advantages, but in the "faculties of reason and speech" that underlie the
capacity for persuasion.[2] Rhetoric – the art of speaking – is the rock on which
the mighty edifice of economics stands.

This is certainly not what most economists would today describe as the
foundation of their discipline. Economics prides itself on its sciencelike character, and economists on their ability to speak like scientists, without color,
passion, or values, preferably in the language of mathematics. Of one hundred
fifty-nine full-length papers published between 1981 and 1983 in the *American Economic Review,* McCloskey tells us, only six used words alone. As I
can testify from my own reading, most articles are "written" in matrix algebra, complex econometrics, formal lemmas, and four-quadrant diagrammat-

A slightly different version of this chapter appeared in the *New York Review of
Books,* April 24, 1986, 46–8.

ics. They would be incomprehensible to anyone not trained in the vocabulary and techniques of advanced economics and are in fact incomprehensible, I venture to say, to a large proportion of the members of the American Economic Association, myself very often included.

McCloskey himself would not be daunted by the pages of the *American Economic Review*. He launches his attack on economics with the confidence of an insider, not the frustrations of an outsider. This enables him to offer a breezy translation of Muth's arguing that public intervention in economic life is rarely effective because individuals "rationally" anticipate government's moves and take self-protective actions that tend to vitiate the effectiveness of governmental action:

MUTH

The hypothesis asserts three things: (1) information is scarce, and the economic system generally does not waste it. (2) The way expectations are formed depends specifically on the structure of the relevant system describing the economy. (3) A "public prediction" in the sense of Grunberg and Modigliani (1954), will have no substantial effect on the operation of the economic system (unless it is based on outside information). This is not quite the same thing as stating that the marginal revenue product of economics is zero, because expectations of a single firm may still be subject to greater error than the theory.

TRANSLATION

In other words, I'm saying that people take appropriate care with their guesses, and economists should credit them with such caretaking. If people take care of guessing, talk about the future would be pointless: people will have allowed for the effects being talked about. For instance, declarations that prosperity is just around the corner will have no impact, unless the declarer really does know something we all don't know. Economists do know something, though not as much as their present notions about guessing imply: they know that a bunch of guesses by individuals average out over a large group to less quirky guesses. (McCloskey 1985: 93)

McCloskey's target is the pretentious scientism in which economists couch their mutual persuasions – a scientism that lingers on as the near-official language of economic discourse long after its inadequacies have been recognized by philosophers and scientists. What McCloskey wants economists to understand is that the language of formalism and mathematics is still a language, and therefore inescapably "rhetorical." Moreover it is a dangerous language in that it conceals or minimizes, although it can never eliminate, the elements of judgment and moral valuation that are an intrinsic part of economics. It therefore becomes necessary, says McCloskey, for economists to recognize that, like all serious inquiry, economics is ultimately a "conversation" – a dialogue conducted among qualified people who share the ethical commitments without which the accumulation of knowledge is impossible: Don't lie; pay attention; don't sneer; cooperate; don't shout; let other people talk; be open-minded; explain yourself when asked; don't resort to violence or conspiracy in aid of your ideas."

This view of science as a "conversation" has been put forward by the philosopher Richard Rorty, and also resembles the philosophic arguments of Paul Feyerabend, who maintains that scientists use whatever method advances their purposes, despite their protestations of methodological purity. In like fashion, McCloskey declares that even the most "scientific" economists use all manner of wiles to persuade one another – leaning on authority (as in my use of Adam Smith in the opening paragraphs of this piece), or relying on the powerful associations of metaphors, such as those of "systems" and "mechanisms," or simply reaching for literary device.

McCloskey's attack on the dominant economic methodology is slashing and witty. Much as with Feyerabend, his prose is itself part of the attack, in that its very gaiety and irreverence challenge the formal citadel of the discipline as much as does the cogency of his argument. To judge by the extraordinary interest aroused by his article in the *Journal of Economic Literature,* in which he first raised the subject of rhetoric, McCloskey has touched a live nerve of the profession. Indeed, if the chief problem of economics were its continued obedience to sterile and antiquated methodology, his book might carry the day, and the *American Economic Review* might again be written in a more articulate prose, comprehensible to the nonspecialist, as it was thirty years ago.

The trouble is that this is not the chief difficulty with economics, at least as I see it. Nor is its chief difficulty its failure to predict the movements of the economy or the effects of government policies. McCloskey is correct when he says that prediction is not possible in these matters, at any rate not with the exactitude that would be commensurate with the conception of economics as a science. The main trouble with economics is its failure to make "sense out of economic experience," to use the criterion that McCloskey himself selects as the proper objective for the profession. This failure, however, does not derive from a tendency to carry on a conversation in the jargon of science. It arises from a failure to ponder what the conversation is to be about.

Let me illustrate this by discussing economics not as a conversation but as an ideology. By ideology I do not mean a knowingly biased or inaccurate description of the way society works, or an attempt to bamboozle the populace with explanations that economists know in their heart of hearts to be false. I mean, rather, an earnest and sincere effort to explain society as its ideologists themselves perceive it: an effort to speak the truth at all costs. What is "ideological" about such an effort is not its hypocrisy but its absence of historical perspective, its failure to perceive that its pronouncements are a belief system, conditioned like all belief systems by the political and social premises of the social order.

From such a perspective let us examine the conversation of the typical conventional economists today. It concerns the workings of a social world that is seen as split into two "sectors," one public, one private. The public sector is regarded as essentially political. That is, its raison d'être is perceived as primarily giving shape and force to the necessary social exercise of authority. The public sector is not viewed as having as vital and inextricable an economic role as the private sector. It is seen as peripheral to the production of wealth – indeed, it is often spoken of in economic conversation as constituting a drain on, rather than a source of, fruitful economic activity. The private sector, by contrast, is perceived as having an exclusively economic function, namely production and distribution of wealth, and it is thought to be entirely divorced from any intrinsic political tasks, lobbying aside.

The conversation also leads us to see activities in the private sector as yoked into social harness through the pushes and pulls of market forces that, as Muth contends, cannot be escaped or outwitted, even by government. Moreover, because we see the market as a "mechanism" for the rational allocation of resources, we are able to speak about its workings without the encumbrances of guilt that inhibited or cramped economic understanding in earlier times. Economists do not dismiss questions of morality, but they do not consider them as lying within the discourse of economics. It makes no sense for economists to converse about which of two equally profitable enterprises is "better" than for scientists to ask which of two experiments is more pleasing to the gods.

Now let us imagine how a historian of the future, wearing a different set of ideological spectacles, may perceive this selfsame economic world. He could well see it as not divided into two sectors, but as comprising a single socioeconomic whole, in which two spheres of responsibility and competence divide the tasks of authority and the tasks of production between them. The economic responsibility of the private sphere can then be described as the production of those goods and services that can be produced profitably, and its political responsibility as the provision of social discipline – steady work habits – through the payment or nonpayment of wages and other renumeration. By way of contrast, the political task of the public sphere appears as an exercise of the ancient prerogatives of state authority – mainly the making of laws, the conduct of war, and the performance of ceremony – while its economic function is seen as the production of all goods and services needed by the socioeconomic whole but unobtainable from the private sphere because they cannot be produced at a profit: mass education, general administration, and the public "infrastructure," for example, roads and dams.

From this point of view one could no longer carry on a conversation that took for granted the absence of political functions in the private sphere and of economic functions in the public sphere. Talk would now concern the manner in which such a curiously bifurcated system of social order arranged its material affairs. It would concern what kinds of output were encouraged and what kinds discouraged, or the nature of political life in a society of two authority structures, one recognized and one not. It might not be easy for economists with these views to find something to converse about with economists of another persuasion.

The appearance of the market mechanism also changes when seen through these new lenses. In addition to serving as an institution by which individuals' activities are integrated into a whole, it now appears as a means by which social perceptions are integrated into a belief system. In this system, the political categories of "land" and "capital," both of which refer to property rights, are made to stand on the same footing as "labor," the social category that embraces the living population, so that economists can converse about land, labor, and capital as if all three entities were on a par. No less remarkable is the fact that the market renders its participants – including the most informed and observant ones, the economic experts – quite unaware that the enthronement of profit as the criterion of economic rationality can only be achieved by the exclusion of basically all considerations of morality or esthetics from the calculus of judgment, so that rationality refers only to the rules for profitable activity, not to the rules for socially useful activity. That is why economists can converse about the efficiency of a firm but not about its social validity, and why they become irritated when soft-hearted people declare that an enterprise judged only by its economic performance is as seriously misperceived as a government judged only by its surplus or deficit.

I do not wish to argue here for the second set of lenses as against the first. I set forth these divergent, and in many ways incompatible, views only to make the point that to my mind the deepest problem of economics is not its failure to shake off an obsolete and damaging rhetoric, but its failure to recognize the inescapably ideological character of its thought. To put the matter the other way, suppose that conventional economists developed overnight the methodological flexibility and the literary skills of McCloskey himself: would their conversations thereupon make sense out of economic experience? Would they illuminate our historic plight, our possibilities for social evolution? *The Rhetoric of Economics* does not raise these questions; indeed it professes a certain satisfaction with the state of economics as it now exists, murky rhetoric aside. Donald McCloskey would, I believe, find much to write about if he turned his attention from the style of economics to its substance.

Notes

1. Adam Smith, *Lectures on Jurisprudence.* Oxford: Oxford University Press/Clarendon Press, 1978, 352.
2. In the "Lectures," Smith showed an early propensity to "truck" in "the natural inclination every one has to persuade." In the *Wealth of Nations,* published in 1776, he is more cautious: The propensity to "truck, barter, and exchange" may be "one of those original principles in human nature, of which no further account can be given," or it may, "as seems more probable, . . . be the necessary consequence of the faculties of reason and speech" (Ch. 2).

References

McCloskey, Donald. 1985. *The Rhetoric of Economics.* Madison: University of Wisconsin Press.

PART II

Economic rhetoric:
Further arguments

CHAPTER 5

Marxian theory and the rhetorics of economics

Stephen Resnick and Richard Wolff

Marxism contributes something quite distinctive to the growing awareness among economists that theirs is a kind of theory or discourse or rhetoric and that it is therefore unavoidably embroiled in the intensely argued disagreements over the nature of theory(ies), truth(s), science(s), and so forth. These issues have been debated as well within the Marxian tradition under the heading of epistemology. We will outline several Marxian positions on epistemology, with special stress on the one we find compelling. It partly resembles the positions, for example, of Rorty (1979) in philosophy, McCloskey (1985) in economics, and Gould (1981) in biology. However, there are also significant differences, since our position emerges from the Marxian tradition while theirs do not.

Marxian and non-Marxian economists usually think of their respective approaches as illuminating some basic (essential) set of social forces operating in economic reality. Typically each group produces its particular explanation focused on that set: scarcity and individual preferences for the neoclassicals and relations and forces of production for the Marxists. Each proves the validity of its explanation and, when pressed, proves the other's explanation to be in error.

We have been struck by the willingness of economists operating in these clearly different approaches to share nonetheless two key ideas: (1) one can discover a set of social processes that determines the behavior of all the other processes in society, and (2) one can discover some absolute standard that will prove to every honest thinker which of the alternative approaches to (theories of) society is, singularly, *the truth*. For some time we have raised questions about both of these ideas. More often than not we receive a common response from Marxist and non-Marxist economists alike. They ardently defend an almost religious search for the essential cause of social development and/or the absolutely true explanation (knowledge) of social life. Indeed, the passion accompanying the defenses led us to believe that questioning each of these ideas touches something profoundly personal and private in such individuals. For many, more seems to be at stake in their clinging to these two ideas than to the rest of the Marxian and non-Marxian traditions. We shall suggest some reasons for this behavior in the conclusions to this paper.

We are hardly alone in raising critical questions about the roles of such ideas in Marxian and non-Marxian approaches. In the non-Marxian tradition, for example, Rorty (1979) criticizes the attempts to locate some particular mental or physical processes, for example, reflections or sensory observations, which serve as a universal standard to determine the true among alternative theories of social or natural life. Rorty and others attack such attempts as "foundationalism," the claim to have found some absolute foundation for adjudicating among alternative explanations. McCloskey's (1985) arguments share this antifoundationalist orientation. His work and that of Klamer challenge economists' searches for incontestable measures of the truth.[1]

In Marxism Althusser (1970a, b) presents a major critique of traditional epistemology parallel to the antifoundationalism of Rorty. However, Althusser goes beyond Rorty's critique to suggest a distinctive and, we think, original way to think about the relationship among different theories and the nontheoretical aspects of social life; he calls it "overdetermination." His term has little to do with its use in mathematics; it traces its meaning rather to the work of Freud. Overdetermination implies a strictly antifoundationalist position (we prefer and thus will use the related term, "antiessentialist"). At the level of epistemology, this position rejects the rationalism (or "apriorism") and empiricism (or "positivism") that mark so much of current Marxian and non-Marxian thought.

Our work, while influenced by Rorty, follows more in the tradition of Althusser. It parallels, in Marxian economics, McCloskey's intervention in the neoclassical economics tradition. The first part of this paper examines overdetermination as an antiessentialist rejection of traditional epistemology – the hunt for absolute truths of social life – within the Marxian tradition. To accept strictly antifoundationalist theories of knowledge of the sorts advocated by Rorty and Althusser undermines, we have found, the belief that there are some essential (foundational) processes of life that determine all others. Thus, the second part of this chapter elaborates the related rejection of essentialism within social theory, the hunt for the ultimate determinant(s) of social development.

The critique of essentialist or foundationalist approaches in theories of knowledge *and* theories of society seems intolerable to many. They infer from the critique a condition of being unable to choose correctly among different and contending theories and being unable to state anything definitely meaningful about the world. Much of our effort in recent years has been aimed at disputing this inference. In the final part of this chapter we propose a criterion of choice among theories, namely the analysis of their social consequences on our lives. We also introduce the idea of each theory's entry-point concept as key to its particular knowledge construction. We argue for a nonessentialist epistemology informing a distinctively Marxian social theory, one capable of articulating (as well as being thoroughly self-conscious about) the definite meaning of its particular knowledge of social life.

Epistemology within the Marxian tradition

Marx had to deal with the problem of the scientific status of different theories of economics. He understood that his critique of classical political economy – of Smith, Ricardo, Malthus, Mill, and so on – was itself an alternative economic theory. Trained as a philosopher and having been a close student in particular of Hegel, Marx recognized the problem of theorizing about the relations between two different theories of how capitalist economies work and change.

Marx, in short, entered the terrain of epistemology. The Marxian theoretical tradition has ever since included debates over epistemological issues, often with intense partisanship. Is there one economic science to which classicals, neoclassicals, and Marxists variously contribute? Is there a singular set of established economic truths we may use as a standard or test for adjudicating the competing claims of alternative economic theories? Is there one correct logic or system of rules for linking propositions in economics that all theories must utilize if they are to be true? Or are some economic theories perhaps irreducibly different ways of conceiving, seeing, studying, and interpreting that part of reality called the economy? And if so, how do we theorize about their coexistence and interrelationships?

Unfortunately, most Marxists as well as most non-Marxists have either ignored the debates and issues of epistemology or, when pressed, taken very conventional, unexamined epistemological positions. That is, they presumed that truth was singular, a matter of using the right logical rules (''the scientific method'') to draw the correct inferences from ''the relevant'' data. Marxists and non-Marxists pursued their investigations, each group more or less confident that their particular theory was the closest (then available) to the presumedly singular truth.

The Marxists considered the non-Marxists as at best ignorant of the greater proximity of Marxist theory to truth (or at worst mere ideologues and apologists for capitalism). The non-Marxists held the reverse perspective. If, from both perspectives, truth, science, and logic are singulars confronting different theories, then one theory must be true or truer while the others are false.

The Marxian theoretical tradition always contained a dissenting epistemological voice. This voice appears in the writings of Lenin, Georg Lukacs, Antonio Gramsci, Mao, and most recently and powerfully in the French Marxist, Louis Althusser (Resnick and Wolff 1987a). It mounts a critical attack upon traditional epistemology. It demands instead the acceptance of Marxian theory's irreducible difference from both classical and neoclassical theories. It envisions a world in which alternative ways of thinking about economics challenge and contest with one another. Alongside struggles over class and politics, the world contains as well struggles over how to think about everything, including economics.

This position within Marxism rejects notions of truth as singular. It claims rather that its version of Marxian theory is no more true than other, very different theories both within and without the Marxian tradition. It elaborates its differences from them and emphasizes that its propositions have social consequences distinct from theirs. An examination of this position within the Marxian epistemological debates offers a new perspective on current discussions about what economists do, what economic theories are, and what scientific status these theories can claim.

The epistemological standpoints of the majority within Marxism are familiar because they are identical to the majority standpoints outside Marxism. The first of these is often referred to as empiricism or positivism. This epistemology holds that we can find the true one among contesting theories by appealing to the facts, to empirical reality. Our senses provide reliable access to factual reality. Alternative theories are to be tested for their "fits" to that factual reality. The best-fitting theory wins the accolade for "truth" or "being most true." Many Marxists, past and present, affirm their commitments to Marxism on the grounds of its achieving such a best fit.

The prevalent form of Marxian empiricism celebrates the "facts of history." Theories are seen as mere cerebral efforts at explanation that deserve no loyalty unless and until they are verified by actual "human practice" in the concreteness of "history." Theories are judged to be realistic or not according to their conformity to "actual history." Their accession to the status of truth depends then on the extent of their realism: how fully, adequately, and precisely they conform to the facts of history. Whether theories actually "work" determines their truthfulness. Current empiricist work in economics, non-Marxian as well as Marxian, stresses a variant of this notion: the "predictive power/accuracy" of theories is the ultimate test of their validity.

Like other empiricisms, the Marxian variant implies a notion that ever more empirical tests cumulatively approach "the truth." Successive verifications and falsifications are thought to purify the theory as it approaches "the truth." Empiricist epistemologies are comforting in their view that theory today is necessarily truer than it was before, that propositions falsified are absolutely discardable, and that greater truth lies ahead.

The other major epistemological position is rationalism or apriorism. Like empiricism, it views truth as singular, "the" objective of all theories. It also shares empiricism's view that there is an essential cause of true knowledge. However, it rejects empiricism's criterion by which we are to select the true one among competing theories. Rationalists typically deride empiricists for their "fetishism of facts." They enjoy pointing out that "the facts" touching upon any object of investigation and theorization are always infinite in number. No investigators could possibly canvass all the facts and then test theories against them all; the very project is absurd.

Rationalists insist that all people must and do select *some* from among the infinite facts they will consider pertinent for any purpose, including the testing of alternative theories. Empiricists' "facts" are always and necessarily "selected facts," and empiricists are to be attacked whenever they claim otherwise. Hence what matters are the principles of selection used by different "fact gatherers." Rationalists insist that prefactual principles of reason guide everyone's fact gathering. Therefore, for rationalists, to get at the truth requires attention not primarily to the selected facts gathered around some proposition, but rather to the underlying reasoning that produced both the proposition and the fact-selection process.

Rationalists research the long history of human inquiry to find true prefactual principles of reason; those that have stood the test of time and of innumerable efforts to find faults in them. Human reason (whether divinely inspired or not is a debate between religious and nonreligious rationalists) has critically purified certain principles of thought that can lead theory to the truth. This includes guiding our selections of the facts relevant to our theories. Rationalists propose human reason as a test of facts (i.e., their relevance) while empiricists test reason (theories) against facts.

For Marxian rationalists, the highest achievement of human reason to date lies in the Marxian theoretical tradition. Marxian theory supersedes – in the Hegelian sense of absorbing as it supersedes – all previous social theory including, for example, all that was important in the theoretical discoveries of Smith, Ricardo, et al. Marx took it all further, thereby bequeathing to us the purest available principles for studying society, that is, inventing propositions, selecting facts, and juxtaposing them.

Both rationalists and empiricists are epistemological essentialists: They presume an essential order in the world about which they theorize. They both generally presume the human mind's capacity eventually to grasp and express this essential order. They differ over whether factual reality ultimately determines (is the essence of) the truths we reason or whether reason ultimately determines (is the essence of) the truths we construct and those facts we consider. Both epistemological positions – which often occur mixed together in individual Marxian works – rank Marxian theory's approximation to truth ahead of all other theories. Both have criticized devotees of such other theories as ignorant or ideological in the fullest negativity of the terms.

By contrast, the Marxian tradition has always contained a different epistemological position radically opposed to both empiricism and rationalism

(Resnick and Wolff, 1987a). Borrowing a term from Sigmund Freud's psychoanalysis of dreams, Lukacs and then Althusser made "overdetermination" a central concept of this different epistemological position and indeed of Marxian social theory in general. Theories, this argument claims, are so many different ways of making sense of the world. Theories are not determined by *either* certain facts *or* certain principles of reasoning, but rather by both of these and beyond them by each and every other aspect of society. Human beings think about their environments by conceiving particular relationships among whichever particular parts of those environments attract their reflections. Which parts are attractive and which relationships seem plausible depend on the totality of influences impacting particular human beings. Since individuals and groups live different lives, that is, are impacted by different sets of social influences, they correspondingly invent and develop different theories.

In a word, theories are overdetermined by everything else. They are not, for example, determined by facts or by acts of reason any more or less than by climate, diet, cultural fashions, political confrontations, or anything else occurring within society. Theories are stories people tell as one way to cope with their environments alongside other ways, such as housing they build, love relations they enter, and political systems they invent. Each of these is likewise overdetermined by everything else. As it makes no sense to ask which kind of housing, love, or politics is true, so it makes no sense to ask that of theories either.

The truth or falsity of alternative theories is a nonissue for the overdeterminist epistemological position, rather like comparing different cuisines to determine which one is true. From this perspective, the Marxian tradition encompasses multiple, different theories or stories, much as other traditions have always done. These theories differ because they have been overdetermined by different combinations of social influences.

This notion of overdetermination clashes profoundly with conventional, that is, essentialist notions of causality, both in matters of epistemology and in social theory generally. Overdetermination means something very different from complex interaction, systems of simultaneous equations, interdependence, mutual causality, or any of the other variant forms of conventional cause-and-effect logic. It goes far beyond these conventional concepts to propose a basically different approach to cause and effect. The key word to express the uniqueness of overdetermination is "constitutivity."

Every aspect of society is understood as totally constituted by all the influences emanating from every other aspect. Nothing is self-created; nothing can exist independent of these influences. Autonomous objects do not influence each other, as in the variant forms of cause-and-effect logic. Rather, objects only exist as effects of and by virtue of influences from all the other similarly constituted objects in a society. Every aspect of society is simultaneously a cause and an effect.

Overdetermination transforms the idea of causality. It becomes futile to try to explain the cause of A by searching for the essential B and/or C and/or D that best or most explain it. That essentialist effort is in principle unacceptable. Overdetermination begins instead with the presumption that event A is caused by innumerable influences emanating from all the other events in the social totality. In principle, then, the full or final explanation of A's causes is impossible. Theories cannot and do not provide explanations of events in the sense of the true, adequate, comprehensive, and complete account of their essential causes. This includes Marxian theories, of course.

Since theories cannot do what conventional epistemologies insist they can and must do, from an overdeterminist standpoint, the latter formulates an alternative concept of thinking and theories. Theories are inherently partial, distinct stories or rhetorics about portions of social reality. None grasps the totality, however shrill its claims to do so. All are stories built around particular emphases on aspects of society deemed worthy of theoretical attention. Theories differ partly according to what they focus upon. They differ in their rules or logics for linking various propositions into particular knowledges, sciences, truths, and so on that they produce. Finally, they also differ in the criteria they erect – definitions of truth – to guide their practitioners in deciding whether to accept, reject, or change propositions they invent or encounter. Indeed, such criteria include the epistemological notions we have been discussing: whether truth is singular or plural and whether it inheres in facts or in reason or is a discardable fantasy.

One difference, then, between an overdeterminist Marxian theory and alternative theories inside and outside the Marxian tradition is a difference over epistemology. Empiricism and rationalism are essentialist epistemologies: They agree that theories all share an essential goal (*telos*) of uncovering the singular truth of the world, and they agree that truth has an essential component, but they disagree on what the singular truth is and on what the essence of truth is. Overdetermination, in contrast, specifies a strictly anti-essentialist epistemology. Truths are plural, not singular; and they have no essences since facts and reason are but two of the infinite social influences that quite literally produce them.

This distinctive epistemology connects to other distinguishing marks of an overdeterminist Marxism. For example, it follows from this approach that another way to distinguish theories is by noticing the particular partiality of each. We have called this the issue of entry points. Different theories all confront the chaos of the infinite diversity of aspects and processes, factors making up any possible object of thinking. Faced with this enormity, all theories commence by focusing their attention on some particular aspect or process: their entry point into the web of interactions among many aspects they aim to articulate.

Theories differ in their entry-point concepts. For example, as we shall argue below, Marxian theories typically enter into their analyses of economies by focusing on class and power, whereas neoclassical theory focuses on individuals' preferences and productive capabilities. Theories also differ in the logics used to link their propositions, for example, overdeterminist rather than determinist or reductionist. An overdeterminist logic in social theory means that no social events are presumed to have essential determinants and hence no effort is made to reduce events to essential causes. By contrast, the determinist logic favored by most Marxian and neoclassical economists seeks to reduce social events to some essential determinants. Simply put, the overdeterminist theory is antiessentialist in the logical structure of its propositions, while determinist or reductionist theory is strictly essentialist.

After World War II particularly, essentialist and antiessentialist (overdeterminist) positions battled within Marxism. The issues: how to think about what theories are, and how to think about what societies are. A growing voice inside Marxism, shaped and exemplified by Althusser, propounded a kind of antiessentialism (antireductionism) that has deeply influenced literary theory (e.g., the works of Macherey [1978], Jameson [1981], and Eagleton [1983]), philosophy (e.g., the works of Foucault [1976] and Lyotard [1984]), and biology (e.g., the work of Levins and Lewontin [1985]). We propose to examine how antiessentialist Marxian theory bears directly on the issue of the rhetorics of economics.

Anti-essentialist Marxian theory

Alongside their differences, much of the Marxian and non-Marxian economic traditions share a common methodological theme: They take some aspect(s) of society to be the essential determining cause or origin of the behavior of all other aspects of society. Such essences are thought to cause the existence of the other social aspects; they are never thought to be constituted by them. These essences represent objects for social theory parallel to those sought in some physicists' dreams: the ultimate building blocks of the universe. Most economic theorizing has turned this natural scientists' vision into reality: The ultimate particles that cause economic life have been discovered, named, and observed.

From the perspective of overdeterminist (i.e., antiessentialist) Marxian theory, we propose to explore the nature and effects of this dream. We will consider its presence first within the broad Marxian economics tradition and then within neoclassical economic theory.

In the hundred years since Marx's death, individuals thinking within that tradition have debated, often ferociously, the issue of how to connect the economic with the noneconomic aspects of society. Three broad positions emerged and contest to this day. All find support for their views in Marx's texts. The first is an economic determinist position in which economic govern noneconomic aspects. The second position reacts to the first by reversing the order of governance: Noneconomic parts of society (most often political aspects) shape and determine the economic. A third and middle position allows economic and noneconomic aspects of society to affect each other but affirms an *ultimately* determining influence of the economic upon the interaction between economic and noneconomic.

Much of the debate has turned on the relation between the so-called base of society (its economics) and the superstructure (its politics, culture, and ideology). The first position claims that two economic aspects, the forces of production (read technology) and the relations of production (read class), combine together as the base. So combined, they determine the forms and development of the superstructure. The latter includes laws passed and enforced, music created and performed, economic theorizing written and taught, and so on. Called the mode of production, this basic combination of forces and relations of production comprises what is thought to be a self-reproducing totality. The mode of production determines superstructural laws, cultural processes, and so on, so as to reproduce itself. In effect, noneconomic aspects of society are relegated to a clearly secondary role. They become phenomena of and functional to the reproduction of a governing economic essence: the economic base or mode of production.

Some Marxian economic determinists ask the next logical question for any essentialist: Between the forces and relations of production, which is the ultimate or last instance determinant of the other and a fortiori of the rest of the superstructure? In answer, some essentialize the forces (Cohen 1978) while others prefer to essentialize the relations (Dobb 1947). They too struggle over which is the true essence.

Noneconomic determinists essentialize some aspect(s) of the superstructure taking it (them) to be the most powerful governing force in society. Two broad approaches of this sort may be identified. The first treats the forms and distribution of power over individuals and property as the essential causes of economic classes, technology, culture, and so on (Poulantzas 1978; Bowles and Gintis 1982). The second focuses instead on human consciousness as the ultimate determinant of economic and social behavior (Thompson 1963). In contrast to economic determinism, these alternative determinisms tend to relegate economics to a secondary or derivative position in society and history.

The middle position allows the mode of production and the superstructure both to affect one another and variously to *dominate* one another. The mode of production ultimately determines whether and when economic and non-economic aspects variously dominate one another across history (Hirst and Hindess 1975). For example, in a noncapitalist society, politics or religion may dominate in the sense of shaping and guaranteeing economic exploitation, but that dominating role is itself determined by the particular mode of production present in such a society. This middle position represents the most sophisticated variant of economic determinism yet devised within Marxism.

An idea common to these three Marxian positions is that the preferred governing aspect of society is always a cause and never itself an effect of the other aspects of society. The mutual overdetermination of these aspects – the idea that the existence of each is the combined effect of all the others – is ruled out of inquiry and out of their debates. Instead, each orders the aspects of society according to its ranking of causal importance, reducing them to its preferred final, ultimate cause.

Essentialisms in Marxian social theory parallel the essentialisms in traditional epistemologies. The former insist on a final determinant of social history, while the latter insist on a final determinant of ''the'' truth. Essentialist Marxian social theories, of course, hold no monopoly on such views. Neoclassical economic theory affirms its determining essence(s) with every bit as much confidence and bravado as do any Marxists.

Parallel to the Marxian tradition, neoclassical theorists' attempts to link the relation of the economy to the rest of society have produced formulations in which the economy determines society. Since they tend to limit themselves more strictly to economics as a discipline, it is within economics that their essentialist theorizing is most clearly visible. Indeed, classical and neoclassical economic thought since Adam Smith displays a concerted effort to discover the minimum set of driving forces – essences – that determine economic events.

These essences have been reduced to three: inherent human preferences, given private endowments of productive resources, and a given technology. These essential attributes of human beings are understood to interact in markets to generate individuals' supply and demand behaviors. These in turn produce patterns of prices and incomes. In the last instance, then, the interaction between human beings' preferences and productive capabilities determines the wealth of modern society and its distribution among citizens.

Interestingly, neoclassical economic theory resembles the Marxian approach that affirms the determining influence of a human being's power or consciousness on economic events. Both essentialize the struggle of people to realize innate potential in the face of societal or natural constraints. They only disagree over which characteristics of human beings are to be treated as determining

essences: power or consciousness in the Marxian approaches versus preferences and productive capabilities in neoclassical theory. Given their common
essentialization of human nature, we may call both of them humanist approaches, in contrast to the economic determinism of the traditional Marxist
approach. The tendency toward a convergence of Marxist and non-Marxist
humanists has surfaced recently in writers who marry the kind of Marxist
theory that essentializes power to the neoclassical essentialization of individual utility or profit maximization (Roemer 1982; Bowles 1985; and Elster
1985).

Our understanding of Marx is decidedly antiessentialist in its approach
both to socioeconomic analyses and to knowledge. It grows out of dissent
from the Marxist determinist debates and from the contending neoclassical
theory. It rejects the notion that any one of society's aspects, chosen from the
infinite set of class, culture, power, technology, preferences, resources, and
so forth, could be the governing essence of the rest. There is no essence in
society from which the behaviors of all other social aspects can be derived as
necessary effects. Rather, each aspect of society is understood to exist, to be
constituted, as the site of the combined influences emanating from all the
others.

It follows for Marxian theory as we understand it that each aspect of society, the economic as well as the noneconomic, exists only in and through its
interrelations with all the other aspects; it has no independent existence. From
such an overdeterminist perspective, neither the base nor the superstructure
nor any element within them can be ranked as a cause without being simultaneously an effect. Likewise, the preferences and productive capabilities of
neoclassical theory must be conceived to be constituted effects, as well as
constituting causes of incomes, prices, and all the other aspects of society.

An overdeterminist Marxism offers a new way to differentiate one theory
from another. It focuses on each theory's relational logic (determinist versus
overdeterminist) and on its specific entry-point concepts. Using this taxonomy
we may diagram differences among the economic theories surveyed here as
shown in Figure 1.

Practitioners of each theory depicted in Figure 1 posit their respective conceptual entry points and logics to construct their distinct stories of society
(their objects of knowledge). Unidirectional arrows indicate determinist logics, while the bidirectional arrow indicates overdetermination. Each theory's
object, society, is given a different number to underscore that the knowledges
of society produced are as different as the entry points and logics used to
construct those knowledges. Of course, this diagram is itself but one story
constructed by one theory about the structures of different theories, including
itself.

Each of the theories in Figure 1, except the overdeterminist Marxian the-

Theory	Point of entry		Object
	Mode of production $\Big\}$	Relations Forces - - - - - - - - ⟩	Society 1
Marxian Tradition	Human power $\Big\}$	Over people - - - - - - ⟩ Over property	Society 2
	Human consciousness	- - - - - - - - - - - - - - - ⟩	Society 3
Neo- classical	Human nature $\Big\}$	Preferences Technology - - - - - - ⟩ Endowments	Society 4
Overdeterminist Marxism	Class	⟨ - - - - - - - - - - - - - - ⟩	Society 5

Figure 1

ory, embraces an essentialism in its story. Each except the latter offers its entry point as *also* the essential determinant of the structure and dynamic of society.

Let us focus briefly on some differences between the overdeterminist Marxian theory that has been developed recently and neoclassical theory (Resnick and Wolff, 1987b). For this Marxian theory, a particular notion of class is the conceptual entry point that focuses its story or rhetoric. Class is understood not as a matter of power or property, but rather as a process in which surplus labor is performed and its fruits distributed to others than those who performed it. As Freud (1938) conceptualizes an unconscious as a repressed aspect of individual life, so this Marxian theory sees the production and distribution of surplus labor (which it dubs "the class process") as a repressed aspect of social life. This class process needs to be admitted, recognized, studied, and changed in order to accomplish a just and egalitarian social order: much as Freudian psychoanalysis and psychotherapy permit the individual to admit, recognize, study, and change his or her unconscious as a means to a better life.

By theorizing with the class process as entry point, Marxists hope to change society in particular ways. For neoclassical theory, the notions of human preferences and productive capabilities push society to change (its institutions, laws, and so forth) in the particular ways it prefers: toward the optimal outcome of the wealth-seeking interactions of individuals. These two radically different theories produce different understandings of the same society; there is a Marxian capitalism and a neoclassical capitalism in the United States.

Moreover, these two different stories shape our economic and noneconomic lives in different ways. Our politics, culture, and economy are all influenced by the complex effects of these different ways of making sense of our lives.

From the neoclassical standpoint, the production and distribution of surplus labor does not exist. The Marxian entry point has no status as a concept within the neoclassical knowledge of social life; hence it is a nonissue in society and in social analysis. From the overdeterminist Marxian standpoint, the neoclassical entry-point concepts of preferences and productive capabilities do exist, but they, like all other aspects of society, are overdetermined by, among all else, class – that focal Marxian idea that is completely absent from the neoclassical view. Given such differences, is it any wonder that practitioners of the two theories have been at one another for the past hundred years?

The two logics deployed are different, too. Neoclassical theory reduces virtually all economic events to its ultimately determining preferences: technology and endowments.

Overdeterminist Marxian theory makes its entry-point concept of class into merely one of the infinite aspects of society that mutually and collectively constitute one another. Class, human preferences, productive capabilities, music, economic theories, and so on – all interact, mutually shaping and thereby changing the existence of each.

Radically different consequences follow from these two different approaches that, as noted, shape our lives in different ways. For example, in the neoclassical view, wealth and poverty result in the last instance from human preferences (and their derived choices), initial resources endowments, technological possibilities, and whatever barriers in society may constrain the proper working of these essential determinants of economic life. The neoclassical notion of optimum solutions to each individual's struggle for wealth and happiness recognizes that barriers may arise to block such solutions, for example, power-seeking individuals, irrational behaviors, and extramarket phenomena interfering with markets.

In the Marxian theory emphasized here, wealth and poverty are explained in terms of, but never reduced to, the class process. So Marxian theory stresses how class and nonclass aspects of life combine to distribute incomes across society. Its approach emphasizes the overdetermination of income distribution versus the neoclassicals' reduction of distribution to but three of what Marxian theory sees as its many determinants. Its approach emphasizes class, while neoclassical theory ignores it.

These different understandings of the wealth and poverty of our society influence our attitudes toward one another, toward social justice, toward politics, toward state programs to aid the rich and those to aid the poor, toward U.S. foreign policy in third-world nations, and so on. Different theories matter tangibly and practically in terms of their consequences for our thinking and our actions.

Consequences of rejecting essentialist theories

Rejecting essentialist epistemologies (the search for the absolute truth) and essentialist social theories (the search for essential causes of social life) carries serious consequences. It seems to open a door to a discursive field that few want opened. The open door would have to admit some of the most outrageous conceptualizations in the history of social theories as simply other rhetorics affirming their particularly produced stories. All theories would have to be considered as alternative, socially contrived stories typically displaying not only distinctive knowledges of social life but also distinctive claims about truth. With the door opened in this way, the urgent questions become why some theories prevail over others for periods of history and what social consequences flow from the prevalence of one rather than another.

For most Marxists and non-Marxists alike this is a door few ever want to open. Each of them seems much more comfortable affirming that their particular rhetoric is the right one, the most exact mirror of the singular objective reality, and that therefore it is not mere rhetoric at all. It is other theories that are wrong or misguided and thus merely rhetorics or ideologies: tales to convince the unwary and naive. Essentialists on all sides seem much more comfortable proving time and again that their respective essences in social theory are warranted by the facts and/or by the wisdom of Marx or Smith, depending on which tradition holds their loyalty. Therefore, we do not have intertheoretic conversations in which alternative stories offering their different entry points, logics, and objects challenge and cross-fertilize one another. Rather we have the vain trumpeting at cross purposes of theories that each claim to hold privileged communion with the truth and that denounce other theories as dogmatic, logically invalid, not warranted by the facts, and so on.

Even those who approvingly recognize theories to be alternative rhetorics or idea systems or language games often fall back in their own work to positions of epistemological essentialism, assertions that their rhetoric is somehow closer to "the truth." We wonder why. Perhaps the reason is the aforementioned conscious or unconscious fear that if all we have are but rhetorics, we will lose the boundaries between ideology and science, Marxism and neoclassical theory, fantasy and reality, physics and poetry. Would scientific order give way then to discursive anarchy and the tyranny of ideology or nonsense? One way to close this door is to privilege, as "the truth," one particular discourse or its logic or its point of entry – and so close the door to unwelcome theories.

Perhaps another part of the reason lies in particular historical events. Non-Marxists tend to view whatever Marx and Marxists have to offer theoretically through particular interpretations of the Soviet experience. Put simply, Marxism is equated to Stalinism. This equation generates significant consequences. For example, the Marxian tradition is then often collapsed into economic determinism, which is only one of the many theories contesting within that tradition. Equating Marxism with Stalinism makes no more sense than equating Catholicism with the Spanish Inquisition or neoclassical theory with the Vietnam war. Nonetheless, what is acceptable as an idea at any moment is influenced partly by the concurrent interpretations of historic events. One way to close the door on unwelcome theories is to conflate them with disliked historical events.

Perhaps still another part of the reason involves clinging to the notion that it is possible to prove that other theories are logically flawed and hence necessarily rejected. Surely there must be some way to establish, to agree upon, some minimum set of ideas that could serve as a standard of truth and falsehood across all theories. If not, how could we ever be convinced that our own is better than alternative theories? We would be left with whatever we find convincing or satisfying at that moment because of our own personal politics, culture, and economics.

We are all products in part of the historic influence of religions that proclaim the existence and power of absolutes. Science and the language of mathematics have become the new religion and its holy script. They give subtle aid and comfort to those who discount the "old" deities while they rush to discover godlike essences in social theory and in knowledge theory. To ask individuals to give up their beliefs in absolutes and in specific methods/rituals that capture such absolutes has always been one of the most dramatic, difficult, and personal requests that can be made of them.

Suppose however that the rejections of essentialism in epistemology and in social theory were widely accepted. Suppose that the implications of Rorty's and other like works were convincing and led us to embrace finally a democracy of theoretical differences. We would then treat every theory as a story about the nature of society – never complete, never more or less true than other stories, merely different from them. Does this mean that thinking no longer really matters as we lapse into indifference about the different stories? Does this door opening lead inevitably into a retreat to Nietzsche?

We think not. Different social theories matter enormously. They do not matter in terms of the futile and fetishistic game of asking which one is closer to some absolute truth. They do matter in the different ways they affect our lives. Neoclassical theory affects the ways we do and do not see things in society, the ways we view recessions, wealth, poverty, and in general the complex interrelations of daily life. In other words, neoclassical theory shapes our existence. It matters. Each of the Marxian theories discussed in this paper has changed our lives in still different ways. Those theories matter, too.

Therefore we cannot remain indifferent before this onslaught of different theorizings, each offering its own knowledge, truth claim, standards of proof, and distinctive social consequences. We choose among them not on the basis of a discovered essence, "the truth," but rather because of the different consequences each produces in and on our lives. Because those different social consequences matter urgently to us, so, too, must the theories linked to them.

We find some theories horrific, others magnificent, and still others at various points in between. We form close theoretical alliances with some theorists, while we fear or ignore others. We do this through our theory's assessment of the conjunctural connections between *all* theories and the rest of the society in which we live. We are not lost in a relativist limbo, but are rather partisans of some theories as against others.

Note

1. See especially Chapter 1 by Klamer and McCloskey.

References

Althusser, Louis. 1970a. *For Marx.* Translated by Ben Brewster. New York: Vintage Books.

———. 1970b. *Reading Capital.* Translated by Ben Brewster. London: New Left Books.

Bowles, Samuel. 1985. "Post-Marxian Economics: Labour, Learning and History." *Social Science Information* 24: 3.

Bowles, Samuel, and Herbert Gintis. 1982. "On the Class-Exploitation-Domination Reduction." *Politics and Society* 11: 3.

Cohen, G. A. 1978. *Karl Marx's Theory of History: A Defense.* Princeton: Princeton University Press.

Dobb, Maurice. 1947. *Studies in the Development of Capitalism.* New York: International Publishers.

Eagleton, Terry. 1983. *Literary Theory: An Introduction.* Minneapolis: University of Minnesota Press.

Elster, Jon. 1985. *Making Sense of Marx.* Cambridge: Cambridge University Press.

Foucault, Michel. 1976. *The Archaeology of Knowledge.* Translated by A. M. Sheridan Smith. New York: Harper & Row.

Freud, Sigmund. 1938. "The Interpretation of Dreams." In *The Basic Writings of Sigmund Freud,* Translated by A. A. Brill. New York: The Modern Library (Random House).

Gould, Stephen Jay. 1981. *The Mismeasure of Man*. New York: Norton.

Hirst, Paul Q., and Barry Hindess. 1975. *Pre-capitalist Modes of Production*. London and Boston: Routledge and Kegan Paul.

Jameson, Frederic. 1981. *The Political Unconscious: Narrative as a Socially Symbolic Act*. Ithaca, N. Y.: Cornell University Press.

Levins, Richard, and Richard Lewontin. 1985. *The Dialectical Biologist*. Cambridge, Mass.: Harvard University Press.

Lukacs, Georg. 1978. *The Ontology of Social Being*, vols. 1 and 2. Translated by David Fernbach. London: Merlin Press.

Lyotard, Jean-Francois. 1984. *The Post-Modern Condition: A Report on Knowledge*. Translated by Geoff Bennington and Brian Massumi. Minneapolis: University of Minnesota Press.

Macherey, Pierre. 1978. *A Theory of Literary Production*. Translated by Geoffrey Wall. London and Boston: Routledge and Kegan Paul.

McCloskey, Donald N. 1985. *The Rhetoric of Economics*. Madison: University of Wisconsin Press.

Poulantzas, Nicos. 1978. *State, Power, Socialism*. London: New Left Books.

Resnick, Stephen, and Richard Wolff. 1987a. *Knowledge and Class: A Critique of Political Economy*. Chicago: University Chicago Press.

————. 1987b. *Economics: Neoclassical Versus Marxian*. Baltimore: Johns Hopkins University Press.

Roemer, John. 1982. *A General Theory of Class and Exploitation*. Cambridge, Mass.: Harvard University Press.

Rorty, Richard. 1979. *Philosophy and the Mirror of Nature*. Princeton: Princeton University Press.

Thompson, Edward P. 1963. *The Making of the English Working Class*. New York: Vintage Books.

CHAPTER 6

Economic rhetoric:
The social and historical context

A. W. Coats

I

By comparison with the situation in literary studies, the discussion of economic rhetoric or discourse (the terms will be used interchangeably here) is still in its infancy. In this respect economics clearly lags behind other branches of science studies,[1] which is hardly surprising, considering economists' general lack of interest in cognate fields of inquiry and their manifest disdain for the history of their own discipline. Notwithstanding the pretensions of some of its proponents, it is still too early to judge whether the study of economic discourse will eventually grow up to become a mature research program with a recognized place and influence on its parent discipline. The preliminary results are promising, even exciting, and as budding research programs require nurturing, it is appropriate at this stage to focus on the constructive possibilities.

To the present writer this self-denying ordinance imposes severe constraints, for the Klamer/McCloskey (KM) agenda incorporates a number of negative features that constitute serious impediments to a balanced appraisal of its implications for an understanding of the development and functioning of economics as an academic discipline and a profession. The KM campaign is based on, and actively propagates, a currently fashionable radical epistemology (or antiepistemology) that directly conflicts with widely accepted views of the nature and purposes of the scientific enterprise. In particular, McCloskey's exaggerated and misdirected attack on economic methodology (rather than the abuse of it) – in which he has lumped together and caricatured various intellectual positions under the blanket label "modernism" – is both "alarming"[2] (as he intends) and confusing. He willfully blurs the distinction between familiar and useful categories, for instance, declaring, "Economics is a collection of literary forms, not a science. Indeed, science is a collection of literary forms, not a science. And literary forms are scientific." Moreover, lest the reader should infer that economics (like science) is not a science, he adds helpfully a page later, that "economics *is* science, a successful sort at that." Elsewhere he also terms it "a peculiar variant of social history," "humanism," equivalent (identical?) to "sociology," and "literary too."[3]

No doubt these terminological maneuvers are designed to have a shock effect, to disturb the reader's complacency prior to changing the conventions of established economic discourse, and, indeed, the initial impact may well be salutary. Whether in the long run this practice promotes "good" disciplinary conversation – that is, mutual comprehension as a basis for intersubjective agreement in the advancement of knowledge – is another matter.

Unfortunately the concepts of "rhetoric," "conversation," and "persuasion" that figure so prominently in the KM campaign are not sufficiently clear, precise, and comprehensive to provide a basis for understanding the distinctive character, operation, and social significance of economics or any other intellectual discipline. The initial applications of discourse and rhetorical analysis in case studies of rational expectations, economics textbooks, the use of statistical significance tests, and the writings of Muth, Fogel, et al., have undoubtedly been illuminating, providing a useful addition to the repertoire of concepts and techniques already available to serious students and practitioners of the discipline. Whether the techniques of literary criticism can significantly enhance our knowledge and understanding of the substance of a purportedly "scientific" discipline remains an open question.[4] It is appropriate to recall the intellectual historian's quip that "text without context is pretext," and to suggest that the KM campaign has so far lacked the depth of insight and evidential richness to be found in numerous recent history and sociology of science studies.

Critics of the KM program who sense that the preoccupation with rhetoric and discourse is, indeed, "mere" conversation, that it lacks adequate contextual substance or "thick description" (in Clifford Geertz's sense), are unlikely to be reassured by the accompanying all-out attack on empiricism and the moderate realist interpretation of science. Among other controversial claims, KM reject the philosopher's concept of a demarcation criterion by which to differentiate science from other species of knowledge, they appear to deny the possibility of any "objective" knowledge of the world, and they dismiss or belittle the notion that truth is the (or a) goal of scientific research. These views faithfully reflect the uncertain and volatile postpositivist state of the philosophy of science and economic methodology, raising questions too fundamental and far-reaching to be treated adequately here. Nevertheless they demand some attention, however brief, before turning to the more mundane purpose of this chapter, which is designed to suggest how a more direct and conventional sociological approach can add depth and content to the KM campaign.

II

One obstacle to good conversation between KM and their critics is the coexistence of conflicting concepts of discourse, currently a topic of active discussion among historians and sociologists of science. According to the so-called Anglo-Saxon view, discourse is epiphenomenal and clearly distinguishable from actual scientific practice (*praxis*), whereas KM, in conformity with continental authors like Foucault, deny or seek to dissolve the distinction between language and action. To Foucault, for instance, discourse is *constitutive:* While it does not actually prohibit a distinction between a thing and what is said about a thing (which is crucial for realists), it insists that the distinction is actively created rather than an inescapable feature of reality.[5] KM apparently view knowledge simply as an ongoing, ever-changing product of conversation that can be usefully studied virtually without reference to what is "out there" in the world. Nevertheless it is entirely possible to accept the constructivist's account of knowledge as an active, creative process without at the same time denying the existence of "reality." To the historian and sociologist the concepts of language-community and speech-community, cited by Klamer, are useful in analyzing past and present economic "schools" (as will be suggested below in Part VI), and the same applies to Clifford Geertz's ethnographic approach[6] which recalls Axel Leijonhufvud's light-hearted but brilliantly incisive anthropological account of the economics tribe.[7] The concepts of initiation rites and the socialization of new recruits into economics are familiar, but they have not been systematically utilized.[8] Yet when Klamer goes on to approve Geertz's argument that scholarly disciplines are not simply "coigns of vantage," but also "ways of being in the world . . . forms of life . . . or varieties of noetic experience," and Nelson Goodman's idea of the "multiple actual worlds" presupposed indifferent conversations, it is time to plant our feet more firmly on the ground and reemphasize the subject matter (i.e., content) variations between (and indeed within) disciplines.[9]

Curiously enough, the aura of philosophical (or literary) abstraction in some parts of the KM writings sharply contrasts with much recent research in science studies. At one time sociologists of knowledge (for example, Karl Mannheim) were justly accused of dealing in vague general categories that were not amenable to historical research. Nowadays, however, the focus has shifted markedly as the effort to discover "what scientists actually do" has led to a preoccupation with minutiae, so that the broader purposes of the undertaking are obscured by the details. While one may warmly endorse Richard Rorty's claim on behalf of community "solidarity," expressing "the desire for as much inter-subjective agreement as possible,"[10] it does not follow that this solidarity "is threatened by the pursuit of objectivity which values a relationship with something outside the community above relationships within."[11] On the contrary, Rorty puts the cart before the horse. It is the collective quest for "reliable" intersubjective knowledge that has created the broader scientific community, giving it special, historically identifiable, characteristics.[12] Nor is it necessary (or desirable?) to deny the existence of "one world" simply because there are multiple ways of perceiving and interpreting it. As Mary Hesse observes, in a critique of radical conventionalism (an approach apparently favored by KM):

> Science does not depend on algorithmic rules of methodology, nor on necessary and sufficient conditions for what counts as replicability, and in general, science need not be supposed to exhibit one-to-one correspondence with objects and regularities in the world independently of human categories and classifications.[13]

Nevertheless, science exhibits "order," which reflects the order of the natural world. It stems from the scientists' collective interest in "predictability and control in the natural environment," hence their preoccupation with such matters as "confirmation, falsifiability, instrumentality, objective respectability, technical interest," and so on. The view that these social habits are purely conventional, and do not reflect some actual order in the world, is unnecessarily destructive. The belief in that order is the basis on which we conduct our daily lives; without it there would be personal (psychological) and social disintegration. To Hesse:

> Without the assumption that social habits have grown to reflect some order in the world . . . [we cannot] explain the general success of the expectations we have to rely on for everyday practical needs. Some biological needs are common to all cultures, and would explain why many inductive assumptions are the same in all cultures in similar environments. In other respects different cultures may have different needs and correspondingly different linguistic classifications.[14]

III

The so-called Strong Program (SP) in the sociology of knowledge, a radically relativist conception that asserts the primacy of sociological over all other interpretations of scientific knowledge and procedures, has much in common with the KM interpretation.[15] SP advocates question the supposedly universal and immutable correct principles that have usually figured so prominently in methodology and philosophy of science writings, emphasizing instead the local, contingent, and context-dependent character of scientists' beliefs and activities and arguing that the explanation of beliefs is independent of their status, whether true or false, scientific or nonscientific. They focus on the "internal" sociology of knowledge, arguing that the methodological rules, heuristic principles, basic norms and conventions adopted by any scientific group have no absolute, unique, or universal validity and significance. The language employed, systems of classification, logical conventions and procedures, inferences, and judgments are all learned within the relevant segment of the scientific community. Instead of defining a theory in the conventional manner as "a system of statements perhaps or a formal mathematical structure from which particular solutions are deduced or logically derived . . . the tables are turned, and a theory . . . is defined by its applications: it is simply the cluster of what are called its 'applications' " or problem solutions.[16]

According to the SP – as can be the case with the rhetorical or discourse approach – there is a general correspondence between knowledge and "reality," but reality can be perceived, described, and interpreted in a variety of different ways. There is no single criterion of truth acceptable in all cultures, and scientific concepts, theories, paradigms, tests, judgments, and so on are simply conventions approved by the scientific community. However, this does not mean that these conventions are either arbitrary or lax: On the contrary, they derive from stringent rules and procedures that cannot easily be mastered or changed. Science is based on order, continuity, authority and control, and while it is neither rigid nor inflexible the scope for novelty and innovation is strictly limited by the recognized conventions (tradition) and by the specific circumstances of the scientist's field.[17] Tradition governs the accepted theories, methods, and techniques in any discipline, and also the selection, training, qualification, and socialization of recruits.

This account, which in many respects resembles Kuhn's description of "normal" science, provides the context for disciplinary "conversation" and the persuasive deployment of techniques and forms of argumentation – a state of affairs that depicts "many characteristics of cognition and culture which it is difficult to imagine could be otherwise."[18] Radical criticism is possible "only where there are more than one set of standards and conventions and more than one conceivable definition of reality."[19] This does not mean that normal disciplinary conversation is static. On the contrary, acceptable usage and procedure is "developed step by step in a succession of on-the-spot judgments. Every instance of use, or proper use, of a concept must in the last analysis be accounted for separately, by reference to specific, local, contingent circumstances,"[20] and "there is no basis for validation superior to the collective contingent judgment of the paradigm-sharing community itself."[21]

Needless to say, several features of the SP are highly controversial. Critics complain of the overemphasis on sociological determinants, the particularistic description of scientific work, and the relativistic denial of an epistemological distinction between science and other forms of knowledge, making it difficult to explain why modern science has developed as a peculiar and crucially important species of knowledge. The tendency to treat the social process of knowledge production as chaotic makes the eventual emergence of agreement on results appear mysterious or inexplicable; hence it is necessary to provide a more generalized and comprehensible account of scientific work and its significance both for the growth of knowledge and for society at large. An impressive step in that direction has been taken by Richard Whitley, who insists on the interdependence of the content of science at any stage and the concepts, propositions, reasonings and methods employed by the relevant group of scientists. Whereas the SP treats scientists' judgments and scientific change merely as epiphenomena of material causes and interests, Whitley claims that these interests and scientific beliefs are reciprocally interrelated, so that

> . . . the sociology of knowledge should concern itself with the configuration of relations linking beliefs, rationalities, social structures, and the organization of knowledge production. Sociological accounts of the genesis, elaboration and acceptance of scientific beliefs . . . need to reconstruct the procedures and practices through which it made sense to particular groups to believe one theory or set of statements rather than another.[22]

IV

McCloskey's conception of rhetoric as a complex blend of literary devices and styles, persuasive arguments, and modes of communication can, in principle, be applied systematically to the structure of audiences for the economist's output, in combination with Klamer's analysis of "levels" of discourse. In his stimulating book, *Conversations with Economists,* Klamer identified the principal components of economic conversation as comprising

1. Core claims
2. Various types of arguments, including
   a. Theoretical
   b. Empirical
   c. Epistemological (methodological)
   d. Philosophical (ideological)
   e. Commonsense
   f. Metaarguments
3. Personal and social factors.[23]

This list is formidable, and perhaps overly subtle. Applied in conjunction with the various types of audiences it offers an irresistible challenge to mathematical manipulators. Without attempting to be exhaustive, a necessary classification of audiences would have to include the following:

1. Undergraduates – differentiating between elementary and advanced students
2. Graduates – including specialists (prospective recruits to the economics profession) and students in other fields (e.g., business, law, engineering, public policy)
3. Professional economists
   a. Academics (in a variety of special fields and doctoral schools, possibly differentiating between elite and nonelite academics)
   b. Nonacademic economists, for example, in business, banking, governments (federal, state, and local), international agencies, and so on
4. Noneconomist academics, for example, deans, promotion committees, research grant committees
5. Nonacademic audiences, including "experts" in other fields; government and international agency bureaucrats; business persons, bankers, politicians, journalists; foundation boards; and members of the lay public (intelligent and otherwise)

How far it would be either practicable or fruitful to study these various combinations of economic arguments and audiences is a question that need not concern us here. Some groupings are clearly more feasible and promising than others, being instructive in analyzing the spread of economic ideas, a long neglected topic that is now beginning to attract serious scholarly attention.[24] Rather than pursuing this line of inquiry, however, the remainder of this chapter will focus on some issues in the KM agenda that have been considered in earlier economic literature. While pointing to contextual matters that have previously been considered, sometimes inadequately, the following examples may suggest topics for future investigators armed with the new rhetoric and discourse (r&d?) apparatus.

V

One of the economist's greatest assets – the fact that his discipline deals with questions of obvious public interest and importance – has also been a major source of vulnerability, for economists have rarely been able for long to enjoy the measure of insulation from external pressures considered essential to sustained intellectual and scientific inquiry. In other words, the internal and external sociology of economics have invariably overlapped and interpenetrated in various ways. Consequently economists have long recognized that open disagreements within their ranks, especially those involving fundamental issues of principle and policy, were bound to impair their individual and collective reputations as scientists or experts, and they have accordingly proposed various means of reducing, suppressing, or eliminating unnecessary controversy. The nature of these means has obviously varied contextually, according to the state of the discipline, the number of practitioners, and their relations with the general public.

Richard Whitley has recently provided a systematic analysis of scientific fields in terms of the degree of their "reputational autonomy" from competing organizations and the wider social structure over such matters as the setting of performance standards, the assessment of problems, and the development of research strategies.[25] Fields can be characterized by references to their domain, problems, and descriptive language, and the last of these is especially pertinent to economics and the KM campaign. As Whitley has observed:

> . . . the topics which economics purports to deal with are important everyday issues and the terminology of economic analysis is close to ordinary language even if technical definitions of these terms are quite distinct. Profit, for example, has a technical meaning in microeconomics which is not the same as usages in conventional accounting – which themselves vary. In their internal discussions and rankings of intellectual significance of contributions economists use their technical concepts and their own standards of evaluation, yet they also make policy pronouncements and seek to intervene in everyday debates and discussions where terms are not technically defined and they do not control usages. Indeed, it seems unlikely that economics could receive so much financial support if it was not thought that its subjects and problems were strongly connected with everyday phenomena. Thus, within the professional fraternity, performance and significance standards, and technical terminology, are fairly strongly controlled by the reputational elite but there is also considerable overlap with common sense terms and concerns which legitimates public support and sometimes affects standards. As with the problem of demonstrating effective technical control over phenomena, this difficulty is resolved to some extent in economics by separating analytical economics by fields of application and elevating the former to a position of dominance and insulating it from external influences to a very high degree. Thus economics is a hybrid science in which divergent features are combined so that the core exhibits different characteristics to the peripheral subfields.[26]

Early nineteenth-century British economics provides a wealth of examples of economists' desire for unity, the difficulties of achieving it, and their concern to protect the intellectual authority of the *cognoscenti* against criticism from the lay public.[27] There was at that time virtually no formal training in economics and no clear demarcation between those who were qualified to write or speak on economic topics and those who were not. Most of the leading economists, "the gloomy professors of the dismal science," as Thomas Carlyle termed them, spent only a small proportion of their lives in academic chairs, if that, and their decision to found the Political Economy Club of London, in 1821, to disseminate "sound" ideas, can be viewed both as a professional and political act. Most of the club's members shared common values about the ends of economic activity, as well as other liberal moral philosophical ideas, and although the boundaries of the "scientific community" were blurred, there was at least a clear distinction between the economists and their most articulate opponents, the literary critics – interestingly enough, at a time when the emergence of a distinct literary "profession" is clearly discernible.[28] The question whether economics was a purely logical discipline, as Robert Torrens implied in claiming that its arguments constituted "proof amounting to strictly mathematical demonstration," or a science of "fact and experiment," as John Ramsay McCulloch argued, need not detain us.[29] But the interdependence of methodology and professionalism, a much neglected theme in the history of economics, clearly underlays James Mill's insistence on the need to establish "the criteria and tests of a science" in his essay on the usefulness of political economy. Mill claimed:

> Among those who have so much knowledge on the subject as to entitle their opinion to any weight, there is wonderful agreement. . . . A reasoner must be hard pressed when he is driven to quote practical men in aid of his conclusions. There cannot be a worse authority, in any branch of political science, than that of merely practical men.[30]

Mill grudgingly conceded the existence of some dispute "on the minor questions involved," but the economists' desire for collective solidarity was such that another member of the Political Economy Club, Thomas Robert Malthus, whose differences with Mill and David Ricardo were by no means minor, was also concerned to minimize damaging public dissension. In his *Definitions in Political Economy* (1827),[31] the first work of its kind in English, he made a sustained attempt to prescribe rules designed to eliminate purely verbal disagreements among economists on the following grounds:

> Till some steadiness is given to the science by the greater degree of care among its professors not to alter [terminology] without improving – it cannot be expected that it should attain that general influence in society which (its principles being just) would be of the highest practical utility.[32]

Malthus acknowledged that the frequent complaints about "the differences of opinion among political economists" might be reduced by introducing "a new and more perfect nomenclature," thereby enabling that subject to approach more closely "to the strict science of mathematics," but he also conceded that a change "would not be submitted to" in a science like morals and politics, "where the terms are comparatively few, and of constant application in the daily concerns of life."[33]

Needless to say, Malthus failed to achieve his objective, and the same is true of innumerable later schemes, including the American Economic Association's early action in establishing a committee to explore ways of reaching agreement on the use of terms, and the recent proposals to standardize the use of symbols in economic models.[34] To cite a different type of activity, the refusal of American journal editors to agree on uniform conventions (e.g., in the use of citations and footnotes), so that an author could send a rejected typescript to a succession of periodicals without extensive revisions, is testimony to the strength of individualism in a discipline traditionally hostile to all forms of collusion and monopoly practice. Professional solidarity obviously has distinct limits.

The basic defect of schemes to standardize language on some French Academy–type model, was acknowledged in Lindley Fraser's classic *Economic Thought and Language* (1937), namely:

> If economists as a whole were to adopt a corpus of technical terms, each one with an unalterable meaning and content, there would be a real danger of their being left behind by the march of events. A static terminology is not well suited to the study of dynamic phenomena.[35]

It was also vital to maintain contact with "ordinary life," to cite Alfred Marshall's self-consciously pedestrian expression. Nevertheless, like many of his contemporaries and predecessors, Fraser was keenly aware of the errors and confusions resulting from uninhibited individualism in terminological usage, some of which reflect deliberate authorial efforts to differentiate a theoretical product. Oddly enough, his attempt to demonstrate "the frequency with which economists have not merely misunderstood each other's arguments but have even failed to grasp the implications of their own contentions"[36] was published during a major controversy over the terms *savings* and *investment*, which John Maynard Keynes had defined in the *General Theory* (1936) in direct contradiction to the definitions he had used six years earlier in his *Treatise on Money*. How far the differences were "merely" terminological rather than substantive and theoretically significant was a question actively debated in the leading economic journals.

In recent decades the most assiduous and perceptive student of economic language has undoubtedly been Fritz Machlup, whose collected *Essays on*

Economic Semantics were published a quarter of a century ago.[37] Machlup was not only concerned with terminological inconsistencies, vagueness, and similar sources of misunderstanding, focusing on targets like kaleidoscopic and weasel words, jargon, and misplaced concreteness, he was also eager to expose the unintentional or deliberate employment of persuasive definitions and disguised politics lurking behind a cloak of scientific respectability. Machlup was anything but authoritarian, insisting that "the semanticist may analyze, but not dictate," and against those who sought to make economics an exclusively mathematical discipline he pleaded on behalf of "polylingual scholarship."[38] With respect to the choice of language he was pragmatic, acknowledging that the selection of definitions must be "appropriate to the purpose" at hand,[39] and while strenuously appealing for linguistic precision and consistency he conceded that

> . . . standards of clarity are not uniform. . . . I cannot be sure whether, when I complain about vagueness, my perception is too poor, my sense of discrimination too fine, my insistence on unambiguous expression too pedantic – or whether the writings in question were just too wooly.[40]

Machlup was acutely sensitive to the role of personal values and judgments in economics, not simply in terminological matters. In an exceptionally self-revealing passage he confessed:

> . . . my suspicion is aroused by the strange coincidence that I have found crypto-apologetic meanings of structure [one of the fashionable terms he analysed in detail] only in pleas for policies which I do not like: restrictions of competition, price and allocation controls, import barriers, exchange restrictions. Have I perhaps failed to notice similar aberrations in policies I happen to like? . . . [To] grasp an argument that leads to conclusions hitherto rejected is much more difficult than to grasp an argument supporting a preconceived conclusion. Where I do not like the results, I am more eager than otherwise to question the validity of the premises, the consistency of the argument, the clarity of the concepts. . . . Aware of these influences of one's philosophy upon one's understanding of concepts, I must concede the possibility that my judgment has not attained the degree of fairness to which I aspire.[41]

VI

The KM approach offers rich possibilities for a deeper analysis of the nature, content, and historical significance of doctrinal or professional schools in economics. As Schumpeter observed in his classic *History of Economic Analysis,* the scholarly or scientific workers in any particular field

> . . . tend to become a sociological group . . . [with] other things in common besides the interest in scientific work. . . . The group accepts or refuses to accept co-workers also for reasons other than their professional competence or incompetence. . . . In economics this group took long to mature, but when it did mature it acquired much greater importance than it did in physics.[42]

Schumpeter did not attempt to justify or document this intriguing claim, but he was particularly impressed by the cohesion and durability of the group that emerged in late nineteenth-century Cambridge under Marshall's leadership. This economic "profession," he noted

> . . .developed attitudes to social and political questions that were *similar also for reasons other than similar scientific views.* The similarity of conditions of life and social location produced similar philosophies of life and similar value judgments about social phenomena.[43]

In this passage Schumpeter appears to favor a crudely deterministic sociological interpretation of Marshall's remarkable influence on British economics in the half century or so following his inaugural, in 1885.[44] The explanation is, of course, more complex than this; it involves factors like his quality as a deep and original thinker, his personality, the state of the discipline, and the position of his university at the time. Marshall's deference to the authority of the British tradition in economic thought, his reluctance to claim priority for his own contributions or to acknowledge his contemporaries' originality, and his efforts to shield his pupils and colleagues from disturbing foreign influences, combined with the architectonic character of his own system to establish him as the embodiment and culmination of the wisdom of the past. Of particular interest here, however, is his insistence on the careful use of language in economics, and his development of a distinctive mode of argumentation that created unusual problems of interpretation both for his associates and for later generations of commentators and critics.

As is well known, Marshall emphasized the limitations of pure theory and mathematical reasoning in economics, and attached great importance to the economist's ability to communicate effectively with the laity, especially businessmen. Special significance therefore attaches to his contention:

> Continuity of tradition is important everywhere; it is nowhere more important than in our use of terms; while in our use of terms it is even more important as regards the *tone* or *flavor* which they connote, than as regards the boundaries marked out by them.[45]

The sociological significance of this distinction between the connotation and the denotation of economic terms can only be fully appreciated by reference to other distinctive Cambridge characteristics. For example the "oral" tradition, which has been described as "quite unique in the history of economics,"[46] developed largely because Marshall's own ideas were familiar locally long before they were published, and access to this insider's knowledge directly contributed to his pupils' and colleagues' sense of privilege and intellectual superiority. Beyond this, indoctrination into the subtle connotations of Marshallian language played an integral part in the training of novitiates, training that could hardly be acquired without personal contact with the fount of wisdom and insight. For the uninitiated, Marshall's terminology was full of pitfalls, resulting from his efforts to combine the linguistic precision required by the expert with the comprehensibility demanded by the layman.

Some of the implications of the Marshallian approach have been explicated in Wassily Leontief's critique of "implicit theorizing" and Lawrence Fouraker's discussion of the "Cambridge didactic style." Leontief focused on the distinctive mode of reasoning that, he complained, enabled Cambridge economists to defend themselves against accusations of error by adopting subtle shifts of meaning or by employing illegitimate modes of argument.[47] Fouraker demonstrated that this procedure was a calculated method of disseminating subtle, technically complex arguments in a form accessible to a wider audience.

> Instead of leading the reader through the intricate processes that their own minds had traversed . . . [the Cambridge economists, following Marshall's lead] would provide a short cut, in the form of an assumption whose purpose was to eliminate consideration of the intricate problem they had solved.
>
> This is an admirable method for bringing the fruit of intellectual labor to the attention of the largest number of people in the shortest time. It has a major shortcoming however. The most capable of one's [non-Marshallian] professional colleagues may point to the bypassed terrain and question whether that path leads to the same conclusion as the short cut. Marshall and Keynes covered this contingency with a bit of literary gamesmanship. Their major works are infested with oblique passages that the novice dismisses as manifestations of a poor writing style. It is only after he has seized upon some apparent flaw in the system and followed its implications that such passages lose their opaque quality. They are then recognized as admirably constructed defenses of the author's flank, indicating that he has already considered and resolved the objection. Many a criticism of the *Principles of Economics* and *The General Theory* has been trans-

formed into an interpretation of some obscure paragraph by a rereading of the pertinent chapters. . . .[48]

whence the well-known Cambridge dictum that "it's all in Marshall" (or in
Keynes, as the case might be).

Fouraker's exercise in literary deconstruction represents a telling example
of the difficulties of designing a language suitable for communicating simultaneously with two or more very different audiences. To the sociologist of
science, the Cambridge didactic style is but one of several practices that combined to create a sense of intellectual solidarity and communion among the
cognoscenti.[49] As Michael Polanyi has convincingly argued, scientific training calls for the acquisition of semi-intuitive skills, "tacit knowledge" and
"connoisseurship," as well as more conventionally explicit kinds of comprehension.[50] The Marshallian style can be maddening to economists who value
logical rigor over realism, whose ideal in economics is mathematical formalization, complete specification of all terms and steps in the argument, and
conclusive empirical tests.[51] No wonder they prefer the precision and apparent
completeness of general equilibrium analysis rather than Marshallian partial
equilibrium analysis, the successful application of which depends on the analyst's skill in distinguishing relevant from irrelevant variables, and in knowing how far to pursue the implications of a given problem.[52]

It is no coincidence that Keynes fully appreciated the nature of Marshall's
method and the difficulties "contained in the concealed crevices of that rounded
globe of knowledge which is Marshall's *Principles*."[53] Many of the same
qualities appear in Keynes's own writings, especially in his *magnum opus,*
which has been the joy and exasperation of generations of students and full-
fledged professional economists. As Don Patinkin has so effectively demonstrated, Keynes displayed an ambivalent attitude toward mathematical analysis in economics, substantial reservations about the use of econometrics, and
a "genuine concern with integrating his theoretical analysis with the data of
the real world . . . [and] strong intuitive feelings for the proper orders of
magnitude of the various data."[54] Keynes was, of course, a genius and arguably
sui generis. Nevertheless the beliefs he shared with Marshall suggest the importance of a continuing scholarly and scientific tradition, one that was fully
in harmony with the cultural heritage and the prevailing conception of the
economist's role in British society.

VII

The standpoint adopted in this paper is that the study of the discourse
(or rhetoric) of any scientific or scholarly discipline is and should be treated

as subordinate to the study of its intellectual content and the social and historical context in which it occurs.[55] In other words, the so-called Anglo-Saxon approach (referred to earlier) is accepted here, according to which there is a clear and essential distinction between content and discourse (or form), although the interrelationships between these elements are subtle, varied, and changing over time.

This is not to deny either the validity or the value of the KM agenda. Indeed, its value is enhanced by the general neglect of economic rhetoric in the past although, as the two immediately previous sections of this chapter demonstrate, questions of language, types of argumentation, and audience have by no means been entirely ignored. The examples provided here are of course merely illustrative. A search of the literature armed with some of the KM tools could be highly illuminating. The Cambridge tradition, as briefly sketched [56] above, is but one unusually revealing case. How far it is exceptional is yet to be determined. And it seems clear that, for example, a comparative analysis of orthodox and heterodox versions of economics on KM lines would add much to our understanding of the past development and current functioning of the discipline.

As is so often the case with innovations, the KM campaign has been accompanied by exaggerated claims; it is still much too early to assess its long-term value. In this connection the experience of historians and sociologists of science may be helpful, for a number of scholars in these closely interrelated fields have approached scientific research from the standpoint of how scientists construct accounts of what is going on during the research process. In conformity with the current tendency to treat this process as problematic, they contend that "reality" cannot be distinguished from the scientist's account of it, and that by analyzing scientific discourse they can not only shed new light on such familiar topics as the nature of discovery, theory choice, scientific consensus, and the role of norms in scientific work, but also provide insights into neglected topics, such as accounts of error, the structure of formal texts, the use of pictorial representations, the practical applications of scientific knowledge, and even the role of scientific jokes.[57] The similarities to the KM agenda are clear, but this suggests a much richer range of possibilities than has been tried out in economics. As in some other contemporary work, this so-called social-accounting approach emphasizes, as do KM, the substantial gap between how scientists go about their work and how they present it as finished, public knowledge. We are all familiar with the expression "writing up" research, and this phase of the operation has acquired added depth and significance through studies emphasizing that scientific knowledge does not emerge spontaneously in a pristine, objective, neutral form, but is consciously *constructed* in accordance with the researcher's aims, interests, and conception of conventionally acceptable procedures and results.

Some proponents of scientific discourse analysis go further, making an unwarranted epistemological claim by viewing it as a means of circumventing the interpretative difficulties arising from the remarkable variety to be found in scientists' accounts of their actions and beliefs. This, of course, is mistaken: There are no grounds for assigning privileged status to discourse or, indeed, to any other species of data, and the problem of interpretation is inescapable.[58] An even more radically empiricist and relativist approach to scientific work in Karin Knorr-Cetina's "constructivist" program, which involves microscopic internalist studies of scientists' behavior on the grounds that research is essentially idiosyncratic, contingent, and context dependent. However it should be noted that this program is designed not simply as an end in itself, but as a means to a deeper – and eventually presumably more general – understanding of the nature and processes of scientific knowledge production.[59]

Needless to say, like the KM agenda, none of these approaches has privileged status. Moreover, pace McCloskey, all have epistemological and methodological implications, and there is need for scholarly cooperation even, may it be suggested, with modernists!

Notes

1. See, for example, the discussions of scientific discourse in various volumes of *Social Science Information* and *Social Studies of Science*. Also, especially, the references in note 5, infra.
2. Donald McCloskey, *The Rhetoric of Economics* (Madison: University of Wisconsin Press, 1985), 51; also p. 4. For criticism of McCloskey's treatment of methodology, see Bruce Caldwell and A. W. Coats, "The Rhetoric of Economists: A Comment on McCloskey," *Journal of Economic Literature* 22 (June, 1984): 575–8; also see my "Why Bother with Methodology?" (forthcoming), being a revision of a paper delivered at the History of Economics Society's 1986 meetings in New York.
3. McCloskey, *The Rhetoric of Economics,* 55–7, italics in original. Also Donald McCloskey, "Economics as an Historical Science," in *Economic History and the Modern Economist,* ed. William R. Parker (Oxford: Basil Blackwell, 1986), 69; "Thick and Thin Methodologies in the History of Economic Thought," mimeographed, to be published in de Marchi volume (December, 1985), 15, 17.
4. In *Rhetoric of Economics,* 57, McCloskey cites Charles Bazerman, "What Written Knowledge Does: Three Examples of Academic Discourse," *Philosophy of the Social Sciences* 11 (September, 1981): 361–87, as evidence that "the workaday methods of economic scientists . . . are literary." But Bazerman's analysis focuses on the *differences,* rather than the similarities, between the critical methods appropriate to the analysis of imaginative literature, as contrasted with those

appropriate to the natural and social sciences. However, a sample of three hardly constitutes a sufficient basis for generalization.

5. For example, Steve Woolgar, "On the Alleged Distinction Between Discourse and Praxis," *Social Studies of Science* 16 (1986): 309–17, and the sources cited therein. Also Ellsworth R. Fuhrman and Kay Oehler, "Discourse Analysis and Reflexivity," *Social Studies of Science* 16 (1986): 293–307.

6. Cited by Arjo Klamer, "As If Economists and Their Subjects Were Rational," in John S. Nelson, Allan Megill, and Donald N. McCloskey (eds.), *The Rhetoric of Human Sciences* (Madison: University of Wisconsin Press, 1987), 165.

7. Axel Leijonhufuud, "Life Among the Econ" (1973), reprinted in his *Information and Coordination: Essays in Macroeconomic Theory* (Oxford: Oxford University Press, 1981), 347–59.

8. For a revealing pioneering study, see David Colander and Arjo Klamer, "The Making of an Economist," *Journal of Economic Perspectives* (Fall 1987): 95–112.

9. Cited by Klamer, "As if economists . . . ," 165; also see his "Economics as Discourse" (December 1985), 20–1 (to be published in de Marchi volume).

10. Cited by Klamer, "Economics as Discourse," 25.

11. Ibid., Klamer's paraphrase of Rorty.

12. See, for example, John Ziman's admirable study, *Reliable Knowledge: An Exploration of the Grounds for Belief in Science* (Cambridge: Cambridge University Press, 1978), passim. For his comments on the socialization of recruits into physics see pp. 128–30. The idea that science is a unique cultural institution with unequalled cognitive authority has been forcefully argued by Robert Merton and his followers.

13. Mary Hesse, "Changing Concepts and Stable Order," *Social Studies of Science* 16 (1986): 725. Her review of Harry Collins's *Changing Order: Replication and Induction in Scientific Practice* (1985) argues that Collins's radical conventionalist interpretation of scientists' activities conflicts with his "realist" conception of science in general. Such an inconsistency is not unusual nowadays.

14. Hesse, "Changing Concepts," 717, 723.

15. The following section is based largely on my "The Sociology of Knowledge and the History of Economics," published in Warren Samuels, ed., *Research in the History of Economic Thought and Methodology,* vol. 2 (Greenwich, Conn.: JAI Press, 1984), 211–34. The principal differences are that the SP is based on a more elaborate and explicitly relativistic epistemology than the KM program, which focuses more narrowly on literary styles and modes of argument. Proponents of the SP have undertaken more detailed, sociologically and historically rich empirical studies of past and present science, dealing with both "internal" and "external" influences on its development.

16. Barry Barnes, *T.S. Kuhn and Social Science* (New York: Columbia University Press, 1982), 121.

17. Cf. W. B. Gallie, "What Makes a Subject Scientific?" *British Journal for the Philosophy of Science* 8 (August, 1957): 118–39.

18. Barnes, *T. S. Kuhn and Social Science,* 57.

19. David Bloor, *Knowledge and Social Imagery* (London: Routledge and Kegan Paul, 1976), 38.
20. Barnes, *T. S. Kuhn and Social Science,* 30–1.
21. Thomas S. Kuhn, *The Essential Tension: Selected Studies in Scientific Tradition and Change* (Chicago: University of Chicago Press, 1977), 51.
22. Richard Whitley, "From the Sociology of Scientific Communities to the Study of Scientists' Negotiations and Beyond," *Social Science Information* 22 (1983): 694. See also ibid., 687–94, and Whitley's general study, *The Intellectual and Social Organization of the Sciences* (London: Oxford University Press, 1984.)
23. Arjo Klamer, *Conversations with Economists: New Classical Economists and Opponents Speak Out on the Current Controversy in Macroeconomics* (Totowa, N. J.: Rowman and Allanheld, 1983), especially Ch. 13. An earlier, less complex clarification appeared in his "Levels of Discourse in New Classical Economics," *History of Political Economy* 16 (1984): 263–90.
24. A conference on "The Spread of Economic Ideas," organized by David Colander, was held at Middlebury College, Vermont, in October 1986. The papers presented are being prepared for publication.
25. Cf. Whitley, *Intellectual and Social Organization of the Sciences.*
26. Ibid., 225–26. On the problem of the influence of "lay images" in the social sciences, see Cornelis Lammers, "Mono- and Poly-paradigmatic developments in natural and social sciences," in Richard Whitley, ed. *Social Processes of Scientific Development* (London: Routledge and Kegan Paul, 1974) 123–47.
27. For a more extended treatment of this topic, see my "The Role of Authority in the Development of British Economics," *Journal of Law and Economics* 10 (1966): especially 85–95.
28. Raymond Williams, *Culture and Society* (London: Chalto and Windus, 1958), 49.
29. Robert Torrens, *On Wages and Combinations* (London, 1834), 73; John Ramsay McCulloch, *A Discourse on the Rise, Progress, Peculiar Objects and Importance of Political Economy* (London, 1824), 9.
30. James Mill, "Whether Political Economy Is Useful?" *The Westminster Review* 30 (1836): 553, 554. The last passage is from his "War Expenditure," *The Westminster Review* 2 (1824): 45.
31. The full title was *Definitions in Political Economy, Preceded by an Inquiry into the Rules Which Ought to Guide Political Economists in the Definition and Use of Their Terms, With Remarks on the Deviations from These Rules in Their Writings* (London, 1827). Republished in *Reprints of Economic Classics* (New York: Kelley and Millman, 1954). Malthus's rules are stated in Chapter 1. He was not alone in his concern. Nassau W. Senior, in *An Outline of the Science of Political Economy* (London, 1936), declared: "If Economists had been aware that the Science depends more on reasoning than observation, and that its principal difficulty consists not in the ascertainment of its facts, but in the use of its terms, we cannot doubt that their principal efforts would have been directed to the selection and consistent use of an accurate nomenclature" (p. 5). He regarded this as a major reason for the slow progress of political economy.

32. Ibid., p. 124. Curiously enough, this appeared at the end of a severe criticism of McCulloch's usage, hardly an indication of professional solidarity!
33. Ibid., 3–4.
34. Cf. the early *Publications of the American Economic Association*. Also, see J. Mars, "A Note on a Problem of Notation," *Economic Journal* 73 (June, 1963): 226. Contrasting economics with the natural sciences, Mars argued that "the curse of Babel still hangs over the social sciences." But although the *Journal's* editors invited readers to comment on this "important" issue, no further discussion occurred.
35. Lindley Fraser, *Economic Thought and Language* (London: A&C Black, 1937), vii–viii.
36. Ibid., 20.
37. Fritz Machlup, *Essays in Economic Semantics* (New Jersey: Prentice-Hall, 1963).
38. Machlup, "Issues in Methodology," *American Economic Review, Papers and Proceedings* 42 (1952): 70–1; "Positive and Normative Economics: An Analysis of the Ideas," in Robert L. Heilbroner, ed. *Economic Means and Social Ends, Essays in Social Economics* (New Jersey: Prentice-Hall, 1969), 100n; "Concepts of Competition and Monopoly," *American Economic Review, Papers and Proceedings* 45 (1955): 483.
39. Machlup, *Essays on Economic Semantics*, 251.
40. Ibid., 82. He nevertheless proposed a number of procedural rules on semantic matters on pp. 71–2.
41. Ibid., 96.
42. Joseph A. Schumpeter, *History of Economic Analysis* (New York: Oxford University Press, 1954), 47.
43. Ibid. Italics in original.
44. For general background see my "Sociological Aspects of British Economic Thought (ca. 1880–1930)," *Journal of Political Economy* 75 (October, 1967): 706–29. Also the recent, brilliant study by John Maloney, *Marshall, Orthodoxy and the Professionalization of Economics* (Cambridge: Cambridge University Press, 1985).
45. Alfred Marshall, "Distribution and Exchange," *Economic Journal* 8 (March, 1898: 43. At that time there was much terminological product differentiation in the theories of value and distribution in a number of different countries.
46. Ben B. Seligman, *Main Currents in Economics, Economic Thought Since 1870* (New York: The Free Press, 1963), 457.
47. Wassily Leontief, "Implicit Theorizing: A Methodological Criticism of the Neo-Cambridge School," *Quarterly Journal of Economics* 51 (February, 1937): 337–51.
48. Lawrence A. Fouraker, "The Cambridge Didactic Style," *Journal of Political Economy* 66 (February, 1958): especially 67. He illustrates his general case by analyzing Marshall's concept of consumer's demand, and Keynes's concept of the propensity to consume.
49. Other aspects include agreement with respect to the important questions for study, and distaste for purely theoretical and methodological discussion.
50. See, for example, Michael Polanyi, *Personal Knowledge: Towards a Post-Critical*

Philosophy (Chicago: University of Chicago Press, 1958), especially Ch. 4 and 5.

51. For a penetrating general critique of these "modernist" tendencies see, for example, Henry Woo, *What's Wrong with Formalization in Economics* (Newark, Calif.: Victoria Press, 1986). Also Nicholas Georgescu-Roegen on the urge to make economics an "anthropomorphic" science, in his *The Entropy Law and the Economic Process* (Cambridge, Mass.: Harvard University Press, 1971), Ch. 11.

52. Henry W. Briefs, *Three Views of Economic Method* (Washington, D.C.: Georgetown University Press, 1960), 13–17, provides shrewd comments on this type of analysis.

   Colander–Klamer, "The Making of an Economist," a study of graduate training in economics, reinforces the impression that prevailing practice both attracts and helps to form "convergent" mental attitudes unsuitable for developing the kind of judgment required in dealing with practical problems. This is one reason for stressing the historical dimensions of economics. The helpful distinction between "convergent" and "divergent" minds is elaborated in Liam Hudson, *Contrary Imaginations: A Study of the English Schoolboy* (London: Methuen, 1966).

53. Quoted by Fouraker, "The Cambridge Didactic Style," 67, from Keynes's classic memorial essay on Marshall.

54. Don Patinkin, "Keynes and Econometrics: On the Interaction Between the Macroeconomic Revolutions of the Interwar Period" (1974), reprinted in his *Anticipations of the General Theory? And Other Essays on Keynes* (Chicago: University of Chicago Press, 1982), 238. Patinkin adds that Keynes was "indeed, so strong and so confident that he did not hesitate to pit these feelings against the systematic estimates made by the specialists in the field. Not unrelatedly, it shows him as a person who was not too meticulous in his handling of data, and who sometimes succumbed to the temptation to bend the data to fit his preconceptions . . . not exactly a phenomenon which has since disappeared from the face of the earth" (pp. 238–9).

55. It would, for example, be worth examining the components of knowledge production in economics in terms of training employment reputational assessment and funding, as Whitley suggests in *Intellectual and Social Organization of the Sciences*.

56. This term is employed deliberately. An adequate treatment of any such tradition would require much more depth and detail.

57. Cf. for example Michael Mulkay and G. Nigel Gilbert, "What Is the Ultimate Question? Some Remarks in Defence of the Analysis of Scientific Discourse," *Social Studies of Science* 12 (1982): 309–19; also their earlier "Contexts of Scientific Discourse: Social Accounting in Experimental Papers," in Karin D. Knorr, Roger Krohn, and Richard Whitley (eds.), *The Social Process of Scientific Investigation, Sociology of the Sciences Yearbook* vol. 4 (1980) (Dordrecht, Holland: D. Reidel, 1981), 269–94; and "Joking Apart: Some Recommendations Concerning the Analysis of Scientific Culture," *Social Studies of Science* 12 (1982): 585–613.

58. This issue has been extensively discussed in *Social Studies of Science,* especially in the 1982 and 1984 volumes.
59. Cf. Karin Knorr Cetina's *The Manufacture of Knowledge: An Essay on the Constructivist and the Contextual Nature of Science* (Oxford: Pergamon Press, 1981); also her "The Constructivist Program in the Sociology of Science: Retreats or Advances?" *Social Studies of Science* 12 (1982): 323;

   For criticism see, for example, Thomas F. Gieryn, "Relativist/Constructivist Programs in the Sociology of Science: Redundance and Retreat," *Social Studies of Science* 12 (1982).

CHAPTER 7

The ideas of economists

Robert W. Clower

In the concluding chapter of his engaging *Conversations with Economists*, Arjo Klamer (1984) aptly summarizes the flavor of the answers elicited by his questioning:

> Economists do not only construct models and conduct empirical tests, they also argue on what a good model should look like. Moreover, they philosophize, appeal to common sense, and talk about other economists and their work. Economics involves the art of persuasion. In the absence of uniform standards and clearcut empirical tests, economists have to rely on judgments, and they argue to render their judgments persuasive. This process leaves room for nonrational elements, such as personal commitment and style, and social discipline.

This description conveys a picture of "scientific" economics quite different from Milton Friedman's 1953 essay on "The Methodology of Positive Economics," but it accords well with the portrait of physical science suggested by Hanson's 1958 *Patterns of Discovery*. My impression is that the Friedmanian view – sometimes construed in ways that Professor Friedman probably would be loath to accept – played an unhealthily prominent role in economics throughout most of the past quarter-century. As the present conference suggests, the influence of that view now appears to be waning and seems likely before long to be replaced by the more relaxed and nondoctrinaire views endorsed by McCloskey, Klamer, and other modern students of "the rhetoric of economics."

The essay reprinted here* is in some respects a precursor of recent work by McCloskey and Klamer, but it was conceived as a natural offshoot of "revisionist" accounts of the history of physical science by Hanson (1958), Kuhn (1962), and others. Correspondingly, its primary emphasis is on the rhetoric of science; only incidentally does it deal with the rhetoric of economics. I do not count this a shortcoming, because to my mind there is no signif-

---

*Originally presented at Monash University on September 4, 1972, and later published by Monash University as the Sixth Monash Economics Lecture. It is reprinted here with only minor editorial changes.

icant difference between the methods of economics and those of other sciences, but, then, some may regard my view of science as mildly singular.

* * *

Nearly a half-century ago, the noted British economist and statesman, J. M. Keynes, remarked rather wistfully how splendid it would be if economists could someday manage to get themselves thought of as "humble, competent people, on a level with dentists." So it would be – if the reputation were deserved. Unfortunately there is a kernel of truth in the popular view that regards economics as "the science whose practitioners, even if laid end to end, still would not reach agreement." Personally I doubt if economics has more than its fair share of arrogant quacks; it must be admitted, however, that contemporary economics is more accurately regarded as a way of thinking about certain kinds of problems than a settled body of knowledge. In these circumstances, ideological and methodological biases occasionally have as much influence as factual evidence in determining what some economists think and say – so much so that economists themselves are generally loath to lend credence to any but narrowly technical pronouncements by fellow economists. We can hardly be surprised, therefore, if the public at large is disposed to view economists and their work with a certain amount of suspicion.

Granted that the ideas of economists are not generally held in high esteem, wherein lies the fault? Is economics, by its nature, essentially different from other sciences in outlook, method, and logical structure; or is the problem simply that economists have somehow failed to convey to the general public an accurate impression of the nature of their discipline and the reliability of the conclusions to which it leads?

In my opinion the explanation lies in the second of these alternatives. In everyday discussion of economic problems – and even in academic instruction – economists tend to proceed on the supposition that those they presume to instruct have a good general background knowledge about economic phenomena as well as a clear appreciation of the nature of scientific inquiry. This procedure is natural: After all, economics is concerned for the most part with thoroughly commonplace phenomena – consumption, production, and related activities with which everyone may be presumed to be more or less directly familiar; and we live in a society where Science (definitely with a capital S) is almost a part of the air we breathe. In these circumstances, most people would think it perverse if economists insisted on treating their discipline as anything more than systematized common sense. But would it really be so perverse? Let us examine the issue more closely.

We all have some notion about the nature of the economic system, just as we all have some notion about the nature of the solar system. In the latter case, we realize that our personal knowledge is not sufficiently connected or reliable for us to explain how it is, for example, that ocean tides occur twice each day when the earth revolves just once about its axis, or what is the precise nature of the forces that generate observed patterns of planetary motion. In matters of this kind, most of us are willing to admit that common sense is no substitute for the accumulated wisdom of generations of professional astronomers. In the former case, however, many of us take it for granted that things are just as they appear to us – that what we know from our personal experience is as good a guide to correct understanding of economic events as the "fanciful speculations" of professional economists. The presumption is natural – as natural, in fact, as it once was to suppose that the stars revolve every twenty-four hours around an Earth that stands still at the center of the universe. All the same, we should not really be surprised to discover that in order to make sense even of the most elementary "facts" of economic experience, we may have to begin by acknowledging that things are not exactly as they appear to us, which would require (among other things) that we start by discarding intuitive preconceptions about the nature of economic phenomena in favor of an abstract framework of ideas that might initially seem unnatural, artificial, and offensive to common sense.

Science: Fact or fiction?

Contrary to popular opinion and the pretensions of some scientists, the bulk of all knowledge commonly regarded as "scientific" is expressed in terms of stories that differ little from stories told by writers of serious novels. The resemblance is not accidental. The aim of the novelist is to persuade us that his story might almost be true, while that of the scientist is to persuade us that outwardly chaotic sense data fall into meaningful patterns. We might argue that the two situations differ in that the scientist doesn't invent his facts (at least, he is not supposed to) whereas the novelist is not so constrained. On further reflection, however, the two cases seem to be indistinguishable. Although the scientist does not invent his facts, he does choose them. More precisely, he selects from an infinity of possible facts collections in which (for reasons best known to him) he is able to "recognize" interesting patterns. In exactly the same manner, the novelist chooses from an infinity of possible characters and situations just that combination about which he thinks a good story can be told. In both cases, therefore, it is strictly true to say that the artist "invents" his story. We need not be surprised, therefore, to find "order" in economic or social phenomena any more than we are surprised to find "order" in natural phenomena – or in any good novel. Scientists would not bother to write about "nature" or "society" any more than novelists would bother to write about "life" unless they were first convinced that what they had to say made a story that was worth telling.

How do scientists go about the business of selecting facts in order to "discover" or "invent" intellectually satisfying stories about "designs in nature?" Procedures vary greatly from one discipline to another and also from one area of inquiry to another within any given discipline. The construction of scientific stories is a creative art rather than a technical skill. Little of a specific nature can be said about such matters, therefore, except in relation to the practice of particular investigators working with particular problems. We may clarify our general understanding of the creative process, however, by considering an example from the dawn of modern science.

Science as we now understand the term is generally acknowledged to begin with Galileo's studies of the motion of freely falling bodies. Before Galileo, science (known then as "natural philosophy") was just a minor part of an all-embracing conceptual scheme that Aristotle and the Scholastic philosophers had erected to give unity to all fields of human thought and knowledge – politics, poetry, ethics, theology, public administration, domestic housekeeping, and natural philosophy. Underlying this scheme was a quasi-religious presupposition that the meaning of things is to be found in the purpose they serve in the affairs of God and Man. As F. S. Taylor observed in *Science Past and Present:*

> It was transparently clear . . . that the world and all that's in it was created for the service of man, and that man had been created for the service of God. That was a perfectly intelligible scheme of the world. The sun was there to give us light and to tell the time and mark out the calendar by his motions. The stars and planets were a means of distributing beneficient or maleficient influences to the things on earth to which they were sympathetically linked; plants and animals were there to give us food and pleasure, and we were there to please God by doing His will.

Students of nature before Galileo's time would have found it not only unreasonable but nearly inconceivable that anyone should be so lacking in good sense as to be concerned *only* with the kind of phenomena that obsess modern scientists.

Galileo did not attempt to challenge or refute the Aristotelian scheme (he hardly could, for its essentially religious nature insulated it from serious criticism by any kind of argument or evidence); instead he turned his back on the "large issues" of his time and wrote a series of stories about narrowly circumscribed aspects of experience. The key to his achievement, and also to all later progress in science, lies not so much in what he took into account as in what he chose to ignore.

The kernel of Galileo's method is contained in a short passage of his *Discourses* (Crew and deSalvio 1914) where the motion of freely falling bodies is discussed by three men (*Simplicio* representing an Aristotelian, *Salviati* representing Galileo, and *Sagredo* representing a disinterested but helpful friend):

> *Salviati:* I greatly doubt that Aristotle ever tested by experiment whether it be true that two stones, one weighing ten times as much as the other, if allowed to fall, at the same instant, from a height of, say, 100 cubits (150 feet), would so differ in speed that when the heavier had reached the ground, the other would not have fallen more than 10 cubits. . . .
>
> *Sagredo:* . . . I, who have made the test, can assure you that a cannon ball weighing one or two hundred pounds, or even more, will not reach the ground by as much as a span ahead of a musket ball weighing only half a pound. . . .
>
> *Simplicio:* Your discussion is really admirable; yet I do not find it easy to believe that a bird shot falls as swiftly as a cannon ball.
>
> *Salviati:* Why not say a grain of sand as rapidly as a grindstone? But, Simplicio, I trust you will not follow the example of many others who divert the discussion from its main intent and fasten upon some statement of mine which lacks a hairbreadth of the truth and, under this hair, hide the fault of another which is as big as a ship's cable. Aristotle says that an iron ball of one hundred pounds falling from a height of one hundred cubits reaches the ground before a one-pound ball has fallen a single cubit. I say that they arrive at the same time. You find, on making the experiment, that the larger outstrips the smaller by two finger breadths . . . ; now you would not hide behind these two fingers the ninety-nine cubits of Aristotle, nor would you mention my small error and at the same time pass over in silence his very large one.

We could hardly have a clearer example than this of the confusion that can result from supposing that a naive first glance at "the facts" is a sufficient basis for understanding observed phenomena. Bodies of different weight falling freely in air indeed *do not travel precisely the same distance* in a given interval of time, but this is much less significant than the fact that *they do travel almost the same distance*.

Galileo's work leads us to what is perhaps the most fundamental principle underlying the modern scientist's search for "order in nature." In choosing a set of facts and weaving them into a story, the scientist views observed phenomena not as they *actually appear* but rather as he thinks they *would appear* if Nature were so gracious as to spare him the trouble of "thinking away" extraneous complications by omitting them in the first place. Unfortunately, Nature is seldom so gracious. To see patterns in phenomena, the scientist usually must remove himself at least one step from reality. He must use his imagination to invent artful caricatures of experience that he knows to be literally false in the hope that he may thereby see designs that might otherwise be overlooked because they lack "a hairbreadth of the truth." This is seldom as easy as it sounds. In most cases, the task of recognizing patterns entails much more than an act of creative imagination. Galileo had to "think away" not only air resistance but also an entire philosophical tradition. Copernicus had to "think away" God's concern with Man before he could simplify the description of astronomical events by putting the sun at the center of the solar system. Darwin had to "think away" the Creation to make sense of evolution. And Einstein had to "think away" the very existence of matter in order to fit electromagnetic energy into a story that would simultaneously accommodate Newton's laws of motion.

Scientific explanation

I have been concerned so far more with artistic than with routine aspects of scientific inquiry, my aim being to emphasize the essentially fictional nature of the stories that scientists tell. Unlike the "characters" found in works of fiction, however, the "characters" that appear in scientific stories (phenomena associated with observable objects and events) appear again and again with essentially unchanged identities in the writings of successive generations of scholars. Scientific stories thus exhibit a cumulative character that is lacking in ordinary works of fiction. Stories told by one scientist are seized upon by others, reworked, expanded, and passed on to other scientists with similar subject matter interests.

Obviously this kind of community enterprise could not long be sustained unless all scholars engaged in it subscribed to certain common ground rules governing the arrangement, analysis, and communication of ideas among themselves. In fact we find that just such rules prevail in every established science. Since no two sciences deal with exactly the same phenomena or problems, each has certain procedures that are peculiar to it (the "experimental method," for example, has little place in astronomy or economics but plays a crucial role in physics and chemistry). By and large, however, different sciences are more like different breeds of cat or dog than members of different species, for though they differ in details of scope and content, they all conform to a common pattern in fundamentals of logical structure and conceptual orientation.

The nature of this common pattern of scientific explanation may be clarified by considering a second important milestone in the development of modern science: Isaac Newton's "discovery" of the theory of universal gravitation. According to tradition, Newton stumbled upon the basic ideas of his theory late one autumn evening as he was preparing to take a nap under an apple tree in the garden attached to his family home in Woolsthorpe, England. By some strange coincidence, a full moon was rising just as an overripe apple fell to the ground, narrowly missing Newton's head. Tradition deserts us here, the story scarce begun, but from evidence contained in the *Principia* (Motte 1946) and some of Newton's other writings, we may imagine that Newton's subsequent chain of thought must have gone something as follows:

> How odd . . . the moon going up and the apple down! Why don't the moon and the apple obey the same natural laws . . . or do they? Hmmmm . . . now, let me see . . . Yes! Damme me, I believe they do! (*At this point Newton takes a twig and sketches a diagram on the ground, of which a facsimile is shown in Figure 1.*) Suppose I threw the apple towards my aunt's house. Galileo's studies and the feebleness of my arm convince me that the apple would follow a parabolic path (N in the figure), and fall to Earth long before it broke any windows. But suppose I had the strength of Atlas; then the apple would describe a similar path, but it might not fall to Earth until it had reached the shores of France . . . or Greece . . . or even the outer reaches of the Antipodes (*paths F, G, and S*). Indeed, if Atlas were as mighty as some legends suggest, then even though the apple fell constantly towards the center of the earth – attracted there like all natural bodies – it might at the same time transverse such a vast lateral distance as to circle the globe before coming to ground (*path C*). Hah! Yes! So if I were Atlas (and if I'd had a little more sugar and milk with my afternoon tea), I could impart such force to the apple that it would circle the earth endlessly, its path paralleling that of the moon. So the moon *does* obey the same laws as the apple . . . but who in the world could have thrown it up there . . . ? You don't suppose those old legends . . . No! *Hypotheses non fingo!* It's time I had my snooze.

Our reconstruction of Newton's story accurately expresses the main outlines of a train of thought that Newton himself presented in the *Principia*. The story is of general interest for historical reasons as well as for its own sake. For our purposes, however, it is significant mainly as a classic example of a category of scientific stories called *conceptual experiments* (also *thought experiments* and *gedankenexperimenten*) that exhibit in miniature the logical structure and conceptual orientation of scientific stories generally.

Though Newton's conceptual experiment consists of nothing more than an

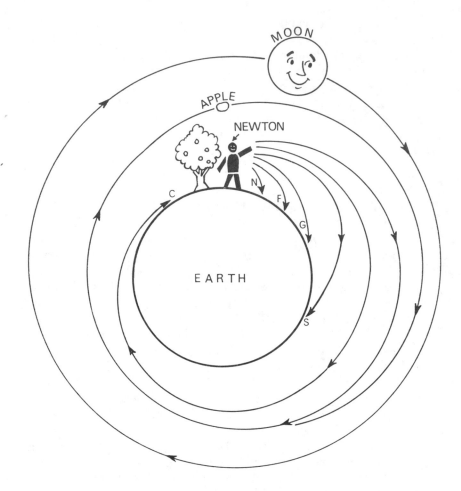

intuitively persuasive story and a related diagram (both of which grossly distort ''the facts''), the experiment neatly captures the essential features of an extremely complex problem. The theory of universal gravitation, an elaborately technical and intuitively incomprehensible system of ideas, is at bottom merely a complicated variation on the simpler theme discussed in the conceptual experiment. Given the conceptual experiment, one can ''understand'' the theory of universal gravitation; without the conceptual experiment, the general theory is just analytical gibberish. A similar observation applies quite generally to all scientific stories. Certain portions of every science are expressed in formal mathematical language. Specialists may become so bemused with the precision and logical elegance of these creations that they come to think of themselves not as empirical scientists who make use of mathematical ideas but rather as mathematicians who employ a peculiar terminology. This results not in science but in nonsense. A scientific story cannot be considered acceptable unless it provides the reader with enough information to figure out not only what the teller of the story is saying but also what he is talking about. An important virtue of conceptual experiments is that they serve both purposes simultaneously.

Although the results of Newton's experiment may seem "obvious" to modern minds, they could not have been reached in his day by anyone but a great genius. They were *not* reached, for example, by Galileo or Kepler, both of whom had at their disposal all the "facts" that were available to Newton. As in our earlier discussion of Galileo's work, so also here we are reminded in the strongest possible manner that *what we are able to see by looking at "the facts" depends in an essential way on what we expect to see before we look at them.* The key to Newton's achievement lies in the kind of questions that his conceptual experiment prompted him to pose. He did not ask, "Why does the apple fall?" or "Why does the moon circle the earth?"; instead, he asked questions of the form, "If we suppose, . . . then what may we conclude?" The difference in language may be slight, but the difference in perspective is monumental. An acceptable scientific story should be so phrased as to force us to ask "if–then" rather than "why" questions. Another important virtue of conceptual experiments is that they force us to do just this.

Two additional aspects of Newton's work merit special comment. First, although our version of Newton's story does not suggest this, the logical structure of his conceptual experiment is the same as the description of a parlor game like parchesi or chess. The description of such a game consists in every case of a set of *rules* (assumptions) that prescribe the manner in which specified *pieces* (apple, moon) may be *played or moved* (acted upon) by the various *players* (Newton, gravity). Of course, it is one thing to know the rules of a game and be able to play it, quite another to figure out the rules by observing it being played. The purpose of a conceptual experiment – like that of any good scientific story – is to provide a provisional solution to the second of these problems. The person conducting the experiment starts with factual data, which may be regarded as various moves in a game directed by Nature. Unfortunately, the experimenter has no way of knowing in advance if the "moves" as he sees them are truly associated with any set of "rules." Neither has he any way of knowing the object of the game (how could one discover that the object of chess was to checkmate the king if one never observed the game being played out?). Moreover, he cannot be sure that the "moves" he sees come from just *one* game (consider the predicament of a person who tries to make sense of the actions of a group of bridge players who are simultaneously playing chess to keep their minds occupied between hands!). To add to his difficulties, he cannot tell if he has identified either all relevant "pieces" (phenomena) or all of the "players" (natural and human forces) that Nature sends into the game. Considering just these difficulties (there are many others), we must surely count it remarkable that anyone has ever managed to arrive at even a partial set of rules by the route that Newton pioneered. But the fact is that they have and, indeed never by any essentially different route.

My second comment is closely related to the first. It has been said that half the battle in solving any problem consists in formulating it so that one can recognize its solution if one is fortunate enough to find it. Explicit recognition of the analogy between parlor games and conceptual experiments (more generally, between parlor games and scientific stories) effectively provides the basis for just such a formulation. Equally important, the game formulation permits one to communicate accurately to other scientists not only his conception of a problem but also the precise rules that he has managed to infer from the facts at his disposal or has imposed on the basis of other considerations. Without such communication among scholars, the scientific enterprise could hardly be purposeful, much less cumulative and fruitful. A scientific story that cannot be expressed explicitly as a "game" must therefore be counted a dubious contribution to scientific knowledge.

Economics: The vision of Adam Smith

I have emphasized four main themes in the preceding remarks: the deceptiveness of appearances as a guide to rational understanding of observed events; the fictitious nature of the stories scientists tell; the dependence of scientific inquiry upon agreed upon ground rules for analyzing and communicating ideas about experience; the crucial role that informal conceptual experiments (scientific parables) play in scientific explanation. It remains for me to relate these themes to the ideas of contemporary economists.

Let us begin by looking once more to the past, this time to the history of economics. The origins of economics, like those of every other intellectual discipline, may be traced back to early Greece and Rome, but economics was regarded then as a branch of domestic science dealing with matters like the management of slaves and the allocation of manure among alternative agricultural uses. In the revival of learning that followed the Middle Ages, economics emerged in a new guise as a branch of "moral philosophy" concerned with such issues as the ethics of loan interest and the justness of market-determined wages and prices. By the beginning of the eighteenth century, the subject had lost most of its theological overtones and had started to take definite shape as a science, but largely as a branch of political theory dealing with questions of government intervention in economic affairs. Then in 1776 the Scottish moral philosopher Adam Smith published the first edition of his monumental *Inquiry into the Nature and Causes of the Wealth of Nations,* and economics began to assume its modern form as an essentially independent science.

Smith lived in an age when the traditional right of rulers to impose arbitrary and oppressive restrictions on the political and economic liberties of their subjects was coming under increasingly strong attack in all parts of the civilized world. As other men of that time were arguing that democracy could and should replace autocracy in the sphere of politics, so Adam Smith argued that laissez-faire could and should replace government direction and regulation in economics. The "should" is so mixed with the "could" portion of Smith's analysis as to make his book seem almost as much a political tract as an economic treatise. What has given the book lasting significance, however, is the cogent case Smith made for believing that the economic activities of individuals could be more effectively coordinated through the indirect and impersonal action of "natural forces" of competition and self-interest than through the direct and often ill-conceived action of government authorities. In effect, Smith opened the eyes of humankind to the existence of a "grand design" in economic affairs similar to that which Newton had earlier shown to exist in the realm of physical phenomena. The impact of Smith's ideas upon his contemporaries was quick and widespread; as Alexander Gray has observed in his *Development of Economic Doctrine:* "Before Adam Smith there had been much economic discussion; with him we reach the stage of discussing economics."

That Smith's vision of the economic system should ever have been considered "original" may well seem strange to modern minds, but that is only because we now "see" economic phenomena in the light of his conception. As Arrow and Hahn have remarked in the *General Competitive Analysis,* "The immediate 'common sense' answer to the question, 'What will an economy motivated by greed and controlled by a large number of different agents look like?' is probably: there will be chaos." That is certainly the answer that would have been given by most of Smith's contemporaries – at least before they read his book. The greatness of Smith's accomplishment lies precisely in the fact that he, unlike his predecessors, was able to "think away" extraneous complications and perceive an order in economic affairs that common sense could never reveal.

It is one thing, of course, to say that Smith's conception of economic phenomena is original, another to suggest that it corresponds to contemporary facts of experience. According to Smith, society in its economic aspect is a vast concourse of people held together by the desire of each to exchange goods and services with others. Each individual is concerned directly only to further his own self-interest, but in pursuing this aim each is led as if by "an invisible hand'' to promote the interests of others. Forbidden by law and social custom to acquire the property of other people by force, fraud, or stealth, each individual attempts to maximize his own gains from trade by specializing in the production of goods and services for which he has a comparative advantage, trading his surplus produce for the produce of others on the best terms he can obtain. As a consequence, ''natural forces'' of market competition – the result of each individual attempting to ''buy cheap and sell dear'' – come into action to establish equality between demand and supply for each commodity at rates of exchange (prices) that reflect supplies forthcoming from relatively efficient producers and demands forthcoming from relatively eager consumers. Common sense to the contrary notwithstanding, therefore, the economic system is an essentially self-regulating mechanism that, like the human physiological system, tends naturally towards a state of ''equilibrium'' (homeostasis) if simply left to itself. Such, in essence, is the message of Adam Smith.

The contemporary scene

Nearly two hundred years have elapsed since Adam Smith's death. In the course of these two centuries, the superstructure of economic science has grown apace. To say that Smith would hardly recognize the science he is credited with fathering would hardly do justice to the changes that have occurred. If we look behind outward appearances and focus attention on Smith's initial vision, however, we can hardly help feeling that things have not, after all, changed that much. The foundations of contemporary economic analysis are, in truth, remarkably similar to those laid down originally by Adam Smith. Specifically, it must be recognized that at the present time, just as in Adam Smith's day, what we have by way of theoretical understanding of the working of a market economy is strictly in the nature of a magic castle: satisfying to the imagination but not much use for solving a housing shortage.

Let me be more explicit. A convincing demonstration of the logical consistency of Smith's conception of the economic system even under highly idealized conditions was not forthcoming until the 1950s. As a result of more recent work, it is now recognized that even this weak result (i.e., logical consistency) cannot be established for an economy in which trade takes place in decentralized markets and involves the use of money and other financial instruments as exchange intermediaries. Thus our most powerful contemporary tools of theoretical analysis appear to be applicable only to economic systems that are devoid of just those institutional features that seem to lie at the heart of our most pressing practical problems.

Now I should not like to assert that this body of knowledge is worthless. Among other things, it has a certain value as an instrument for analyzing weaknesses in piecemeal programs of economic intervention: pointing out the dangers of minimum wage laws as devices for improving the economic well-being of lower-income groups, tracing out the probable consequences of fixed exchange rates and inflationary government financial policies, suggesting possible adverse effects on per capita national income of tax policies that aim at a more equal distribution of income and wealth, and so forth. In no sense, however, is contemporary economic theory a suitable instrument for elaborating positive programs of social reform and economic control. For that purpose, we need a body of knowledge that has far more empirical content than the theory we presently possess – a body of knowledge that permits us to predict major features of the economic future, say, six months or a year ahead, with at least as much accuracy as meteorologists are currently able to predict the general character of next month's weather.

To some extent, our problem is one of inadequate factual knowledge. For reasons that I need not go into here, economists have always had to rely for the most part on data collected by governments and business firms for their own purposes. The kind of data that is urgently needed to improve our present understanding of economic events – mainly information about holdings of money and other financial assets by individual households and business firms and related information about stocks of goods in process, trade credit, and overdraft facilities – currently is not available in sufficient detail to be of any use or is simply not collected at all. But it really is no good to fulminate at the powers that be for failing to meet this need. The sad fact is that the relevance of this kind of information cannot be documented by reference to established theory.

Let me conclude by recalling another remark by J. M. Keynes, this one from the concluding chapter of his *General Theory*. "The ideas of economists," said Keynes, "are more powerful than is commonly understood. Practical men, who believe themselves to be quite exempt from any intellectual influences, are usually the slaves of some defunct economist. Madmen in authority, who hear voices in the air, are distilling their frenzy from some academic scribbler of a few years back." Personally I doubt if there was much truth in Keynes's remark at the time he made it – some thirty-five years ago. In recent years, however, economists have come to play an increasingly prominent role as advisors to governments. Whether this indicates that "madmen in authority" or the public at large are beginning to take the ideas of economists more seriously is an open question; the record in most countries indicates that after economists give their advice, the local "madmen" go ahead and do what they intended to do regardless. There can be no doubt, however, that economists are beginning to take *themselves* more seriously, and to my mind *this* is dangerous.

I should not like to be accused of fouling my own nest or even of the less heinous crime of obscurantism. As a specialist in economic theory who has dealt from time to time with practical problems of economic policy, however, I am tempted to say of my advice-giving colleagues what Wellington is reputed to have said of his foot soldiers: "I don't know how they strike you, but by God, sir, they surely frighten me." The basis for my fear is not personal and professional knowledge of instances in which policy action recommended by economists has turned out to be misguided. I should no more think of burdening the economics profession with the sins of its practitioners than of burdening the medical profession with the sins of its quacks. My misgivings derive from a deeper source: professional awareness of the unsettled and uncertain state of contemporary intellectual understanding of forces governing the coordination of economic activities in the world in which we actually live. To put the matter bluntly, we do not know enough to distinguish cases of economic toothache from cases of social lockjaw. In economics as in dentistry, intelligent diagnosis is a prerequisite for effective treatment. Lacking a secure basis for such diagnosis, we are about as likely to maim as cure the patient. So economists who are anxious to offer policy advice, and people – madmen in authority or otherwise – who are quick to seek and follow such advice, fill me with uneasiness if not terror. Economics has, I think, a great future as a science that produces results. Like Keynes, therefore, I look forward to a time when economists will be known as humble, competent men, on a level with dentists. For the immediate future, however, it seems to me that the proper business of economists is to advance their own understanding of how the economic system works. It will be time enough for economists to bring light to the world when they are able to convince themselves that they are no longer groping in the dark.

References

Arrow, K. J., and F. H. Hahn. 1971. *General Competitive Analysis.* San Francisco: Holden-Day.

Crew, Henry, and Alfonso de Salvio, trans. 1914. *Galileo Galilei, Dialogues Concerning Two New Sciences.* New York: Macmillan.

Friedman, Milton. 1953. "The Methodology of Positive Economics." In *Essays in Positive Economics,* 3–43, edited by Milton Friedman. Chicago: University of Chicago Press.

Gray, Alexander. 1931. *The Development of Economic Doctrine.* London: Longmans, Green.

Hanson, N. R. 1958. *Patterns of Discovery: An Inquiry into the Conceptual Foundations of Science.* Cambridge: Cambridge University Press.

Keynes, J. M. 1936. *The General Theory of Employment, Interest and Money.* New York: Macmillan.

Klamer, Arjo. 1984. *Conversations with Economists*. Totowa, N.J.: Rowman and Allanheld.

Kuhn, Thomas S. 1962. *The Structure of Scientific Revolutions*. Chicago: University of Chicago Press.

Motte, Andrew, trans. 1946. *Isaac Newton, Mathematical Principles of Natural Philosophy*. Revised by Foren Cajori. New York: Greenwood Press.

Taylor, F. S. 1949. *Science Past and Present*. New York.

Watson, J. D. 1968. *The Double Helix*. New York: Norton.

CHAPTER 8

Should a scientist abstain from metaphor?

Cristina Bicchieri

1. Introduction

Positivism is dead, we all agree. Gone is the rigid set of dichotomies purporting to define what can be meaningfully said and what is deprived of meaning, what is literal and what is expressive, figurative, or whatever. Abandoned, too, is the pretense of a unique, authoritative system of conditions defining scientific rationality once and for all. I could continue this necrology forever, since almost all of the tenets of the received view have been relinquished. We are left without a system, without a large and encompassing view of knowledge and cognition. Indeed, many of those who have given up positivism also doubt that these categories, knowledge and cognition, should prominently figure in an account of what we do when we engage in a scientific activity.

If scientific method is not the exhaustive list of procedures positivists pretended it to be, *then* – it is argued – it is just the set of practices adopted by given communities. Such practices are manufactured and relative, and science as a human activity should be considered from a whole series of perspectives, including the sociological, anthropological, and rhetorical ones. When one engages in a scientific practice, or for that matter in any other social practice, one enters into a complex web of power relations, has to learn the norms regulating research and the publication of results, has to master the tools of the trade, which include not only knowing how to do research but also, as McCloskey argues, knowing how to present one's findings in appropriate ways (McCloskey 1985). If methodology is thus collapsed into social practices, it is meaningless to search for a unique standard of scientific correctness, since we are likely to find many, and even incompatible ones.

To this extent, methodological relativism is appropriate. What is reasonable to believe is relative to goals, experiences, and means that are inescapably "local." Likewise with the means by which we assess what is true: They are variable and subject to change. But to recognize all that, we do not need to relativize truth. We may approach the world in many ways. The links between the language and the world undergo constant change. These changes, however, are cognitive, not just linguistic. The challenge one faces is thus to try to reconcile methodological relativism with the idea that language refers and hence that there is something it refers to. I cannot meet the challenge here, but mentioning it is pertinent to our present topic, the rhetorical analysis of science.

McCloskey's attack on positivism takes the form of a rhetorical analysis or, as he puts it, a "literary criticism of science." The study of scientific practices is identified with an analysis of the language of science, the means by which scientists communicate with each other and the general public, both in writing and speaking, and the literary tropes they favor. Rhetoric deals with communication and conversation that is intended to persuade. The rhetoric of economics is thus a study in persuasion, the point of the matter being *how* economists persuade, not *why* they succeed in doing so.

There is nothing wrong in saying that scientific language has an expressive, figurative dimension. But it would be excessive to claim that this is its only dimension. It is dangerously close to positivism to interpret the scientific vocabulary as made of purely literary devices. Positivists, of course, held an exactly opposite view; they maintained that scientific language is entirely literal, that it does not need embellishment to persuade. But when confronted with metaphors and other literary tropes they would agree with McCloskey: These are quintessential literary devices, devoid of cognitive content. The risk of the rhetorical analysis of science is thus that of throwing away only half of the positivist bequest, the idea that scientific language is exclusively literal. The risk is that of substituting the once discredited figurative uses of language for their literal counterparts, of saying that all language is metaphorical, and in so doing to *maintain* the traditional separation between literal and figurative, cognitive and expressive.

I believe that the separation is too narrow and ultimately impairs our understanding of science. Literal and figurative are the two poles of a continuum; they differ not in kind, but in degree. The distinction we may want to draw is pragmatic, a matter of the relative familiarity we have with certain words, sentences, or analogical connections. The figurative corresponds to the unfamiliar, that which is not yet entrenched in our system of knowledge. An illustration of the inadequacy of the figurative/literal distinction is provided by a consideration of economic metaphors and how they work. According to McCloskey, because economists make extensive use of metaphors and analogies, they are rhetoricians. Maybe they are. But are metaphors *only* literary devices? Is that true that there is no difference between poetic and economic metaphors, as he repeatedly claims? Are metaphors merely ornamental, or do they convey some knowledge? I believe that they do, and that is the reason why some of them persuade.

2. Metaphor: the traditional view

The traditional suspicion toward metaphor could not be better expressed than Bishop Berkeley did when he stated that "a philosopher should abstain from metaphor." Indeed, how could a philosopher say *"A is B"* and mean *"A is O"* instead? If a word uniquely refers to an object, metaphorical usage is not just confusing, it is against the rules of language. Literal language is the only vehicle for expressing meaning and making truth claims, and metaphor is a deviant use of words in other than their proper senses.

Old-fashioned empiricism separates literal and figurative language, associating the latter with rhetorical purposes or stylistic embellishment. This antithesis between the literal and the rhetorical found its classic formulation in Locke. In his *Essay Concerning Human Understanding,* he asserted that rhetorical statements aim "to insinuate wrong ideas, move the passions, and thereby mislead the judgement; and so indeed are perfect cheats." Rhetoric is contrasted with informative and truth-conveying discourse, a discourse where words signify ideas, so that by using them we can convey our ideas to the mind of the listener. Such communication plays an essential role in science, the main feature of which as rational discourse, according to empiricists, is that it is not rhetorical.

Consistent with this contrast is the idea that metaphor, the chief rhetorical trope, is an elliptical simile that can be translated into a literal paraphrase without loss of content. This interpretation of metaphor goes back as far as Aristotle, who understood metaphor to be a deviation from literal usage, the transfer of a name to some object to which that name does not belong. An underlying similarity makes the transfer possible. Thus when we say, in a Hobbesian vein, "man is a wolf," we indirectly present some literal meaning, such as "man is fierce, avid, cruel, and deceitful." The meaning of the metaphor is a literal set of similarities indicated by the context of the utterance. Consequently, figurative discourse is used only for rhetorical purposes or stylistic embellishment; metaphor is denied any autonomous cognitive content.

Modern positivism did not change the picture. Its distinction between the cognitive and emotive aspects of language, coupled with the belief that scientific knowledge can be reduced to a system of literal sentences, implies that metaphor has no cognitive import. Again, metaphor is a deviation from literal discourse, an elliptical simile, so that if we want to attribute to it any cognitive content, we have to look for its literal paraphrase. For the positivist, the language of science *refers*. It refers directly, in the case of observational terms, while the reference of general or theoretical terms like "electron" or "equilibrium" has to be fixed by explicit conventional definitions. The consequence is that the meaning of these terms is fixed. By breaking linguistic rules, by saying something and meaning something else, metaphor can have no literal meaning; it cannot refer.

It must be noticed that the idea that metaphor is an elliptical simile does not depend upon the neopositivistic theory of language nor on the cognitive/ emotive dichotomy. We may, for example, hold a *comparison view* of metaphor, and this would suffice to deprive it of any *autonomous* cognitive content. As to this view, when we metaphorically say *"A is B,"* we mean *"A is like B in the following respects . . .";* this implies that there are two objects being compared, that there are similarities between them, and that these similarities are obvious in the given context. Sufficiently obvious, at least, as to allow understanding of what the utterer means by using the metaphor.

But if we pay attention to how metaphors work, in literary or in everyday language, we see that many of them do not fulfill these conditions. For one, there might not exist two objects that are being compared, as when we say, "John is an angel." Or the asserted similarity might be false, as in the case of "Tom is a swine," if it is not true that pigs are dirty, voracious, and prone to improper sexual behavior, while these are the qualities that the speaker intends to attribute to Tom. (These points are discussed in Searle 1979.) Also, similarity is anything but an objective relationship, and since any two objects are similar at least in some respect, it might be very difficult to compute the meaning of a metaphor (cf. Black 1962, Ch. 3). Finally, there might not be any literal similarity between the two objects that are being compared, as when one says, "Qaddafi is a paper tiger". From these examples we may conclude that, though similarity plays a role in comprehending a metaphor, a metaphor cannot be just an assertion of similarity.

Such criticisms are the basis for the *interaction view* of metaphor, a view first introduced by I. A. Richards (1936) and subsequently adopted by Max Black (1962). According to this theory, understanding a metaphor is not just a matter of comparing objects in order to determine the similarities between them. In any metaphor there are two constitutive elements: the primary subject and the secondary subject. In an effective metaphor the two subjects are taken from different domains or modes of discourse and are brought together interactively.

In the statement "Sally is a dragon," the system of commonplaces one associates with Sally interacts with that of the dragon to produce a new metaphorical meaning. These commonplaces are whatever properties and relations are *believed to be true* of Sally and dragons, respectively. It does not matter if they are not actually true. What happens in this metaphor is that we use the entire system of commonplaces associated to dragons to "organize" our conception of Sally, to see her in a different light. The interaction between the primary and secondary subjects of a metaphor, therefore, generates a new perspective on both, it reorganizes our conceptual structure. An important consequence of this interaction view is that metaphors, rather than expressing preexisting similarities, *create* new ones. A further consequence is that metaphor has a meaning of its own that cannot be reduced to literal paraphrase, since the meaning results from the interaction of two different contexts.

So far I have not mentioned economic metaphors, or for that matter scientific metaphors. Is the same process at work in literature, science, and everyday language? Is the interaction view appropriate to scientific metaphors? After all, it is easier to admit that poetic metaphors create new and striking similarities than to attribute the same power to scientific metaphors. Indeed, Max Black thought there was a difference between explicit scientific usage of language and metaphorical usage. According to him, we need metaphors in those cases where the precision of scientific statements is not possible. Hence metaphor is appropriate to the prescientific stages of a discipline or, in the case of developed sciences, to heuristics.

Early economics is full of examples of such conceptual reorganizations. Both the Physiocrats and Adam Smith described the relations among the spheres of production, circulation, and distribution in terms of functional relations among the parts of the human body. Economic society was described as a "social body," from which the division of labor and specialization of the parts naturally follow. The development of the metaphor brought together concepts from two conventionally different domains – the world of natural history and the artificial products of human society. The orderly work of the human body mirrors the organization of economic activities, but unlike the body, the latter are manufactured. The metaphor thus uncovers a tension and draws attention to those features of the economy that are like the functioning of a human body, regular and well organized; it points to those organizational features that are beneficial to the whole society. It is precisely this "naturalness" of the economic sphere that directs one to find the underlying causes of such regularities, to state the principles that account for the coordination of economic activities.

This is an example drawn from the early stages of economics. At this stage everything was still needed – a new vocabulary as well as a model of how to proceed – and the physiological metaphor provided for both. As the field grew, the metaphor was substituted by a far more rigorous, self-contained economic vocabulary. Should we conclude that metaphor plays no role in a mature field? Or isn't it rather the case that metaphors also evolve, change content, become internal to a field, therefore less visible? Indeed, I want to argue that metaphors play an essential role even in mature fields, in the development of new theories as well as in the extension of old ones. They are *constitutive* of scientific discourse. This does not happen because, in rejecting the distinction between literal and metaphorical, one has to come to the conclusion that all language is metaphorical. Quite to the contrary, it is possible to appeal to a different theory of meaning and reference, a theory that makes metaphors an essential part of the linguistic machinery of theories.

Those who, like Black, do not believe that the role of metaphor should be thus furthered, hold the related view that sentences can have two separate meanings, literal and figurative; the secondary, figurative meaning is creative and is chosen by rejecting the primary, literal meaning. Unfortunately, this view does not account for what happens even in relatively unproblematic everyday usage. Many figurative meanings are not secondary and are not even creative. For example, if I tell somebody, "Your idea is a joke," the figurative meaning is immediately preferred, despite the plausible literal counterpart. On the other hand, "I have lost my temper," though figurative, is anything but creative.

Can one say the same of scientific language? In this context it is even more difficult to see how there could be two separate meanings, while it is often the case that a statement that was previously used in a figurative sense later becomes literal: It gets "entrenched" into the language of the theory. Consider an economic expression like "The market is in equilibrium." Nowadays it is obviously taken to be literal; it means that excess demand is zero, something that can in principle be verified. The same expression, two hundred years ago, was taken to be figurative; it evoked an unspecified gravitational process of prices toward their "natural" values. The example is not meant to suggest that an expression counts as literal only when it becomes amenable to some sort of operational definition, testing, or other empirical procedure. There are many other economic sentences, such as "agents' preference sets are convex" or "Oligopoly is an n-person noncooperative game," which are meant to be literal, yet have no obvious empirical counterpart. What makes them literal, I want to suggest, is their being well entrenched into economic theory.

The intuitive idea of something being "entrenched" into a theory can be replaced by the more precise notion of "generative entrenchment," which has been introduced in biology by W. Wimsatt to replace the innate/acquired distinction. According to Wimsatt (1986), early evolutionary features have a higher probability of being required for features that will appear later and will generally have a large number of "downstream" features depending upon them. A feature is thus "generatively entrenched" in proportion to the number of features that depend upon it. In the same vein, one might say that the above economic sentences are generatively entrenched, in that they state connections between preferences and convex sets, and oligopolistic markets and games, upon which a large number of "downstream" connections depend.

That the literal/figurative opposition is only pragmatic has already been suggested by Mary Hesse (1976), who conceives of literal usage as use in a familiar context. Indeed, if the literal and the figurative are but the two extremes of a continuum, the distinction one wishes to draw is a matter of degree: It has to do with the level of entrenchment of a sentence into our cognitive structure. For example, sentences expressing connections between preferences and convex sets are well entrenched while those connecting speculative bubbles and price movements are still "figurative." Metaphors thus express a provisional connection, a link between the primary and secondary system that is new and suggestive but might as well turn out to be uncongenial. What remains to be explained is why some metaphors meet with success, how some of them succeed in becoming so well entrenched as to grow into literal statements. Becoming literal is not just a matter of time.

3. Models and metaphors

Economic texts are full of metaphors. As McCloskey (1985) pointedly argues, words like *equilibrium, depression, stagflation, elasticity,* and so on are highly evocative, they impress the reader with their gloom or convey a simpler and immediate visual image of the more complex idea that is introduced (p. 76). These are not, however, the metaphors I deem to be relevant to a discussion of how economic theories work. The above cases only tell us that the vocabulary of economics consists largely of words introduced by *catachresis,* the use of an idiom to fill a gap in the lexicon. Moreover, confining our attention to single words makes it difficult to see how metaphor might play any cognitive role in the development of theories.

McCloskey, however, draws further and more interesting examples from human capital theory and Gary Becker's economics of the family. In the first case the novelty consisted in treating people's expenditures on health and education as analogous to investment in physical capital. People, that is, spend on themselves in diverse ways, not only for present enjoyment but also for the sake of future benefits. This borrowing of ideas from investment theory had important consequences; for example, the demand for postcompulsory schooling was no longer seen as demand for a consumption good and thus presumably a function only of taste, income, and the cost of instruction. Human capital theory suggests that this demand should be a function both of variations in direct and indirect private costs of schooling and in earning differentials associated with additional education. This metaphorical redescription of the demand for instruction creates new similarities, and introduces a new dictionary. New predictions are made possible, for example that there should be a correlation between age and demand for instruction, which made no sense under the previous approach.

The same can be said for the extension of utility theory to family decisions.

For example, a similarity is asserted between children and durable goods: We plan to enjoy them for a long time, derive utility from them, and choose to have them on the basis of a cost–benefit calculation. The similarity is indeed *created* by using the economic vocabulary to describe family choices. New predictions, such as that family income is positively related to the utility derived from child services or that rich people will have fewer, better-educated children, are made possible by the introduction of a new dictionary, which redescribes the primary subject (children) through predicates drawn from the secondary subject (consumers' choice).

These examples are perhaps better described as instances of the use of models in economics. A number of philosophers of science, among them Mary Hesse, Thomas Kuhn, and Richard Boyd, have argued that the use of models in science resembles the use of metaphors, inasmuch as it requires analogical transfer of a vocabulary and creates similarities. By "model" here is meant a set of assumptions about a system attributing to it a given structure, so that many of its properties are explained by reference to this structure. Indeed, it has been argued that scientific explanation can be interpreted as a metaphorical redescription of the domain of the explicandum (Hesse 1966: 157–77).

While all extensions of the theory of consumer choice to new fields are obvious examples of explanatory models, this is by no means the only such case in economics. Game theory, as applied to market structures, is another example of the use of models with explanatory purposes, as is the recent microfoundations program in macroeconomics. In all these cases, we represent objects or phenomena "as if" they possessed certain properties or satisfy certain relations. Such properties and relations are borrowed from another theory, which is familiar and manageable. The analogy with metaphorical processes is straightforward: In a scientific theory, the primary system is the domain of the explicandum, while the secondary system is a theory that is already well known and relatively unproblematic.

Paradigmatic examples of such models are the mechanical models of nineteenth-century physics; gases were described as collections of moving particles obeying newtonian laws, and atoms as miniature solar systems. The conventional wisdom in philosophy of science did not deny the usefulness of such models. Still, it saw them only as heuristic devices, belonging to the context of discovery, to be eliminated as soon as a field progresses and a direct and complete description of the primary system can be given. In fact, many of the nineteenth-century models have been replaced in modern physics but, as Kuhn (1979) has argued, not so the metaphorical process that underlay them. When Bohr's model replaced the solar system metaphor, the new model was not intended to be taken completely literally:

> Electrons and nuclei were not thought to be exactly like small billiard or Ping-Pong balls; only some of the laws of mechanics and electromagnetic theory were thought to apply to them: finding out which ones did apply and where the similarities to billiard balls lay was a central task in the development of the quantum theory. [. . .] The model remained essential to the theory. Without its aid one cannot even today write down the Schrödinger equation for a complex atom or molecule for it is to the model, not directly to nature, that the various terms in that equation refer. (pp. 414–15)

Models, and the metaphorical processes underlying them, are an integral part of science. They help in structuring the primary system, allow one to deal with it in a manageable way and to explain some of its features. In addition, by providing something like a linguistic extension, a new vocabulary, the model introduces new predicates in the domain of the primary system, allowing new predictions to be made.

A further question is whether we are completely free to introduce whatever model we please, or whether instead we can say there are better and worse models, and whether this has to do with some "fit" between the two systems that are brought together. If we were free to introduce whatever model we pleased, we would have to say that models perform no cognitive function; we would have to endorse the logical empiricist's claim that models and metaphors do not refer.

To say that there must be some fit between the two systems does not mean that there must exist analogies on which to ground the metaphorical redescription of the primary system. What is the analogy between an oligopolistic market and a noncooperative game? There is no evident preexisting analogy. It is precisely the description of this market structure through game theory that makes us aware that there can be structural similarities. But it is not the case that we can substitute for the model an exhaustive list of all the analogies existing between oligopolies and noncooperative games, any more than we can substitute for any metaphor a list of all the underlying similarities between the primary and secondary subjects.

Generally, the only prior constraint imposed on the system we borrow from is its relative familiarity and manageability. Thus the fact that most of the time models are not grounded in preexisting similarities and are interpreted in a nonrealistic way, might suggest that not only the construction, but even the persistence of a model are largely chance events. Quite to the contrary, I believe there are good reasons why a model is thought to be successful, even if "successful" or "well entrenched" does not mean dropping the *as if* clause.

Some of the most successful economic models are mathematical models. By this I do not mean sets of quantified relations or simple diagrammatical representations. Mathematical models are rather applications of mathematical theories to economic phenomena; they tie the phenomena to descriptions in the mathematical theory by redescribing economic objects as mathematical objects. A classic example of such redescription is to be found in Debreu's *Theory of Value* (1959). Economic actions are described as points in the commodity space, which is mathematically represented as a finite-dimensional real vector space. Prices are similarly represented by a point in the price space, the real vector space dual of the commodity space. Finite dimensional commodity and price spaces are then identified as Euclidean spaces, which allows a geometrical representation of most economic phenomena.

Yet the use of mathematics in economics does not just offer a more convenient representation of what is already known. Mathematics is not a mere shorthand language; neither, however, is one bound to assume realistically that the "true" structure of economic phenomena is that depicted by the mathematical theory. What, then, makes a mathematical model "successful"? Invoking criteria like predictability will not do, since these general models are often used to refine and evaluate specific predictive theories, but are not themselves predictive. (A similar view is expressed in Green 1979.) Even the idea of explanation needs to be qualified, since what are explained are not observable market phenomena, but rather conditions are stated under which an ideal market configuration can exist.

A good example is the Arrow–Debreu model of general equilibrium with uncertainty. In this model, allocations are represented as points in vector spaces, and production and consumption sets as real valued vector spaces. Randomness, too, is represented through a vector space structure. These assumptions allow the economist to use results from convex analysis to prove the existence, Pareto optimality, and local uniqueness of equilibria. A crucial feature of the model is that its way of treating uncertainty not only makes it compatible with the former model of general equilibrium under certainty, but also generalizes its results to economies where there is uncertainty about the future state of the world. Hence one obvious reason for its success is its fit with a previous, well-established model. Another is that it explains under which conditions an equilibrium exists and what sort of properties it may possess. Finally, it is general enough to allow for many different assumptions about agents' objectives, technology, production processes, and so on.

Such models do not pretend to be realistic. They are *fictional* descriptions, in that they attribute to economic objects what Nancy Cartwright (1983) has aptly called "properties of convenience," that is, properties having the effect of bringing the objects modeled into the range of the mathematical theory (pp. 158ff). These properties may be idealizations or just pure fictions. In the above example the commodity space is represented as a real vector space so that the property of convexity can be attributed to production and consumption sets. Assuming convexity might not just be an idealization, though. As it happens, many observable economic phenomena *lack* the property, as when increasing returns to scale in production exist. This restricts the applicability of the model, and indeed it may even happen that a model's conditions of applicability are never found in the economy. Or, as has been suggested by Wimsatt (1985), a model may be purely "phenomenological," describing phenomena without making any claims as to the existence of the variables in the model.

Fictional models are not, as many economists would have it, shortcuts to deal with the complexities of the real world. They do help in understanding the phenomena, whether they act in an organizing role or as benchmarks that focus attention on the points where the models deviate from reality, leading to the hypothesis of mechanisms of how and under what circumstances the excluded variables act and are crucial. In these cases, too, one would say that there is some fit between a mathematical structure and certain economic phenomena, even if there is no obvious preexisting structural analogy between the two and the fit cannot be measured in terms of realism.

The fictional character of such models is well captured by the idea of a metaphorical description, attributing a provisional similarity to structures otherwise very different. The metaphorical process reveals new relationships, suggests new ways of looking at the phenomena. Some of them may later come to be rejected. These are the unsuccessful models, the failed metaphors. They can fail precisely because they have cognitive content and are not merely rhetorical devices.

4. Can metaphors refer?

Should one then conclude that metaphors (and models) make truth claims? Can metaphors be assimilated to factual statements, though irreducible to literal paraphrases? If one answers in the affirmative, one is bound to say that models and metaphors have referents, and the obvious candidate is the primary subject. However, Tom is not literally a swine, children are not commodities, and gas particles are not billiard balls. One cannot really identify the referent of the metaphorical expression, taken in its literal meaning, with the primary subject.

Let's take the idea of modeling agents as having rational expectations. The question is not whether an extension of the principle of rationality to people's beliefs is realistic or has to be taken in a literal sense, but whether it is fruitful in generating new information about macroeconomic phenomena, in coordinating previously uncoordinated aspects of the field, in suggesting refinements of previous theories. What happens is that rationality is provisionally assigned to people's beliefs, and the consequences of this assignment are explored. This is the way scientific metaphors work. Theory-constitutive metaphors are invitations to future research, in that they introduce terminology for features of the world that seem probable, but whose properties have yet to be discovered.[1]

The reference of a term like *rationality* is not fixed once and for all by a stipulated convention, as logical empiricists would have it. Rather, it is fixed by dubbing ceremonies or acts of ostension, involving the association of the term with samples of its referent.[2] Just as we learn the meaning of the word *game* from a juxtaposition of a series of exemplary games, so we can point to different aspects of the same property we call "rationality." To be rational is to choose the action that one believes will maximize the chances of attaining the desired goal, to entertain noncontradictory beliefs, to use all the available information in the best possible way. The term is introduced by appealing to situations in which we *believe* it is exemplified, often prior to "discovering" whether it is in fact appropriate.

Metaphors fix reference in precisely this way. Indeed, according to Boyd (1979: 368), one of the important roles of theory-constitutive metaphors "is to accomplish nondefinitional reference fixing of this sort. If the fundar..ental properties of the metaphorical secondary subjects of a body of related metaphors are sufficiently well understood, then these metaphors can be employed – together perhaps with exemplary circumstances of application – to fix non-literal referents for the metaphorical expressions they contain." The extension of a rationality principle to people's expectations is a case in point. By calling them rational, we intend to refer to some postulated aspect of expectations. We "guess" there is an analogy between practical rationality, that is, the rationality of an action, given one's beliefs, and epistemic rationality, that is, the rationality imputed to the belief itself. Then we start investigating this guess and its consequences.

On a purely formal level, we require beliefs to be consistent, as preferences should be. When beliefs are probabilistic in nature, we expect them to satisfy the axioms of probability calculus. Unlike economic preferences, beliefs and expectations must also be substantively rational, in that they must be grounded on some evidence, and the evidence at agents' disposal must be "processed" in an appropriate way. "Evidence," of course, includes other people's actions, which in turn depend on whatever beliefs those people hold. In rational expectations models, rational beliefs thus defined are always assumed to be correct beliefs. And correct beliefs, in this context, mean equilibrium beliefs; that is, agents have no reason to change them, assuming other agents' beliefs stay the same. This equilibrium assumption has prevented for some time a further question to be asked: How can different prior beliefs come to converge to the same posterior beliefs?

The discovery that there can be multiple equilibria, each depending on different initial sets of beliefs, has made the above question crucial. It is not just a problem for the economist, to decide which set of beliefs economic agents start with. It is a problem for agents, too, to guess which beliefs other agents entertain, to learn from aggregate outcomes (what else?) what the others' beliefs might have been. Is learning possible in interactive (that is, social) environments? Is there such a thing as rational learning? These are meaningful questions that have been brought about by the metaphorical extension of the principle of rationality to expectations. It is precisely this capability of opening new problems and indicating research avenues that makes the metaphor so successful.

Through interaction with many different primary subjects, rationality itself has come a long way. Throughout these extensions, it has come to be more precisely defined. Even if it obviously lacks an explicit and univocal definition. Contrary to what logical empiricists (and Friedman) would claim, rationality refers, and so do its metaphorical extensions to new primary subjects, such as types of behavior or beliefs. We may come to discover that some of its imputed applications are indeed wrong. For example, we may come to see that it is not possible to form any justifiable belief about other people's actions in an interactive context where actions are open to many possible interpretations. In these circumstances, there would be no rational expectations, and the provisional commitment we made to their existence would be retracted. Just as Russian roulette is no longer considered a game, so we might eventually drop the word *rational* from expectations. The class of things of which rationality is predicated would shrink, and this would be in itself a cognitive step forward.[3] These changes are not purely linguistic, however; they are cognitive: They are changes in the links we posit between our language and the world.

If we accept an ostensive, or ''dubbing'' theory of reference, we can use it to support the claim that metaphorical terms refer. *Rationality* in this interpretation is a term that can be used in different contexts, in different paradigms, and still be coreferential. When used metaphorically, be it as an extension of a given theory or as an explanatory device, it does refer, even if provisionally, and indicate a research direction concerning its referent.

5. Why do metaphors persuade?

If scientific metaphors were only literary devices, ornaments, or embellishments superimposed on an otherwise dry and boring language, we would be justified in treating them as we do poetic metaphors. We would grow restless and upset at hearing rationality being predicated for the nth time of whatever the economist in question is talking about, much as we react to a piece in which a woman's teeth are compared to pearls or her eyes to suns. We find such metaphors banal, overexploited; they have lost usefulness through overuse. A good literary metaphor should be surprising and unexpected, as Mary Hesse (1966), discussing precisely this difference, has pointedly argued.

Scientific metaphors, on the contrary, are to be overused. They undergo public articulation (indeed, this is the mark of a good metaphor), and the proposed similarities between the two subjects are extensively explored, sometimes by entire generations of researchers. Of course, these metaphors must be intelligible, but not so much so as to discourage research.

In literary metaphors, the characteristics associated to the secondary subject are commonplace. We all know (or believe we know) what pigs, diamonds, and pearls are like. The metaphorical connection might surprise us, but it hardly encourages thorough probing; indeed, a successful metaphor is a combination of unexpectedness and immediate apprehension. In scientific metaphors we are left open to explore how expectations can be rational or how gas particles behave like small elastic spheres. Indeed, one is invited to investigate the metaphor. Paradoxically, a successful scientific metaphor is a "dead" metaphor: It has become well entrenched, literal, part of our body of knowledge. On the contrary, I do not believe that literary metaphors benefit from overuse.

Linguistically, both poetic and scientific metaphors may function in the same way. But their contexts are very different, and so are their goals. One has a cognitive goal, the other does not attempt to extend our "theory" of the world. Thus, the conventions of speech will be different, as will be the expectations about what is said. Pace McCloskey, no scientific metaphor persuades only because of its beauty, elegance or simplicity. If it did, one would be justified in denying it cognitive content, as generations of philosophers of science have maintained.

Notes

1. On this point and what follows, cf. Boyd (1979).
2. What I am talking about is, in essence, the Kripke–Putnam account of reference, which maintains that reference of natural-kind of "theoretical" terms in science, is fixed ostensively or casually rather than by definitional convention. Kripke (1972). Cf. also Putnam (1975).
3. I have extensively discussed these points in Bicchieri (forthcoming).

References

Bicchieri, C. Forthcoming. "Rationality and Predictability in Economics." *The British Journal for the Philosophy of Science.*

Black, Max. 1962. *Models and Metaphors.* Ithaca, N.Y.: Cornell University Press.

Boyd, R. 1979. "Metaphor and Theory Change: What Is 'Mctaphor' a Metaphor For?" In *Metaphor and Thought,* edited by A. Ortony, 356–408. New York: Cambridge University Press.

Cartwright, N. 1983. *How the Laws of Physics Lie.* Oxford: Clarendon Press.

Debreu, 1959. *Theory of Value: An Axiomatic Analysis of Economic Equilibrium.* New Haven: Yale University Press.

Green, Edward. 1979. "Fundamental Theory in Positive Economics." In *Philosophy in Economics;* edited by J. C. Pitt Boston: D. Reidel.

Hesse, M. B. 1966. *Models and Analogies in Science.* Notre Dame, Ind.: University of Notre Dame Press.

———. 1976. "Models Versus Paradigms in the Natural Sciences." In *The Use of Models in the Social Sciences,* edited by L. Collins. London: Tavistock Publications.

Kripke, S. A. 1972. "Naming and Necessity." In *The Semantics of Natural Language,* edited by D. Davidson and G. Hartman, Dordrecht: Reidel.

Kuhn, T. 1979. "Metaphors in Science." In *Metaphor and Thought,* edited by A. Ortony. Cambridge: Cambridge University Press.

Locke, John. *Essay Concerning Human Understanding,* Book 3, Ch. 10, 34.

McCloskey, D. N. 1985. *The Rhetoric of Economics.* Madison: The University of Wisconsin Press.

Putnam, H. 1975. "The Meaning of Meaning." In *Mind, Language and Reality.* Cambridge: Cambridge University Press.

Richards, I. A. 1936. *The Philosophy of Rhetoric.* Oxford: Oxford University Press.

Searle, John. 1979. *Expression and Meaning.* Cambridge: Cambridge University Press.

Wimsatt, W. "Functions of False Models as Means to Truer Theories." Mimeographed. Chicago: University of Chicago, November.

———. 1986. "Developmental Constraints, Generative Entrenchment, and the Innate/Acquired Distinction." In *Integrating Scientific Disciplines,* edited by N. Bechtel. Dordrecht, Boston: Martinus Nijhoff.

PART III

Economic rhetoric among economists

Shall I compare thee to a Minkowski–Ricardo–Leontief–Metzler matrix of the Mosak–Hicks type?

Or, rhetoric, mathematics, and the nature of neoclassical economic theory

Philip Mirowski

They have endeavor'd, to separate the knowledge of Nature, from the colours of Rhetorick. . . .

> – Thomas Sprat, *History of the Royal Society*

The greatest thing by far is to have a command of metaphor.

> – Aristotle, *Poetics*

I. Easy Rider

Is rhetoric just a new and trendy way to *épater les bourgeois?* Unfortunately, I think that the newfound interest of some economists in rhetoric, and particularly Donald McCloskey in his new book and subsequent responses to critics (McCloskey 1985a; 1985b), gives that impression. After economists have worked so hard for the past five decades to learn their sums, differential calculus, real analysis, and topology, it is a fair bet that one could easily hector them about their woeful ignorance of the conjugation of Latin verbs or Aristotle's six elements of tragedy.[1] Moreover, it has certainly be-

I would like to thank Arjo Klamer, Roy Weintraub, and Ken Dennis for their comments, as well as Warren Samuels, Daniel Hausman, and Bruce Caldwell for rescuing me from some errors. Undoubtedly, they all still believe I resist from being rescued from all error. I would also like to acknowledge the editors of the *Journal of Economic Literature* for demonstrating that the bounds of polite philosophical discourse are located at the perimeters of the defense of neoclassical theory. I am also aware that it is gauche to explain literary allusions, but I fear that the average economist has become so ignorant of the history of his discipline, and therefore claims to understand only the most literal of phrases, that I would direct those seeking the inner meaning of the title to consult Samuelson (1966, p. 1499). This chapter was revised in August 1986 and then in September 1986. Reprinted with permission from *Economics and Philosophy* 3 (1987): 67–96.

come an academic cliché that economists write as gracefully and felicitously as a hundred monkeys chained to broken typewriters. The fact that economists still trot out Keynes's prose in their defense is itself an index of the inarticulate desperation of an inarticulate profession.

There is nothing new in all of this: The average economist knows it in his or her bones. Hence the exasperation that must greet a passage like that found in McCloskey (1985a: 29): ". . . the overlapping conversations provide the standards. It is a market argument. There is no need for philosophical lawmaking or methodological regulation to keep the economy of the intellect running just fine." Isn't this just what the average neoclassical economist believed anyway? So what else is new?

I would like to argue that there is more to rhetoric than that. There is something in McCloskey's original 1983 *Journal of Economic Literature* article that touched a nerve but is in danger of getting smothered amid all of the small-*r* rhetoric. McCloskey's "rhetoric" can only be fully understood in its dual historical contexts: the older context of the decline of classical rhetoric and the more modern context of the ongoing methodological defense of neoclassical economic theory. Examination of these trends will lead us directly to a prosaic discussion of mathematical expression as a species of metaphor and its dominant influence upon the rise of neoclassical theory. In a visceral way, "rhetoric" is often invidiously contrasted with mathematical expression among neoclassicals; this conviction is the most important clue in understanding the nature of neoclassical economic theory. Meditation upon this sequence of events shall redouble our curiosity concerning the philosophical implications of rhetorical analysis in the penultimate section of this chapter.

II. War of the worlds

Don McCloskey has asserted that the canons of rhetoric provide a suitable set of concepts for understanding how arguments among economists fail or succeed. On a superficial reading, he appears to be concerned solely with "style." To be sure, this is one connotation of the term *rhetoric:* It is *l'art de bien dire,* defined as the correct and agreeable demeanor of address in conformity with the rules of communication in a civilized society. But there is another connotation of rhetoric, one that is also relevant: This is the art of persuasion. In a civilized society, it should be possible to change another person's mind without force or coercion. Hence rhetoric is also a form of a theory of social order, a prototype of morality, statecraft, and of philosophy itself. As the great philosopher himself said, "The perfection of style is to be clear without being mean" (Aristotle 1961: 101).

Classical rhetoric was one of the pillars of education until the seventeenth century, the others being grammar and logic. Rhetoricians sought to instruct the student in the techniques of the arts of persuasion, beginning with drills in Greek and Latin and continuing on to translations of the ancient masters, such as Aristotle, Cicero, and Quintilian. Advanced exercises included practice in declamation and disputation and instruction in the tropes appropriate to the three duties of the orator, which were to instruct, to please, and to move.

This situation began to change in the seventeenth century, when rhetoric came under severe attack from the partisans of the new sciences. In France, for instance, the primary antagonists of the rhetoricians were recruits from the Cartesian camp, who insisted that the conviction of certainty arose from introspective knowledge, mathematical expression, and the reduction of all the epiphenomena of the world to a few simple rules of matter in motion. Malebranche, for one, feared that audiences were too frequently swayed by what he termed nonrational considerations, and he denounced the appeal by rhetors to the senses, the imagination, and the passions (France 1965, pp. 19 et seq.). The archetypical complaint of the new scientists was that the rhetor engaged in an irrelevant display of verbal or literary pyrotechnics; he aimed more to provoke applause and admiration than to get on with the real business of analysis and tutelage. Some critics went so far as to insist that all embellishment got in the way of communication, whereas others suspected that rhetorical refinements served to convince people against their wills. The Cartesian antidote to all of this puffery was immersion in the bracing environment of austere mathematics and rational mechanics. As Descartes wrote to Mersenne in 1629, "Order is what is needed: All the thoughts that can come into the human mind must be arranged in an order like the natural order of numbers." A goodly dose of that purgative would reveal a truth that was self-evident and independent of the authority and eloquence of others.

We are all aware that the Cartesian idea of a natural science has had its instrumental and tactical successes, and as a consequence it has displaced rhetoric. The rise of the modern university further encouraged a tendency toward professionalization more attuned to the Cartesian ideal (Pyenson 1983). One salient aspect of the process was the cultivation of an arcane jargon in each little department, both for purposes of differentiation and to prevent the intrusion of outsiders. The *lingua franca* of the natural sciences became mathematics, and its influence became apparent in every discipline that pined for the status and legitimacy of the Cartesian natural sciences. Eventually, a mathematical and self-consciously scientistic style became conflated with the ideal of legitimate suasion, a format McCloskey calls "modernism," but given its genealogy, is more aptly called "the Cartesian Vice."

There now exist quite a few competent descriptions of the Cartesian Vice (Tiles 1984; Rorty 1979). In simple terms, for the Cartesian, the only reasoning is formal reasoning and the only thought is conscious thought. Reasoning is formal when knowledge of the subject matter is deemed irrelevant to the principles of formal demonstration, and therefore irrelevant in any acknowledgment of the validity of an argument. Indeed, it is claimed that the formal principles of reason are embodied in mathematics alone, a computational scheme that could ideally be programmed into an automaton that could then settle all disputes "objectively." Moreover, the Cartesian tradition is hostile to the idea that the social process of argumentation and persuasion should have any bearing upon rational knowledge, since only the individual mind can convince itself; it is also hostile to the idea that there is an inextricable social component to the growth of knowledge, suspicious of appeals to historical authority and suspicious of the slippery connotations of words in the vernacular. In short, it is hostile to rhetoric. Assent of an audience of rational individuals is only to be expected upon the demonstration of the impersonal and self-evident truth of the mathematical syllogism (Gaukroger 1980).

The irony of McCloskey's article on the rhetoric of economics was that he opted to champion the vanquished foe of Cartesianism as the best methodological defense of the social science most addicted to the Cartesian Vice, neoclassical economic theory. The neoclassical school of economics had only recently adopted all the trappings of the Cartesian world view – mathematical formalism, axiomatization, derogation of literary narrative, and mimesis of natural science terminology and attitudes – but had also endowed their mannequin of rational economic man with exclusively Cartesian powers and abilities: transparent individual self-knowledge, mechanical algorithms of decision making, independence from all historical determination, and all social action ultimately explained by rational individual assent. In fact, one could easily make the argument (although I shall decline to do so here because of the necessity of the citation of too much historical evidence) that in neoclassical economics ontogeny recapitulated epistemology, in the sense that the prior Cartesian conception of science dictated the model of man, and not vice versa (cf. Mirowski 1985a, 1988, forthcoming). Suddenly, along came McCloskey, insisting that neoclassical economists had been too long caught in the thrall of the Cartesian Vice. Irony was piled upon irony when he further asserted that addiction to the Cartesian Vice was nonlethal. If only economists would acknowledge that the persuasiveness of their arguments hinged upon rhetorical considerations, they would discover that orthodox theories now in the ascendant would be preserved, if not actually strengthened.

McCloskey's crusade could not help but sound dissonant and appear self-contradictory. One common reaction was to view it as just another installment in the continuing decline of the West, the dissolution and squandering of our rational heritage. Another common reaction was the American admonition: If it ain't broke, don't fix it. Both reactions were really beside the point, although they did stoke the swirling fires of controversy. What was missing from the controversy was an appreciation of the historical determinants of this seemingly iconoclastic crusade.

Since the 1930s neoclassical economic theory has increasingly allied itself with the natural sciences – or more exactly, an image of physics (a claim documented below) – in the process of inquiry, imitating both style and substance. Examination of neoclassical manifestos, from Robbins's *Essay* (1952) to Koopmans's *Three Essays* (1957) from Friedman's *Essays* (1953) to Blaug's *Methodology* (1980), reveals an escalation in the appeal to scientific legitimacy through citation of the practices that purportedly constitute the core of the scientific method, be they prediction, falsificationism, axiomatization, or the use of mathematical formalism. In deference to the Cartesian Vice, these practices were portrayed as self-sufficient, abstract methods, independent of any examination of what physicists actually did or how they did it.

It was precisely this oblivion when it came to the actual practices of scientists that set neoclassical economics up for a fall in the 1970s. Physics itself had been going through a period of turmoil, trying to assimilate the dual disturbing implications of quantum mechanics and the proliferation of subatomic particles. The increasing politicization of science had fostered the growth of political movements skeptical of the claims of scientists (Krimsky 1982). These first two trends led to a third, the revolution in the philosophy of science and the explosion of science studies in previously neglected areas, such as the history and sociology of science. Everyone who was not intellectually moribund in the 1970s had at least heard of Thomas Kuhn's *Structure of Scientific Revolutions;* and many who were not professional philosophers took to reading the works of Paul Feyerabend, Stephen Toulmin, Imre Lakatos, David Bloor, and others. It was the combined project of these and other authors to explode the myth of a single scientific method by means of detailed historical investigations into the origins and development of specific scientific theories.

In this context the neoclassical appeals to *the* scientific method appeared anachronistic and almost naively quaint (McCloskey 1985a: 12). Testimonials of faith in the faultless rudder of falsificationism ran smack into the Duhem–Quine thesis, which states that every test is so inextricably imbedded in auxiliary hypotheses that rational adjustment of some subset can reverse the verdict of any adverse test (Harding, 1976). Proponents of austere axiomatic formalism were chastened by Gödel's Theorem and Wittgensteinian puzzles of interpretation (cf. Mirowski 1986). Prophets of prediction were humbled by the appearance of ARIMA models as statistics with little or no a priori theory. And, to add insult to injury, physicists began to undermine some of the neoclassical economists' most cherished tenets of faith, such as the supposed impossibility of a free lunch. By the 1980s some cosmologists were claiming that the entire universe was itself a free lunch, nothing more than a vacuum fluctuation.[2]

Eternal verities were crumbling; the barbarians were at the gates. From this one should not infer that most economists heard the rumblings from their posts on the barricades or even had their ear to the ground. Nevertheless, the rumblings on the frontier were just beginning to be audible to a few, however indistinct and jumbled, and neoclassical economists felt their force as part of the continuous lay litany that economists are charlatans and economics is not a science. Earlier defenses of neoclassical economies based on the progressively discredited conceptions of science were rendered ineffectual.

The genius of McCloskey's 1983 manifesto was that it promised an escape from this impasse. McCloskey's advocacy of a rhetorical defense was an exhortation to abjure all reliance upon "science" or the "scientific method." In criticizing scientism – what he called "modernism" and Hayek (1979: 24) called the "slavish imitation of the method and language of science" – he made use of many of the philosophical theses of Kuhn, Feyerabend, and Rorty on the radical underdetermination of scientific theories by data, the absence of a neutral observation language, and the importance of "external" considerations for the acceptance or rejection of scientific theories. Many historians of science – most notably, those associated with the Edinburgh school – had interpreted those external conditions as mediated by sociological forces, but McCloskey introduced his own innovation here, substituting classical rhetoric for sociological or anthropological theories. As he later admitted in the book-length version of his work, "The project here is to overturn the monopolistic authority of science in economics by questioning the usefulness of the demarcation of science from art" (McCloskey 1985a: 57). The bottom line was that, while neoclassical economists were not the most artful of souls (or artful of dodgers?), they did manage to improve the tenor of their conversations over time. Hence, basically, I'm OK and you're OK.

This solution to the problem of the methodological justification of neoclassical economics was not destined to please everyone. Of course, some will cling to their outdated scientism, blind to both rhetoric and science.[3] Others will pronounce a plague on all methodological houses as long as their own career meets the market test – that is, they get paid for doing economics. The remainder who do detect some valuable insights in McCloskey's work, however, will eventually find their curiosity frustrated and stymied by some deep contradictions inherent in his overall program. The first, already alluded to, is the painful incongruity of the assertion that a Cartesian model of economic man can be justified with an anti-Cartesian paradigm. This argument displays an antisymmetry that could easily be used against it: If people in general are neoclassical optimizers, and if economists are people, then should not economists also maximize over a set of personal objectives that might be contrary to the pursuit of open and honest conversations?[4] In other words, classical rhetoric embodies a specific theory of social order. Should not theory be consistent and congruent with the theory of social order in the theory it was intended to defend?

Second, there is an extreme incompatibility between the ideal of rhetoric as the study of all the various techniques of persuasion and McCloskey's own study of the rhetoric of particular arguments in economics. In one place he insists that economics itself is "a historical rather than a predictive science" (McCloskey 1985a: xix); yet elsewhere in the same volume he insists that the rhetorical analysis of economists' arguments, as well as the content of the arguments themselves, are necessarily ahistorical (McCloskey 1985: 64–5, 93). The problem with this position is that rhetoric, by most accounts, is intrinsically and essentially a hermeneutic and historical form of inquiry, whereas it is neoclassical economics that is generally conceded to be an ahistorical explanation of social activity. Some of the best examples of rhetorical analysis of economic arguments, such as Klamer (1983), are by their very nature historical inquiries: investigations into the "external" determinants of theory rejection or acceptance beyond the acknowledged arguments to be found in the economic literature.

I believe that McCloskey understood that the implicit theory of social order in classical rhetoric is diametrically opposed to the atemporal existence of the neoclassical *Homo economicus,* and therefore a full rhetorical analysis would be congenitally critical of neoclassical economic theory. Of course, this would never do for his purposes, so in order to restrain and repress this tendency, McCloskey tried to restrict his definition of rhetoric to an atemporal consideration of the style of argumentation of economists independent of all historical context. Thus, in his chapter on the impact of Robert Fogel upon the discipline of economic history, he arbitrarily quarantines any discussion of the historical fact that Fogel and his cliometrics movement were the vanguard of the penetration of neoclassical economics into a stronghold of institutionalists, historicists, and other disgruntled types united by their distaste for the atemporal character of neoclassical economics. In his chapter on John Muth and rational expectations theory, he neglects entirely the running controversy over whether Keynesian economics was (or could be) consistent with the premises of neoclassical theory, as well as the relevant psychological literature that had suggested that the process of learning could not be adequately captured by neoclassical theory. It is not all inconceivable that what starts out as a rhetorical immunization of neoclassical theory could rapidly become a poison pill, if all the directions on the label were followed. Perhaps this explains some of the disdain that greeted the appearance of McCloskey's original article.

I should like to take very seriously McCloskey's primary thesis – that "the scientific method'' is inadequate to explain how economists choose to advocate the theories they do – but to maintain that his subsidiary hypotheses are false. I would like to suggest some amendments to his manifesto:

i. Rhetorical analysis can provide valuable insights, but only when it is diachronic as well as synchronic.
ii. The style of economic arguments cannot be adequately understood independent of their content or context.
iii. Rhetorical analysis is innately critical and will never constitute a satisfactory defense of neoclassical economic theory.

I am aware that the spirit of these assertions runs counter to contemporary deconstructionist credos in literary theory, but then, what would you expect coming from an economist? If economists, with their ''pig philosophy'' as Carlyle called it, do not insist on the existence of a world outside the text, then who will?

Rather than shuffle a deck of methodological fiats and slap them down on the table one by one, it may be more edifying and instructive to focus attention on just one of McCloskey's rhetorical claims: that ''mathematical theorizing in economics is metaphorical, and literary'' (McCloskey 1985a: 81). This assertion is almost certainly correct, but extended rhetorical analysis shall reveal it has implications undreamt of in McCloskey's market argument.

III. The absentminded professor

The most subversive doctrine (from the vantage point of neoclassical economics) in the armory of McCloskey's rhetoric is the idea that mathematical expressions are ''merely'' metaphorical. In a discipline that has arrayed its pecking order largely on the basis of the appearance of mathematical sophistication, this must surely sound like the tic-tic-tic of the barbarians pecking at the gates. In order to drive home the inversion of conventional values, McCloskey has written that, ''What is successful in economic metaphor is what is successful in poetry, and the success is analyzable in similar terms'' (McCloskey 1985a: 80). The average neoclassical economist might be willing to agree with Bentham that pushpin is as good as poetry, but would resist to the death the idea that poetry is as good as polynomial.

It is important to realize that McCloskey himself does not think this is a disruptive doctrine and, indeed, thinks it a defense of the behavior of neoclassical economists in some of their most recent *contretemps,* most notably in the erstwhile Cambridge capital controversies.[5] These sometimes acrimonious controversies forced certain neoclassical theorists to admit that their Cambridge U.K. cousins' criticisms did possess some merit; however, it remains somewhat of an embarrassment that this has not curbed the ubiquitous appearance of neoclassical production functions in mathematical models. Whatever happened to the bracing discipline of the austere logic of mathematics? McCloskey would respond that, if one regards the production function (and, indeed, capital itself) as merely a metaphor, there is little harm done. No metaphor is premised upon the precise identity between the object and the thing compared, or, as he put it:

> The reason there was no decision reached was that the important questions were literary, not mathematical or statistical. The debate was equivalent to showing mathematically or statistically that a woman cannot be a summer's day. Yet no one noticed (McCloskey 1985a: 82).

Such a cavalier summary of what was an extremely labyrinthine and subtle dispute cuts two ways. Superficially, it seems to say that the differences that divided the two Cambridges were *merely* metaphorical and therefore inconsequential. Surely this cannot be McCloskey's message, because such an interpretation implies an invidious comparison between questions literary and questions mathematical contrary to the spirit of his rhetoric. On the other hand, neither can this be interpreted to suggest that the disputants be absolved of the respective pigheadedness merely because they neglected to subject the metaphorical content of their respective mathematical models to sustained analysis. Simply because Paul Samuelson (1966) insisted that J. B. Clark–style capital was a "parable" did not get him off the hook: He had made mathematical errors that were doubly grievous because so much of his authority derives from mathematical expertise. Surely the rhetor is not satisfied to mumble that "everyone has her own opinion, and there is nothing you can do to change it"? On the contrary, one would reasonably expect the proponent of rhetoric to plumb the depths of the metaphorical sources of apparently technical disagreements, with the eventual goal of clarifying the points of the dispute. There is no getting around it: Some parties are going to be criticized. Yet this is precisely the sort of analysis that McCloskey is not inclined to do.

The metaphorical character of mathematical analysis is not a novel idea. The great mathematician Henri Poincaré defined mathematics as the art of giving the same name to different things, a phrase more than adequate to do double duty as a definition of metaphor (Kline 1980: 273). Wittgenstein (1976), with his characteristic acuity, got to the crux of the matter:

> Mathematical conviction might be put in the form, "I recognise this as analogous to that." But here "recognise" is not used as in "I recognise him as Lewy" but as in "I recognise him as superior to myself" (p.63).

The problem of what enforces the acknowledgment that one set of mathematical relationships is "the same" as another set is a major theme of Wittgenstein's later philosophy. One profoundly disturbing implication of this inquiry is that mathematics cannot be considered an independent mechanical decision procedure (as portrayed in the Cartesian tradition), because there are no self-enforcing rules concerning the sufficiency of mathematical analogy. Why is a geometric circle "the same" as the equation $(x-a)^2 + (y-b)^2 = r^2$? Does one still consider it the same if the y-coordinates are complex numbers, or if we are concerned with a non-Euclidean geometry? In what sense is matrix multiplication "the same" as the multiplication of integers or rational numbers? These types of questions led in the later nineteenth century to the concepts of "iso-morphism" and "homeomorphism" as an attempt to codify some of the principles of "sameness" and to reveal the analogies between various branches of mathematics (Kline 1972: 767). While this in turn led to very profound results in the theory of groups and semigroups, one should not conclude from it that the principles of metaphor and analogy in mathematics are formalized and settled for all time. The fact that Hesse (1966: 64–77) tried to formalize the process of analogic reasoning in science using abstract algebra and failed should warn us that the latter has not sufficiently subsumed the former. There can be no more poignant illustration of this fact for economists than the case of the writings of William Stanley Jevons.

Although it is not common knowledge, Jevons was at least as famous as an expositor of the philosophy of science (such as it was in his day) as he was renowned as an economist. The second edition of his textbook *The Principles of Science* devotes an entire chapter to the role of analogy in science, and he specifically discusses the function of analogy in the development of mathematics. He admitted that "generalization passes insensibly into reasoning by analogy," but as a good Cartesian, he could not bring himself to express unrestrained enthusiasm over the method of reasoning by analogy. The stumbling block was the same as that indicated by Wittgenstein: When could one say metaphorical relationships were really "the same"? How does one decide that a resemblance or lack thereof is fundamental, and when incidental? Jevons chose to illustrate the problem of analogical reasoning with an example from mathematics:

> . . . analogical reasoning leads us to the conception of many things which, so far as we can ascertain, do not exist. In this way great perplexities have arisen in the use of language and mathematical symbols. . . [Mathematicians] have needlessly puzzled themselves about the square root of a negative quantity, which in many applications of algebraic calculation, is simply a sign without any analogous meaning, there being a failure of analogy (Jevons 1905a: 643).

This passage was anachronistic when it was written; its error is glaringly apparent today. In the nineteenth century there were reasons to think that the square root of a negative number should not be accorded the same treatment as the square root of a positive number, but these reasons were not written in stone, and in some cases the pure aesthetic appeal of the metaphor induced some mathematicians to persist in its development and elaboration. Quite unexpectedly, these "imaginary numbers" were then found to have applications in periodic functions, in probability theory, and in quantum mechanics. Jevons had suspected that analogy was pernicious, luring the unwary onto false paths. Instead, the analogy had become a sort of self-ratifying reality, with curious analytical constructs being developed for their own sake and later further analogies being forged with physical phenomena.

The profound ramifications of the thesis that "mathematics is analogical reasoning" are being debated in the philosophical literature; a summary of those debates would carry us too far afield from our present concern, which is to analyze the rhetoric of mathematics in neoclassical economics. However, there is one fascinating thesis that we cannot pass by and that may prove useful. Mary Tiles (1984) has recently argued that it is the metaphorical character of mathematics that can explain the uncanny feeling that the mathematician "discovers" platonic essences and grasps preexisting mathematical relationships independent of the process of inquiry – that is, that the widespread conviction that the mathematician is a discoverer, not an inventor (Wittgenstein 1978, Part 1: 99).

While the fact that two separate mathematicians arrive at the same solution for the problem $x = \sqrt{(56)(32)}$ may be traced either to a mechanical calculation procedure or to the heavy hand of authority, the discovery of new mathematical structures cannot be explained by the same means. Bachelard and Tiles claim that the new structures are a by-product of the drive of the mathematician to unify her discipline (Tiles 1984: 87). The scheme for creating this unity is to apply the theory of one existing mathematical structure to the domain of another – that is, to reason by analogy. Because the two domains are never identical, there will be some ways in which the initial analogy appears to be a bad fit: The heterogeneity of domains produces "analogical interference." Tiles uses the example of a ratio of integers and the idea of a ratio between the diameter and the circumference of a circle, an analogy that induced cognitive dissonance and resulted in the discovery of π and other "irrational numbers" (Tiles, 1984: 93). She could have used the noncommutativity of the multiplication of quaternions or any of a plethora of similar instances in the history of mathematics. The fact that the analogies are not perfect and can never attain perfection leads mathematicians to ask novel questions. The answers to these questions are curious, in that they do not seem to be predetermined by the previous corpus of mathematics and yet produce answers that have the aura of objectivity, in the sense that the will of the mathematician to impose an analogy has been frustrated. Hence, the mathematics appears to "resist" the original drive to unify the subject matter, fostering the impression that it exists independent of the objectives and choices of the researcher. In a rhetorical twist worthy of O. Henry, it is the metaphorical practices of mathematicians that conjure the impression of the cold objectivity of mathematics.

The practice of analogical reasoning is of course not restricted to the activities of mathematicians. This should appear self-evident to the neoclassical economist whose time and energy is spent constructing "models" of increasing levels of complexity and abstraction. What the neoclassical economist may not realize is that a substantial proportion of the activities of the physicist also consists of the transport of analogy from one domain of science to another. This has been recognized by numerous historians and philosophers of science from Duhem to Hesse to Pickering, including W. S. Jevons. Those forced to suffer through courses on electrical engineering will recall the light that dawns when one realizes that any mechanical or acoustical system can be reduced to an electrical network and the problem solved by circuit theory, or vice versa (Olson 1958). The very success of the theory of energy in the nineteenth century was owing to the newfound capacity to see analogies between phenomena that had previously appeared distinct and unrelated (Mirowski, forthcoming, Ch. 2). Now one could state that mass was "like" inductance and that velocity was "like" current and hence use the mathematical formalisms developed in the sphere of rational mechanics to describe other phenomena in novel spheres, such as electricity and light.

Other analogies that were critical for the development of physics in the nineteenth century were comparisons between heat and electro-statics and comparisons between light and the vibrations of an elastic medium. The physicist James Clerk Maxwell was so impressed with the fecundity of these analogies that he elevated the postulation of analogy to a principle of research method, a method he conceived as a middle way between the sterility of a strictly mathematical analysis and the excesses of pure speculation. His method paid off handsomely with the postulation of the famous Maxwell equations and the subsequent discovery of the electromagnetic nature of light (Nersessian 1984). Examples of the role of analogy and metaphor in physics could be multiplied indefinitely.

The prevalence of metaphor and analogy in the history of the physical sciences is no accident. It is a corollary of another trend, the increasing use of mathematics as the preferred mode of communication within the disciplinary matrix. Mathematics, as we have observed, is the method *par excellence* for the transfer of metaphor. Once mathematical expertise has come to be the badge of the theorist in any science, theory becomes isolated from that subset of the discipline responsible for empirical implementation and experiment. The mathematical theorist is given *carte blanche* by her prestige and her separation from the nitty-gritty of everyday observation to prosecute any mathematical analogy or metaphor that captures her fancy. The negative component of any of these metaphors (for instance, the fact that light waves are not "really" like water waves because we cannot identify the substance that light waves move through) can be effortlessly set aside for the time being, or dismissed as irrelevant, impounded in *ceteris paribus* conditions or otherwise neutralized, because for the theorist, it is only the mathematics that matters (Colvin 1977).

Many appeals to "beauty," "simplicity," "clarity" and suchlike by the mathematical community can be rendered comprehensible as comments upon the esthetic qualities of analogies. Ironically, it is the existence of the closed community of those fluent in mathematics that permits the mathematical theorist to indulge in wilder flights of fanciful metaphor than might be condoned were they expressed in the vernacular. As it stands, the closed community of mathematical theorists can independently invest a metaphor with legitimacy, and leave it to the "applied scientists" to clean up the negative components of the analogy and make the messy bits fit with recalcitrant reality. It should go without saying that this constitutes an excellent sociological structure for the protection of a theory from its critics.

Before we get too carried away with the image of the cabal of mathematicians foisting off a whole load of rubbishy metaphors on a sheeplike and uncomprehending world, it will be prudent to recall that mathematical formalization is an ideal method of the transfer of metaphor and that metaphor is an indispensable tool of human reasoning, "scientistic" or not. Metaphors are necessary because they provide us with ready-made linkages of concepts, and with ready-made reasons to justify those linkages. Metaphors differ from the "assumptions" that economists profess to hold with such cool agnosticism because they represent a web of propositions that have withstood testing, elaboration, and criticism in a different context. Knowledge is not an agglomeration of discrete and interchangeable propositions, like some tub of Lego blocks that can be indifferently snapped together and broken apart. If that were the case, research would be a chaotic and anomic proposition, doomed to a random walk in a strange landscape. The lesson of philosophy in the age of Duhem, Quine, and Hesse is that propositions are networks of meaning (Hesse 1974; Quine and Ullian 1970). Metaphors gingerly extricate a web from one context and drape it over the phenomena in another context. Some aspects of the metaphor may not fit the new context, but when that inevitably happens, we do not necessarily abandon the entire theory, but rather use the metaphor to help us decide which conceptual aspects could be adjusted and which are indispensable. There are some situations that would counsel abandonment of the entire theory; but there would be no way of knowing what they were without metaphors.

IV. Don't look back

Fortified with these observations, we now return to explicit consideration of neoclassical economics and McCloskey's thesis that mathematical models are metaphors. The preceding considerations suggest that there is substantial truth to this claim, simply because most extensions of mathematical formalism proceed by metaphor and analogy. Nevertheless, this simple observation has little cash value, because there are a potentially limitless number of possible metaphors that might have been proposed and a myriad of mathematical metaphors that might have been deemed to warrant sustained elaboration. These are the questions that should concern the rhetor: Which metaphor(s) were chosen? Why were they thought plausible when they were adopted? What happened to the negative components of the analogy? Are they still thought to be plausible? Why? Are the metaphors "dead" or "alive"? The very process of persuasion dangles without rational support in the absence of such an inquiry.

There already exists a metaphorical analysis of this format that can stand as an alternative to McCloskey's "rhetoric" of neoclassical economic theory. This analysis claims that there is a coherence to neoclassical theory because all of it has grown out of a single metaphor, a mathematical metaphor. It asserts an empirical hypothesis, that the progenitors of neoclassicism did what all mathematical theorists do: They appropriated a mathematical model lock, stock, and barrel from somewhere else, in the guise of a metaphor. In particular, the early neoclassicals took the model of "energy" from physics, changed the names of all the variables, postulated that "utility" acted like energy, and then flogged the package wholesale as economics. The author has filled many pages documenting this claim (Mirowski 1984a, 1984b, 1985a, forthcoming) and will spare the reader a rehearsal of the prodigious parade of evidence here. In lieu of a sustained attempt to convince the skeptical reader, we shall merely sketch in the main outlines of the metaphor, restricting ourselves to what is needed to evaluate our later rhetorical theses.

At one point in his *Three Essays* Tjalling Koopmans notes in passing, "A utility function of a consumer looks quite similar to a potential function in the theory of gravitation. . . ." (Koopmans 1957: 176). Although he opted not to elaborate the analogy, let us explore it further. Suppose we are to describe a mass point moving in a three-dimensional Euclidean space from point A to point B.

The conventional physical description, developed in the mid-nineteenth century, postulates a "force" decomposed into its orthogonal components, each multiplied by the spatial displacement, also suitably decomposed. In order to incorporate cases of nonlinear displacement and acceleration, the "work" done in the course of motion from A to B was defined as the summation of the infinitesimal forces F multiplied by their displacements:

$$T = \int_A^B (F_x dx + F_y dy + F_z dz) = \left. (1/2)mv^2 \right|_A^B$$

The writings of Lagrange and Hamilton insisted that the total energy of this system depended in a critical way upon the position of the mass point in a gravitational field. This was subsequently clarified in the following manner: Suppose that the expression $(F_x dx + F_y dy + F_z dz)$ was an exact differential equation. This would imply that there exists a function $U(x,y,z)$ such that:

$$F_x = \partial U/\partial x; \; F_y = \partial U/\partial y; \text{ and } F_z = \partial U/\partial z.$$

The function $U(x,y,z)$ so defined was asserted to represent a gravitational field, which by the 1860s was also identified as the field of potential energy. The sum of the kinetic energy $(1/2mv^2) = T$ and the potential energy U was understood as being conserved in the confines of a closed system. The law of the conservation of energy, in turn, clarified and encouraged the use of constrained maximization techniques (such as the Principle of Least Action, Lagrangean multipliers, and the Hamiltonian calculus of variations) in the description of the equilibrium motion of a mass point under the influence of impressed forces.

As Koopmans indicated, the similarity between this model and the conventional canonical neoclassical model is quite striking. Let the forces "F" be the prices of individual goods x,y,z, and the displacement be infinitesimal changes in the quantities of the goods dx, dy, dz. The rest of the metaphor falls into place: "Kinetic energy" is the sum of prices times quantities, and hence is the total expenditure or budget constraint; the potential field defined over the commodity space is clearly "utility."[6] Constrained maximization (or minimization) of an imponderable quantity over a conservative field leads directly to the equilibrium configuration of forces/prices.

Is this remarkable similarity merely an accident? Koopmans is prudently silent on this issue, but examination of the origins of neoclassical theory reveals that its progenitors consciously and willfully appropriated the physical metaphor in order to render economics a "mathematical science" (Mirowski, 1984a, forthcoming). Jevons (1905b: 50), Walras (1960), Edgeworth (1881), and nearly every other early neoclassical economist admitted this fact. Here the rhetor pricks up his ears; his blood starts to race: Could this be a "rhetorical ploy"? And they all admitted it? Then why is it such news a century later? Could this be a "dead" metaphor – has it become so fully detached from its sources of inspiration that is is now effectively independent of the connotations and conditions of its genesis? Curiously enough, this was the position of the most pugnacious defender of economic mechanics (or mechanical economics?), Pareto:

> Let us go back to the equations which determine equilibrium. In seeing them somebody – and it might be the writer – made an observation of the kind above and said: ''The equations do not seem new to me, I know them well, they are old friends. They are the equations of rational mechanics.'' This is why economics is a sort of mechanics or akin to mechanics. . . . [Mechanics] can be studied leaving aside the concept of forces. In reality all this does not matter much. If there is anyone who does not care to hear mechanics mentioned, very well, let us disregard the similarity and let us talk directly about our equations. We shall only have to face the drawback that in certain cases we shall have to labour greatly in order to deduce from those equations certain consequences that we would have perceived at once had we kept in mind the fact that mechanics has already deduced them from its own equations, which are similar to ours. All told this does not alter the consequences (Pareto 1953: 185).

The rhetorical analyst, forewarned and forearmed by our previous discussion, smells the Cartesian Vice in the neighborhood. Here is the insistence that sources of inspiration are irrelevant; the actual process of inquiry is irrelevant; the composition of the audience is irrelevant. All that purportedly matters is the formal mathematical expression, which alone renders truth more transparent. The fact that the mathematics was appropriated wholesale from physics merely speeds up the research and does not influence the content of the theory. However much Pareto wishes to appear a pragmatical and nononsense type of guy, the fact is that his prosopopoeia is eminently rhetorical, in that it is meant to persuade, and *not* to be a literal account of his activities or the activities of other neoclassical economists.

I should like to argue that the physics metaphor in economics is not a dead metaphor and that the attendant mathematics have not served as the simple heuristic device, pace Pareto. In the first place, neither Pareto nor any of his comrades in the marginalist revolution made explicit use of the mathematical analogy for the purposes of speeding up the process of inference, or even to provide an independent check upon their analytical prognostications. This was not because the metaphor was dead on arrival; rather, it was because none of the neoclassicals understood the physics well enough to follow up on the detailed implications of the metaphor. This fact is illustrated by the numerous occasions when physicists, upon recognizing the physical equations, wrote letters to the neoclassicals to query them upon various points. The early neoclassicals – Walras, Fisher, Pareto – to a man replied with bombast, far-rago, and finally a frustrated and sullen silence, simply because they did not understand what was being asked of them (Mirowski 1985a, forthcoming).

In the second place, no neoclassical economist has ever seen fit to plumb the energetics metaphor for its ''positive'' versus ''negative'' components, weighing those parts of the metaphor that seemed relevant against those that appeared odd, strained, or even downright perverse. This could not be at-tributed to the possibility that the metaphor of utility as energy was so elegant, so felicitous, and so very right that it would be futile to look for its negative aspects. Yet with only minor effort we can generate six profound disanalo-gies:

1. There is nothing obvious about the definition of human rationality as the maximization of an objective function over a conserved entity (Mirowski 1985b). This elevation of the significance of extrema did not arise first in social theory, but rather in physics, as the principle of least action. The physics of constrained extrema were interpreted as evidence for the exis-tence of a God who had constructed the world in the most efficacious and coherent manner. That maximization or minimization was global in the most comprehensive sense, and encouraged an attitude that ''efficiency'' could be defined in some absolute framework. In its evolution from Mau-pertuis to Euler to Hamilton, the principle of least (or varying) action shed its theological skin, but the notion of absolute efficiency persisted, and it was this connotation that was recruited to tame the multiform and unruly concept of rationality.

   The predisposition of the modern neoclassical economist to ''optimize'' over someone's ''objective function'' is neither an empty tautology nor a harmless metaphor: It surreptitiously presumes an inordinately large amount of structure about the nature of desires and objectives, the role of time, the understanding of causality, the unimportance of process, the conservation of the domain of the objectives, the relative construction of the world of the actor vis-à-vis its reconstruction by the social analyst, the strict sepa-ration of the thing desired and the act of choice, and much, much more (Bausor 1986; Mirowksi 1984b). And, of course, it resonates with this Western theological tradition without ever making reference to it.

2. The metaphor of energy/utility that was appropriated by neoclassical eco-nomics was derived from the physics of a specific historical moment, namely, the years of the midnineteenth century just prior to the elaboration of the second law of thermodynamics. The mathematics of preentropic physics is now thought to have been the pinnacle of the development of static mechanism (Prigogine 1980). In this vintage of physics, all physical phe-nomena are portrayed as being perfectly reversible in time; there was no

room in theory for hysteresis. In other words, nineteenth-century physical law could have no history. This stubbornly antihistorical bias of neoclassical economics has frequently been excoriated by critics, such as Joan Robinson, and bemoaned by partisans, such as Hicks (1979) and Shackle (1967). What the latter have not realized is that it is futile to attempt to inject history into neoclassical stories without thoroughly wreaking havoc with the very physical metaphor that was its inspiration and the mathematical techniques that were responsible for its success. The mathematical metaphor of "equilibrium" is incoherent when a process exhibits a fundamental dependence upon its temporal location. In other words, economists misunderstand the dictates of their chosen metaphor of equilibrium.

3. In preentropic physics all physical phenomena are variegated manifestations of a protean energy that can be fully and reversibly transformed from one state to another. When this metaphor was smuggled into the context of economic theory, it dictated that all economic goods be fully and reversibly convertible into utility and thence into all other goods in the act of trade. Now, most economists would admit that the introduction of money into neoclassical economic theory has been an awkward marriage at best and a shotgun marriage at worst (Clower 1967). The problem has been, curiously enough, metaphorical. In the mathematics, the analogue to money has not been some lubricant that greases the wheels of trade but rather a superfluous intermediate crypto-energy that all other energies must become in transit to their final state. The mathematics say one thing; the accompanying commentary, something else.

4. As a prerequisite for the application of techniques of constrained extrema, it has long been recognized that energy must be conserved as a mathematical rather than an empirical imperative (Theobald 1966). If one takes the neoclassical metaphor literally, it would dictate that the sum of realized utility plus the money value of the budget constraint be equal to a constant, that is, $T + U = k$ (Mirowski 1984a, forthcoming, Ch. 5). Since this sum has no coherent interpretation from an economic point of view, the early neoclassicals avoided it. But there is no constrained optimization in the absence of a conservation principle, and neoclassicals discovered a mathematical imperative to impose various "unobstrusive postulates," such as the conservation of the utility field, the conservation of income, or the constancy of the marginal utility of money.

5. There was a flurry of activity in the 1940s and 1950s that portended the liberation of neoclassical value theory from any dependence upon the utility concept. The motivations behind this self-denying ordinance were never openly discussed, although a rationally reconstructed history (Wong 1978) can be organized by asking how our understanding of the folk-psychology of utility makes it dissimilar to energy. It can also explain why economists

cannot bear to take psychology seriously. The failure of this abortive research program can be gauged by the extent to which axioms of revealed preference are isomorphic to those of a gravitational field.
6. Problems with the energetics metaphor can also assume less lofty and philosophical proportions. For example, the components of physical forces can assume negative values without disrupting the physical intuition; but negative prices really do seem beyond the pale (cf. Mirowski 1986a).

The more one is willing to become embroiled in the history of physics and mathematics, the more one could expand this list. For our present purposes, I hope it proffers sufficient evidence to counter the claim that it makes no difference where the mathematical analogies come from, because once appropriated, they are freely amended to express only what was consciously intended. Mathematics is not a colorless and secure cloak into which the analyst can slip in order to shield himself from the vagaries of human discourse.

There is a vast rhetorical process going on here, and it cries out for analysis. It is not simply a matter of writing style or conversational tactics or an incident in which a single individual flashes into fleeting fame. It is not the sage of a John Muth or a Robert Fogel. It is the narrative of the displacement of all other schools of economics (with the obvious exception of Marxism) by means of a single mathematical metaphor appropriated from nineteenth-century physics. It is the story of the persuasion of the majority of Western economists to pledge allegiance to a particular ideal construction of economic life by means of a single rhetorical technique.

This is where the idea of mathematics as metaphor takes us. It takes us to the historical origins of neoclassical theory, into its content. Inexorably, it also draws us into *critique,* into looking at the present with something far short of warm admiration and cozy satisfaction. This is where rhetorical analysis takes us, but it is a place where Don McCloskey does not want to go.

V. Blow-Up

Don McCloskey claimed he rode into town on his Donald Davidson (McCloskey 1985b). I suppose that this means he subscribes to Davidson's thesis that, "metaphors mean what the words, in their most literal interpretation, mean, and nothing more" (Davidson in Johnson, 1981: 201). Neoclassical economists have been trying to use this trick to get out of some of the nastier embranglements resulting from their physics metaphor since the beginning. Witness Pareto:

> [Social scientists] . . . can therefore derive no advantage from words. They can, however, incur great harm, whether because of the senti-

ments that words arouse, or because the existence of a word may lead one astray as to the reality of the thing it is supposed to represent, and so introduce into the experimental field imaginary entities such as the fictions of metaphysics or theology. . . . Literary economists . . . are to this day still dilly-dallying with speculations such as "What is *value?*" "What is *capital?*" They cannot get it into their heads that things are everything and words are nothing. . . (Pareto 1935: 61–2).

This search for the perfect essence, the real stuff, has been frustrated for over a hundred years now. This tough-minded attitude about words and things is itself the last refuge of a scientistic scoundrel. The not-so-subtle innuendo, that the common vernacular is fettered with clinging frivolous associations while the mathematics is not, really will not wash either.

Neoclassical economic theory is founded upon a single mathematical metaphor that equates "utility" with the potential energy of mid-nineteenth-century physics. From Walras to Pareto to McCloskey the tendency has been to admit the metaphor in a coy and indirect manner, hedged about with the qualification that it is merely a matter of words, and therefore of no consequence to evaluations of the content and significance of the theory. If a "good metaphor depends, too, on the ability of its audience to suppress incongruities," and "What is successful in economic metaphor is what is successful in poetry, and the success is analyzable in similar terms" (McCloskey, 1985a: 79fn and 80), then the prognosis is clear. All that modern neoclassicals must do is to suppress all the uncomfortable or silly bits of the founding fathers' metaphor – and this they have done by their blinkered concentration upon the technical aspects of the mathematics, come hell or high water – and to evaluate the "artfulness" of the resulting product using their own internally generated criteria. This, of course, is nothing other than the "market test" in sheep's clothing. Just as the realpolitik version of great art is the art that still sells, the realpolitik version of great economics is the stuff that neoclassicals still flog in the classroom. If the metaphorical genesis of neoclassical theory is no longer mentioned in the classroom, well, then, it must have been expendable.

One of the virtues of the broader conception of rhetoric advocated here is its mandate to describe the *process* of persuasion in all its multiform splendor, from the literal reference of "mere words" to the social construction of the object of discourse. In the more narrow case that concerns us here, the importance of metaphor (vernacular or mathematical) is that its role, contrary to Donald Davidson, is *never* limited to a literal representation of the concept of reference (Bicchieri 1986). The use of metaphor sets up a field of secondary and tertiary resonances, contrasts, and comparisons that do not merely describe, but also reconstruct and transform the original metaphorical material.

It is commonplace among philosophers that there are no rules for definitively identifying metaphors because the original thing compared and the object of comparison frequently undergo figure/ground reversal, and the forcefulness of a metaphor often derives from the unstated synergistic implications. This is not to say that the analysis of the efficacy of metaphoric reasoning is a hopeless project, trapped at the ineffectual level of esthetic appreciation.

The foundational metaphor of mathematical neoclassical economic theory is palpably different from poetic metaphor, and therefore must be analyzed in a distinct manner. Mary Hesse, who has considered the role of metaphor in physics at great length, has described the fundamental distinctions between metaphors in science and metaphors in poetry (Hesse, 1966; 1974; 1980: 118–23). It is a distinguishing characteristic of successful poetic metaphor that the images chosen be initially striking, unexpected, shocking, or even perverse. (One here might recall Baudelaire's comparison of his lover's body to a piece of carrion.[7]) A poetic metaphor is largely meant to be savored, to be entertained in the way one sips a wine, and not to be further analyzed in pedantic detail. (This most certainly explains the pariah status of literary critics in certain quarters.) The poetic metaphor sports a penumbra of further metaphors and implications that may themselves be contrary to conventional usage and the tacit knowledge of the reader, flagrantly contradictory with one another, and fly in the face of previous comparisons in the same text. Far from being considered an error, this is part of the calculated impact of poetic language. Finally, only the confused pedant takes a poetic metaphor to be a research program. A poem is intended to be self-contained; it is a rare occurrence for a poem to recruit missionaries who go out to remake the world in its image – at least, in the twentieth century.

Scientific metaphors clearly have different criteria of efficacy and success. Although a scientific metaphor may initially appear incongruous, this is not generally conceded to be a point in its favor, and much of scientific activity can be interpreted as an attempt to render unseemly metaphors intelligible and pedestrian. A distinguishing characteristic of scientific metaphors is the fact that they are considered failures if they can only muster temporary impact and do not become the object of pedantic explication and elaboration. (Here one might cite examples of mathematicians rooting out the most obscure and arcane implications of the idea of a continuous function or of the metaphor of "infinity"; cf. Dauben 1984.) Scientific metaphors should set in motion research programs that strive to make explicit all of the attendant submetaphors of the original. They should provoke inquiry as to whether the implications are consistent one with another, as well as consistent with the background tacit knowledge.

There is no such thing as a perfect scientific metaphor that has no negative aspects. It is the job of the scientist to reconcile these inconsistencies with the tacit knowledge of the profession as well as with the "facts." Scientific metaphors can fail, but this is not generally because of some mythical *experimentum crucis,* but rather because of an increasing realization on the part of the scientific participants that the metaphor is cumbersome, awkward, and throws up intractable inconsistencies with its penumbra of meanings. However tentative and nonteleological this process seems, metaphors are an indispensable component of the scientific vocabulary, because they are a means that permits the expansion and adaptation of theory to a changing world.

Thus a rhetorical analysis of scientific and mathematical metaphor will diverge from the rhetorical analysis of a poem in distinct and critical respects. The former must ask: Is the metaphor consistent with itself? Is it consistent with the rest of the science? What properties of the metaphor are essential, and which expendable? Which aspects are those of similarity, and which of causality? (Hesse 1966: 86–7). In these areas McCloskey's version of rhetoric gets low marks, because it abdicates all responsibility for the tough questions. The probable cause of McCloskey's watered-down rhetoric is that neoclassical economic theory does not fare well under more intense cross-examination.

As already indicated, the progenitors of neoclassical theory did admit that they were asserting that something in economics was "like" energy in physics, but not one of them ventured beyond coy references to the examination of the consistency of the metaphor in any detail. When various physicists and mathematicians challenged the consistency and adequacy of the metaphor, particularly with respect to what they considered to be the most fundamental property of energy (i.e., its conservation), the neoclassicals responded with nonsense and incomprehension (cf. Mirowski, 1985a). This situation did not improve over time. Later neoclassicals wavered between affirming and denying that the metaphorical "utility" was required by the very structure of their economic theory or quibbled about whether it only needed to be ordinal rather than cardinal, as if the denial of the metaphor as the very rock upon which the theory was founded would somehow exorcize all of the negative components of the analogy with energy (Wong 1978; Schoemaker 1982; Mirowski, forthcoming, Chs. 6 and 7). Hence, twentieth-century neoclassicals tried to suppress the negative components of the energetics metaphor by trying to suppress the metaphor itself, to the extent that contemporary neoclassicals are still surprised and a little shocked when confronted with the fact that their economic theory was unabashedly and directly appropriated from nineteenth-century physics. It was a curious sort of repression, basking in the warm sensation of being "scientific" because what twentieth-century neoclassicals did so resembled what physicists did, without evincing the least curiosity about how it all came to pass, or whether it all made a difference. This was not science, and it was not even passable poetry.

Because of this fact, critics of neoclassicism over the past century have been put in the unenviable position of having unwittingly to reinvent the wheel. When Veblen complained that man was not a lightning calculator of pleasures and pains who oscillates like a homogeneous globule of desire of happiness under the impulse of stimuli that leave the man intact, or when Schumpeter complained that the firm would not exist as a static maximizer, or when Sraffa complained that there are no increasing or decreasing returns, or even when the exceptional undergraduate frowns skeptically at the idea of a utility function, they are all unwittingly questioning the scientific propriety of the metaphor of utility as energy. The fact that the modern proponents of utility were innocent of the genealogy of the theory and its implications resulted in a palpable degeneration in the quality of discourse. The critics were testing the limits of the physics metaphor, whereas the defenders felt free to tender any response that was convenient, since they had no clear conception of what was necessary and what was superfluous in their adopted model. If care had been exerted in metaphorical reasoning, it would have eventually become apparent that once utility had been equated with potential energy, neoclassicals were not free to advocate anything they liked about production or psychology or equality – or even ''justice'' (Mirowski, forthcoming). If attention had been paid to the physics metaphor, then it would have become apparent that there are some attributes of the energy concept that are indispensable: that it be conserved in a closed system; that it is a variable of state, and therefore cannot be time dependent; that it posited a fundamental symmetry between the past and the future; that it was not a substance but a relation; that it was an integral, and therefore only determinate up to a constant of integration. Many acrimonious debates in the history of economics, including the Cambridge capital controversies, would have been clarified tremendously if these tenets had been kept in clear view. The purpose of Pareto's tough-guy sermon on words and things, as well as McCloskey's more tender-minded rhetoric, was precisely to deny that metaphors have consequences.

VI. The discreet charm of the bourgeoisie

Unhappily, neoclassical economists have not used their metaphor the way scientists generally use metaphors. But if this has been the case, the rhetor feels a duty to ask, then why has neoclassical economic theory been so persuasive over the course of the last century, to the extent of ''marginalizing'' all other schools of economic thought? The answer takes us outside the realm of McCloskey's rhetoric but remains well within the bounds of our broader notion of rhetoric as the social construction of knowledge. This expanded rhetoric draws its theoretical inspiration from fields disparaged by the neoclassical economist because they have remained relatively impervious to the siren song of the Cartesian Vice; namely, anthropology and the sociology of knowledge.

Tracing their influence from Durkheim and Mauss on primitive classification, Mary Douglas and David Bloor have recently argued that the act of persuasion in any human culture is intrinsically metaphorical and social:

> I feel we should try to insert between the psychology of the individual and the public use of language a dimension of social behavior. . . . Persons are included in or excluded from a given class, classes are ranked, parts are related to wholes. It is argued here that the intuition of the logic of these social experiences is the basis for finding the *a priori* in nature. The pattern of social relations is fraught with emotional power; great stakes are invested in their permanence by some, in their overthrow by others. This is the level of experience at which the gut reaction of bewilderment at an unintelligible sentence is strengthened by potential fury, shock, and loathing. Apprehending a general pattern of what is right and necessary in social relations is the basis of society: this apprehension generates whatever *a priori* or set of necessary causes is going to be found in nature (Douglas 1975: 280–1).

In other words, *all* societies must appeal to their understanding of natural order for the purpose of legitimizing their social order. The works of Douglas (1973, 1975, 1982) describe how this process operates in non-Western societies; the fascinating work of Bloor (1982) and Barnes and Shapin (1979) applies the same sort of analysis to the history of Western physics, mathematics, and medicine. The relevance of this work to a revitalized theory of rhetoric is that it unites social theory with the original quest to understand how audiences are won over by certain general techniques of communication. The appeal to nature and to a natural order pervades our discourse in ways neither literal nor transparent; this submerged content accounts for many of those subversive and troublesome emotions that color any rational argument. The Cartesian plot to banish emotional discourse and to denigrate the process of argumentation was yet another instance of this general pattern of appeal to natural order.

Thus the appropriation of a mathematical metaphor from physics and its reification as neoclassical economic theory is rendered comprehensible as part of a much larger pattern, one that we share with such precapitalist societies as the Tiv and the Lele, as well as with our predecessors in earlier Western social formations. The success of neoclassical economic theory cannot be traced to the scientific criticism and elaboration of the positive and negative aspects of the original physics metaphor. Rather, it can be traced to the fact that the appropriation of a physics metaphor expresses a basic principle of human understanding, that social order must be understood as being rooted in and a reflection of natural order. Because this principle has been expressed in economics indirectly as a metaphor, it has proven profoundly more effective than if it had been stated baldly and prosaically, perhaps as a philosophical dogma or a tenet of faith. The Cartesian predispositions and the scientific pretensions of economists would in that case have clashed with an explicit authoritarian fiat. It has proven more felicitous to allow the individual scientist through reflective contemplation to discover the implied metaphors of natural order inherent in the mathematical model appropriated from physics.

So what precisely is this metaphorical content of neoclassical economic theory that has proved so very successful in displacing all other schools of economic thought? Our expanded rhetorical analysis can only be adequately carried out in the detailed analysis of texts and conservations, but the architectonics can be briefly summarized. The physics metaphor implies that economics is a *science* and deserves all the legitimacy that is granted to physics itself because there exists no great difference between the two modes of inquiry. The economy is portrayed as a self-contained and separable subset of social life, and as such has the character of a stable natural process. "Capitalism" as a natural entity is implied to be timeless; that is, it has always existed and will always continue to exist. Human beings within this sphere of social life behave as if they were automatons, in that their rationality is conflated with the existence of mechanical decision rules, most notably constrained maximization over a conserved vector field. Humans may behave differently in other spheres of social life, but since that behavior is "irrational" by definition, there is nothing left to be explained. Finally, the physics metaphor endows differential ontological validity upon sets of social phenomena: The "individual" is taken to be more real than any other social formation, be it the family, the firm, the nation-state, and so on.

VII. Portrait of a lady

Let me tell you why I hate critics. Not for all the normal reasons: that they are failed creators (they usually aren't; they may be failed critics, but that's another matter); or that they're by nature carping, jealous and vain (they usually aren't; if anything, they might be accused of over-generosity, of upgrading the second-rate so that their own fine discriminations might thereby appear the rarer). No, the reason I hate critics – well, some of the time – is that they write sentences like this:

"Flaubert did not build up his characters, as did Balzac, by objective, external description; in fact, so careless is he of their outward appearance that on one occasion he gives Emma [Bovary] brown eyes (14); on another deep black eyes (15); and on other blue eyes (16).''

– Julian Barnes, *Flaubert's Parrot,* p. 74

Surely here is an opportunity to get rid of that great stick of a character *Homo economicus* and to replace him with somebody real, like Madame Bovary.

– Donald McCloskey, *The Rhetoric of Economics,* p. 66

Notes

1. For the curious, they are plot, character, diction, thought, spectacle, and song in Aristotle (1961: 62).
2. I mean this literally, not figuratively. See Guth (1983, p. 215): ''I have often heard it said that there is no such thing as a free lunch. It now appears possible that the universe is a free lunch.''
3. A good example of the argument *''après moi, le deluge''* may be found in Hahn (1986: especially 834): ''But the theory which Arrow and his coevals and successors have built is all that we now have of honest and powerful thinking on the subject. It is doubtful that politicians and intellectual speculators can act and speak sensibly without its help.'' It is also doubtful they can derive any guidance for action with its help, he neglects to add.
4. McCloskey (1985a: 126) admits this possibility, but does not seem to realize the extent to which it could cripple his entire thesis:
   ''. . . the Announcement, the more bold, unargued and authoritarian the better, is the favored form of scholarly communication. . . . One wonders why unargued cases are accepted more readily than argued ones, even among professional arguers. . . .''
   Others have already noticed the possible symmetry between the neoclassical theory of social behavior and a neoclassical theory of the behavior of scientists. See, for instance, Garner (1979).
5. The best blow-by-blow commentary is still Harcourt (1972) supplemented by Harcourt (1982). Does it say something about the tenor of American rhetoric that the most cogent defense of the Cambridge, Massachusetts, position also comes from the other side of the Atlantic (viz. Blaug 1974)?
6. Fisher (1926: 85–6) presents a table that lists the correspondences between the physics and economics labels for the variables in the same mathematical formalism. For a detailed commentary, see Mirowski (forthcoming, Ch. 5).
7. ''Une Charogne'' in Baudelaire's *Les Fleurs du Mal.* In the Pleiade *Oeuvres Completes* it can be found on pp. 29–31.

References

Aristotle. 1961. *Poetics,* New York: Hill and Wang.

Barnes, B., and S. Shapin, editors. 1979. *Natural Order.* Beverly Hills: Sage.

Bausor, Randall. 1986. "Time and Equilibrium." In *The Reconstruction of Economic Theory*, edited by P. Mirowski, pp. 93–136. Boston: Kluwer-Nijhoff.

Bicchieri, Cristina. 1986. "Should a Scientist Abstain from Metaphor?" Unpublished manuscript.

Blaug, Mark. 1974. *The Cambridge Revolution: Success or Failure?* London: IEA

———. 1980. *The Methodology of Economics*. Cambridge: Cambridge University Press.

Bloor, David. 1982. "Durkheim and Mauss Revisited." *Studies in the History and Philosophy of Science* 13:267–97.

Clower, Robert. 1967. "A Reconsideration of the Microfoundations of Monetary Theory." *Western Economics Journal* 6:1–9.

Colvin, Phyllis. 1977. "Ontological and Epistemological Commitments in the Social Sciences." In *The Social Production of Scientific Knowledge*, edited by E. Mendelsohn, P. Weingart, and R. Whitely, pp. 103–28. Boston: Reidel.

Dauben, Joseph. 1984. "Conceptual Revolutions and the History of Mathematics." In *Transformation and Tradition in the Sciences*, edited by E. Mendelsohn. Cambridge: Cambridge University Press.

Douglas, Mary. 1973. *Natural Symbols*. London: Barrie and Jenkins.

———. 1975. *Implicit Meanings*. London: Routledge and Kegan Paul.

———. 1982. *In the Active Voice*. London: Routledge and Kegan Paul.

Duhem, Pierre. 1977. *The Aim and Structure of Physical Theory*. Translated by P. Wiener. New York: Atheneum.

Edgeworth, F. Y. 1881. *Mathematical Psychics*. London: Routledge and Kegan Paul.

Fisher, Irving. 1916. *Mathematical Investigations in the Theory of Value*. New Haven: Yale University Press.

France, Peter. 1965. *Racine's Rhetoric*. Oxford: Clarendon Press.

Friedman, Milton. 1953. *Essays in Positive Economics*. Chicago: University Chicago Press.

Garner, C. 1979. "Academic Publication, Market Signalling and Scientific Research Decisions." *Economic Inquiry* 17:575–84.

Gaukroger, Stephen, editor. 1980 *Descartes: Philosophy, Mathematics and Physics*. Totawa, N.J.: Barnes and Noble.

Guth, Alan. 1983. "Speculations on the Origin of Matter, Energy and the Entropy of the Universe." In *Asymptotic Realms of Physics*, edited by A. Guth, K. Huang, and R. Jaffe, pp. 199–216. Cambridge, Mass.: MIT Press.

Hahn, Frank. 1986. "Living with Uncertainty in Economics." *Times Literary Supplement* 4348 (August 1): 833–4.

Harcourt, Geoffrey. 1972. *Some Cambridge Controversies in the Theory of Capital*. Cambridge: Cambridge University Press.

———. 1982. *The Social Science Imperialists*. London: Routledge and Kegan Paul.

Harding, Sandra, editor. 1976. *Can Theories Be Refuted?* Boston: Reidel.

Hayek, Friedrich. 1979. *The Counter-Revolution of Science*. Indianapolis: Liberty Press.

Hesse, Mary. 1966. *Models and Analogies in Science*. Notre Dame: Notre Dame University Press.

———. 1974. *The Structure of Scientific Inference*. Berkeley: University of California Press.

————. 1980. *Revolutions and Reconstruction in the Philosophy of Science*. Bloomington: Indiana University.

Hicks, J. R. 1979. *Causality in Economics*. New York: Basic.

Jevons: W. S. 1905b. *The Principles of Science,* 2d ed. London: Macmillan.

————. 1905b. *The Principles of Economics*. London: Macmillan.

Johnson, Mark, editor. 1981. *Philosophical Perspectives on Metaphor*. Minneapolis: University of Minnesota Press.

Klamer, Arjo. 1983. *Conversations with Economists*. Totawa, N.J: Allenheld and Rowman.

————. 1985. "Economics as Discourse." Unpublished manuscript. Wellesley College.

Kline, Morris. 1972. *Mathematical Thought from Ancient to Modern Times*. New York: Oxford University Press.

————. 1980. *Mathematics: The Loss of Certainty*. New York: Oxford University Press.

Knorr-Cetina, Karin. 1981. *The Manufacture of Knowledge*. New York: Pergamon.

Koopmans, Tjalling. 1957. *Three Essays on the State of Economic Science*. New York: McGraw-Hill.

Krimsky, Sheldon. 1982. *Genetic Alchemy*. Cambridge, Mass.: MIT Press.

————. 1985a. *The Rhetoric of Economics*. Madison: University of Wisconsin Press.

————. 1985b. "Sartorial Epistemology in Tatters." *Economics and Philosophy* 1:134–7.

Mirowski, Philip. 1984a. "Physics and the Marginalist Revolution." *Cambridge Journal of Economics* 8:361–79.

————. 1984b. "The Role of Conservation Principles in 20th Century Economic Theory." *Philosophy of the Social Sciences* 14:461–73.

————. 1985a. "The Sciences Were Never at War?" Unpublished manuscript.

————. 1985b. "Institutions as Solution Concepts in a Game Theory Context." In *Microeconomic Theory,* edited by Larry Samuelson. Boston: Kluwer-Nijhoff.

————. 1986. "Mathematical Formalism and Economic Explanation." In *The Reconstruction of Economic Theory,* edited by P. Mirowski. Boston: Kluwer-Nijhoff.

————. 1987. "The Philosophical Foundations of Institutionalist Economics." *Journal of Economic Issues* (forthcoming).

————. Forthcoming. *More Heat Than Light*. New York: Cambridge University Press.

Neressian, Nancy. 1984. *From Faraday to Einstein*. Dordrecht: Nijhoff.

Olson, Harry. 1958. *Dynamical Analogies,* 2d ed. Princeton: Van Nostrand.

Ortony, A., editor. 1979. *Metaphor and Thought*. Cambridge: Cambridge University Press.

Pareto, Vilfredo. 1935. *The Mind and Society*. New York: Dover.

————. 1953. "On the Economic Phenomenon." *International Economic Papers* 3: 180–96.

Pickering, Andrew. 1984. *Constructing Quarks*. Chicago: University of Chicago Press.

Prigogine, Ilya. 1980. *From Being to Becoming*. New York: Freeman.

Pyenson, Lewis. 1983. *Neohumanism and the Persistence of Pure Mathematics in Wilhemian Germany*. Philadelphia: American Philosophical Society.

Quine, W., and J. Ullian. 1970. *The Web of Belief*. New York: Random House.

Robbins, Lionel. 1952. *An Essay on the Nature and Significance of Economic Science*. London: Macmillan.

Rorty, Richard. 1979. *Philosophy and the Mirror of Nature*. Princeton: Princeton University Press.

Samuelson, Paul. 1966. *The Collected Scientific Papers*, 2 vols., edited by J. Stiglitz. Cambridge, Mass.: MIT Press.

Schoemaker, Paul. 1982. "The Unexpected Utility Model." *Journal of Economic Literature* 20:529–63.

Shackle, G. 1967. *Time in Economics*. Amsterdam: North Holland.

Theobald, D. 1966. *The Concept of Energy*. London: Spon.

Tiles, Mary. 1984. *Bachelard: Science and Objectivity*. Cambridge: Cambridge University Press.

Walras, Leon. 1960. "Economique et Mécanique." *Metroeconomica* 12:3–13.

Wittgenstein, Ludwig. 1976. *Lectures on the Foundations of Mathematics, Cambridge, 1939*, edited by Cora Diamond. Ithaca: Cornell University Press.

———. 1978. *Remarks on the Foundations of Mathematics*, rev. ed. Cambridge, Mass.: MIT Press.

Wong, Stanley. 1978. *The Foundations of Samuelson's Revealed Preference Theory*. Boston: Routledge

CHAPTER 10

On the brittleness of the orange equilibrium

E. Roy Weintraub

I want you to remember that words have those meanings which we have
given them; and we give them meanings by explanations.

Ludwig Wittgenstein, *The Blue Book*

The proof . . . changes our concepts. It makes new connexions and changes
the concept of these connexions.

Ludwig Wittgenstein, *Remarks on the Foundations of Mathematics*

"Equilibrium"

Mathematical economists are members of an interpretive community
(Fish 1980). It is sometimes suggested that the creation of mathematical texts
in economics is associated with the community's desire to avoid serious issues
of interpretation: Mathematics is thought to produce a text that allows little or
no variability in a reader's response (e.g., a real number is not a metaphor).[1]
My own argument, however, will show that a mathematical text *established*
one of several competing interpretations and forced readers to select one image from a set of images; mathematical work has in at least one case shifted
economist-readers' use of a word.

At issue is the word *equilibrium* and how its meaning evolved in a sequence of papers published between 1939 and 1954. Although *equilibrium* is
a term that appears in the hard core of the neo-Walrasian program, and *hard
core* suggests linguistic fixity, that connotation is misleading. I am not, of
course, interested in the "true" meaning of equilibrium. I am instead interested in how an interpretative community read the word *equilibrium* over a
fifteen-year period. In McCloskey's terms (1983, 1986) one must examine
the rhetoric associated with some writings about equilibrium. Unlike his case
studies of purchasing power parity, and unlike Robert Fogel, I want to study
change, to paint over the austere Lakatosian landscape with the bright colors
of language.[2]

In preparing this version of the paper, the author has been helped by conversations
with Neil de Marchi, Philip Mirowski, Nancy Wulwick, Alex Rosenberg, Don Mc-
Closkey, Axel Leijonhufvud, Arjo Klamer, and Stanley Fish.

146

Hicks's *Value and Capital*

Two passages from *Value and Capital* (Hicks 1939) prefigure many later themes:

> If a small rise in price does not make supply greater than demand, when all its repercussions have been allowed for, then there will be no tendency at all for equilibrium to be restored. The market will move away from equilibrium rather than towards it. (p. 66)

> A market is in equilibrium, statically considered, if every person is acting in such a way as to reach his most preferred position, subject to the opportunities open to him. This implies that the actions of different persons trading must be consistent. (p. 58)

Sir John Hicks offers two images of "equilibrium." The first is associated with mechanics, impersonal in tone and hard in texture: "in balance," "equally opposed forces." The second brings to mind individuals acting as if in harmony one with another, and is called forth with language like "coordination of activity," "the invisible hand," "rational agents," and so forth. The first passage above speaks of "market," the second of a "person"; the two different ways of characterizing equilibrium arose from two different traditions.[3]

Hicks recognized that the market equilibrium was associated with Marshall, while the more individualistic alternative was associated with Walras and Pareto: "In deciding to treat the general theory of exchange before dealing with production, we are following the example of Walras rather than Marshall" (p. 57). In one case studied by Hicks individual persons traded, and perhaps reached equilibrium.[4] In the other case production creates supply, which is a force opposed to demand; supply and demand together determine an equilibrium position of rest for the economic system.[5]

Hicks's language induced two images of equilibrium. *For Hicks, indeed, the two ways of imagining equilibrium define the tension that his book was presented to resolve.* That is, he believed that his method of analysis added a Marshallian dynamic theory to the static theory of Walras and Pareto. That static theory could not address problems in monetary economics, for the business cycle literature was concerned with the time path of processes that worked themselves out in a monetary economy. Static or mechanical equilibrium notions failed to encompass monetary theoretic ideas. Consequently Hicks's stability analysis tried to reconcile the two images of equilibrium. His ideas of perfect and imperfect stability were a flawed[6] attempt to blend the imagery of agents acting to make themselves better off with the image of a state of rest of the set of relative prices in the economy.[7]

Paul Samuelson

Paul Samuelson's mathematical training is discernible in his earliest writings, in which *equilibrium* was defined in the language of dynamical systems. Consider "Dynamics, Statics, and the Stationary State" (1943), which was an applied companion piece to the two-part *Econometrica* paper "The Stability of Equilibrium" (1941, 1942) in which he introduced both dynamics and the correspondence principle.[8]

In this 1943 paper Samuelson states that there is a problem distinguishing between "statics" and "dynamics"; he develops his argument by citing writers who had, like Marshall, been confused by the distinction. He writes: "We may say that a system is dynamical if its behavior over time is determined by functional equations in which 'variables at different points of time' are involved in an 'essential' way" (1943: 59). Samuelson attributes this definition to Frisch (1935–6). The Frisch–Samuelson definition was introduced by an important paragraph:

> In defining the term dynamical, at least two possibilities suggest themselves. First, it may be defined as a general term including statical as a special rather degenerate case. Or on the other hand, it may be defined as the totality of all systems which are not statical. Much may be said for the first alternative; the second, however, brings out some points of controversy in the literature and will be discussed here. This decision involves no point of substance, since only verbal problems of definition are involved. (p. 59)

This important passage has a simple meaning, and one much more complex as well:

1. The simple idea is that, from a mathematical point of view, consider any general *dynamic* system of the form $F_i(x_1, x_2, \ldots) = 0$; if x_i is of the form dx_i/dt, then in the sense defined by the conditions of the implicit function theorem, F_i can be simplified as $dx_i/dt = f_i(x_1, x_2, \ldots)$ for $i = 1, 2 \ldots n$. Thus a static system of the form $f_i(x_1, x_2, \ldots) = 0$ is a special case of the general (possibility dynamic) system; the specialization requires that, $\forall i, dx_i/dt = 0$.
2. Alternatively, define the set of all nonstatic systems as the set of dynamic systems. Then "nonstatic" means that $F_i(x_i, x_2, \ldots x_n) = 0$, where the x_i may be time dependent. Then if *no* x_i is time dependent, we have the static system $f_i(x_1, x_2, \ldots) = 0$, which equation does not involve time directly.

Suppose we adopt the second definition of a static system. Since such a system is fundamentally nondynamic, we must have that equilibrium is defined by $f_i = 0$; the balance of forces defines the equilibrium. Alternatively, if we adopt the first point of view, the static system is the limiting case, or the special case, of a degenerative dynamic system. "Equilibrium" is then interpreted as the limit of the dynamic behavior of the system. That is, a solution of the dynamic system involves time, so as time is allowed to pass out of the picture as it were, or is integrated out by a limiting process, or if we wait until time is no longer meaningful to the statement of the problem, $\lim_{t \to \infty} x_i(t) = \bar{x}$, the equilibrium.

To reiterate, for the system $dx_i/dt = f_i (x_1, x_2, \ldots x_n)$ we can define "equilibrium" $\bar{x}$ *in two ways:*

1. If $x_i(t)$ is any motion or solution of the system, "equilibrium" is defined by $\lim_{t \to \infty} x_i(t;t_0) = \bar{x}$; in this case of the degenerate dynamic problem, equilibrium is linked to the eventual playing out of certain behaviors over time. We "settle into" equilibrium, or we can conceive of "agents reaching equilibrium" over time. These images lead to characterizations of equilibrium that associate ideas like "coordination" and the "process whereby agents" with the idea of *equilibration;* the activity of achieving equilibrium plays a larger role than does the terminal state of rest.
2. If $\bar{x} = (\bar{x}_1, \ldots, \bar{x}_n)$, where $\bar{x} = \bar{x}(t;t_0), f_i(\bar{x}) = 0$ defines "equilibrium." Here "equilibrium" is characterized by the satisfaction of a set of static conditions; we speak of a language of "equilibrium conditions," "balances of forces" of supply and demand, "market clearing," and so forth. Even if the equilibrium conditions are maximization conditions for households and firms, there is no mechanism that establishes the position of equilibrium.

Thus by the early 1940s Samuelson had clarified the distinction between statics and dynamics. The formalization he used to present and organize his analysis was that of dynamic systems, taken in part from the mathematician Garrett Birkhoff. This comprehensive theory obliterated the distinction between equilibrium as a behavioral outcome and equilibrium as a mechanical rest point. In the class of models Samuelson used to present his analysis the two images of equilibrium are merged: Either can characterize the state of the system $f_i(x_1, x_2, \ldots) = 0, i = 1, 2, \ldots n$ and any distinction truly "involve[d] no point of substance . . . but only verbal problems of definition. . . ."

Samuelson's work on dynamics was but one part of a larger theme that concerned him in this period: finding "meaningful theorems of observational significance" (1941: 97). By this he meant that observations in economics, that which was shown by data, were changes in equilibrium positions resulting from changes in a parameter; in later econometric language Samuelson was concerned with the identification problem. If a price was in equilibrium before and after a parameter change, it was not necessary to say anything about the equilibrium save the predicted direction of the price change induced by the parameter change. Except for his interest in comparative statics, Samuelson was uninterested in the equilibrium position. Neither was he interested in untangling the differing interpretations of "a position of an economic system in an equilibrium position." He believed that the two conflicting interpretations of equilibrium were illusory, for if one were careful in defining (mathematically) the notion of a static system, both interpretations would collapse to a single formal definition.

To reiterate, Samuelson's approach to analysis was to emphasize maximization and the correspondence principle. He wrote:

> Within the framework of any system, the relationships between our variables are strictly those of mutual interdependence. It is sterile and misleading to speak of one variable as causing or determining another. Once the conditions of equilibrium are imposed, all variables are simultaneously determined. Indeed, from the standpoint of comparative statics, equilibrium is not something which is attained; it is something which if attained, has certain properties. (1947: 9)

In Samuelson's work the distinctions between the use of and images associated with the word *equilibrium* were lost in the mathematical structure; that structure allowed one to talk of "equilibrium positions characterized in the following manner" but did not have a grammar for usages like "the equilibrium arises from" or "equilibrium is achieved when."

As Hahn (1983) notes, "Samuelson does not appear to have committed himself to a formal description of what we are to understand by intertemporal equilibrium. . . . In particular, he maintains that in general there is no privileged motion of the economy (no sequence that we want to designate as equilibrium and the stability of which deserves particular attention. Rather it is the asymptotes of 'each and every motion of the system' (Samuelson, 1947: 330) that he proposes to study" (in Hahn 1983, p. 33). That is, the behavior of the system, specifically how it responds to change (comparative statics) is of more importance than any particular point designated "equilibrium."

This suggests that Samuelson, having reduced the study of equilibrium to a study of the properties of the solution to a set of equations (which solution was assumed in all cases to exist), was unconcerned with equilibrium as an organizing concept and rather used the properties of systems as that organizer. His approach is one of a physicist, not that of a mathematician: "[In] a series of papers on the partial differential equations of mathematical physics . . .

[the mathematician Richard] Courant's primary concern was *existence*. The significance of this concern on the part of mathematicians is sometimes questioned by even quite sophisticated physicists. They are inclined to feel that if a mathematical equation represents a physical situation, which quite obviously exists, the equation must then of necessity have a solution" (Reid 1976: 95). Like physicists mistrustful of mathematicians, Samuelson believed his equations characterized "reality" or the "real economic situation." Samuelson linked "equilibrium" and the mathematical analysis of solutions of equation systems; his work was the stepping stone to the papers by McKenzie (1954) and Arrow and Debreu (1954).

Arrow and Debreu

The text for discussion is "Existence of an Equilibrium for a Competitive Economy" by Kenneth J. Arrow and Gerard Debreu, which appeared in *Econometrica* in July 1954. (Cf. Weintraub 1983.)

Who were the readers of the Arrow–Debreu paper in 1954? The readers of *Econometrica* in 1954 did not have the photocopying machine available, nor did they have discussion papers "on-line" for circulation of research work prior to publication.[9] For 1954 we may presume that the function of a scientific journal was to propagate new research findings, and to serve as the repository of record for the settling of priority claims to new results. The Econometric Society was not large in 1954, so the journal of that association was not read by large numbers of economists. Members were a mixed group, with young postwar-trained economists probably predominating. The research traditions were not heavily mathematical; there were few places where training in calculus was required, and a student who had some calculus was placed on the mathematical track.

The early part of the paper itself provides many clues to its readers' interests and backgrounds. The first paragraph begins with "L. Walras" which defines the continental tradition in economics, and places the article in opposition to the Marshallian partial equilibrium approach. The second paragraph provides some reasons for studying the problem and justifies itself to its readers on the basis of both descriptive and normative considerations: "The view that the competitive model is a reasonably accurate description of reality, at least for certain purposes, presupposes that the equations describing the model are consistent with each other" (p. 265).

Since every competitive equilibrium is Pareto-efficient, and every Pareto-efficient allocation can be considered to be a competitive equilibrium, an interest in efficiency-promoting social actions requires analysis of the existence of equilibrium for competitive economies. Thus the fourth paragraph of the introduction presents, in ordinary language, the major theorems and the assumptions that entail those conclusions, while the fifth paragraph comments on those assumptions. The sixth introductory paragraph specifies what the reader needs to know to read the paper: "Mathematical techniques are set-theoretical. A central concept is that of an abstract economy, a generalization of the concept of a game" (p. 266). The introduction ends with the sentence: "The last section contains a detailed historical note."

The initial Arrow–Debreu paragraphs locate the readership and the manner in which the readers will partition themselves among ways of reading. The introduction provides a guide for the interested reader who has little mathematical skill beyond rudimentary mathematical analysis; such an individual would note the "Walrasian tradition," acknowledge the reasons for proving existence of equilibrium, think a bit about the economic assumptions that were used to get the theorem proved, and then skip over to the two-page historical note. That note tied the current paper to a series of past contributions of economists whose work would have been casually known to all readers of the journal.

The introductory paragraphs are thus inclusionary; they invite all readers of the journal to participate in the article, to construct the text for their own purposes. The material of Section 1 of the article, however, restricts readership, serves an exclusionary function.

Three paragraphs into that section the reader is met with:

1.2.1 $x \leqq y$ means $x_h \leqq y_h$ for each commodity h;

$x \leq y$ means $x_h \leqq y_h$ but not $x = y$

$x < y$ means $x_h < y_h$ for each component h.

R^ℓ is the Euclidean space of ℓ dimensions . . .

$\Omega = \{x | x \in R^\ell, x \geq 0\}$ . . . (p. 267)

Any reader unfamiliar with the emergent notational conventions in linear algebra would be baffled by these lines, and possibly would not even notice the difference between $\leq$ and $\leqq$. This notation, and the set-theoretic background, was not part of an economics curriculum in 1954; in the mathematics curriculum, this vector-order notation was specialized to the theory of games, which was not an established mathematical subdiscipline in the early 1950s.

Equilibrium was formally defined by:

1. y_j^* maximizes $p^* \cdot y_j$ over the set Y_j, for each j;
2. x_i^* maximizes $u_i(x_i)$ over the set:
   $\{x_i | x_i \in X_i, p^* \cdot x_i \leq p^* \cdot \zeta_i + \Sigma_{j=1}^n \alpha_{ij} p^* \cdot y_j^*\}$
3. $p^* \in P = \{p | p \in R^\ell, p \geq 0, \Sigma_{h=1}^\ell p_h = 1\}$
4. $z^* \leq 0, p^* \cdot z^* = 0$, where $x = \Sigma x_i, y = \Sigma y_i, \zeta = \Sigma \zeta_i, z = x - y - \zeta$.

These four conditions define the Arrow–Debreu equilibrium. The first condition states that at the equilibrium price vector p^* and input–output vector

y^* profits are maximized. The second condition says that at the equilibrium price vector p^* and consumption vector x^* utility is maximized. The third condition defines feasible prices, and the fourth condition states that at the equilibrium price vector, all markets clear in the sense that net excess demand is zero on all markets.

The approach that Arrow and Debreu take to show that the competitive model has an equilibrium in the sense of the previous paragraph is to apply the notion of a Nash equilibrium for noncooperative n-person games. A Nash equilibrium is defined by the idea that, at an equilibrium, each agent is maximizing the payoff to him, given the equilibrium actions of the other agents.

The proof of the existence of equilibrium is done in a straightforward manner.

> [Each] of the first m participants, the consumption units, chooses a vector x_i from X_i, subject to the restriction that $x_i \in A_i(\bar{x}_i)$, and receives a payoff $u_i(x_i)$; the jth out of the next n participants, the production units, chooses a vector y_j from Y_j (unrestricted by the actions of the other participants), and receives a payoff $p \cdot y_i$; and the last agent, the market participant, chooses p from P (again the choice is unaffected by the choice of other participants), and receives $p \cdot z$. (p. 274)

Informally, each consumer makes an restricted consumption choice and receives a provisional utility payoff, which leads to demands for goods and supplies of factors; each firm makes a restricted input–output choice, which leads to a provisional profit payoff, which leads to supplies of goods and demands for factors. The fictitious market maker chooses prices in the markets, and compares the demands and supplies that are induced in those markets by the actions of the agents who are reacting to the prices the market maker chooses. That is, the "center" selects market prices, all agents make their choices on the basis of those prices, and their choices lead to supplies and demands. The center compares supplies and demands and changes prices accordingly. Does this process of price → supply–demand → new price → . . . . ever lead to a price → supply–demand → same price? If so, that "maintained" price is an equilibrium. In other words, an equilibrium price, were it to exist, is one that would mediate among the conflicting desires of the agents, who then would have no incentive to take further action.

This proof strategy forces the reader to accept the idea that an equilibrium is a set of prices and quantities that will not be "objected to in practice" by the agents in the economy. The supply–demand balance only serves as the mechanism by which agents compare notes to see whether they are going to be satisfied; the language is not "equilibrium *is* a supply–demand balance" but rather "when in equilibrium, supply and demand are in balance." Still another way to put it is to go back to the definition, and note that conditions 3 and 4 are necessary for an equilibrium, but that 1 through 4 are the necessary and sufficient conditions for the equilibrium. *In the Arrow–Debreu model, the coordination of agents' plans through optimization is necessary for equilibrium, and the clearing of markets as a balance is necessary for equilibrium, but they jointly are necessary and sufficient for equilibrium.*

The "supply–demand balance" is thus what remains of the older images of balance beams and forces. It serves, simply put, as a reference point for some fictitious market maker to tell the players to keep on playing, for they are not yet coordinated. If, indeed, all agents were to get this information for themselves, from their own actions, the supply–demand balance idea would not be associated with equilibrium except after the fact; that is, if the message "lack of coordination" could be triggered directly by the lack of harmony among agents' plans, and that message would lead to a revision of those plans in a self-correcting manner, then there would no longer be any need for the "market" to function as an information dissemination device that says "keep on trading."

Conclusion

The positivist argues that the idea of equilibrium is associated with some aspect of the real world, and that the task of the scientific analysis of competition equilibrium is to create better, or more realistic, models of equilibrium; the test of the theory of equilibrium is thus verisimilitude, correspondence with the real world in which equilibrium is to be found. The postpositivist, the pragmatist, maintains that there is no meaning of equilibrium except as that word is used by the community of economists who read and write texts in which the word *equilibrium* appears; the meaning of equilibrium is derived from the use to which the word is put by the community of readers of the texts of equilibrium analysis. More directly, as equilibrium is dependent for its meaning on the context in which it is found, the meaning of equilibrium changes over time as the texts change. No meaning has a privileged status because of its presumed correspondence to the true equilibrium out there in the world.[10] Equilibrium is associated with a Wittgensteinian language game, and the meaning of the word is dependent on the players of the game and the rules they decide to play by at a particular moment in the history of economic thought.

The foregoing exercise paid attention to a rhetorical issue. We saw that analysis of a shift in the meaning of the word *equilibrium* was associated with a change in the images called forth in the reader's mind when the word *equilibrium* appeared on the page. We saw that the image change was induced by a mathematical proof strategy, and that the mathematical tool itself foreclosed a set of language options, effectively terminating a particular line of inquiry.[11]

The fundamental shift in the imagery of equilibrium was created by Arrow and Debreu's linking of an equilibrium price vector in a general equilibrium model with a Nash equilibrium, which was really the fixed point of a mapping from prices "given" to prices "induced by the actions of agents." Thus the equilibrium metaphor shifted from a balance between market forces to a price that, once established by the desires of the agents, would not be modified as long as the desires of the agents remained unchanged.

The ordinary language of economic analysis was, in this case at least, modified by the metaphors associated with a mathematical theorem.[12] The influence of mathematical economics on the corpus of standard economic analysis goes deeper than is usually acknowledged by both friends and opponents of the mathematization of economics.

Discussion

STUDENT: I have listened to the arguments you have been presenting, Teacher, and I must tell you that I can hold my comments to myself no longer. You have argued as though there has been a change in the way we talk about equilibrium. You have traced the various ways that the word *equilibrium* has been embedded in models and theories. You have argued that there are images that change over time, associated with the word equilibrium. But nowhere have you had the courage to say that one use, or another, is the correct one. Your unwillingness to say whether equilibrium is used by Samuelson is an improvement over its use by Hicks pushes scholarly objectivity to its limits. You must sooner or later commit yourself to some position.

TEACHER: On what must I commit myself?

STUDENT: To the view that one use of "equilibrium" is correct and another is not correct, or is at least less correct.

TEACHER: Why must I assert that one use of a term is correct?

STUDENT: Because our theories are not whimsical. We construct theories to explain the real world, to help us predict phenomena in the real world. Equilibrium is a characteristic of the world, and we want models and theories to explain that phenomenon.

TEACHER: Where is equilibrium?

STUDENT: What?

TEACHER: Where is the equilibrium that you want to explain by the use of theoretical analysis? Is it in my garden, or is it in France? Where may I observe it?

STUDENT: Every time you observe a price you are observing an equilibrium, since that price is a market outcome.

TEACHER: Then why call it an equilibrium instead of just a price?

STUDENT: I call them equilibrium prices because they do not change.

TEACHER: What about a price of wheat that changes when there is a drought?

STUDENT: Supply has changed, so the equilibrium price changes.

TEACHER: It sounds to me more like you have a theory about prices that leads you to call some prices equilibrium prices and others not. Your equilibrium is a theoretical construct, not a feature of reality. In general, equilibrium is a feature of our models, not the world: You should agree with Dorfman, Samuelson, and Solow that "It is the model we are analyzing, not the world" (p. 351).

STUDENT: But what about the truth of the theory? Aren't you in the least concerned with the truth of falsehood or your theory of equilibrium? Surely you cannot call a tree an "equilibrium" and then argue that an equilibrium has leaves. Don't you think that economics must explain the real world if it is to be useful?

TEACHER: Why are you distinguishing between "the real world" and a "useful theory"?

STUDENT: Because I want to know whether my economic theories are correct; how can the theories be judged true or false if there is no reality independent to confirm or disconfirm those theories?

TEACHER: Reality does not disconfirm theories; data or observations or evidence do. There is a lot of evidence around, and the choice of what evidence is appropriate to the discussion generated by a particular theory is a feature of the discussion, not "reality."

STUDENT: You cannot possibly believe that there is no world out there, a world of people working at jobs, factories producing goods, governments taxing and spending, central bankers fighting inflation, and so on. That is the economy, the real world of relevance to economists, and the world our theories must explain.

TEACHER: Of course I am not denying that there are objects in the sense that we talk about objects. I am simply saying that our theories are "in" language and that our explanations are "in" language, and not "in" stones or trees or factories. Our explanations are conversations we have with ourselves and with each other, not monologues directed to rocks and machines.

STUDENT: But don't those explanations have to be connected to reality, to the rocks and machines and unemployed workers?

TEACHER: Perhaps, or perhaps not. The only point I wish to emphasize is that there is nothing productive to be said about those connections, about the truth of theoretical propositions.

STUDENT: Are you saying that there is no criterion that distinguishes truthful from untruthful propositions or explanations?

TEACHER: What have been the criteria proposed? For many centuries we had the criterion of conformity to the word of God; for other periods we have had the criterion of Truth as scientific knowledge, or what was scientifically established by scientific theories was true, and all other propositions were either tautologies or meaningless noises. This positivism runs through to the cult of science today. My argument is simply that there is nothing constructive to be said about Truth, and so we should stop talking about it. The success of the enterprise, the human activity, we call "science" does not depend on Truth at all; rather, it depends on the wonderful richness of the propositions and statements and claims and arguments and counterarguments that are created by individual scientists.

STUDENT: I cannot believe you mean what you are saying. If your science, or in this case economics, stands totally apart from the real economy, why should I bother with it; why should I study an economics that cannot explain real events?

TEACHER: In any useful sense of the term "explanation" I am sure that economics explains various data and observations and facts and phenomena. What I am calling into question is your notion that there are two worlds, one of phenomena, the other of theory, and that there must be criteria *independent of the phenomena and the theory* to answer the question of whether the theory explains the phenomena. I simply do not believe that there can be any useful discussion of such independent criteria: In nearly twenty-five hundred years we have not found anything worth saying about such criteria, and I want to stop wasting my time talking about such correspondence theories of Truth. I am perfectly happy agreeing that there are many truths but nothing that can be called Truth. There is no characteristic shared by true propositions that can be abstracted from those propositions and called an attribute, Truth. Aside from saying that proposition *A* is true and proposition *B* is true, and both *A* and *B* are true, there is no attribute that is shared by *A* and *B* and all the other true propositions, at least nothing can be said about them that is philosophically interesting.

STUDENT: What are the implications for science? You argued that there were some.

TEACHER: The major implication is that science, or Science, is not an enterprise defined by success in uncovering Truth, nor does Science stand in any privileged position with respect to Truth. For if there is nothing useful to be said about Truth, there is no reason to defend Science as a Truth-seeking, and -finding, enterprise. The justification for Science, or the various sciences, such as botany, chemistry, economics, physics, and so on, must be different from their ability to search for Truth and find it. The success of physics is independent of Truth and should be discussed with reference to the various true propositions that physicists can utter, the prediction successes of physicists, and the richness of the theories and experimentation that physicists engage in.

STUDENT: For economics, this means that there is no meaning to be attached to "the economy," I presume.

TEACHER: Not so. It is just that we do not justify, or rather appraise the merit of, our theories, our research programs, on the basis of the truth of those theories, the degree to which they correspond to the reality of the economy as it were. Just as in physics, we find theories plausible or not, interesting or not, *true or not,* independent of the success of the theories in possessing the attribute called Truth.

STUDENT: But why should the method of conjectures and refutations, the usual process of scientific investigation, lead to all the interesting or plausible or true propositions about the economy, about economics? Why, in other words, should the use of mathematics, statistics, theory, testing, *et hoc genus omne* be taken to define the appropriate way to do economics?

TEACHER: They should not be so taken.

STUDENT: Should astrologers and Wall Street chartists be thought of as productive economists?

TEACHER: Be careful. If you are talking about the profession "economist" I think that it is at least in part defined by a common training of its members, a common language, and so forth. These issues are well known to sociologists of science who study the scientific communities. Your question could mean something a bit different however, and that is, "Can an astrologer ever speak a true proposition about the economy or uncover a true proposition about economic phenomena?"

STUDENT: Can poets be sources of interesting propositions about the economy in the same sense that econometricians are sources of interesting propositions about the economy?

TEACHER: An answer might turn on the meaning of the phrase "in the same sense." For if you refer to the ability to utter true propositions, I must say that the poet and the econometrician are symmetric in my view of things; neither, because of their expertise, has an inside track on the Truth (which is uninteresting) while each can utter plausible but different truths. The truths that Marx wrote down about child labor in England early in *Capital* do not differ in their truthfulness from the truths that Milton Friedman wrote about in his studies of the consumption function; the prose of Marx was close in places to poetry – the prose of Friedman was never close in any place to poetry. Did the high comic style of Veblen prevent his uncovering and writing true propositions, interesting propositions, useful propositions? Does the austerity of Lucas's theoretical writing make his ideas more true? I think the answer to both questions is "No."

STUDENT: Progress is thus associated with the augmentation of the stock of true, useful, and interesting propositions.

TEACHER: Nicely said.

Notes

1. Mathematization is also associated with the professionalization of economics as a social science. A. W. Coats (1985: 1698–9) cites Thomas Haskell's observation: "[Professionalization involves] a three-part process by which a community of inquirers is established, distinguishes itself from other groups and from the society at large, and enhances communication among its members, organizing and disciplining them, and heightening their credibility in the eyes of the public. Any act which contributes to these functions, which strengthens the intellectual solidarity of this very special kind of community, is a step towards professionalization" (Haskell 1977: 19). It should be clear that the mathematization of economics was a step towards professionalization in this sense. This is another set of arguments concerning mathematization about which I shall have nothing to say.
2. It was my intention in my earlier studies of general equilibrium analysis (Weintraub 1983, 1985, 1986) to show how the Lakatosian vision required significant augmentation to explain the growth and development of a literature in economic theory.
   "A asks 'How many slabs?' and B answers with a numeral. . . . Systems of communication [like this] we shall call 'language games'. . . . Children are taught their native language by means of such games. . . . We are not, however, regarding the language games which we describe as incomplete parts of a language,

but as languages complete in themselves, as complete systems of human communication'' (Wittgenstein 1960: 81).

This chapter can thus be read as an exploration of a Wittgensteinian language game, the game of ''What is the meaning of equilibrium?''

3. I am not unmindful of the force of Mirowski's (1986) claim that the central mechanical imagery was simply lifted, as a piece, from classical field theory in physics. Indeed, I think that the broad substance of Mirowski's argument is not only correct, but of paramount importance for understanding modern economics. The details of how the field theory worked in particular arguments, such as the ones I present here, are crucial to understanding and corroborating Mirowski's work.

4. ''Of course, this ideal state of equilibrium never exists; but a sense of mutual advantage is perpetually bringing about approximations to it, by prompting both of any two men whose scales of marginal significance do not coincide, directly or indirectly to effect exchanges and readjustments until they do. . . . When a state of equilibrium has been reached – that is to say, when the conditions for exchange and readjustment no longer exist . . .'' (Wicksteed 1910: 144–5). Thus it is not just the distinction between Marshall and Walras that is at issue, but the distinction between Marshall on the one hand, and Wicksteed and Edgeworth on the other.

5. ''When demand and supply are in stable equilibrium, if any accident should move the scale of production from its equilibrium position, there will be instantly brought into play forces tending to push it back to that position; just as, if a stone hanging by a string is displaced from its equilibrium position, the force of gravity will at once tend to bring it back to its equilibrium position. The movements of the scale of production about its position of equilibrium will be of a somewhat similar kind'' (Marshall 1890: 346).

6. Oskar Morgenstern (1941) took Hicks to task for ignoring the published solution to the equilibrium existence problem (see Weintraub 1985: 85), and Samuelson, as we shall see, made an early reputation untangling Hicks's mathematically monstrous distinctions concerning ''stability.''

7. Thus by 1939 there were certainly two distinct sets of images used to characterize equilibrium. In stating this as a fact, I am not committed to stating that this disjunction did or did not originate with Hicks, nor am I saying that there was any conscious tension in the minds of economists between these two sets of images. I am simply noting the discrepancy and identifying its dimensions.

8. These papers form Part 2 of his book *Foundations of Economic Analysis,* which appeared in 1947.

9. But it is worth nothing that Debreu was alerted to Arrow's interest in the problem of equilibrium by his being asked to referee a Cowles Paper written by Arrow; for Debreu's memory of this origin of their collaboration see Weintraub (1983: 28–29), and (1985: 95).

10. This view is, in the literature, most recently associated with Thomas Kuhn (1962, 1977), who documented the manner in which many concept words in science are theory dependent; the correspondence view, the idea that science is an epistemological enterprise, is the target of Rorty (1979, 1982).

11. Although I have been presenting this argument as if it were an entirely original one, it is not that at all. The quotes from Wittgenstein should suggest to the alert reader that, even for mathematics, the rhetorical analysis was done by Wittgenstein. For an absolutely first-rate discussion of these points, and a full discussion of two other case studies of mathematical language games in "real" mathematics, see Chapter 5, "Mathematics: An Anthropological Phenomenon," in Bloor's (1983) *Wittgenstein: A Social Theory of Knowledge.*

12. In this case, the Nash equilibrium theorem (Nash 1950) is equivalent to the Brouwer Fixed Point Theorem (von Neumann 1936) or the Kakutani Fixed Point Theorem (Kakutani 1941). It should be recognized that the Brouwer theorem itself is presented to mathematical readers with an image of some power: The theorem is sometimes called the "cowlick theorem." For if a head is a sphere, and a scalp is convex and compact, then hair is associated with the points of a compact convex set. "Combing hair" is thus a transformation or mapping of the points of the scalp to itself. "Combing" is certainly a continuous mapping. The Brouwer theorem can then be stated as "There is always a cowlick after every combing." (A continuous mapping of a compact convex set to itself always has a fixed point.)

References

Arrow, K. J., and G. Debreu. 1954. "Existence of an Equilibrium for a Competitive Economy." *Econometrica* 20: 265–90.

Bloor, D. 1983. *Wittgenstein: A Social Theory of Knowledge.* New York: Columbia University Press.

Coats, A. W. 1985. "The American Economics Association and the Economics Profession." *Journal of Economic Literature* 23: 1697–1727.

Dorfman, R., P. Samuelson, and R. Solow. 1958. *Linear Programming and Economic Analysis.* New York: McGraw-Hill.

Fish, Stanley. 1980. *Is There a Text in This Class?* Cambridge, Mass.: Harvard University Press.

Frisch, R. 1935–6. "On the Notion of Equilibrium and Disequilibrium," *Review of Economic Studies* 3: 100–6.

Hahn, F. H. 1983. "On General Equilibrium and Stability." In *Paul Samuelson and Modern Economic Theory,* edited by E. C. Brown and R. Solow. New York: McGraw-Hill.

Haskell, T. L. 1977. *The Emergence of Professional Social Science: The American Social Science Association and the Nineteenth Century Crisis of Authority.* Urbana: University of Illinois Press.

Hicks, J. R. 1939. *Value and Capital.* Oxford: Oxford University Press.

Kakutani, S. 1941. "A Generalization of Brouwer's Fixed Point Theorem," *Duke Mathematics Journal* 8: 457–9.

Kuhn, T. S. 1962. *The Structure of Scientific Revolutions.* Chicago: University of Chicago Press.

———. 1977. *The Essential Tension.* Chicago: University of Chicago Press.

Marshall, A. 1980. *Principles of Economics*. Variorum edition, edited by C. W. Guillebaud. Reprinted 1961. London: Macmillan.

McCloskey, D. N. 1983. "The Rhetoric of Economics." *Journal of Economic Literature* 21: 481–517.

———. 1985. *The Rhetoric of Economics*. Madison: University of Wisconsin Press.

McKenzie, L. 1954. "On Equilibrium in Graham's Model of World Trade and Other Competitive Systems." *Econometrica* 22: 147–61.

Mirowski, P. 1988. *More Heat Than Light*. New York: Cambridge University Press.

Morgenstern, O. 1941. "Professor Hicks on Value and Capital," *Journal of Political Economy* 49: 361–93.

Nash, J. 1950. "Equilibrium Points in N-Person Games." *Proceedings of the National Academy of Science* 36: 48–49.

von Neumann, J. 1936. "Ueber ein ökonomisches Gleichungssystem und eine Verallgemeinerung des Brouwerschen Fixpunksatzes." Reprinted 1937 in *Ergebnisse eines Mathematischen Kolloquiums, 1935–36,* edited by K. Menger. Leipzig and Vienna: Franz Deuticke. Reprinted 1945–6, translated by G. Morton. "A Model of General Economic Equilibrium," *Review of Economic Studies* 13:1–9.

Reid, C. 1976. *Courant*. New York: Springer-Verlag.

Rorty, R. 1979. *Philosophy and the Mirror of Nature*. Princeton: Princeton University Press.

———. 1982. *The Consequences of Pragmatism*. Minneapolis: University of Minnesota Press.

Samuelson, P. A. 1941. "The Stability of Equilibrium: Comparative Statics and Dynamics." *Econometrica* 9: 97–120.

———. 1942. "The Stability of Equilibrium: Linear and Nonlinear Systems." *Econometrica* 10: 1–25.

———. 1943. "Dynamics, Statics, and the Stationary States." *Review of Economics and Statistics* 25: 58–68.

———. 1947. *Foundations of Economic Analysis*. Cambridge, Mass.: Harvard University Press.

Weintraub, E. R. 1983. "On the Existence of a Competitive Equilibrium: 1930–1954." *Journal of Economic Literature* 21: 1–39.

———. 1985. *General Equilibrium Analysis: Studies in Appraisal*. New York: Cambridge University Press.

———. 1986. "The NeoWalrasian Program Is Empirically Progressive." Duke University Economics Department Working Paper.

Wicksteed, P. H. 1910. *The Common Sense of Political Economy*. Reprinted 1945. London: Routledge.

Wittgenstein, L. 1956. *Remarks on the Foundations of Mathematics*. Oxford: Basil Blackwell.

———. 1960. *The Blue and Brown Books*. New York: Harper & Row.

CHAPTER 11

The significance of significance: Rhetorical aspects of statistical hypothesis testing in economics

Frank T. Denton

1. Introduction

It may not be immediately evident that statistical hypothesis testing is a proper subject for attention in this volume. The formal testing of hypotheses is a branch of statistics, based on axioms of probability and the strict rules of mathematical logic. Journals in statistics, as well as in biometrics, econometrics, and other statistically oriented disciplines, are full of highly technical articles on the theory of hypothesis testing, emphasizing mathematical rigor and logical precision. Surely statistical hypothesis testing has little if anything to do with the rhetoric of economics.

So it may appear at first glance. But let us take a second one. The abstract framework of hypothesis testing provides a set of input boxes and a logical structure for drawing inferences once the boxes have been filled. The boxes have names like Null Hypothesis, Data, and Assumed Sampling Distribution. In applications in economics these boxes are filled by economists who seek to use the testing framework to provide evidence about regularities in economic life. Most of the data that economists use are perforce nonexperimental, and the framework therefore requires special interpretation. So interpreted, it takes on a particular metaphorical content: A story must be told (or accepted implicitly) so that the data can be treated as if they were a sample from an unseen (and unseeable) parent population or the product of an invisible generating mechanism that was capable of spewing out infinitely many 1986 GNP growth rates but in fact produced only one.

The statistical hypothesis-testing framework can thus be viewed as a rhetorical device for use in the organization and interpretation of real-world observations. When the economist employs this device to persuade others of the reliability of his conclusions he is implicitly asking them (a) to accept the

I am grateful to the following for helpful discussions and comments on the original paper: David Feeny, Peter George, Zvi Griliches, Lonnie Magee, Donald McCloskey, Ernest Oksanen, Leslie Robb, Byron Spencer, Gordon Tullock, and Doug Welland.

underlying metaphor, and (b) to judge as reasonable both what he has put into the input boxes and the manner in which he has interpreted the output.

There is a related issue. To be successful in persuasion, arguments must not only be well constructed; they must also be delivered to those whom one would persuade. It has long been recognized that publication decisions about papers reporting hypothesis tests are likely to be influenced by the results of the tests. I shall argue that biased *information filtering* (as I shall call it) is widespread and not at all surprising. I shall argue also that it is a critical concern in the interpretation of published arguments based on statistical tests of hypotheses.

2. Where we are and how we got here

The birth date of statistical hypothesis testing has been assigned by historians of statistics with some precision. A qualitative argument used by Galileo as part of his refutation of the Ptolemaic system has been cited as an early example of the spirit of such testing (Box 1978: 64), but John Arbuthnot gets credit for being "the first individual to employ . . . a formal probability test of a statistical hypothesis" (Eisenhart 1967: 32; see also Eisenhart and Birnbaum 1967, and Hacking 1965, Ch. 6). Arbuthnot, a Scottish satirist, physician to Queen Anne, and amateur scientist and mathematician, noted that in London in the eighty-two years ending in 1710 liveborn male infants had outnumbered liveborn female infants in every year. He calculated that if male and female births were equally likely occurrences, the probability of observing such a run of male predominance was $(1/2)^{82}$. This number being minute, he was led to reject the hypothesis of "chance" and to argue that the evidence indicated intervention by Divine Providence (on behalf of males). In modern terminology we might interpret Arbuthnot's test as a one-sided test of the null hypothesis that the binomial probabilities are 0.5 against the alternative hypothesis that the male probability is greater than 0.5, at some high level of significance. However, that was certainly not the language or framework of the day.

Modern conventional testing theory stems mainly from the work in the present century of R. A. Fisher, Jerzy Neyman, and Egon Pearson. Fisher has often been referred to as the founder of modern mathematical statistics. His story is well told by his daughter and biographer, Joan Fisher Box (1978). Combining mathematical and logical skills with a practical interest in experimental design and the analysis of data, he developed a consistent body of theory for using probabilities to draw conclusions from experimental data. The notion of the "statistical significance" of an experimental result was formalized by Fisher and procedures for carrying out tests were developed and promoted through his influential writings (especially Fisher 1951 [1935], 1970 [1925], 1973). Much of Fisher's work and practical interest had been in genetics, agricultural experimentation, and the biological sciences generally, but his influence spread to other fields, and eventually induced a general orientation in applied statistics towards rigorous principles in the design of experiments and the application of exact tests of statistical significance.

The general philosophy of present-day hypothesis testing continues to be much like that of Fisher, but the formal procedures and mathematical and logical framework now in common use are attributable to a celebrated series of papers by Neyman and Pearson. The Neyman–Pearson framework was not introduced without controversy. (Good reading on the controversy is provided by Hogben [1968].) Indeed, Fisher himself opposed it to the end of his life. Fisher objected in particular to the Neyman–Pearson requirement that the test of any hypothesis must be a test against an explicitly stated rival hypothesis. He objected also to the strict frequentist orientation of Neyman–Pearson (Dempster 1979). Nevertheless, Neyman and Pearson won the day. Theirs is now the standard testing framework in applied economics (or econometrics, if that is preferred; I shall not make the distinction unless it seems important), as well as other fields of research in which statistical methods are employed.

It was inevitable that statistical hypothesis testing would find its way into economics. Economics was moving in the direction of a greater emphasis on quantitative analysis in the 1920s and 1930s, and quantitative analysis came increasingly to mean the use of the techniques of statistical inference that had caught on in the experimental sciences for which they were originally designed. (See Christ [1985] for a historical account of early work in quantitative economic analysis.) The application of these techniques implied the use of probability models. Clifford Hildreth, in his paper on the work of the Cowles Commission during its Chicago years (1939–55), identifies "the exposition and advocacy of probability models" as one of the two main contributions of the commission to econometrics, the other one being "the development of simultaneous equation models to a usable stage" (Hildreth 1985: 126). Econometrics has never looked back since those pioneering days as far as the use of probability models is concerned, even if there do remain nagging questions and alternative views about the philosophical underpinnings of such models.

An argument based on a probability model of economic behavior requires of the reader or listener the acceptance of certain premises on which the logical structure of statistical inference is erected. Statistical hypothesis testing is usually thought of as a form of analysis to be used by an individual to draw conclusions from empirical observations, but it also serves as a device for persuading others of the consistency of the conclusions with the observations. It is used today to argue about the effects of taxes on investment incentives and a host of other economic relationships in broadly the same way that it

was used in the early eighteenth century to argue about the question of intervention by Divine Providence. As a rhetorical device it is surely one of the
most common ones in present-day debate among economists.

3. Samples, populations, and parameters

The data used in a hypothesis test are referred to as a "sample," and
where there is a sample there must be a population. Survey statisticians earn
their daily bread by designing probability-based sample surveys of human or
other "tangible" populations – the population of the United States, for example, or the population of land under cultivation in some agricultural region
– and by drawing inferences from their samples. They design their sample
surveys in the full belief that the populations exist. To be sure, nobody has
ever seen the population of the United States (just samples of it), but practically speaking, nobody doubts that there is one. Indeed, given a suitable budget, the population could be (and periodically is) enumerated in its entirety
through the taking of a census. The survey statistician who makes an estimate
of the proportion of women over sixty-five in the United States or the rate of
unemployment among teenage males has in mind that he or she is estimating
things for which the true values could actually be obtained, given a sufficiently large budget to work with.

Now consider an experimental situation. A simple one would involve the
throwing of a die a hundred times and the use of the observed proportions of
numbers coming up to make inferences about the "population proportions,"
thereby to judge the fairness of the die. Under a frequentist interpretation, the
population proportions, or parameters of the random process, can be conceived of as those obtained as limiting values in an experiment in which there
is a never-ending sequence of die throws, under constant conditions. In fact
this experiment could not be carried out. Nevertheless, there is little difficulty
in conceiving of it. The principles of inference are the same as those on which
the survey statistician bases his or her work, even though enumeration of the
population is not possible and the true parameters are not strictly determin-
able. The same can be said of an experiment to evaluate the effects of fertilizer on agricultural yields, to take another example. If the experiment involves a randomized design with controlled applications of the fertilizer at
present treatment levels, it may be carried out only once, but there is little
difficulty in imagining an infinite sequence of repetitions based on an underlying stable probability process. The same general principles of inference again
apply.

Considerably more subtlety and conceptual footwork are required to support the idea that these principles are applicable also when working with data

of the "nonexperimental" kind used in economics. Voltaire said, "If God did not exist, it would be necessary to invent him,"and that is just about the situation here. There is no population that could be enumerated in a census, nor any underlying probability process that could be studied by repeated experiments, and so we must invent one. We allude to "unseen parent populations"[1] and "stochastic generating processes." If we are in a particularly metaphorical mood, we talk about the Great Urn of Nature and observe that "Nature does the experiments for us and we must interpret the results." Perhaps we have no need to resort to such figures of speech: When talking among ourselves we are very often preaching to the converted. But if pressed, we tell a story along lines such as these. As with other rhetorical devices, the test of whether the story is convincing is whether it convinces.

The idea of a probability process underlying the balance of trade in the fourth quarter of last year or the latest figures for construction activity does not evoke wild enthusiasm from everybody. There are intelligent and well-educated people who cannot accept that way of thinking about the real world, as they observe it. However, some notion of an underlying process – as distinct from merely a record of empirical observations – has to be accepted for the testing of hypotheses in econometrics to make any sense.

The "Nature does the experiments" story might be seen as a metaphor for the idea that there are regularities in economic life but they are not perfect regularities: The word "Nature" implies some stability – some constancy of parameters in the "underlying process" – while the world "experiments" suggests some uncertain elements in the outcomes. If our inability to find (plausible) exact-fitting models of real-world economic behavior did not force us into a probabilistic way of thinking, we might be using a metaphor like "Nature operates the controls," rather than "Nature does the experiments." Whatever one's metaphorical preferences, appeal to the idea of experimental or probability processes in economics is (if you accept it) a powerful rhetorical device. It is what allows inferential statistics into the arena of economic debate.

4. Hypotheses and data

The standard testing framework requires us to choose a "null hypothesis" and test it against an "alternative hypothesis." On the strength of the result, we may then argue that the null hypothesis should be "accepted" or "rejected" (some would prefer simply "not accepted") at a chosen level of significance (i.e., a chosen probability of making "an error of the first kind" by rejecting when in fact the null hypothesis is true). Most null hypotheses that are tested in this framework in economics are represented by equality restrictions: Two parameters must be exactly equal to each other; the sum of three parameters must be exactly equal to zero; and so on.

The restrictions that give rise to testable hypotheses in economics come from economic theory. Now economic theory is (or should be) based on carefully chosen assumptions that allow us to abstract from issues that are not of central importance, in order to focus on those that are. We hope to be able to obtain sharp conclusions from the theory and then to see whether these conclusions (and hence the theory) are consistent with real-world data. What makes things not quite so straightforward are the initial abstractions, which give rise to the neat theoretical conclusions but almost certainly are out of line with complex reality. So we try to patch things up a bit by introducing some "control variables" into a regression equation, in addition to the ones that the theory says should be there. The theory may not have had much to say about the functional form of the regression equation, beyond (perhaps) some general restrictions on continuity and the signs of some of the first derivatives; perhaps therefore we choose a linear form, in the hope that it is a good enough approximation. The theory may well have had nothing at all to say about the stochastic properties of the equation, leaving us to assume something about those also – a multivariate normal distribution, perhaps, with a shy nod in the direction of the central limit theorem. And then there are the data.

The discrepancies between the definitions of variables in economic theory and the recorded measurements of real-world phenomena can be very large. Variables that are treated in economic theory as if they were uniquely defined to everybody's satisfaction turn out to be quite ambiguous and capable of a wide range of definitions when we come to the point of measuring them (or of using other people's measurements): unemployment, the rate of inflation, the stock of capital, real output, to mention only a few. Definitional problems aside, the measurement processes are unavoidably imprecise, even under the best of conditions, and sometimes downright horrible.[2]

The purpose of the foregoing is (a) not to find fault with economic theory or theorists, (b) not to find fault with economic statisticians or survey statisticians (whose job is to do the best they can in providing data for economists and others to analyze), and (c) not to discourage the testing of economic theories with real-world data. The purpose is rather to provide background for the following question: If so many arbitrary choices and assumptions are necessary to bridge the gap between economic theory and the econometric analysis of real-world data, why should we consider sharp equality-type hypotheses the appropriate ones for testing? I think the answer is that we should not. The tests that are appropriate in economics do not involve precisely defined invariants such as the speed of light, Planck's constant, or the rate of acceleration of a free-falling body at the surface of the earth. The hypotheses are typically better phrased in terms of "close to" than in terms of "exactly equal to."

Consider the famous experiment of a century ago by Albert Michelson and Edward Morley. The experiment involved the splitting of a beam of light into two parts, the transmission of the two parts in directions at right angles to each other, and comparison of the times required by the light to travel identical distances along the two different paths. Contemporary theory in physics postulated the existence of an invisible "ether" and an "ether wind" that would affect the measured speed of light traveling along the two paths differently, depending on the (unknown) direction of the "wind." Refutation of the theory required that the two parts of the initial beam be reflected back to a common point and reach that point at exactly the same time.

Now imagine a situation in which we are repeating this experiment in an ideal form with a measuring device known to produce normally distributed zero-mean random errors. We can think of a formal hypothesis test. If t_1 and t_2 are the times required by the two parts of the light beam to travel identical distances, the null hypothesis is $t_1 - t_2 = 0$, and the alternative hypothesis is $t_1 - t_2 \neq 0$. We repeat the experiment a large number of times, find that the null hypothesis cannot be rejected (at say the 1 percent significance level), and argue that the ether theory is not supported by the evidence. The standard hypothesis-testing theory applies with precision: There is a precise (point) null hypothesis, and it is plausible that this hypothesis could in fact be true.

Contrast this situation with the following. We estimate a demand function using time-series data provided by a central statistical agency according to what it views as feasible and appropriate definitions for practical measurement. The independent variables are household income, the price of the commodity, and the price of some competing commodity. (Both prices are represented by fixed-weight indexes; the income variable is based on a particular set of imputations and conventions for dealing with income in kind.) We assume a log-linear functional form and normally and independently distributed errors. There are other variables that might influence demand, but we have no measurements of these, are unaware of their influence, or have insufficient degrees of freedom to accommodate them, and so we ignore them. The data consist of twenty-five annual observations, and we assume the function to be perfectly stable over the whole of the data period. We theorize that the function is precisely homogeneous of degree zero in income and prices, set up as the corresponding null hypothesis that the coefficients of the three independent variables should sum exactly to zero, and prepare to carry out an F test. *Question:* Does anyone really think that the hypothesis is interesting – that the "true" coefficients of such an equation might be expected to sum *exactly* to zero? *Answer:* I hope not. The homogeneity idea may have theoretical merit and may well be worth testing, but surely the plausible requirement to make the hypothesis interesting is that the sum of the coefficients should be *close to* zero, not exactly zero. "Close to" is an imprecise concept, but it may be a lot more realistic and meaningful in applied econometrics than "exactly equal to."

One can argue that "close to" is generally more meaningful than "exactly equal to" on the basis of the simplicity of models, arbitrariness of assumptions, and crudity of measurements. One can also make the argument on the basis of the economic interpretation of results, as does McCloskey (1985). McCloskey uses as an example the purchasing power parity hypothesis represented by $\beta = 1.0$, where β is the slope coefficient in a regression of a home-country price variable on a foreign price variable (adjusted for the exchange rate). If the estimated value of β is statistically significantly different from 1.0 (at some chosen level of significance), the purchasing power parity hypothesis is rejected according to the standard test procedure; otherwise it is accepted. "But 'exactly' true is not relevant for most economic purposes. What is relevant is merely that β is in the neighborhood of 1.0, where 'the neighborhood' is defined by *why* it is relevant – for policy, for academic reputation, for the progress of knowledge" (pp. 201–2).

There is a common saying in econometrics circles (and in applied statistics circles generally) that if you have a large enough sample you can reject any (equality) hypothesis. If there is a null hypothesis about the exact value of a parameter θ and the parameter space is a continuum, the probability that an estimator of θ will yield a value exactly equal to the one hypothesized is zero. The difference between estimated and hypothesized values is random with a probability distribution dependent on sample size, and (in principle) it will be possible, for virtually any problem of practical interest in economics, to find a sample large enough that the null hypothesis will be rejected at any fixed level of significance. If 100 does not do it, try 1,000; if 1,000 does not do it, try 1,000,000; if not 1,000,000 then 10,000,000. The logical conclusion is stated by Leamer, in a paraphrasing of a statement by Berkson (1938): "[Since] a large sample is presumably more informative than a small one, and since it is apparently the case that we will reject the null hypothesis in a sufficiently large sample, we might as well begin by rejecting the hypothesis and not sample at all" (Leamer 1978, p. 89; see also Meehl 1967).

If we view this situation from within the classical testing framework, the problem lies not with the internal logic of the framework but with the way in which it is used. Taking the time difference $t_1 - t_2$ in the ideal Michelson–Morley experiment as a point in continuous one-dimensional space, we would not expect to reject the "no ether" hypothesis at some high level of significance, if the hypothesis were true, even with an extremely large sample of experimental results, and the point representation of the hypothesis would be entirely appropriate. Taking the slope coefficient β in McCloskey's price equation as also a point in continuous one-dimensional space, we *would* expect to reject the hypothesis $\beta = 1.0$ with a large enough sample. Physicists would not be much impressed by a statement like "The results of the experiment suggest that the difference in light speeds in the two directions is no more than 5 percent" but economists might well be impressed by a similar statement regarding the difference between β and 1.0.

If we decide that the null hypothesis about an individual parameter is more realistically viewed as a statement that the true value lies in some range, rather than that it is a particular number, the standard test becomes that of a composite null against a composite alternative hypothesis, rather than a simple null against a composite alternative. The first problem to be dealt with is then the delineation of boundaries. "Close to" must be given some precise working definition. McCloskey's criterion of how different from 1.0 (or 0.0, or whatever) a parameter would have to be for the difference to "matter" in terms of its economic implications provides a general orientation, but the choice must be rather arbitrary. A particular "close to" definition might be considered by seeing whether all of the points that it implies can be rejected by an appropriate significance test. Or a determination might be made of the smallest region of some shape (centered on the point of interest) that has within it any points that cannot be rejected.

Leamer (1978: 108) noted that the testing of a composite hypothesis can be viewed as an index number problem (a type of problem with which economists are certainly very familiar). The points in the parameter space that correspond to a given composite hypothesis can be summarized by a single weighted average of their likelihood-function values. In effect, composite null and composite alternative hypotheses are each augmented to include a specified weighting function or, in Bayesian terms, a prior probability distribution over the region corresponding to the hypothesis. The Bayesian requirement that a prior distribution must be fully specified seems less threatening when couched in the language of index numbers.

Other ways can be found to reduce composite hypotheses to single ones. "Representative" points can be chosen by some appropriate criterion and tested against each other. For example, Maxwell King has proposed an approach of this kind for tests involving composite hypotheses about autoregressive and moving average error processes (King 1983, and several other studies by the same author). Alternative "representative" points can be tried to see how sensitive results are to the particular choices.

5. Significance, action, and the consequences of making a mistake

The standard hypothesis testing framework requires us to specify null and alternative hypotheses, choose a level of significance, and compute a test statistic with known probability distribution. Under a decision-action interpretation of the framework, if this statistic exceeds a *critical* value (corresponding to the level of significance) we are to *reject* the null hypothesis and take action appropriate to that result; if the statistic does not exceed the critical value, we are to *accept* the null hypothesis and take different action. On no account are we allowed to peek at the data or the computed value of the test statistic before choosing the significance level or specify the hypotheses or to change our minds once we have seen the results of the test. The language is that of a strict, predetermined decision process with firm rules for action.

There are situations in which such decision-action rules are in fact followed quite literally. In a quality control application to an industrial process there may be regular sampling, and if a computed statistic exceeds a preassigned critical level the process may be shut down immediately for inspection and remedial action (with implied costs). But what happens in an application in economics? The answer is generally "not much." If I have carried out a test of some economic hypothesis at the 5 percent level of significance and the statistic exceeds the critical level, I do not sell my holdings of French francs and buy Japanese yen, move to Florida, or change my occupation. I may decide to write a paper, but nothing much else of any well-defined character is likely to occur – nothing that would lend itself to explicit cost–benefit evaluation, let us say.

The point (well known) is that generally the results of hypothesis tests are not used in economics as decision criteria but rather as indicators suggestive of the correspondence between real-world observations and particular economic theories, and perhaps as further contributions to a stock of evidence inherited from the past. The journals are full of apparently highly significant results (in the statistical sense) but we generally view them in a way quite different from that implied by the language of formal testing. The interpretation of test results is more a matter of cautious sifting of evidence than of sudden probability-based decisions to believe this theory or disbelieve that one.

There are more or less conventional levels of significance in the reporting of test results. Levels of 1, 5, and sometimes 10 percent are often reported. Why these? The best answer to why such significance levels are so commonly used this year is probably that those are the ones that were used last year, implying a perfect serial correlation process that allows us to work our way back, year by year, by repeated substitution, to the era in which R. A. Fisher was doing his pioneering work on significance testing. "It is usual and convenient for experimenters to take 5 percent as a standard level of significance," wrote Fisher, having in mind no doubt experimental biology and other areas of science in which there were extensive early applications.[3] If 5 percent was "usual and convenient" many decades ago in agricultural yield experiments, we are surely entitled to ask what bearing that has on applications to nonexperimental data in economics today, or more generally why any widely used level should be regarded as appropriate for the testing of some *particular* economic theory with some *particular* concerns and objectives in mind.

It is hard to disagree with McCloskey's (1985) suggestion that greater attention should be paid to the notion of loss in the design and interpretation of statistical tests in economics (in the tradition of Neyman, Pearson, and Abraham Wald). The difficulties of formulating explicit loss functions for most applications in economics seem so formidable that I think the prospects for widespread adoption of a formal loss-function framework are not promising. However, a general orientation that would involve thinking about problems in terms of what matters from the point of view of their economics, rather than just their statistical aspects, seems clearly desirable.

A related issue has to do with how we put the questions in the conventional testing framework. A high level of significance is specified for testing one hypothesis against the other, but which way should the test go? Which should be the null and which the alternative hypothesis? If one hypothesis is represented by an equality restriction (e.g., $\theta = 0$) and the other by an inequality restriction (e.g., $\theta > 0$), standard practice in most situations requires that the equality one be designated as the null hypothesis. Unless the equality hypothesis fails the test it is then declared winner.

This asymmetric treatment of two competing hypotheses may be consistent with the logic and goals of an investigation, or it may not be. There are cases in which one might prefer simply to determine which of two hypotheses were favored by the data, rather than basing a judgment on the pass–fail performance of one of them. There are also cases in which it would make more sense to let the inequality hypothesis have the "null" role and the quality hypothesis the role of "alternative," were it not for the difficulties of doing that within the standard framework. Bayesian procedures, and evaluations of hypothesis support based on likelihood functions, need not be restricted by the asymmetry of the null–alternative designation, but they have other characteristics that to date have kept them from being widely used in practical applications with economic data.

6. Information filtering

I turn now to a quite different set of issues. Many years ago Theodore Sterling (1959) found overwhelming evidence of publication bias in favor of test results that indicate rejection of the null hypotheses that were tested. (See also Tullock 1959; 1966, Ch. 6.) What Sterling did was to examine issues of four psychology journals in 1955 or 1956. He recorded the numbers of research papers in which tests of significance were reported, and of those, the numbers in which null hypotheses were rejected at the 5 percent or higher level of significance. Of the 294 reports of significance tests, he found that 286 involved null hypothesis rejections and only 8 involved failures to reject. He observed also that "A few minutes of browsing through experimental journals in biology, chemistry, medicine, physiology, or sociology" indicated similar situations. I think it fair to say that we could add contemporary economics to the list. It seems obvious that there is a biased selection process at work.[4] I shall refer to this process as *information filtering*.

It can be argued that biased filtering of information about test results goes well beyond journal acceptance–rejection decisions and applies to book publication decisions, decisions by conference organizers about papers to be presented, and most important of all, perhaps, the decisions of individual researchers about whether or not to write up their results in the first place in a potentially publishable form. While biases in journal publication decisions are the easiest to visualize, they are probably only the tip of the iceberg. I shall argue below that all biases of this kind are in fact quite understandable. Sterling referred to "malpractices" in discussing journal biases, but that is not the way in which I view the situation. First, though, a more explicit development of the filtering idea.

An argument by analogy is as follows. Imagine that there are three individuals. Let us call them Tester, Editor, and Reader, and just T, E, and R, for short. T is busily engaged in carrying out statistical hypothesis tests. He sits at a computer terminal day after day and does test after test, using whatever data sets are accessible and whatever test statistics are appropriate. Each time he does a test he records the result on a piece of paper and puts the paper into an envelope, which he then seals and gives to E. One possibility is that E simply serves as a conveyer. He takes each envelope and passes it to R, unopened. R then opens the envelope and notes whether the null hypothesis tested is accepted or rejected. Obviously there is no selection bias involved in this process: All the information that T has about tests carried out is available also to R. In the standard testing framework, if T has a 5 percent probability of making an error by rejecting a null hypothesis at the 5 percent significance level when in fact the hypothesis is true, then R has the same probability if he accepts T's results.

Now suppose that E comes to believe that there is just too great an outpouring of test results and that R is probably not interested in seeing so many. He therefore decides to pass on only a fraction of the envelopes he receives. His selection is made at random, again without opening the envelopes. R now has less information than T about work carried out, but what he does have has been filtered randomly, and (on average) he is receiving results in the same proportions as the ones given to E. For any given test result that reaches him, the probability of making an error by rejecting the null hypothesis when it is true is still 5 percent for R, as it is for T.

Suppose though that E behaves differently. Suppose that he opens the envelopes and checks the results of the tests before deciding which ones to pass on. He still transmits only a fraction of those that he receives, but now his choices are based on whether he thinks R would find the results "interesting," and more often than not he feels that statistically significant results are likely to be more interesting than nonsignificant ones. The information flowing from T to R has now been filtered in such a way as to alter R's probabilities. To take the most extreme case, if E decides to pass on a result *only* if it implies rejection of the null hypothesis, then R will never see anything *but* rejections. His probability or rejecting a null hypothesis if he takes the results at face value will then be 100 percent, regardless of whether the hypothesis is true or false (which he never knows). The good news is that he has 100 percent power (in the statistical sense): He always rejects a hypothesis when it is false. The bad news is that he has a 100 percent probability of making an error of the first kind: He always rejects a hypothesis when it is true. If E does not go so far as to withhold all nonsignificant results but simply transmits the significant ones in disproportionately large numbers, then R's probability of rejecting true hypotheses will be less than 100 percent, but still greater than the 5 percent level adopted by T when he did the tests.

Now, what is happening to T while all of this is going on? Let us suppose that E returns to T those test results that he has decided not to transmit. Being a perceptive fellow, T comes to realize after a while how the system is working. He observes that whenever he gives E a statistically nonsignificant result he is very likely to get it back, perhaps with a note thanking him for submitting it but explaining that the result is not considered to be sufficiently interesting to warrant passing it on. T therefore comes to the (entirely rational) conclusion that if his goal is to communicate with R there is not much point in taking the time to write down and pass on information about his results to E unless they indicate statistical significance. Better he should use the time to carry out more tests and see whether he cannot generate more results that are significant. Most of the envelopes that E receives from T from now on will therefore contain reports indicating null hypothesis rejection. Even if E now makes his choices for subsequent transmission strictly at random, the damage has been done; the information flow has been filtered in a biased fashion right at the source.

It would be a mistake to argue that in the real world of editorial selection statistically significant results would always be viewed as more interesting than nonsignificant ones. While I think that they would be so viewed in the majority of cases in economics (and probably many other disciplines), one can easily think of circumstances in which just the opposite situation would obtain. If the theory that x is strongly related to y were (a) considered important, (b) widely believed, and (c) apparently supported by previous evidence, then a new test with new data in which the null hypothesis of no relationship could not be rejected might well be considered interesting. Even here, though, the test probabilities for the reader would be distorted. The fact that an author's decision to submit and an editor's decision to publish may be based on the reported test result is sufficient to make the test probabilities for a reader different from those of the author, whichever direction the bias is in.[5]

7. Data mining as a form of information filtering

That standard hypothesis tests are distorted when there is "specification search" over alternative models, using the same (or at least not independent) data sets, was long recognized by econometricians in a general sort of way. However, the dimensions of the problem and the need to take explicit account of it have come to be understood much better in recent years, largely in consequence of well-known work by Leamer (1978, 1983, and elsewhere). Difficulties arise with regard to formal testing when specification search is fully reported by an author, because in practice such search tends to involve informal, hard-to-characterize learning activities and perhaps "flashes of inspiration," which (by their nature) could not possibly have been foreseen. When search activities are unreported, the problem may not be apparent but may in fact be much worse. The reader of an article is then not even given a fighting chance to make allowance for other model specifications that were tried before the final choice was published. Unreported specification search goes by many names and identifying phrases: "data mining," "fishing," or "grubbing," when one wishes to disparage the work of others;[6] "extensive experimentation," "not wanting to impose unwarranted structure on the model," "letting the data speak for themselves," and the like, when one refers to one's own work. But it all comes to the same thing. I shall use the term "data mining."

Data mining is essentially information filtering. Information available to the original tester is withheld when reports of tests are sent to journals or otherwise put into channels of communication. The term "data mining" conjures up an image of people deliberately violating the classical first commandment: In carrying out a hypothesis test thou shalt not allow thyself to be influenced by the data in such a way as to change the original specifications. But in fact data mining may be inadvertent and even unavoidable. Consider the following four cases.

Case 1: "Successful" individual data mining.   An individual researcher has tried many versions of a regression equation and finally found one that "works," in the sense that the t-statistics are significant at the 1 or 5 percent level, the signs of the coefficients are what economic theory says they should be, and so on; in short, the equation is "presentable." The researcher writes a paper and sends it to a journal, making little or no mention of his search activities. He is obviously a true data miner.

Case 2: "Unsuccessful" individual data mining.   Another individual researcher has also tried many versions of a regression equation but has failed to find a presentable one. In spite of heroic efforts he has been unable to get "significant" t-statistics, etc. He gives up and the world never learns of his "failure." We might not recognize this researcher as a data miner if we met him on the street, but he is one nevertheless, perhaps through circumstances rather than choice. The fact that he withheld *all* information about his searching serves to distort the probabilities for test results published by others in the same way that the partial withholding of information in Case 1 does. It represents self-imposed filtering. Had he found a "presentable" equation and written a paper, he might have been fully honest about his search. However, that is irrelevant; it is the fact that his decision to report or not to report any results was based on the "success" or "failure" of the search that does the damage.

Case 3: Coordinated collective data mining.   Suppose that instead of just one researcher there is a team, and that I am the team coordinator. We are working with the same data set as the individual researcher of Case 1. My function is to assign particular regression equations to the members of the team and theirs is to estimate the equations and carry out the associated hypothesis tests. Each member of the team operates independently of the others and within the classical framework: He or she estimates just one equation and then gives the results to me. If his equation is "presentable" I suggest that the member and I write a joint paper in which we report the results. Otherwise I just accept what I have been given and thank the worker for doing a good job. Except for me, no individual is aware of any infraction of the classical rules, but collectively the effect is the same as if I had been working alone as an out-and-out individual data miner. This case is perhaps too artificial to be considered important by itself, but it serves as a lead-in to the next one, which is very important.

Case 4: Uncoordinated collective data mining.   Now assume a population of researchers with no coordinator, but working with a common set of data. Each member of the population is a confirmed classical statistician. Working independently, each chooses a single specification for his or her regression equation, estimates the equation, and does the hypothesis testing exactly as planned. If the researcher is lucky enough to obtain significant t-statistics and to satisfy the other requirements for acceptability, he or she writes a paper and sends it to a journal. Otherwise the researcher gives up and turns to other matters. On no account would he or she consider trying a different model specification. If told that he or she is participating in the mining of data, the researcher would be insulted. But that is the case. Collectively, the population is trying many different regression equations, even though no individual member tries more than one (and even though two or more individuals may, unwittingly, try the same equation). If only those equations that have high t-statistics and other desirable characteristics emerge from this collective activity (i.e., get published), the effect is essentially the same as the effect of individual mining. Uncoordinated collective data mining may be much less efficient than individual mining, but given enough time it can achieve the same result: the trying of all possible models of some process of interest and the reporting to the world about those that "worked."

The consequences of data mining for test probabilities and model selection in the individual researcher setting have been explored by Lovell (1983); collective data mining has been discussed by Denton (1985).[7] The basic problem that gives rise to data mining in either form is that the classical model is quite unrealistic. Search, learning, trial and error, flashes of brilliance, and so on are the essence of processes by which progress is made in science, both by individuals and by scientific communities as a whole, and the filtering of information so as to favor "interesting" over "uninteresting" results and the interpretation of statistical hypothesis tests should recognize these facts.

8. The role of the journals

In a sense, the filtering function performed by journals is also a data-mining function. If referees and editors take account of significance levels and other characteristics of estimated models in making their recommendations and decisions, in such a way that only the most "interesting" results get into print, they are behaving very much like the researchers who chose only the most "presentable" regression equations for submission in the first place. From a reader's point of view they are clearly violating the classical rules. But surely that is just what we expect. The fact that there are biases in the selection of statistical material for publication should not surprise us.

The situation is not unlike that of the general press, television, and radio services in the reporting of "news." The daily newspapers are full of accounts of wars, murders, political announcements, "breakthroughs" in medical science, and other "newsworthy" events, and the selection is certainly not intended to be representative of what is going on in the world or to provide a balanced picture of everyday life. If I read reports of two fires last night I do not expect the newspaper also to provide reports of 100,000 nonfires so that I will get the probabilities right and not think that the whole city was in flames. Similarly, I do not expect the journals to report vast numbers of uninteresting statistical results – and "interesting" in the applied econometrics context very often means "statistically significant." (Surely nobody would long subscribe to a journal containing article after article in which authors stated novel theories and then reported that attempts to find empirical support for them were dismal failures.)

That journals (and other research outlets) distort hypothesis test probabilities by filtering submitted material is, I think, incontestable. To some extent they do this by explicit decisions, but more important, probably, is the self-filtering they induce in researchers. The significance levels that readers should assume in interpreting published test results are clearly not the same as those reported by authors, and by and large they are probably much lower. Given the present style of quantitative economic research, with its mass production of test statistics, I see little possibility of doing much about that, and there is probably little point in trying. The journals may be viewed as a surrogate agency whose function is precisely to try to select for publication only such material as its readers would find interesting.

9. Summing up

Arguments based on the results of formal hypothesis testing (widely used in economics) may be viewed as rhetorical devices. Acceptance of such arguments requires acceptance of the framework developed by statisticians for drawing inferences from experimental data and of the interpretation of that framework by econometricians in ways that are appropriate for the kinds of data they must use. In particular, there must be acceptance of the concepts of unverifiable populations or generating processes and experiments that are repeatable only in the imagination.

The most common testing procedures are ones developed in the Neyman–Pearson framework, on a foundation put in place by R. A. Fisher. Tests of simple against composite (or equality against inequality) hypotheses are generally the most convenient, and by far the most common ones. But hypotheses about economic processes are typically better defined in terms of ranges rather than points or equality restrictions; "close to" is very often a more realistic specification than "exactly equal to." The appropriateness of testing "close to" types of composite hypotheses can be argued on the grounds that the theoretical models to be tested are generally highly simplified or incomplete, and that economic variables are ambiguously defined and imprecisely measured. It can also be argued on the grounds that "close to" is what really matters for economic interpretation. The development of acceptable and easily applicable procedures for handling general forms of composite and "fuzzy" hypotheses would be a valuable contribution to economic analysis and debate.

It would appear that choices of test procedures are very often made on the basis of convention and convenience, without careful consideration of how the test probabilities match with the requirements of the particular problem of applied economic analysis with which the test is supposed to help. The designation of competing hypotheses as "null" and "alternative" and the choice of a significance level typically ignore the fact that the resulting test may have some kind of implied loss function that is inconsistent with the purpose of the analysis. It would appear that attention to underlying probabilities very often takes second place to the adoption of testing rules that may have been set up with goals in mind quite different from those of an economist who has a particular problem to investigate with nonexperimental data, and a particular set of objectives.[8]

The language of the Neyman–Pearson framework is precise and can be interpreted to imply an exact decision-making process. However, in evaluating evidence and debating issues, economists interpret test results quite differently – and so they should. Evidence that is presented as giving strong statistical support to some hypothesis is in fact viewed with caution and skepticism; large discount factors are applied to statements like "the hypothesis is rejected at levels far beyond the 1 percent level of significance."

The nonrandom filtering of information about hypothesis tests can cause large discrepancies between the significance levels appropriate for journal readers and the nominal ones reported by authors. Explicit editorial acceptances or rejections based (in part) on test results are a factor, but implicit self-filtering by researchers is probably much more important. The practice of "data mining" – the selection of only the best statistical results for reporting – represents information filtering and can take different forms. Even if no member of a population of researchers engages in the practice, the population as a whole may inadvertently act so as to produce the same result. In a sense, the journals themselves are "data miners" by virtue of their selection of only the "best" results to pass on to readers. However, the practice of test-based information filtering by journals is both natural and unavoidable. In essence, it is similar to the filtering of "news" by the daily press and other media for the dissemination of information to the general public.

I do not want to leave the impression that I think econometrics has not had a great deal of success in its application of the methods of statistical inference. It has. We have come a very long way in the past half-century, and I think the record of accomplishment is obvious and impressive. I do think that collectively we may have got ourselves somewhat habituated to the use of a particular framework for evaluating empirical evidence, and that consideration of whether that framework is in fact the most appropriate one would be desirable. I find it difficult to get excited about debate over whether classical or (explicitly "subjective") Bayesian analytical approaches should be adopted, as competing and distinct alternatives. It seems to me that more progress will be made if issues of methodology are treated in a less polarized way than seems often to be the case. The classical framework using nonexperimental data already implies a very heavy personal commitment to the entirely "subjective" notion of invisible and unverifiable populations or processes. If allowing in addition the use of "subjective" probability ideas helps to achieve a more useful set of practical tools for organizing and evaluating economic evidence, then so be it. Nobody has to accept somebody else's conclusions; each can question them and evaluate the evidence differently. What matters most is whether different ways of handling data lead to similar conclusions or to quite different ones. If similar, we can have more confidence in the conclusions. If different, we need to await further evidence.

The most convincing test of all in any science is the "interocular trauma test" proposed by Berkson: "[You] know what the data mean when the conclusion hits you between the eyes." [9] Unfortunately, positive results according to this test are scarce in economics. Insensitivity of conclusions over a range of assumptions and methods of analysis would be a good second best.

It is sometimes said, "We are all Bayesians at heart." We never start from scratch; rather we build on earlier work – the whole inheritance of ideas from past history, one might say – and the choice of models to investigate implies some "subjective" prior distribution of probabilities over all conceivable models. Nor do we accept individual test results at face value; we interpret them in light of other information and prior opinions. Perhaps the informal "Bayesianism" that characterizes scientific investigation in the large might be referred to as "bayesianism," with a small b (and apologies to the Reverend Bayes). In any event, "subjectivism" in econometrics is here to say; we are certainly not going to abandon the highly "subjective" concepts and stretches of imagination that are the necessary foundation for probability-based econometric models of any kind. We crossed that bridge a long time ago.

Notes

1. Populations of this kind have been referred to as "superpopulations" in the statistical literature. See Godambe and Thompson (1986).
2. There is much more that could be said about economic data, but too much space would be required. Interesting observations on the subject are provided by Gril-

iches (1985). I think the common separation (in terms of those who do the work) of data provision, on the one hand, from analysis and interpretation, on the other, is a particularly important consideration, as suggested by Griliches.

3. The quotation is from page 13 of the sixth edition of *The Design of Experiments,* which was published in 1951. Without checking, it appears to have been carried forward from the first edition, which was published in 1935.

4. Johnston (1984: 502) refers to "the propensity of editors to publish only significant results."

5. See Denton (1986) for a theoretical treatment of information filtering and some numerical illustrations of its effects.

6. Gordon Tullock has added to this list "data torturing," which is perhaps the best metaphor of all: "if you torture the data long enough, it will confess" (private correspondence). The metaphor is attributed to Ronald Coase.

7. See also the hypothetical data mining example provided by Johnston (1984: 501–4).

8. General concern about the ways in which hypothesis tests are used is found in the statistical literature. Cox (1986) observes, "It has been widely felt, probably for 30 years and more, that significance tests are overemphasized and often misused and that more emphasis should be put on estimation and prediction." Cox's discussion of issues in statistics is of relevance to econometrics.

9. The quotation is taken from Bakan (1970: 251).

References

Bakan, David. 1970. "The Test of Significance in Psychological Research." In *The Significance Test Controversy,* edited by Denton E. Morrison and Ramon E. Henkel. Chicago: Aldine.

Berkson, J. 1938. Some Difficulties of Interpretation Encountered in the Application of the Chi-Square Test." *Journal of the American Statistical Association* 33: 526–36.

Box, Joan Fisher. 1978. *R. A. Fisher, The Life of a Scientist,* New York: Wiley.

Christ, Carl F. 1985. "Early Progress in Estimating Quantitative Economic Relationships in America." *American Economic Review* (December): 39–52.

Cox, D. R. 1986. "Some General Aspects of the Theory of Statistics." *International Statistical Review* (August): 117–26.

Dempster, A. P. 1979. "Life and Work of Ronald Fisher." (A review of *R. A. Fisher, The Life of a Scientist,* by Joan Fisher Box.) *Science* (February 9): 537.

Denton, Frank T. 1985. "Data Mining as an Industry." *Review of Economics and Statistics* 67 (February): 124–7.

———. "Econometric Hypothesis Testing from the Reader's Point of View: The Probabilities Are Not What They Seem to Be." Research Report No. 162. Program for Quantitative Studies in Economics and Population, McMaster University.

Eisenhart, Churchill. "Anniversaries in 1966–67 of Interest to Statisticians, Part I: Introduction and Summary." *American Statistician* (April): 32–4.

Eisenhart, Churchill, and Allan Birnbaum. 1967. "Anniversaries in 1966–67 of Interest to Statisticians, Part II: Tercentennials of Arbuthnot and DeMoivre." *American Statistician* 21 (June): 22–9.

Fisher, Ronald A. 1951. *The Design of Experiments,* 6th ed. Edinburgh: Oliver and Boyd. (Complete set of editions: Edinburgh: Oliver and Boyd, 1935, 1937, 1942, 1947, 1949, 1951, 1960, 1966.)

———. 1970. *Statistical Methods for Research Workers,* 14th ed. Edinburgh: Oliver and Boyd. (Complete set of editions: Edinburgh: Oliver and Boyd, 1925, 1928, 1930, 1932, 1934, 1936, 1938, 1941, 1944, 1946, 1950, 1954, 1958, 1970.)

———. 1973. *Statistical Methods and Scientific Inference,* 3d ed. New York: Hafner. (Earlier editions: Edinburgh: Oliver and Boyd, 1956, 1959.)

Godambe, V. P., and M. E. Thompson. 1986. "Parameters of Superpopulation and Survey Population: Their Relationships and Estimation." *International Statistical Review* 54 (August): 127–38.

Griliches, Zvi. 1985. "Data and Econometricians – The Uneasy Alliance." *American Economic Review* 75 (May): 196–200.

Hacking, Ian. 1965. *Logic of Statistical Inference.* London: Cambridge University Press.

———. 1975. *The Emergence of Probability.* London: Cambridge University Press.

Hildreth, Clifford. 1985. "The Cowles Commission in Chicago, 1939–1955." Discussion Paper no. 225. Center for Economic Research, Department of Economics, University of Minnesota.

Hogben, Lancelot. 1968. *Statistical Theory.* New York: Norton.

Johnston, J. 1984. *Econometric Methods,* 3d ed. New York: McGraw-Hill.

King, Maxwell L. 1983. "Testing for Autoregression Against Moving Average Errors in the Linear Regression Model." *Journal of Econometrics* 21 (January): 35–51.

Leamer, Edward E. 1978. *Specification Searches: Ad Hoc Inference with Nonexperimental Data.* New York: Wiley.

———. 1983. "Let's Take the Con out of Econometrics." *American Economic Review* 73 (March): 31–43.

Lovell, Michael C. 1983. "Data Mining." *Review of Economics and Statistics* 65 (February): 1–12.

McCloskey, Donald N. 1985. "The Loss Function Has Been Mislaid: The Rhetoric of Significance Tests." *American Economic Review* 75 (May): 201–5.

Meehl, Paul E. 1967. "Theory Testing in Psychology and Physics: A Methodological Paradox." *Philosophy of Science* 34 (June): 103–15.

Sterling, Theodore D. 1959. "Publication Decisions and Their Possible Effects on Inferences Drawn from Tests of Significance – or Vice Versa." *Journal of the American Statistical Association* 54 (March): 30–4.

Tullock, Gordon. 1959. "Publication Decisions and Tests of Significance: A Comment." *Journal of the American Statistical Association* 54 (September): 593.

———. 1966. *The Organization of Inquiry.* Durham, N.C.: Duke University Press

CHAPTER 12

The rhetoric of self-interest:
Ideology and gender in economic theory

Nancy Folbre and Heidi Hartmann

Feminism and rhetoric: a parable

Rhetoric and Feminism met on a morning run around the lake at Wellesley College. They were both there to work on Economics, trying to get him into better shape to deal with changing realities.

RHETORIC *(breathing heavily):* This is rough going. I can't seem to make these economists see the underlying assumptions that structure their models. They're all talking about me instead.

FEMINISM *(treading lightly):* I know what you mean. They really cling to this notion that perfect self-interest rules in the market and perfect altruism rules in the home. They're certainly not maximizing our joint utility.

RHETORIC: Let's get together. You concentrate on the ideological substance of their argument, showing how it benefits men. I'll use logic to show them that their assumptions are inconsistent.

FEMINISM: You mean you'll divert them with Latin terms while I take away some of their privileges?

RHETORIC: Well, if it doesn't work, we could always get married and settle down.

FEMINISM: Yeah, but who's going to take care of the kids?

* * *

The contents of basic economics texts and research journals suggest that economists don't like to talk about inequality between men and women (Feiner and Morgan 1985). Most economists seem persuaded that gender inequalities lie beyond the purview of economic analysis, either in the realm of biological givens or sociological imponderables. In this chapter we hope to persuade otherwise and to show how and why this particular economic con-

We gratefully acknowledge the comments and criticisms of Ann Ferguson, Arjo Klamer, John Nelson, Kate Oser, and Helen Smith.

versation has been circumscribed. We argue that certain assumptions embodied in the rhetoric of economics have deafened most economists to the possibility that economic motives help explain inequality between the sexes.

Our strategy is somewhat McCloskeyesque (1985). Rather than developing an empirical or historical analysis, we critically examine the logic and consistency of a set of basic assumptions that have divided the economist's world into two parts, variously designated public and private, market and household, economic and noneconomic, self-interested and altruistic, male and female. Like McCloskey, we are critical of the rhetorical intent of these sharp dichotomies. Unlike McCloskey, we believe this rhetoric has a strong ideological component. Some arguments persuade more than others partly because they deliver greater benefits to those who decide the outcome of the debate. In particular, we argue here that economic self-interest has influenced the way economists think about the concept of self-interest.

Within both the neoclassical and Marxian traditions predominantly male economists have assumed that individual self-interest motivates men's decisions in the capitalist marketplace, but does not motivate men or women in the private sphere of the home. Many economists have explored the relationship between the concept of "rational economic man" and the rise of capitalism (Hung 1986; Elster 1979; Hirschman 1977). But most economists have overlooked the relationship between "rational economic man" and the patriarchal dimensions of capitalist society. At least two rhetorical devices have disguised an important relationship between the rhetoric of self-interest and the rhetoric of gender: Within the neoclassical tradition, the assumption of a joint utility function has obscured the possibility of conflicts between individuals in the family. Within the Marxian tradition, the assumption that class interests are primary has obscured the possibility of conflicts between individuals within the same class.

As a result, both paradigms idealize the family, placing very strict limits on the operation of self-interest there (Hartman 1981; Folbre 1986). By virtue of their association with this distinctly non-self-interested and therefore "noneconomic" domain, women themselves came to be portrayed as relatively "noneconomic creatures." This portrayal played an important part in early arguments against women's political and legal emancipation and is still used as a rationalization of gender-based inequalities. The image of the "selfless woman" initially proved an effective rhetorical device for reconciling male domination with economic theory. But early feminist economists quarreled with this image. And contemporary feminist economists have documented considerable economic conflict between men and women. Their research complements and strengthens other current efforts to overcome the traditional conceptual segregation of self-interest and altruism.

In the first section of this chapter we trace the gender-biased rhetoric of individual self-interest through the neoclassical tradition from its progenitors in eighteenth-century political philosophy to contemporary empirical research. Within this tradition the concept of a moral, altruistic family has been used not only to legitimate inequalities between men and women, but also to fend off the argument that moral and altruistic concerns might apply to the capitalist marketplace. In the second section we turn our attention to the Marxian tradition, where the emphasis on class interests and the desire to apply the ideals of "brotherhood" to the larger economy often led to an idealization of family life and a denial of gender-based inequalities.[1] In the third section we describe a research literature that has emerged from feminist dissent in both major traditions, and review contemporary research that suggests that economic self-interest has shaped many inequalities between men and women. In a brief conclusion we suggest how feminist insights can contribute to the development of a new economics, one in which responsibility for altruism is no longer assigned to women, or confined to the family.

1. The neoclassical rhetoric of self-interest

The economic individualism so central to neoclassical economic theory could better be termed male individualism. Most of the progenitors of economic theory defined women as wives or mothers, not as individuals; modern empirical work often asserts that women are not as economically rational or self-interested as men. A strict rhetorical boundary between the impersonal world of men and the personal world of women has helped protect the marketplace from moral criticism and insulated gender relations from economic scrutiny.

The roots of modern methodological individualism lie in seventeenth-century political theory that emphasized free exchange between individuals. In his classic exploration of the theories of Thomas Hobbes and John Locke, C. B. McPherson (1962) provides an apt description of the emphasis on free exchange, including the concept of human capital:

> Society becomes a lot of free equal individuals related to each other as proprietors of their own capacities and of what they have acquired by their exercise. Society consists of relations of exchange between proprietors. Political society becomes a calculated device for the protection of this property and for the maintenance of an orderly relation of exchange. (p. 3)

The "possessive" quality of this individualism inheres in the concept of man as proprietor of his own person or capacities, owing nothing to society for them. As a result, liberal democratic theory always focused on relations between adult men. Hobbes himself recognized that parental affection was inconsistent with his central metaphor for human society, the "war of all against all." He stipulated that his theory dealt only with adult men, in his words, "men sprung out of the earth and suddenly, like mushrooms, come to full maturity, without all kind of engagement to each other" (DiStefano 1984, p. 6). He ignored the years of nurturance, provision, and protection that men, unlike mushrooms, require.

Both Hobbes and Locke strengthened the presumption that men had no obligation to society by ignoring the types of relationships that might have incurred such obligation. As Nancy Hartsock (1983: 41–2) observes, this "lack of obligation" in liberal democratic theory could be asserted only if family life, and specifically child rearing, were bracketed and excluded from analysis. She writes, "One could begin to see the outline of a very different kind of community if one took the mother/infant relation rather than market exchange as the prototypic human interaction" (1983: 41–2).

Adam Smith, who transposed many of the assumptions of the liberal democratic tradition into his explanation of economic growth and development, also avoided consideration of economic relationships outside the marketplace. He did, however, take pains to counterbalance his praise of the pursuit of individual self-interest in the market with the claim that a natural affection that required no explanation ruled within the family. Smith made the normative implications (and the ideological baggage) quite clear: Individuals should be selfish in the impersonal marketplace, where the invisible hand would ensure that private interests served the public good. In the family, however, the helping hand should prevail. Selfishness there would be unnatural, inefficient, and uncivilized.

The most famous quotation from *The Wealth of Nations* reads: "It is not from the benevolence of the butcher, the brewer, or the baker that we expect our dinner but from their regard to their self interest." (Smith 1937). But Smith never pointed out that these purveyors do not in fact make dinner. Nor did he consider that wives might prepare dinner for their husbands out of regard for their self-interest. He was not the least bit skeptical of the benevolence of fathers and husbands. In *The Theory of Moral Sentiments* Smith (1966) drew a line between public and private primarily to assign economics to the former and morality to the latter. He did not resort to a simple dichotomy, but designated separate spheres or concentric circles, each with their "corresponding mixture of benevolence to oneself and benevolence to others" (Reisman 1976: 70). Family and friends came closest to the innermost circle of the male self.[7]

This confidence in the moral sentiments of family life proved a powerful device for denying women's rights, for it implied that women, as daughters or wives, enjoyed the protection of family membership. Shortly before the passage of the English Reform Act of 1832 in Britain, which extended the franchise to a wider circle of property-owning males, James Mill published an article in the *Encyclopaedia Britannica* that dismissed the argument for female voting rights with what may be the first historical formulation of the concept of a joint utility function:

> One thing is pretty clear, that all those individuals whose interests are indisputably included in those of other individuals may be struck off without inconvenience. In this light may be viewed all children, up to a certain age, whose interests are involved in those of their parents. In this light also, women may be regarded, the interests of almost all of whom is involved either in that of their fathers or in that of their husbands. (Mill 1825: 122)

Women's presumed lack of selfish motivation was not always used against them in such a simplistic way. Some opponents of female emancipation observed that women were not very good at pursuing their own interests, and would therefore only suffer if treated as individuals. Others insisted that women would be corrupted by contact with the world of selfish individualism, and men would suffer the loss of their civilizing influence. Herbert Spencer (1876) cautioned that women's participation in government would lead to a disastrous welfare state, because women's natural altruism might run amok (p. 414).

Contemporary neoclassical economists are more tolerant of the notion of a welfare state, but continue to treat the "female realm" separately from the "male realm" of individualism. For instance, the field of welfare economics largely foundered under the weight of objections to the aggregation of individual utilities in social welfare functions (Arrow 1963), yet prominent economists from Samuelson (1956) to Becker (1976a) have had little quarrel with the aggregation of individual utilities within the family, because they believe consensus and altruism reign there. The historical continuity of the predisposition to confine interdependent utilities to the family is most apparent in Becker's *Treatise on the Family* where "the advantages of altruism in improving the wellbeing of children and parents are contrasted with its disadvantages in market transactions" (Becker 1981b: 1).

Becker advances the argument by conceding that selfishness can rear its ugly head in the family in the form of a "rotten kid." But in order to explain why individual family members do not free-ride on the benevolence of other family members, Becker actually resorts to the concept of a benevolent dictator. In his words, "parents may use contingent transfers of wealth to provide children with a long run incentive to consider the interests of the whole family" (1981b: 188). "Selfishness" in the family is kept strictly in bounds, associated with the immature behavior of kids, rather than the calculating behavior of adults. Those who hold power are altruistic; only those who don't have it, but want it, are rotten (Hirshleifer 1977; Pollak 1985).

Relatively few economists share Becker's interest in explaining the economics of family life. But the assumption of a joint utility function within the family pervades the empirical literature on women's work in the home and in the paid labor force. The most widely accepted model of female labor supply postulates that women simply compare the marginal product of work they could perform in the home with the wage they could receive in the market and measure both against the utility of leisure (Mincer 1980; Gronau 1980). If women earn less than men in the marketplace but are more productive in the home, they will specialize in home production and maximize the family's joint utility. The possibility that there might be unequal distribution of the products of home production or that independent access to market income might affect the allocation of goods and leisure within the home is simply never entertained.

Even a recent study that purports to analyze the allocation of "full income" (market income plus the imputed value of home work) between men and women builds on the joint utility function assumption (Fuchs 1984, 1986). By imputing a value to women's household labor that is based on their wage income, Fuchs assumes that the source of income is irrelevant to the distribution of its benefits. Under the assumption of equal sharing within the household, Fuchs arrives at the conclusion that increased labor force participation actually made most women worse off relative to men in 1983 than in 1959.[3]

Neoclassical approaches to household decisions regarding fertility carry the assumption of joint utility (and concomitant absence of conflict of interest within the family) to an extreme. Fertility decline is attributed entirely to changes in relative prices – a decrease in the economic benefits of young children because of increased education and reduced child labor force participation and an increase in the cost of women's time because of increased education and increased female labor force participation (Schultz 1981). Possible differences in the distribution of costs and benefits of children to mothers and fathers (or even children themselves) are excluded from consideration. For instance Rosenzweig and Schultz (1982) hypothesize that it was "economically efficient" for Indian families to allocate fewer resources to female children because their potential wages were lower than those of male children. The joint utility function approach assumes that female children would have concurred in this decision for "the good of the family" (Folbre 1984).

Building on the argument that women have a comparative advantage in household production and therefore choose to specialize in it, many neoclassical economists argue that women place a higher priority on the welfare of their family than on the level of their wages. In a version of occupational choice that Karen Nussbaum of 9to5, the National Association of Working

Women, calls the "lemming theory" of women's wages, Mincer and Pola-chek (1974, 1978) and Polachek (1981) argue that women choose low-paying female-dominated jobs because they will experience less wage loss in such jobs when they leave and reenter for family-related reasons. Goldin (1985) offers another explanation of how women themselves are to blame for the lower wages they received in the course of U.S. economic development: They underestimated their future labor force participation and therefore underinvested in job-related skills. By these accounts, women are less economically self-interested than men in the marketplace. And men, presumably interested only in maximizing joint utility, have no economic motive to discourage women from gaining job skills that might increase their economic independence.

The policy implications are clear: If neither men nor employers have any reason to discourage women from seeking better-paying jobs, then women must voluntarily choose not to seek better-paying jobs. Responding to a discrimination suit filed by the Equal Opportunities Commission, Sears, Roebuck and Company brought in an expert witness who told the court that women did not want sales jobs that paid a commission because such positions conflict with home and family values (Weiner 1985). Other expert witnesses disagreed. But even those who agree should address the following question: Why are demanding, high-paying jobs for women at odds with traditional home and family values? One possible answer is that men assign the somewhat thankless task of defending those values to women. As women gain economic independence they begin to question the economic double standard that sanctions selfishness only in men. Once extended beyond the male world of markets, the individual pursuit of self-interest not only threatens traditional values, but also seems far less appealing as a principle for organizing production and exchange.

2. The Marxian rhetoric of class interest

Economists of the Marxian tradition have long railed against the abuses created by unbridled self-interest in the market economy. Indeed, Marx and Engels marveled at the contradictory consequences of the rise of capitalism, which in their words "drowned the most heavenly ectasies of religious fervor, of chivalrous enthusiasm, of philistine sentimentalism, in the icy water of egotistical calculation" (Marx and Engels 1972: 337). But the Marxian rhetoric of class interest, like the neoclassical rhetoric of self-interest, excludes women and the family from the domain of economic rationality.

While neoclassical economists confine the concept of self-interest to the marketplace and use the rhetoric of joint utility to avoid consideration of conflicts within the family, Marxist economists confine the concept of exploitation to the capitalist firm and use the rhetoric of class solidarity to avoid the possibility of exploitation in the home. The adjective *patriarchal* sometimes appears in *Capital* before the word *family*, but Marx generally treated the family as a wholly cooperative unit. Influenced, perhaps, by Hegel's vision of the family as a purely ethical realm (Landes 1982), Marx wrote that "Individual labour powers, by their very nature, act only as instruments of the joint labour power of the family" (Marx 1977: 171). Joint labor power, in this context, is clearly analogous to joint utility. And the consequences of the virtually unspoken assumption are just as far reaching. Marx's analysis of capitalism sidestepped the issues of household production and childrearing and made it difficult to even conceptualize the possibility of exploitation in the home (Folbre 1982).

Class interest has traditionally been defined largely in terms of the interests of working-class men. As Benenson (1984) and Taylor (1983) point out, Marx broke decisively from the utopian socialist vision of the moral transformation of both family and work to formulate what he believed to be a more "scientific" theory of the historical role of the industrial proletariat. This theory "incorporated basic elements of the outlook of the organized, mainly skilled working men of the 1840s, including the male worker's conception of himself as the sole, rightful breadwinner for the working class family" (Benenson 1984: 1). Thus, members of families are assumed to have the same class membership and class interests as their male wage earner (Acker 1973).

More contemporary Marxist analyses of the household and the labor market often treat the family as though it were a miniature, idealized socialist society; they tend to minimize potential conflicts between men and women in the home and the workplace (Hartmann 1981). Housework itself has primarily been analyzed in terms of its consequences for capital accumulation (Dalla Costa 1973); much of the debate has revolved around the issue of whether housework produces surplus value for capital (Himmelweit and Mohun 1977; Seccombe 1974; Harrison 1973). The actual labor process of housework is ignored.

In his historical account of the impact of capitalism on the family Zaretsky (1973) goes so far as to suggest that women only "appear" to work for men in the home; in reality they work for capitalists. Many empirical studies of households in developing countries focus on the extraction of surplus from the peasant household as a whole and argue that women's domestic labor primarily benefits capital (Deere 1983; Deere and DeJanvry 1979). These studies largely bypass the opportunity to explore inequality in the allocation of time and goods between men and women within peasant households (Folbre 1986). Marxian analyses of population growth and fertility decisions are also couched in a rhetoric of class interest that presumes no differences between men and women in the economic consequences of children (Mamdani 1972;

Gregory and Piche 1982). Even Seccombe, who devotes considerable attention to patriarchal social relations and their influence on population growth, assumes that the interests of mothers largely coincide with the interests of fathers (Seccombe 1983).

Neither women's interests as individual women, nor their class interests as self-conscious proletarians are themes in the classic Marxian labor history literature. Thompson's (1963) enormously influential study of the development of class consciousness, *The Making of the English Working Class,* never recognizes women as a significant portion of wage earners nor acknowledges male trade unionists' efforts to exclude women from skilled jobs. The rhetoric of class interest simply subsumes the possibility of gender interests. Occasionally, this subsumption is made explicit, as in Humphries' (1979) account of the struggle for a family wage in England. She argues that English women chose to withhold their labor from the market (and thus relinquish the economic independence that wage work might have given them) in order to raise the wages of working-class males and thereby enhance the welfare of the family as a whole. The parallel with Polachek's theory of occupational segregation, discussed earlier, is obvious.

Contemporary Marxist labor economists recognize the importance of gender differences, but never really translate this into an analysis of gender interests. Braverman's (1974) account of the emergence of clerical occupations initiated a welcome reorientation towards service jobs that include many women workers as well as traditional male blue-collar jobs (see also Sacks and Remy 1984). Still, this book never considers the possibility that jobs may appear "deskilled" simply because women, whose skills tend to be undervalued, begin to fill them. Similarly, Gordon, Reich, and Edwards (1982) emphasize the segregation of the labor force along both sexual and racial lines, but largely attribute this segregation to the efforts and interests of capitalists, rather than to white male coworkers, who also played a critical role (Hartmann 1976).

The typical Marxist diagnosis of current economic trends elides over gender interests in a similar way. When Currie, Dunn, and Fogarty (1980) marshal considerable data showing that working-class families are experiencing considerable economic stress, they treat the words *family* and *women* interchangeably. They are certainly correct to point out that working-class families face the double burden of earning wage income and rearing children. But do men and women share the burden equally? They never ask (WMFTSG 1982).

In short, the rhetoric of class interest, like the rhetoric of self-interest, circumscribes issues of inequality between men and women. It protects men's privileges from economic scrutiny even as it protects Marxist theory from a somewhat disabling question. If conflict and exploitation can intrude even in intimate, personal relationships, isn't a theory of economic transformation based on the dialectic of class interests alone seriously incomplete? The feminist answer to that question is a resounding yes.

3. The feminist rhetoric of gender interest

Feminist economic approaches, however diverse, are all suspicious of any rhetoric that describes women as less self-interested than men or automatically places gender interests on a lower level of analysis than family interests or class interests. Early feminist dissenters pointed to the ideological character of the argument that women altruistically choose a subordinate position within the economic division of labor. Much contemporary feminist research focuses on the causes and consequences of unequal power between men and women. And much of this research provides a better explanation of economic trends in households and in the labor market than research informed solely by the two theoretical perspectives described above.

By most criteria, John Stuart Mill and his acknowledged coauthor, Harriet Taylor, fall squarely within the neoclassical tradition. Unlike their contemporaries, however, they refused to respect the artificial boundary between personal economy and political economy. The anomalous quality of their writings on women is evidenced by the virtual absence of any discussion of them in most texts on the history of economic thought. Even those that allude to Mill's socialist tendencies avoid mention of his feminism (Spiegel 1983; Hunt 1979).

With Taylor's assistance, Mill published an entire treatise entitled *The Subjection of Women* in 1869. But the most concise statement of his criticism of received economic theory was made during the parliamentary debates over the Second Reform Bill in 1867. Mill attacked the concept of joint utility that his father had brandished more than forty years before. His blistering irony was directed at socialists who opposed women's rights, as well as at conservatives:

> The interests of all women are safe in the hands of their fathers, husbands, and brother, who have the same interest with them, and not only know, far better than they do, what is good for them, but care much more for them than they care for themselves. Sir, this is exactly what is said of all unrepresented classes. The operatives, for instance; are they not virtually represented by the representation of their employers? Are not the interests of the employers and that of the employed, when properly understood, the same? . . . And, generally speaking, have not employers and employed a common inter-

est against all outsiders, just as husband and wife have against all outside the family? And what is more, are not all employers good, kind, benevolent men, who love their workpeople, and always desire to do what is most for their good? All these assertions are as true, and as much to the purpose, as the corresponding assertions respecting men and women. (Mill 1869: 486)

In order to make his meaning absolutely clear, Mill went on to describe the horrors of domestic violence.

Mill believed there were important differences between men and women. But as far as self-interest was concerned, he attributed the difference to education and socialization: "If women are better than men in anything it surely is in individual self-sacrifice for those of their own family. But I lay little stress on this, so long as they are universally taught that they are born and created for self-sacrifice" (1869: 396). About thirty years later Charlotte Perkins Gilman, a socialist and feminist economist with a distinctively eclectic theoretical perspective, argued that women specialized in household production for "self-sacrifice" largely because they had little choice. "The female of genus homo is economically dependent on the male. He is her food supply" (Gilman 1966: 22).

A feminist voice can also be heard within the nineteenth-century Marxian paradigm. In *The Origin of the Family, Private Property and the State,* published in 1884, Frederick Engels pointed to a analogy between women and workers. Among propertied families, he wrote, "he (the male breadwinner) is the bourgeois; the wife represents the proletariat" (Engels 1948: 74). Engels diluted the analogy by stipulating that working-class families were not patriarchal because both men and women were wage earners and both lacked private property. Furthermore, he ignored the concept and content of household labor, restricting the concept of work to the production of commodities. Nevertheless he introduced the concept of economic self-interest into an analysis of relations between the sexes when he explained the possible origins of women's subordination. The details of his explanation are far less important than the fact that he described historical circumstances that made women less powerful than men, not biological differences that made women more altruistic.

None of the arguments developed by Mill, Taylor, Gilman, and Engels were consistent with the prevailing rhetoric of economic interests. And orthodox economists of both the neoclassical and Marxian traditions were perhaps too embarrassed by the personal, feminine, and therefore "unscientific" tenor of the issue to pursue it further. Indeed, the exclusion of gender interests helped reinforce the boundary between "humanism" and "science" that has lent the profession its positivist credibility (McCloskey 1985). Over the past fifteen years, however, feminist theory has generated a large body of historical and empirical research.

The growing sources of evidence that the household is a locus of economic conflict, as well as cooperation, are summarized in Hartmann (1981) and Folbre (1986). As Bergmann (1981) succinctly puts it, the "economic risks of being a housewife" are extremely high. Time-budget studies that document inequality in the allocation of goods and leisure time suggest that men and women exercise unequal bargaining power in the family because the costs of family dissolution are much higher for women than for men (Weiss 1984; McElroy and Horney 1981).

The balance of power shifts in complex and contradictory ways in the course of capitalist development. Women clearly gain greater economic independence when they engage in wage labor, and increase their incomes as well. Spalter-Roth (1984) recently looked at the dollar earnings of wives per hour worked (including wage work hours and housework hours) relative to husbands and concluded that women had increased their relative return per hour of labor, by transferring their hours from unwaged to wage labor. On the other hand, men gain considerable freedom from child care and child support responsibilities (Pearce 1979; Folbre 1984).

McCrate's (1985) empirical study of marriage rates in the United States suggests they are inversely related to women's opportunities for income outside of marriage. Fertility decline can also be linked to changes in the relative bargaining power of men and women, parents and children. When children increase their economic independence from parents and diminish their economic contributions to their family of origin, they effectively raise their own "price." When women demand help with child care, whether from husbands or from society as a whole, the redistribution of the costs of children can be as influential as changes in the level of costs (Folbre 1983).

Feminist approaches to the labor market do not reject the notion that there may be differences in men's and women's goals, but suggest that these are often overstated and exaggerated because they serve as rationalization for women's lower wages and limited opportunities. Recent reviews of the psychology and sociology literature concerning the extent to which different individuals value financial rewards, status, freedom from supervision, creativity, working with people, helping others, and so on, failed to find significant differences by gender (Reskin and Hartmann 1986: 60). Women's commitment to family is not necessarily a function of their preferences or their productivity. It is often constrained by the reluctance of other family members to help with housework and child care responsibilities.

Feldberg and Glenn (1979) point out that the a priori assumption that women are primarily concerned with family issues can lead to serious misinterpretation of the behavior of women workers. For instance, when absenteeism in a female-dominated job is high, it is often assumed that family obligations are the cause. But wages and working conditions may play a much more important role; when similar jobs are compared, male and female absenteeism rates are not significantly different (Blau and Ferber 1986). Women are more likely than men to work part-time and to drop out of the labor force for extended periods. But contrary to Mincer and Polachek (1974, 1978), women's commitment to family responsibilities does not explain their lower wages. Several studies show that women and men experience little wage loss upon return from a labor market absence and make up the difference quickly. Women do not gain from specialization in "female occupations." They would do better in regard to earnings if they entered male-dominated occupations where earnings gains are greater over a lifetime (Corcoran et al. 1984; England 1984).

Within the Marxian tradition, feminists have begun to explore the ways men's economic interests have shaped the exclusion of women from certain jobs (Kessler-Harris 1982; Hartmann 1976). Foner's (1979) history of the U.S. trade union movement documents the extent to which men resisted competition from women. In contrast to Braverman's argument that class conflict was the primary determinant of "deskilling," Philips and Taylor (1980) cite research on London sewers in garment manufacturing to show how men succeeded in defining women's work as less skilled. Women were not merely restricted to the less skilled and lowest-paid jobs – the jobs they performed were labeled "less skilled" in order to justify lower pay levels. Davies (1982) suggests a similar dynamic was at work in the feminization of the clerical labor force in the United States.

Skepticism about the relationship between women's pay and their actual productivity has fueled the issue of comparable worth. Many job evaluation studies show that women's jobs are remunerated at a lower level than men's jobs with the same characteristics (Hartmann 1985; Remick 1984; Sorensen 1985). Others have pointed out that women's particular skills in human relations and communication, sometimes termed "emotional labor," have been largely ignored (Hochschild 1983; Alexander 1986). Telling women that caring for others is part of their nature, rather than an important form of work, is one way of lowering the cost of getting such care.

4. Towards a better theory of interests

If the traditional rhetoric of economic interest is flawed by its failure to acknowledge the full range of interests in modern society, the remedy does not lie simply in lengthening the list. The feminist approach laid out above might be accused of a masculinist bias in method. If the pursuit of individual self-interest is good for the gander, it should be good for the goose, the gander's protests notwithstanding. But the feminist argument should not be reduced to this retaliatory logic, because it also brings the traditional boundaries between self-interest and altruism into question and suggests that they may be as overdrawn as the traditional boundaries between science and humanism, facts and values, public and private, reason and emotion, male and female (Jagger 1983). A growing body of interdisciplinary feminist research complements the efforts many economists are making to develop a more complete theory of economic interests, one that can encompass concepts like cooperation, loyalty, and reciprocity.

The caricature of irrational, noneconomic woman has always had a counterpart in the caricature of rational economic man. And in recent years, rational economic man has received something of a theoretical battering. Simon (1978) has accused him of satisficing rather than maximizing. Leibenstein (1976) has asserted that his work performance may be partly explained by intangibles, such as his state of mind and motivation. Akerlof (1982) "feminized" rational man even further when he suggested that workers acquire sentiment for each other and for the firm and that labor contracts represent a partial gift exchange. This new emphasis on the complexity of market behavior is perfectly consistent with the feminist insistence on the complexity of family behavior: In both arenas, complex overlays of self-interest and reciprocity are at work.

Neoclassical economists have traditionally been skeptical of any cooperative behavior because of its associated free rider problems (Olson 1975); Marxian theorists have often assumed that the elimination of class differences would be a sufficient condition for effective economic cooperation. In recent years, however, economists have begun to develop more sophisticated models of group behavior and to analyze cooperation in game-theoretic terms. Maital and Maital (1984) argue that appropriate socialization or enforcement mechanisms can make cooperation an effective long-run strategy for optimization. Schotter (1981) among others, suggests that customs and habits may represent a more efficient solution to certain coordination problems than the market. As North (1981) points out, shared ideals are among the most important mechanisms of cooperation that help solve free rider problems. Feminist historians have done an excellent job documenting the evolution of ideals of manhood and womanhood and their influence on both the home and the workplace (Welter 1973; Cott 1977; Ryan 1979).

The lack of attention to feminist theory has actually hampered economists' efforts to recast their methodology. For instance, Elster (1979) argues eloquently that the polarities of irrationality and rationality should be supplanted by a theory of imperfect rationality, one that encompasses coercion, seduction, and persuasion, as well as voluntary choice (p. 36). Yet he partially undermines his intent with the title of his book, *Ulysses and the Sirens: Studies in Rationality and Irrationality*. The metaphor conveys the image of rational (albeit imperfect) Ulysses threatened by the feminine voices of temptation. But Ulysses also knows how to tempt. McCrate's (1985) recent research on changes in marriage rates offers an excellent application of the concept of imperfect rationality: She points out that purely rational men would have responded to increases in women's economic bargaining power by redistributing the burdens of housework and the rewards of marriage. Instead, male resistance to change contributed to the increase in marital dissolution.

Elster redefines the word *solidarity* as "conditional altruism, as distinct from the unconditional altruism of the categorical imperative and the unconditional egoism of capitalist society" (1979: 21). While the concept of solidarity is relevant to an understanding of class definition and cohesion, it can also be applied to an analysis of the kinds of reciprocity and loyalty based on nation, race, gender, and family. Feminist historians have begun to explore the ways in which class and gender interests (Kessler-Harris 1982) and race and gender interests (Jones 1986) cross-cut and interact.

From a feminist standpoint, it is encouraging to see economists step beyond the bounds of positivism to bring other boundaries into question. Serious consideration of both the rhetoric and the ideology of economics can not only enhance awareness of hidden assumptions, but also help to make those assumptions more realistic. The Hobbesian metaphor is wrong. Neither men nor women spring out of the earth as fully mature individuals, ready to exchange or fight. Rather, girls and boys are born into the care of people whose task is to find and to teach a balance between individual self-interest and collective responsibility. That balance cannot be achieved by simply assigning one to men in the marketplace and the other to women in the home.

Notes

1. Our focus here is on a subset of important rhetorical devices: the concepts of self-interest and joint utility, class interest and class solidarity. Other concepts clearly relevant to a better understanding of the ideology of gender in Marxist theory include production, productive labor, and surplus value.
2. Smith's solution remained problematic. How to delimit the boundaries between the public and the private, the impersonal and the personal? Where to draw the line – at immediate kin, all blood relations, or members of the same club? The problem was best solved by elision, and indeed, after Adam Smith, economists proved increasingly reluctant to examine men's behavior anywhere except in markets. Texts on the history of economic thought sometimes casually note that Smith's concerns with morality reflected the immaturity of economics as a science. Because family relationships carry the moral taint, best to delegate them to other, less scientific disciplines.

3. Fuchs does consider one alternative distributional assumption, "proportionate sharing," in which women and men share in total family income according to their proportionate contribution to that income, where income includes the imputed value of housework. By this assumption, most women fared slightly better relative to men over the 1959–83 period. We would argue for a different distributional assumption. Following McElroy and Horney (1981) and England and Farkas (1986), (1) relative bargaining power has an important impact on household distribution, and (2) market income strengthens bargaining power more than the imputed value of household services (which are often nontransferable and household specific). Therefore, our hypothesis would be that increased labor force participation increased women's share in total household income and made them considerably better off. This hypothesis seems more consistent with the observed increases in female labor force participation, whereas Fuchs is largely unable to explain why women's preference for market income was "revealed preferred."

References

Acker, Joan. 1973. "Women and Stratification: A Case of Intellectual Sexism." *American Journal of Sociology* 78 (January): 936–45.

Akerlof, George. 1982. "Labor Contracts as Partial Gift Exchange." *Quarterly Journal of Economics* 97 (4): 543–70.

Alexander, David. 1986. "Gendered Job Traits and Women's Occupations." Unpublished Ph.D. dissertation, Department of Economics, University of Massachusetts, Amherst, Massachusetts.

Arrow, Kenneth. 1963. *Social Choice and Individual Values*. New Haven: Yale University Press.

Becker, Gary S. 1976. "Altruism, Egotism and Genetic Fitness: Economics and Sociobiology." *Journal of Economic Literature* 14 (September): 817–26.

———. 1976. *The Economic Approach to Human Behavior.* Chicago: University of Chicago Press.

———. 1981a. "Altruism in the Family and Selfishness in the Market Place." *Economica* 48(1): 1–15.

———. 1981b. *A Treatise on the Family*. Cambridge, Mass.: Harvard University Press.

Benenson, Harold. 1984. "Victorian Sexual Ideology and Marx's Theory of the Working Class." *International Labor and Working Class History* 25 (Spring): 1–23.

Bergmann, B. 1981. "The Economic Risks of Being a Housewife." *American Economic Review* 7 (May): 81–6.

———. 1986. *The Economic Emergence of American Women*. New York: Basic Books.

Blau, Francine D., and Marianne A. Ferber. 1986. *The Economics of Women and Work*. Englewood Cliffs, N.J.: Prentice-Hall.

Braverman, Harry. 1974. *Labor and Monopoly Capital: The Degradation of Work in the Twentieth Century*. New York: Monthly Review Press.

Corcoran, Mary, Greg Duncan, and Michael Ponza. 1984. "Work Experience, Job

Segregation and Wages." in *Sex Segregation in the Workplace: Trends, Explanations, and Remedies,* edited by Barbara F. Reskin. Washington, D.C. National Academy Press.

Cott, Nancy. 1977. *The Bonds of Womanhood.* New Haven: Yale University Press.

Currie, E. Dunn, and D. Fogarty. 1980. "The New Immiseration: Stagflation, Inequality, and the Working Class." *Socialist Review* 54 (November–December): 7–31.

Davies, Margery W. 1982. *Woman's Place Is at the Typewriter: Office Work and Office Workers, 1870–1930.* Philadelphia: Temple University Press.

Deere, Carmen Diana. 1983. "The Allocation of Familial Labor and the Formation of Peasant Household Income in the Sierra." In *Women and Poverty in the Third World,* edited by Mayra Buvinic, Margaret A. Lycette, and William Paul McGreevey. Baltimore: Johns Hopkins University Press.

Deere, Carmen Diana, and Alain de Janvry. 1979. "A Conceptual Framework for the Empirical Analysis of Peasants." *American Journal of Agricultural Economics* 61(4): 601–11.

DiStefano, Christine. 1984. "In Search of the Missing Mother: Maternal Subtexts in Political Theory." Paper presented to the Eastern Division Fall Conference on the Society for Women in Philosophy, November 3–4.

Elster, Jon. 1979. *Ulysses and the Sirens: Studies in Rationality and Irrationality.* Cambridge: Cambridge University Press.

Engels, Frederick. 1948. *The Origin of the Family, Private Property and the State.* Moscow: Progress Publishers.

England, Paula. 1984. "Wage Appreciation and Depreciation: A Test of Neoclassical Economic Explanations of Occupational Sex Segregation." *Social Forces* 62(3): 726–49.

Feiner, Susan, and Barbara Morgan. 1985. "Hidden by the Invisible Hand: Race and Gender in Introductory Economics Textbooks." Paper presented at the annual meetings of the American Economic Association, December, New York.

Feldberg, R. L., and E. N. Glenn. 1979. "Male and Female: Job vs. Gender Models in the Sociology of Work." *Social Problems* 26(5): 524–38.

Folbre, Nancy. 1982. "Exploitation Comes Home: A Critique of the Marxian Theory of Family Labour." *Cambridge Journal of Economics* 6(4): 317–29.

———. 1983. "Of Patriarchy Born: The Political Economy of Fertility Decisions." *Feminist Studies* 9(Summer): 269–84.

———. 1984. "Market Opportunities, Genetic Endowments and Intrafamily Resource Distribution: A Comment." *American Economic Review* 74 (June): 518–22.

———. 1986. "Cleaning House: New Perspectives on Households and Economic Development." *Journal of Development Economics* 22(1): 5–40.

Foner, Phillip. 1979. *Women and the American Labor Movement: From Colonial Times to the Eve of World War I.* New York: Free Press.

Fuchs, Victor R. 1984. "His and Hers: Gender Differences in Work and Income, 1959–1979." NBER Working Paper No. 1501. National Bureau of Economic Research, Cambridge, Massachusetts, November.

———. 1986. "Sex Differences in Economic Well-Being." *Science* (April 25, 1986), 459–64.

Gilman, Charlotte Perkins. 1966. *Women and Economics.* New York: Harper & Row. Originally published by Small, Maynard and Co., Boston, in 1898.

Goldin, C. 1985. "Understanding the Gender Gap: An Historical Perspective." National Bureau of Economic Research Discussion Paper.

Gregory, J. W., and V. Piche. 1982. "African Population: Reproduction for Whom?" *Daedalus* 111(Spring): 179–210.

Gronau, R. 1980. "Home Production: A Forgotten Industry," *Review of Economics and Statistics* 62 (August): 408–16.

Harrison, J. 1973. "The Political Economy of Housework." *Bulletin of the Conference of Socialist Economists* 4(1).

Hartmann, Heidi. 1974. Capitalism and Women's Work in the Home, 1900–1930. Unpublished Ph.D. dissertation, Yale University 1974. Available from University Microfilms, Ann Arbor, Michigan, 1975.

———. 1976. "Capitalism, Patriarchy and Job Segregation by Sex." *Signs* 1 (Spring, Part 2): 137–69.

———. 1981. "The Family as the Locus of Gender, Class, and Political Struggle: The Example of Housework." *Signs* 6(3): 366–394.

———, editor. 1985. *Comparable Worth: New Directions for Research.* Washington, D.C.: National Academy Press.

Hartsock, Nancy. 1983. *Money, Sex and Power: Toward a Feminist Historical Materialism.* New York: Longman.

Himmelweit, Sue, and Simon Mohun. 1977. "Domestic Labour and Capital." *Cambridge Journal of Economics* 1 (March): 15–31.

Hirschman, Albert. 1977. *The Passions and the Interests: Political Arguments for Capitalism Before Its Triumph.* Princeton, N.J.: Princeton University Press.

Hirshleifer, Jack. 1977. "Shakespeare v. Becker on Altruism: The Importance of Having the Last Word." *Journal of Economic Literature* 15(2): 500–2.

Hochschild, Arlie. 1983. *The Managed Heart: Commercialization of Human Feeling.* Berkeley: University of California.

Humphries, Jane. 1979. "Class Struggle and the Persistence of the Working Class Family." *Cambridge Journal of Economics* 1 (September): 241–58.

Hunt, E. K. 1979. *History of Economic Thought: A Critical Perspective.* Belmont, Calif.: Wadsworth.

Jaggar, Alison. 1983. *Feminist Politics and Human Nature.* Totowa, N.J.: Rowman and Allanheld.

Jones, Jennifer. 1986. *Labor of Love, Labor of Sorrow: Black Women, Work and the Family, from Slavery to the Present.* New York: Vintage Books.

Kessler-Harris, A. 1982. *Out to Work: A History of Wage-Earning Women in the U.S.* New York: Oxford University Press.

Landes, Joan. 1982. "Hegel's Conception of the Family." In *The Family in Political Thought,* edited by Jean Bethke Elshtain. Amherst: University of Massachusetts Press.

Leibenstein, Harvey. 1976. *Beyond Economic Man: A New Foundation for Microeconomics.* Cambridge, Mass.: Harvard University Press.

McCloskey, Donald. 1985. *The Rhetoric of Economics.* Madison: University of Wisconsin Press.

McCrate, Elaine. 1985. "The Growth of Non-Marriage Among U.S. Women, 1956–1983: Neoclassical and Feminist Explanations." Unpublished manuscript, Department of Economics, University of Vermont, Burlington, Vermont.

McElroy, M., and M. J. Horney. 1981. "Nash-bargained Household Decisions: Toward a Generalization of the Theory of Demand." *International Economic Review* 22(June): 333–49.

McPherson, C. B. 1982. *The Political Theory of Possessive Individualism: Hobbes to Locke.* Oxford: Oxford University Press.

Maital, Shlomo, and Sharone Maital. 1984. *Economic Games People Play.* New York: Basic Books.

Malthus, Thomas. 1976. *An Essay on the Principle of Population.* New York: Norton.

Mamdani, M. 1972. *The Myth of Population Control: Family, Caste and Class in an Indian Village.* New York: Monthly Review Press.

Marx, Karl. 1977. *Capital.* New York: Vintage Books.

Marx, Karl, and Frederick Engels. 1972. "Manifesto of the Communist Party." In *The Marx–Engels Reader,* edited by Robert C. Tucker. New York: Norton.

Mill, James. 1825. "Article on Government." Reprinted in *Women, the Family, and Freedom,* edited by Susan Groag Bell and Karen M. Offen. Stanford: Stanford University Press.

Mill, John Stuart. 1869. "Speech Before the House of Commons, 20 May 1869." Reprinted in *Women, the Family and Freedom,* edited by Susan Groag Bell and Karen M. Offen. Stanford: Stanford University Press.

Mincer, Jacob. 1980. "Labor Force Participation of Married Women: A Study of Labor Supply." In *Economics of Women and Work,* edited by Alice Amsden. New York: St. Martin's Press.

Mincer, J., and S. Polachek. 1974. "Women's Earnings Reexamined." *Journal of Human Resources* 13 (1): 118–34.

Mincer, J., and S. Polachek. 1978. "Family Investments in Human-Capital-Earnings of Women." *Journal of Political Economy* 82 (2): 76–108.

North, Douglass. 1981. *Structure and Change in Economic History.* New York: Norton.

Olson, Mancur. 1975. *The Logic of Collective Action: Public Goods and the Theory of Groups.* Cambridge, Mass.: Harvard University Press.

Oser, Jacob. 1970. *The Evolution of Economic Thought.* New York: Harcourt, Brace and World.

Pearce, Diana. 1979. "Women, Work and Welfare: The Feminization of Poverty." In *Working Women and Their Families,* edited by Karen Feinstine, 101–24. London: Sage.

Philips, Anne, and Barbara Taylor. 1980. "Sex and Skill: Notes Towards a Feminist Economics." *Feminist Review* 6: 79–88.

Polachek, Solomon. 1981. "Occupational Self-Selection: A Human Capital Approach to Sex Difference-Occupational Structure." *Review of Economics and Statistics* 63 (February): 60–9.

Pollak, Robert A. 1985. "A Transaction Cost Approach to Families and Households." *Journal of Economic Literature* 23 (June): 581–608.

Remick, Helen, editor. 1984. *Comparable Worth and Wage Discrimination: Technical Possibilities and Political Realities.* Philadelphia: Temple University Press.

Reisman, David A. 1976. *Adam Smith's Sociological Economics*. New York: Barnes & Noble.

Reskin, Barbara, and Heidi Hartmann, editors. 1986. *Women's Work, Men's Work*. Washington, D.C.: National Academy Press.

Rosenzweig, Mark, and T. Paul Schultz. 1982. "Market Opportunities, Genetic Endowments and Intrafamily Resource Distribution." *American Economic Review* 72(4): 803–15.

Ryan, Mary. 1979. *Womanhood in America: From Colonial Times to the Present*. New York: New Viewpoints.

Sacks, Karen Brodkin, and Dorothy Remy. 1984. *My Troubles Are Going to Have Trouble with Me. Everyday Trials and Triumphs of Women Workers*. New Brunswick, N.J.: Rutgers University Press.

Schotter, Andrew. 1981. *An Economic Theory of Social Institutions*. London: Cambridge University Press.

Schultz, T. Paul. 1981. *Economics of Population*. Reading, Mass.: Addison-Wesley.

Seccombe, Wally. 1974. "The Housewife and Her Labour Under Capitalism." *New Left Review* 137.

———. 1983. "Marxism and Demography." *New Left Review* (January–February): 22–47.

Simon, Herbert. 1978. "Rationality as Process and Product of Thought." *American Economic Review* 68(2): 1–16.

Smith, Adam. 1937. *An Inquiry into the Nature and Causes of the Wealth of Nations*. New York: Random House. Originally published 1776.

———. 1966. *The Theory of Moral Sentiments*. New York: Augustus Kelley.

Sorensen, Elaine. 1986. "Implementing Comparable Worth: A Survey of Recent Job Evaluation Studies." *American Economic Review* 76(May): 364–7.

Spiegel, H. 1983. *The Growth of Economic Thought*, rev. and expanded ed. Durham, N.C.: Duke University Press.

Taylor, Barbara. 1983. *Eve and the New Jerusalem: Socialism and Feminism in the Nineteenth Century*. New York: Pantheon.

Thompson, E. P. 1963. *The Making of the English Working Class*. New York: Vintage Books.

WMFTSG (Washington Area Marxist-Feminist Theory Study Group). 1982. "None Dare Call It Patriarchy. A Critique of 'The New Immiseration.' " *Socialist Review* 61 (January–February): 105–111.

Weiner, Jon. 1985. "Women's History on Trial." *The Nation* (September 7, 1985), 175–80.

Weiss, Robert S. 1984. "The Impact of Marital Dissolution on Income and Consumption in Single-Parent Households." *Journal of Marriage and the Family* 46 (February): 115–27.

Welter, Barbara. 1973. "The Cult of True Womanhood: 1820–1860." In *The American Family in Social-Historical Perspective*, edited by Michael Gordon. New York: St. Martin's Press.

Zaretsky, Eli. 1973. "Capitalism, the Family and Personal Life – Part I." In *Socialist Revolution*, 13–14, 66–125.

PART IV

Economic rhetoric in politics and journalism

CHAPTER 13

The heterogeneity of the economists' discourse:
Philosopher, priest, and hired gun

Craufurd D. Goodwin

Causes of variety

To the layperson it seems that an economist is an economist is an economist. When the economists emerge from their lairs they all sound the same and use the same arguments and analytical tools. Superficially, at least, their statements are predictable, with frequent reference to expensive lunches and trade-offs, enlivened only occasionally by obscure internal squabbles and controversies over fine points of theory. To one who is familiar with the confusing history of the discipline, the situation appears infinitely more complex. Not only is the "profession" of "economist" ill defined and riven by methodological and ideological differences, but most members converse professionally with many kinds of partners on a wide range of subjects. Few fields of science reveal such diversity of conversation. Several features of economics are at least unusual, if not unique.

First, paradigmatic cleavages persist for extended periods, reflecting both methodological and ideological differences of a fundamental character, not only between Marxians and neoclassical economists, but among Keynesians, post-Keynesians, neo-Institutionalists, monetarists, and a host of other smaller sects. Second, and probably of greater significance, the community of economists has never fully come to grips with the difference between a scientific "discipline" pursuing truth and a "profession" selling services at market prices. To complicate the situation, the profession's rhetorical products are in demand both in the public sector, where, in principle, the "public good" is the norm, and also in the private sector, where private gain is the objective.

Even though the number of economists has increased dramatically in the last half of the twentieth century there have been few attempts to distinguish formally the larger profession of practicing economists, selling their rhetorical products for many purposes, from the smaller subset, or disciplinary community, of "pure" economic scientists. In consequence there is at best a

I am grateful to Jane Rossetti for help in preparation of this paper and to the Ford Foundation for financial support.

blurred distinction between the practice of persuading scientific colleagues in disciplinary discourse and the persuasion of a wider public, or segments thereof, undertaken by professional economist-practitioners. No distinguishing pairs of words have emerged to reflect the distinctively different objectives of the two communities of economist-scientists and economist-practitioners (such as physicist/engineer, biologist/physician, theologian/cleric, and so on). Nor have guides to conduct (including rhetorical conduct) emerged for economist-practitioners, like the Hippocratic oath for physicians or licensing standards for engineers. It may be that in professional style economists have become most like lawyers, for whom, until recently at least, few distinctions have been made between theorist and practitioner. An important difference from economics, however, is that while in the law the practitioner has been the dominant partner, in economics the scientist has retained the upper hand.

The reasons for the blurred scientist-practitioner distinction in economics lies in the development of the subject. In particular, many scholar-economists have come to fear the effect practitioner-economists may have on the very system that is their subject of study and therefore have not come to grips with their existence. From the time of the Physiocrats and Adam Smith in the eighteenth century economists have seen danger in an ambitious state and in the machinations of well-organized special interests who would subvert a market system and fix prices different from those of competitive equilibria. Administered prices serve the narrow self-interest of some groups in society but injure others overall. A separate economics "profession," distinct from an economics discipline, presented an opportunity for unscrupulous professionals to serve those dubious masters. These "practicing" economists would become engaged in planning either an extension of the public sector or the schemes of special interests to achieve market imperfection. As the ultimate irony economists might become themselves the very rent seekers they had been trained to root out and expose rather than the efficiency and growth seekers they were taught to admire. They would become like those most hated figures in the discipline's dimly remembered past, the Cameralists and the Mercantilists. The proclivity of heretical groups in the backwaters of the discipline to seek careers as practitioners, notably the Institutionalists, Keynesians, and economic historians, gave "economic practice" an especially bad name.

Uneasiness about the growth of a profession of economist-practitioners, oriented toward the sale of services rather than the search for "truth," has not impeded the vibrancy of the market for these services. It has complicated it, however. The dubious reputability of "practice" may, for example, explain the remarkable occupational mobility of prominent professionals. Leading economists are renowned for their movement in and out of academe, government service, think tanks, and private business. This restlessness may be simply a quest for variety. But it may also reflect a sense that true respectability lies alone with the first of these occupations, even though excitement and financial rewards lie with the others. One's conscience and repute must be restored periodically by a return to the scientific Mecca of academe.

An appreciation of this history is important to gaining an understanding of the rhetoric of economics because peculiarities of professional and disciplinary development are reflected in the discourse in which economists engage. Moreover, if the complexity and heterogeneity of style and activity are as great as the history suggests, we should look for fully as great a variety in the conversations.

The complexity of the scientist/practitioner dichotomy is complicated by yet a third rhetorical challenge for economists. In addition to their scientific colleagues and clients, private and governmental, there is a third audience whose importance grows primarily out of the needs of the Western democracies during the past two centuries. Economists have been impelled both by their disciplinary imperatives and by the urgings of others to convey their messages to a large and unsophisticated audience, so that this multitude of decision makers on issues of public policy (voters, legislators, the media, and so on) can be adequately informed when making choices. This third function for economists has meant that they must interpret the science for public policy and persuade a lay audience of the wisdom of this interpretation. These three rhetorical postures of economists may be characterized by analogy as scholar, practitioner, and interpreter or alternatively as (1) philosopher, (2) priest, and (3) hired gun.[1]

A variety of rhetorical modes and styles was recognized, of course, by Aristotle, the father of rhetorical analysis, who distinguished among political, forensic, and ceremonial persuasion, the first two of which concern us here and correspond roughly to the priestly and gunslinging categories. Aristotle noted that political rhetoric, which deals with advocacy of particular paths into the future, is more difficult to carry on than forensic, which concerns interpretations of the past. This simple Aristotelian taxonomy, like the three-part division just proposed, however, conceals much of the complexity of the rhetorical tasks that face a typical modern economist over a career. These include, at least, persuasion of economist colleagues of the merit in contributions to the discipline (represented in journal articles, papers presented to conferences, and claims for tenure); persuasion of skeptical students and college administrators of the value of studying the subject; persuasion of patrons, such as foundations and government agencies, that funds should be directed to it; persuasion of legislators, the media, and a broad lay public that the subject's "answers" to popular questions are worth attending; persuasion of clients that advice based on economic analysis is sound; and persuasion of judges and other arbiters that a client's case is sound while an opponent's is weak.

The reluctance of economists by and large to recognize squarely and self-consciously their diversity of roles has undoubtedly complicated their rhetoric. This complexity, and even a confusion of styles, is compounded when two or even three roles are assumed by a single economist over a career. The careers of just two prominent economists of the postwar years – one in macroeconomics, the other in micro – will illustrate this point. The first is the late Arthur Okun. In the early years of his career as a distinguished scholar at Yale University Okun was the quintessential philosopher/scientist, speaking mainly to his counterparts within the discipline and attempting to persuade them of the value in his scientific contributions. In the second segment of his career as economic adviser to the president, he hoped by his own account for a role as economist-priest, delivering interpretations of economic wisdom to the executive branch. He soon found himself, perforce, acting as hired gun, operating as part of the White House "team" and supporting, even though *sotto voce,* policies and practices with which he did not entirely agree. Then in the third part of his career Okun went to the Brookings Institution, where as senior fellow his role became truly that of the priest, addressing mainly a Washington audience with the policy implications of macroeconomic theory.

The other illuminating career is that of Alfred Kahn, who played the role of microeconomic scientist at Cornell University and moved into that of economist-priest as a member of the Civil Aeronautics Board, where his rhetorical powers became legendary as the principal advocate of airline deregulation. Finally Kahn took on a role as economic consultant to regulated industries, defending rhetorically as hired gun the interests of those whose behavior he had long deplored as philosopher and priest.

These examples suggest that not only can great rhetorical diversity be expected among economists playing the distinct roles of philosopher, priest, and hired gun, but this diversity may be accommodated even in the career of a single individual, either through successive stages of professional development and consecutive appointments, or even through contemporaneous activities in two or all three roles together. Fascinating research opportunities lie open for analysis of the different forms of rhetoric exhibited in these several roles of the economist and perhaps for discovery of the interaction among these roles and the rhetorical demands they create.

Most of the study to date of the rhetoric of economists deals with their efforts as philosophers to persuade each other within the discipline. To get some sense of the different rhetoric that takes place elsewhere, the two sections that follow present examples of economists as priest and hired gun.

Proclamation of sin

Over the two centuries of modern economics the policy questions discussed most often by economists have revolved around proposals for trade protection. One thinks immediately of the Corn Law Debates, Imperial Preference, the Zollverein, the Common Market, and Smoot-Hawley. The notion of placing restraints on flows of goods flies in the face of the principle that efficiency, and perhaps even some measure of distributive justice, can be attained best in a free market system. To be sure, economists from Adam Smith onward have been prepared to make limited exceptions to the rule of free trade. But they have felt required to defend exceptions carefully and with the understanding that they are guilty until proven innocent. Lying always in the professional subconscious has been the memory of those dreadful "mercantilists," willing to sacrifice the public good for private gain, against whom classical economics came to life. If there is the equivalent of anti-Christ in economics, it is the proponent of trade restraint. And if there is a fall from grace, it is demonstrated by an appeal for what economists call "rent seeking."

After the Marginal Revolution of the 1870s the virtues of free trade were explained mainly with terminology and metaphor taken from physics and engineering. The market economy constituted a "system," wherein "forces" led to "outcomes" in equilibrium. Money as the "wheel" or "lubricant" of commerce traveled through the system at a certain "velocity." At the international level economic activity is manifested in "balances" of trade and payments. First, a gold standard of "fixed" rates, and then "flexible" exchange rates acted as "adjustment mechanisms." Alfred Marshall, despite his flirtation with other metaphors, pictured the economy as a battleship, the ultimate engineering accomplishment of his day.

The metaphors of physics as a way to illuminate the virtues of free markets have persisted over two centuries, unto the present day. In the words of one contemporary user of this style while addressing a lay audience, protection amounts to "driving a wedge" into the "delicate balance" of the economic "system."[2] Here the economy is visualized as a machine or a clock into which villains throw sand or even a monkey wrench.

But economists have not persisted universally, or even predominantly, in the use of mechanical images to persuade the lay public of the significance of free trade. Instead, two alternative metaphorical devices, neither of which has a prominent place in the "scientific" language of the economics profession, appear prominently.

The first device is to picture the economy and the units within it as a biological rather than as a physical or mechanical entity. Biological analogies, of course, do have a place in the history of economic ideas. They played a role in the thought of the German Historical School and the American Institutionalists. John Stuart Mill was willing even to contemplate "infant industry" protection, and Marshall liked to visualize firms as trees in the forest, rising and falling and struggling always for nutrients and light. But in general such biological devices were removed from the purified form of neoclassical economics, whether of a partial or general equilibrium variety.

Even in a rather casual survey of only a few modern works we see the biological metaphor return prominently in the presentation by economists of their views about trade protection. And interestingly, the appeal to biology comes from economists of many varied ideological and methodological positions. For example, Lester Thurow pictures the economy more as a Darwinian jungle than a self-regulating machine or a clock. Protection arises, he suggests, when the inefficient, weak, and unselected members of society refuse to accept the purification process under way and seek to impede it. "At the first sign of trouble everyone runs to the government looking for protection."[3]

An extension of this genetic analogy to the global trading system can be found in the report of the Brandt Commission entitled *North-South: A Program for Survival*. The economist authors of this document portray the world economy as an evolving biological organism with interdependent parts, some of which are always becoming obsolete or redundant and in the normal course of events will slough off. Protection is a misguided attempt to keep these dying appendages in place, to sustain an ecosystem that is no longer viable. Protection seeks to preserve the unnatural and artificial and to impede the natural processes of adaptation to change. The international division of labor is, indeed, simply the global dimension of the Darwinian process of natural selection. It is "a dynamic process which calls for continuous adaptation and adjustment on the part of all countries." "Free and growing trade" is the natural result of the survival of the economically most fit, and while natural selection brings discomfort "protectionism hurts."[4]

A normal progression in the economist's use of biological metaphors seems to be from the theory of evolution to applied biology or a kind of social medicine. Alice Rivlin interprets protection as a mistaken therapy of prescribing palliatives to the economy in response to "painful change" and the perception of "injury." Economic evolution does indeed yield "victims of change" whose pain cannot be "avoided." But the economist-physician must be careful not to prescribe treatment that will "obstruct" healing through structural adaptation. The responsible doctor will "facilitate adjustment" and alleviate suffering only if in so doing a return to long-run health is not delayed.[5]

The expository literature of economists on world trade policy is full of such biological, medical, and public health images. Terms like *victim, injury, hurt,* and *loser* abound. The general posture is of sympathy toward those whose health and welfare are negatively affected. But there is a sense also that genetic improvement will be the beneficent outcome of inaction, and while it is proper to minister to the sick and dying, society must be ever on guard against proclamations of false cures (like protection) for what is in truth not really a disease. The profession of quack medicine may attract the gullible and give them false hope, but it will also damage them and the society in which they live in the long run.

The other rhetorical technique that some economists use to explain issues of trade to the larger public has an even thinner history in the scientific literature than the biological and medical metaphors. Advocates of some form of limitation of trade often convert the notion of beneficent struggle present in the genetic simile to a picture of predatory conflict, suggesting the need for national defense and requiring for its understanding the use of notions taken over from a study of warfare. Typically those modern economists who favor some form of interference with trade use the vocabulary of strategy and warfare to make their case. Indeed, the very term "protection" itself comes out of this tradition. Words long embedded in the terminology of international economic policy reflect this position that mutually beneficial relations can degenerate quickly into conflict and require recourse to unilateral action. "Dumping," "trigger-price mechanisms," "predatory pricing" are only a few examples. Joan Robinson, whose descendants at Cambridge argue still for some measure of commercial autarky for Britain, pictured world trade in 1967 as head-to-head struggle among combatants that Britain had once "dominated." Now the nation had to "defend" itself from "rivals" who threatened to "knock out" its exports. In the face of "stiffened" competition Britain had to put up "powerful resistance" and redress the "balance of power." Protection, she argued, was not a long-term solution to Britain's weakness, but it was a short-term "check."[6]

The metaphors of conflict are used by some critics of trade protection as well as by its advocates. A volume growing out of the Council on Foreign Relations' "1980s Project" speaks of the world "retreating" into protectionism and erecting "barriers" in a misguided attempt to "safeguard" industries and employment. Nations offer "concessions" and plan "intervention."[7] Gary Hufbauer and Jeffrey Schott also discuss "the strategic goal" of extending GATT in the face of "an armada of contingent protection that can be easily deployed to impede the flow of free trade." They reflect on how to overcome "entrenched barriers" and avoid tariff "escalation." Mixing their metaphors somewhat, they see free trade areas as "a useful foil against protectionist pressures."[8]

George Schultz and Kenneth Dam, who later in the department of state had the opportunity to practice what they preached, describe the controversy over trade policy within the United States as analogous to warfare. The clear implication of their statements is that free trade, which in their view needs no further justification, is under serious attack from the forces of darkness and the challenge is to "hold them at bay" and keep the "danger" "under control." It is necessary "to fight the recurrent tendency" toward protectionism, to resist demands to raise trade "barriers." In this regard "the best defense is a good offense," and efforts must be made to prevent trade legislation from becoming "a protectionist weapon" that ultimately would "threaten" exports. They wished to "arrest" protection, "attack" nontariff barriers, and "avoid losing ground in the battle to maintain open trade channels."[9]

Alice Rivlin, too, uses the metaphors of warlike conflict as well as of biological struggle to explain trade policy. She refers to "strategies," "tactics," "fail-safe systems," "deterrent effects" and "challenges."

This brief review of a set of texts that illustrate the rhetorical efforts of economists as priests rather than as philosophers raises questions and only suggests tentative answers. How did metaphors from biology, genetics, and military conflict come to dominate the rhetorical treatment of a subject at the policy level long illuminated by economists through allusion to physics at the scientific level? Was this transformation conscious or unconscious? Was it a reaction to the rhetorical successes and failures of others, on other topics and in other fields? Were the precise policy implications of the science changed by the shift in rhetorical style? Was the content of "scientific" discussion affected by these excursions at the policy level into novel rhetorical territory? Aristotle suggests that determinants of an effective rhetorical style are the capacities to demonstrate "personal goodness" (in this case scientific disinterestedness), to put the audience in a congenial frame of mind (here through the use of familiar metaphors and lines of argument), and to demonstrate proof or apparent proof (in this case by analogy to biological processes and health, with which any large audience is familiar). These priestly economists certainly did not read Aristotle before approaching their rhetorical tasks. But instinctively they may have pursued an Aristotelian strategy, or at least a strategy that is easily comprehended from a reading of Aristotle's insights.

Persuasion of patrons

The strongest case of gunslinging by professional economists is service as consultant-witnesses before regulatory commissions and boards of inquiry. Here economists act like lawyers, engaging in forensic rhetoric on behalf of a client, with the search for truth a secondary or even inconsistent consideration. The client has a certain clear objective: to be granted higher prices, a change in legislation, a license, or some other favor. The economist's task is to use all the means of persuasion at hand to gain this objective. If the client's interests are forgotten for long the economist's fat consulting fees will certainly disappear, which tends to concentrate the mind and discipline the rhetoric.

A much less militant style of gunslinging can be seen in relations between economists and less overtly self-interested patrons of their teaching and research. Unquestionably dependence and deference can be found in this relationship, too, but in more subtle form. At least since the mid-1940s economists have become skilled at addressing actual and potential patrons, in part because the kind of training and research they conduct require substantial amounts of money, but in part also because they enjoy the wide stage on which thereby they step. They have gained a mounting sense that they have answers to important questions and they relish the opportunity, through access to resources, to put them into effect.

In order to gain a feeling for how economists present their case to those from whom they seek support, a series of documents from the 1960s and 1970s were examined in the Archives of the Ford Foundation, which were directed by their economist authors (consultants and staff members) to the management and trustees of the foundation concerning some aspect of the economics field. They all deal, directly or indirectly, with whether to subsidize the development of economic science in the United States and elsewhere in the world. The papers were commissioned by the foundation; they were not direct applications for aid. But they were exercises in rhetoric all the same. These are just a small sample of the flood of paper that came to the foundation from economists during these years. Their function was neither to importune nor to implore, but to persuade and direct foundation programming if they could.

As one might expect, economists here do use conventional economic arguments extensively to make the case for support of the field. "The demand for economists is already so large and it is increasing so rapidly, . . ." said T. W. Schultz in a report on economic education in Latin America, that further additions of trained economists were highly desirable.[10] Another perspective consultant suggested, however, that with philanthropic intervention in the market for the training of economists "Say's Law will operate in reverse; given a firm Foundation statement of its demand, demand will create its own supply."[11] Schultz argued that foundation intervention could increase "institutional competition to provide criticism," which was an "essential safeguard" to quality among economists.[12]

In offering advice to the foundation about how to disburse its resources on economics in the developing world two consultants (Nancy and Richard Ruggles) advised against using universities unless they underwent major reform. "The marginal productivity of efforts in this direction" they wrote "is therefore likely to be low relative to what might be accomplished in other directions."[13] In allocating money for the training of economists, as in all other things, another team of consultants advised that the foundation should seek "efficiency, i.e. with the greatest benefit for a given cost, or the least cost for a given benefit."[14] Lest anyone wonder whether these conditions were present for the support of economics, a staff member (Richard Dye) reported that in contrast to support of the "hard" sciences, "the marginal return on our investment in the social sciences may be higher."[15]

The familiar economist's metaphor of the social "mechanic" appeared prominently and often in these papers. A good economist, the foundation was told, had "competent command of the analytical tools" that he kept in good repair through regular use in "research workshops." In an appraisal of one university it was noted that "fourth year students in undergraduate economics are thought to be as competent as those finishing in engineering. . . ." The general picture of economics that is painted is of a tough discipline with a "received basic analytical core," knowledge of which leads to "competence in using tools." The empirical "physical sciences" are presented as the standard by which economics should be judged in Latin America as elsewhere. The adjective *real* is used repeatedly to modify all kinds of approved activity by economists (for example, research), which was presented as a contrast to "literary" and philosophical speculation and other undesirable endeavors.[16] Excellent centers for research and training were described typically as high-powered and strong with well-defined standards.

Efforts are made repeatedly to identify economics with hard sciences both by describing comparable "tools" among them and by eschewing any substantial remaining links with the humanities. Indeed, the failure of one university to make substantial progress in economics is attributed to the stubborn and anachronistic desire of the dean to retain such contacts. "Much as his humanistic inclination is valuable in the formation of students, of economics or of anything else, his apparent lack of awareness of the greater precision that must be given to the teaching of economics has prevented a radical reform from being carried out. . . ."[17]

Even though within the discipline itself in the 1960s the issue of economics "practice" as distinct from science was far from settled, these consultants accept the notion of some schools (for example, Yale, Williams, Vanderbilt) turning out "practitioners" on the engineering model, for service at least in developing countries. Just as engineering schools should avoid curriculum that is "too high powered," so these economic practitioners should be "trained in techniques and equipment." Taking the analogy to engineering still further, a team of advisors made up of Martin Bronfenbrenner, Charles Kindleberger, and Ben Lewis worried that the practitioners headed for new countries should not be exposed "to an environment of . . . high-powered abstractions without ever getting their hands dirty."[18]

An identity that is often fostered in these documents is between economic knowledge and citizen education in some fundamental sense. Richard Ruggles made the case for economic literacy as "a buffer against the specific special interest groups." Indeed, he argued that a "general economic understanding" was necessary "for a democracy to survive."[19]

The newness of modern economics is stressed repeatedly: a representative economist-commentator on economics in Latin America applauded one country with "a missionary spirit in the air" where "there is little tolerance for traditional solutions." In another "the inspirational atmosphere . . . is to some degree contagious."[20]

Yet in addressing the philanthropic patron these economists, like the writers on trade protection, were not fully at ease with the physics–engineering metaphor alone. Especially when considering the application of economics to the problems of new countries the style became more varied and more biological. The American graduate school was compared to an evolutionary struggle for which the foreign student "by individual temperament or cultural background" might be "unfit." The central concept of progress tended to be framed in terms more complex than those that carry over from physics and engineering. Growth became development, and "extending the frontiers of knowledge" rather than simple research became a goal, albeit a rather vague one.[21]

Twenty years and eight examples cannot make a trend. Nevertheless there does seem to be a discernible change in the content and style of these documents over the period. In the early years when self-confidence among the economist authors was high, the parallels of economics in theory and practice to physics and engineering are drawn often, both explicitly and implicitly. In the later years, however, as economic problems mount at home and abroad for which economists have few easy answers, the posture of the economist advisors seems to change, and with it their style. In the 1970s the notion of the 1960s is seldom pressed that economics is a neat self-contained science with its own well-defined kit of "tools." Instead the papers begin to suggest that economics may, in fact, not be "universal in concept, logic, data, or methodology." Moreover, this science is neither "value nor culture free." In particular, admitted one economist staff member (Edward Edwards), "the growing disillusionment with production and growth as the sole criteria for economic progress and social development has led governments and the Foundation to become more concerned about the inputs which economists and other social scientists can provide on other dimensions of development. . . ." Put positively, the foundation found it increasingly desirable "to integrate physical, economic and social planning" and to seek devices for "recombining the non-economic social sciences with economics."[22]

One result of this change of mood and attitude toward economics among its patrons seems to have been a shift in the posture of the economists toward the promise of their subject, and incidentally in their use of metaphor. Instead of suggesting as they did in the 1960s ''we have the tools, let us finish the job,'' they suggested in the 1970s that the economy was in fact full of mystery that required much study to understand and great art to attend. From the engineering analogies of the 1960s there is a shift to the metaphors of medicine and even of the new, burgeoning field of microelectronics.

A background paper on ''Economics and the Ford Foundation'' prepared by Vice President Marshall Robinson (economist and former business school dean) speaks of the economy as a ''black box,'' whose innards might now be usefully opened to view.[23] The paper stresses the ''woefully deficient'' ''store of factual information about the economy.'' Regrettably, in the face of deep concerns about ''economic health'' the discipline of economics remained ''preoccupied with abstract models and . . . 'closed system' thinking. . . .'' A comparison is drawn between economics and population studies, the latter ''enriched and transformed by medical people, biologists, sociologists and, of all things, anthropologists. . . .'' The implications are clear: ''[The] needs of a healthy economy'' continue to dictate widespread ''economic literacy'' but also a broadened economics discipline doing more than ''narrow puzzle-solving in the niches of the economic literature'' and prepared to cope with the darkest corners of that ''enigmatic black box.''

These few observations about a small number of pieces of evidence about a particular form of economists' forensic rhetoric suggests considerable complexity. Some findings are unsurprising – the use of the economist's own jargon and analytical devices as a way of persuading patrons. But there are also surprises – the recourse to biological, medical, and microelectronic metaphors coincident with the loss of self-confidence. Undoubtedly closer and more sophisticated scrutiny of this and similar material would uncover further anomalies.

Conclusion

This chapter suggests that few conclusions can be reached about economists' rhetoric without disaggregation and detailed examination. It appears from this dip into the literature of economics beyond the strict disciplinary conversations that for different audiences, and for different partners in various colloquies, economists use varied rhetorical styles and forms of argument. When attempting to persuade laypersons, economists abandon to some degree the physical and mechanical metaphors they employ so widely in their own research and either pick the forbidden fruit of biology and medicine or move into realms one might think they were ill equipped to understand, such as the analysis of human conflict.

One explanation may be that in a shrewdly calculating fashion economists find the rhetorical style that will work most effectively with laypersons, be it reference to public health, warfare, or microelectronics. They cleverly translate the substance of their discipline, where the style of physics prevails, into forms that others can understand through the rhetorical structures currently fashionable or at least prevalent. This explanation is of limited use simply because there is no evidence that this kind of rational calculation occurs.

A second and more plausible explanation is that economists subconsciously find themselves thinking, when dealing with their field outside their discipline, in the forms that are predominant among their audience rather than in the science. As members of society they, too, worry about their health and nuclear destruction, and when they are freed from the strict conventions and rules of conversation within their scholarly discipline they slip into these colloquial forms of thought when they explain and interpret their subject for a wider audience.

Still a third explanation is that a confrontation with a lay audience is where economists can let their minds soar and where they may visualize problems in ways that, at the moment, their profession prohibits. If this is true, the very heterogeneity of economists' conversation may be the means whereby ultimately the search will be enriched. The confining rules through which disciplinary progress is made are relaxed when philosophers become priests or even hired guns, and in the process they become better philosophers.

Attention to the rhetoric of economics need not be an alternative to more traditional historical, sociological, and philosophical attempts to understand how the discipline and profession now operate and have evolved. But it does have the capacity to supplement and to inform these more traditional approaches with new questions and new answers.

Notes

1. George Stigler has used part of this terminology for a narrower purpose. He finds that some economists act as "preachers" but he doubts their effect: "We are well received in the measure that we preach what the society wishes to hear." *The Economist as Preacher and Other Essays* (University of Chicago Press, 1982), 13.
2. Gottfried Haberler, *Essays in Contemporary Economic Problems, 1985* (Washington, D.C.: American Enterprise Institute, 1985).
3. Lester Thurow, *Zero-Sum Society* (New York: Basic Books, 1980).
4. Brandt Commission, *North South: A Program for Survival* (Cambridge, Mass.: MIT Press, 1980).
5. Alice Rivlin, *Economic Choices* (Washington, D.C.: Brookings Institution, 1984).
6. Joan Robinson, *Economics: An Awkward Corner* (New York: Random House, 1967).

7. Miriam Camps, ed., *Collective Management* (New York: McGraw-Hill, 1981).
8. Gary Hufbauer and Jeffrey Schott, *Trading for Growth* (Washington, D.C.: Institute for International Economics, 1985).
9. George Schultz and Kenneth Dam, *Economic Policy Beyond the Headlines* (New York: Norton, 1977).
10. T. W. Schultz to Reynold Carlson, September 26, 1963, p. 2, ACC 000007.
11. Martin Bronfenbrenner, Charles Kindleberger, and Ben Lewis, et al., "The Adequacy of Facilities in the United States for the Training of Economists from Underdeveloped Countries," April 27, 1963, p. 23, ACC 000418.
12. Schultz to Carlson, p. 3.
13. Richard Ruggles and Nancy Ruggles, "Economic Research and Training in Latin America," Summary, ACC 000252.
14. Bronfenbrenner et al., "The Adequacy of Facilities," p. 1.
15. Richard W. Dye, "The Ford Foundation and Economics in Peru," December 1970, p. 2, ACC 001967.
16. Schultz to Carlson, pp. 3, 4, 5, 7.
17. Victor Urguidi, "Report on a Project to Expand Economic Research and Improve the Training of Economists at the University of Costa Rica," March 14, 1963, p. 6, ACC 001717.
18. Bronfenbrenner et al., "The Adequacy of Facilities," pp. 9, 15, 16.
19. Richard Ruggles, "Evaluation of the Joint Council on Economic Education," May 1961, pp. 1, 2, PA 54–72.
20. Ruggles and Ruggles, "Economic Research."
21. Bronfenbrenner et al., "The Adequacy of Facilities," pp. 2–4.
22. Edward Edwards to John Bresnar, "Some Thoughts on the Economics Review," August 19, 1974, pp. 3, 4, 11, ACC 008609.
23. Marshall Robinson, "Economics and the Ford Foundation: Some Background," ACC 009111.

CHAPTER 14

The grammar of political economy

James K. Galbraith

This chapter explores the rhetoric of political debate about economic issues. Evidently, the art is thriving; seldom in history have madmen in authority distilled such frenzy from scribblers. Still, economists seem to devote little systematic thought to the politics of persuasion.[1]

Rhetoric is a matter of language, and language is dual, a matter of transmission and of reception. Between economics and politics, transmission and reception must occur across a cultural divide. The rhetoric of political economy, of "economic discourse in the political arena," is, linguistically speaking, a rhetoric of translation, of intercultural communication. To understand it properly you have to have a sense of nuance in both cultures.

One issue – not the primary topic of this chapter – concerns the tactics, the modes of expression, the idiosyncratic professional styles of economists themselves, their manner of comportment in the political arena, for example, in congressional hearings. Take the question of metaphor: What are the images that economists think legislators find persuasive?

On January 19, 1982, the Joint Economic Committee held a hearing of singular distinction. Three witnesses appeared: Professor Wassily W. Leontief of New York University, Nobel Laureate in Economics for 1973; Professor James Tobin of Yale, Nobel Laureate for 1981; and Professor Lawrence Klein of the University of Pennsylvania, Nobel Laureate for 1980. Professor Leontief testified first. The following quotation is long but requires its full length to be savored properly:

> The captain is dismissing a large part of his crew and has ordered the sails set so that the canvas would catch the full force of the wind, that is, that means pursuit of the highest possible profits. He has also directed the helmsman to take his hand off the tiller so that, unimpeded by an attempt to steer it, the ship could sail in the direction in which the wind happens to propel it. Most passengers seem to be enjoying the cruise except, of course, the poor, the old and the sick who are being lowered in leaky dinghies overboard. This, the captain explains, has to be done to lighten the load.
>
> But the mood will change, and I think quite soon when everyone

I thank Arjo Klamer for valuable comments.

hears and feels the rocks scraping the bottom of the vessel. Emergency measures will certainly be taken, but after having been pulled out into deeper water, should we resume experimentation with the same kind of policies based on the same kind of theories that permitted the American economy to reach the stage in which it finds itself today? Let's hope not. The waters that we are about to enter are much more treacherous than those we were navigating up until now.

Professor Tobin spoke next. There is no evidence that he had colluded with Professor Leontief in preparation of the following:

This is the season for reviewing the course of the U.S. ship economy and reconsidering the directions in which its officers are steering it. By general agreement, course corrections are urgently required right now. The captain, his navigators, and the helmsmen are getting plenty of advice from the crew and the passengers, and from other vessels in the convoy, too. But the kibitzers do not agree on the destination. Some want to continue straight ahead on the route to "price level flats," cold and rocky though it may be; they urge the captain to resist the lure of detours and side excursions lest we lose our way. Some are nostalgically preoccupied with reaching once more the comfortable high ground of "long bond island." Others say that if the ship is just steered out of the "red sea" into the "straights and narrows of black ink," all other destinations will be easily within reach. A few speak up for "full recovery mountain," beyond which stretch the gently rising "plateaus of stable growth." The mountain is a once fashionable landmark that has been receding from view for so long it is almost forgotten.

Finally Professor Tobin came round to his point:

Block that metaphor, the *New Yorker* used to say. Now that the hopeful assurances of a year ago that all destinations could be reached easily and quickly simultaneously have been revealed to be costly illusions, Federal policymakers have the opportunity and responsibility to plot a new macroeconomic course.

Nor is the ripe use of literary device confined to economists of one particular theoretical school or set of political leanings. On October 21, 1981, Dr. John Rutledge of the Claremont Economics Institute, in an effort to convey the lessons of rational expectations for price stabilization policy, testified as follows:

> You may have wondered why God put zero in the middle of all the numbers. That's because that's the optimal inflation rate.

This use of the appeal to authority (strong form) provoked JEC Chairman Henry Reuss (D-Wis.), as follows:

> Mr. Reuss. Well, now to examine on that, is zero the optimal unemployment rate, too?
>
> Mr. Rutledge. No, I would not say that.
>
> Mr. Reuss. Did God switch signals on that?
>
> Mr. Rutledge. No, God never made a target for unemployment so far as I know, in the King James version anyway.

As these examples illustrate, economists leave the special languages of their profession at home. Their use would, indeed, be futile, since those not trained to the internal devices of economics tend not to be impressed by them. Instead, economists speaking to politicians adopt the conventions of political discourse, in which wit and analogy and casual empiricism and arguments from introspection predominate, buttressed by authority, whether personal ("experience shows that . . ."), deriving from professional status ("most economists believe . . ."), celestial (as above), or from a black box ("according to the DRI Model . . .").

This is not bad. Indeed, the testimony of economists in public debate is strikingly direct, uninhibited, and free of the cant about style that often characterizes professional communication – and that McCloskey so well exposes. Congressional hearings are, in McCloskey's phrase, "healthy conversation." And the skill of certain economists in lay exposition is the basis of an influence shared by no other scholarly discipline, spawning much (too much!) subscholarly imitation. To borrow again from McCloskey, politicians get the rhetoric of the lunchroom, not the pedantry of the chalkboard. Still, the rhetorical techniques need not be overly subtle.

A second and more subtle issue concerns the perceptions and behavior of politicians who must dispose of the issues on which economists are called to consult. Politicians in this position are guided by their self-interest and by the customs and procedures of the political process in which they work. All these together define a grammar, or implicit rules of discourse, for the consideration of economic topics. Economists tend not to be close students of the political grammar and hence are commonly unaware of the forces that govern the degree of influence their rhetoric may enjoy.

The following discussion bears solely on this issue of grammar, on the culture of political customs and institutions. It is limited within that culture to the specific case of the legislative process of the United States. This further limitation is that of the author. My choice of example is dictated by personal experience and knowledge: As a former member of the congressional staff, I lack experience with argument on economic issues elsewhere, such as within the executive branch or at the Federal Reserve. And if there is a *general* science of adjudication in the political sphere, independent of particular institutions, settings, and patterns of precedent, I have not (yet) discovered it.

Do ideas matter?

First, a preliminary. It is my position, pace the public-choice school and the Marxists, that policy ideas are an independent ideological force.

Some economists, and more political scientists, disbelieve this. Many doubt there exists any role whatever for intellectual persuasion in politics, whether deductive, inductive, or "purely rhetorical." Models, characterized by their attention to the self-interest of bureaucrats and legislators, have been advanced in volume to explain the imperatives of political decision making. If these models are wholly right, then special interests govern all, the scope for discretion and hence persuasion in politics is negligible, and the study of the rhetoric of such discussion can be of only iconological interest.

To be sure, special interests are important. Ulterior motives *are* endemic in politics. And not all of the scholarly cynicism is misinformed. Council of Economic Advisers Chairman Murray Weidenbaum, when asked directly[2] what weight of influence, on a scale of one to ten, economists had enjoyed in drafting the original tax program of the administration, replied, "Zero."

But special interests do not exhaust the interesting phenomena of politics. There is the opposing view of Keynes on ideas: "the world is ruled by little else." In my experience, ideas and interests interact; neither fully dictates any outcome. Interests are never absent from the discussion and often prevail. But there was always a sense that there was discretion, there were choices, and that the interests occasionally could be outsmarted by ingenuity in rhetoric, including as part of rhetoric various tricks of policy design.

Incentives and procedures

Two forces drive the policy process. There are the diverse incentives of individual political leaders, each according to his circumstances. The United States Congress is a highly structured institution. A legislators' role within the whole – what committees he serves on, what parliamentary office he holds, on what issues his views are respected – is determined by many factors, including luck, political skill, disposition, interests, expertise, and seniority. Each individual's career is a cumulative process, conditioned by all the accidents of personal and institutional history. Contrary to the assumptions of much social science, therefore, no two legislators are exactly alike.

And then there are the rules of procedure. These are established so as to provide for the smooth coexistence of diverse individual politicians, to keep the institutions of legislative government functioning. Procedures are formal or informal. Formal procedures establish rituals of legislative process for the disciplined consideration of particular, recurring issues. Informal procedures provide general guidance on such matters as collegiality, courtesy, reputation building, legislative effectiveness, and public image projection.

Economic ideas enter the political arena through portals defined by procedure, and they spread within it along the grooves and channels that procedure lays down. Accordingly the structure of an idea affects its political potential. Where an idea fits smoothly into the grooves of an established procedure, consideration and disposition will be more rapid, and the probability of action greater, than otherwise. When existing procedures are inadequate to cope with the problems for which they were designed, crisis results. Where a new idea carries such force that legislators respond to it by altering established procedures, we have the characteristic signature of a wave of reform.

Individual incentives

We may think of a typical legislator as an investor, a Keynesian speculator in an uncertain world, investing in a sequence of policy choices. As in the standard metaphor, he starts with a unique endowment – call it political capital or *ex ante* probability of reelection. He chooses a portfolio of positions, designed to maximize the expected return (a flow of utility) on this endowment, subject (usually) to the constraint that the discounted probability of defeat (bankruptcy) at the next election remain low.

Legislators may have many alternative arguments – alternative, that is, to constituency service, in their utility function. They may wish to curry favor with their colleagues, their leadership, or the administration. They may wish to establish reputation. They may wish to repay a debt or exact revenge. Or they may wish to "do right and face consequences."[3]

While some objectives are complementary, others are substitutes: Currying favor with the leadership can be costly at home base; standing too often on principle can impair parliamentary effectiveness; a fondness for playing the galleries can damage internal reputation. Actions that enhance reelection probabilities may be thought of as by definition forms of constituency service. Other actions may diminish that probability but are nevertheless not irrational

– at the margin, their utility return exceeds the utility value of the political risk. Rational politicians take political risks when they can afford to.

Given periodic elections, these general observations lead to a variable that accounts for many differences between otherwise like-minded legislators: their payback period. This is, in loose language, the period over which they are prepared to plan. A legislator has a long payback period if he is prepared to support policies whose political costs are immediate and whose benefits are deferred, while a short payback period indicates a strong insistence on seeing political benefits in the short term and meanwhile pushing political costs back. But the important point is that payback periods are strongly affected by institutional rules and institutional position.

U.S. senators serve for overlapping, renewable six-year terms and rarely face their constituencies more than four times over a long senatorial career. But turnover in the Senate is nevertheless quite high as a proportion of the membership exposed in each election. Accordingly, to a senator each election is a major milestone. Senators rarely consider themselves wholly secure in their seats: Each election must be faced as though it carried a nonnegligible risk of defeat. On the other hand, victory brings with it the assurance of a substantial gain in seniority and institutional position, since two more elections must roll by, with all of the turnover that they entail, before any newly elected senator is exposed to the voters again.

For these reasons, senators' payback periods tend to vary directly with the time to the end of their terms. After each election a new crop of forward-looking statesmen, one-third of the Senate, newly elected or reelected, takes office. At the same time, a hapless cohort of thirty-three or thirty-four soon-to-be-exposed incumbents turns, singlemindedly, from relative statesmanship to the fund raising and crowd pleasing of the impending campaign.

In the House of Representatives, there is always an impending election. House members serve for nonoverlapping, renewable two-year terms; over a long career a surviving incumbent will face his or her voters a dozen times or more. This situation strongly affects the distribution of payback periods across members, creating a two-tiered system in the House that does not exist in the Senate.

To a newly elected House member, the political situation is exiguous: The next election is a milestone beyond which the planning period does not extend. And the next election is always less than two years away. Junior House members are for this reason incurably short sighted, and usually willing to prostrate themselves in the effort to make a good impression at home.

As time passes, though, attitudes change. Each succeeding election disproportionately eliminates those members whose *ex ante* probability of reelection was low, while providing survivors with both better information about their standing at home and greater confidence in it. Any member serving over the turn of a decade will also – unlike Senators – face a redistricting, the effects of which usually consolidate senior members in their districts.[4] Senior members thus become secure, and their payback periods lengthen. Those at the top – subcommittee chairmen nearing seniority levels sufficient to bring them major chairmanships or leadership positions – tend to develop payback periods that extend at least to the expected end of their senior colleagues' careers.[5] Except in rare political climates when the effective Democratic majority in the House is under threat, these officials have, easily, the longest time perspectives of any officials in government, solely excepting judges appointed for life.

These elements of structure tell us something about decision-making performance in the House and Senate. The House possesses what the Senate lacks: an institutional subculture with a radically longer time horizon.[6] Hence the relevant political market in the House, particularly on economic issues, often involves the exchange of political goods with differing time streams of benefits and costs: The leadership offers the followers opportunities to make short-term points (for example, pork-barrel benefits for the local district), in return for which the followers support the leaders on matters of policy, whereas in the Senate exchanges must be arranged among members whose institutional positions are far more nearly equal.

Informal procedures

In any group, customs are set by habit and those with long tenure set the habits. Thus we would expect the force of informal and formal procedure to lend added weight to the leadership, again particularly in the House, where leadership is strong.

Informal legislative procedures are governed by the need of legislators (and their staffs) to communicate and make decisions efficiently. Legislative business is complex, yet the time allotted for study, learning, and authentic reflection is minute. And the U.S. system lacks the device of party discipline that substitutes for full information in Parliament. Informal procedures substitute by allowing, under favorable circumstances, delegation of decision-making power from followers to leaders.

The informal codes of Congress are based on specialization, reputation, and mutual trust. Legislators learn, from short experience, on whom to rely for better judgment. Leadership roles are assumed, over the years, by reputation builders, whose reputations rest on a precise service they render their colleagues. The service is the reduction in perceived political risk associated with embracing a proposal about which one is substantively in the dark.

Reputation and trust lubricate congressional consideration of a wide range of issues, virtually all, indeed, of intermediate importance: sufficiently so that they must be addressed, but not so important that each legislator feels the need to hold a definite personal view. These issues are the minor insurable risks of politics; reliance on experts is the mode of insurance. Henry Reuss's authority on international financial questions for many years was an example, while in later Congresses I have seen the same at work in the respect accorded Hamilton on intelligence, Downey on arms control, and others.

Specialization is more thorough, and trust a more powerful force, in the House than in the Senate. Greater numbers and a greater diffusion of substantive responsibility among senior members (especially since the reforms of 1975) are the main reasons. House members are both less likely to know well a subject outside their own area of committee assignment and more likely to assume that the subcommittee chairman (or ranking member) does in fact know about it. Senators are not specialists, so they are likely to think less of their colleagues' authority and more, relatively speaking, of their own. Formal procedures reinforce these informal biases. House members not intimately familiar with a committee bill are routinely restricted from offering amendments to it, whereas Senators may offer amendments on virtually any topic at any time, irrespective of the legislation to which it is attached or the qualifications of the source.

Staff members further reinforce leadership power. Their prime function is not, as often thought, to provide expertise. Mainly, staff members deepen institutional memory and strengthen leadership power. Substantive staff, in their overwhelming numbers, work for senior members: In the House it is rare for a member below the rank of subcommittee chairman to have any substantive specialists whatsoever on personal staff.

On some questions reputation, trust, and confidence in staffwork are not enough; the rank-and-file legislator must occasionally be prepared to think for himself. Indeed there are issues that pit the rank-and-file, or more usually an insurgent subleadership, against the established leaders. On such questions original protagonists must, lacking the reputational crutch, take into account the limited information-processing capabilities of the rank-and-file.

Apparent simplicity of policy design is the key to broad-based appeal in a legislative program – the substitute of choice where the reputation of the initiator will not suffice. This has been especially true in the tax area, where no proposal is truly simple, but all compete to appear so: the ten percent "across-the-board" reductions of Kemp–Roth, the "10-5-3" depreciation reforms of Jones–Conable, and more recently the proposals that led to income-tax reform (the Bradley–Gephardt Bill) and a minimum corporate tax. The apparent comprehensibility of such systems makes them tractable in public debate, even if there would be nothing truly simple about their operation in practice.

Tax reform also illustrates the limitations of apparent simplicity and hence of insurgent legislation. Following the chaotic period of early Reagan tax policy, it became clear to some legislators that the idea of general tax reform would appeal, provided the proposal was presentably simple. Hence the "handles" of Bradley–Gephardt and Kemp–Kasten: reduced numbers of tax brackets and loopholes. Complex legislation rode on its association with simple ideas, which was good for momentum in the early phases. Later on, however, when the final bills came to be drafted, complexity was inevitable and the illusion of simplicity could not be sustained. The key transition was therefore a transition of leadership – from Bradley to Finance Committee Chairman Packwood in the Senate, and from Gephardt and Kemp to Ways and Means Chairman Rostenkowski in the House. Only with the authority of leadership could the complex issues be resolved and particular compromises put through both bodies.

The legislative appeal of the monetarist idea in the 1970s – for those interested enough to pay attention – also lay substantially in its simplifications. Money growth targets are, of course, not simple, but legislators did not need to trouble themselves with multiple aggregates, inconsistent targets across differing objectives, shifts of money demand or velocity, or base drift. The monetary targets gave them something to discuss, which, after all, was better than having nothing, and the monetarist prescription – reduce the growth rate of the monetary aggregates over a period of years – actually gave them something to propose, in the safe knowledge that no one would ever hold them responsible for what happened.[7]

To summarize: Other things equal, effective legislation usually requires the sponsorship of legislators known for their care in respecting the political sensitivities and vulnerabilities of their colleagues. Insurgent legislation must be simple. The tension between simple ideas and complicated ones parallels the tension between short and long payback periods among members: It is hard to reap near-term political benefits from nonsimple legislative enactments. This gives further definition to our market in political goods: The leadership is inclined to be oriented toward substance, while the followership leans toward symbols.

Formal procedures

Procedures established for legislative reasons strongly affect whether a particular economic argument, once having persuaded a legislator and acquired the patina of political respectability that comes after a period of public exposure, can find an outlet within the political process. Again, procedures are framed by the leadership in its own interest – though whether they work that way in practice is often open to question.

Budget process

The budget process provides a famous illustration of the effect of procedure on debate. I will argue that the budget process obscures and obstructs rational debate over desired economic outcomes. A key reason has to do with the mesh, or lack of it, between the payback periods of legislators and the time horizon over which budget decisions are structured to be made.

From this standpoint the core of the existing budget process is its system of rolling multiyear spending and revenue targets. These five-year (and longer) projections for each functional area have a useful microeconomic, program-evaluation function, in particular guarding against the "camel's nose" syndrome in the introduction of new expenditure programs. But in the budget process, three- and five-year projections for expenditure, revenue and especially deficits take on a different role. They become, effectively, in and of themselves, the final *goals* for budget policy itself.

This happens because budget process participants, who must evaluate alternative revenue and expenditure streams, find it necessary to place each alternative on as nearly comparable a basis as possible. To establish ground rules for comparability, they have created the Congressional Budget Office, a nonpartisan organization commanding general respect. CBO generates cost estimates for expenditure proposals and revenue estimates for tax proposals, following standard professional methodologies. However, there is no standard, professional, nonpartisan methodology for evaluating the most important aspect of the effect any tax/expenditure program might have, namely its consequences for macroeconomic performance. In the Congress (as, I would argue, elsewhere) competing economic theories are political. CBO is obliged to skirt this difficulty, and it does so by assuming that all budget programs have the *same* long-run economic impact. Hence, at any given time, the same (baseline) economic projection underlies every budget alternative brought before Congress.

Consequently, it is impossible to use the budget process to design policies for their macroeconomic effect. All efforts to do so are thwarted, quite automatically, by the procedure. Submit the program to CBO for "costing out," and the program comes back with any presumed economic improvements removed. Refrain from submitting your program, and your revenue and expenditure estimates will carry no weight with your colleagues. In recent years only budget programs worked out in conjunction with the Joint Economic Committee staff have sought to incorporate in an explicit and professional way their own macroeconomic implications, and these plans (Moynihan–Rie-gle–Sasser in 1982, Hart–Moynihan in 1983) were short lived.[8]

Since economic performance therefore cannot be a target, the budget deficit itself becomes the target as it were by default. Each year the president's budget, along with every congressional alternative at every level, is geared to hitting, under specific economic assumptions, an "out-year" target for the budget deficit. The target may have a general logic – economists agree that deficit reduction is desirable – but its quantitative value is a matter, at best, of habit. Yet all alternatives are judged by the ability to meet or better the deficit target, and not according to whether they promise better or worse economic performance.[9]

Complicating matters further is the rolling aspect of the multiyear target system. Each year is year one of a new five-year plan. Deviations from the previous year's targets, for whatever reason, are forgotten and superseded with each new budget message. Hence the end-point of the current process never falls under the time horizon of the sitting legislature, and political accountability is impossible. In the year before each election the administration and Congress are just as far from ultimate realization of their current goals as they were the day they took office. And the goals it issued then have been, by then, long since rendered obsolete by the failure of the economy to track its previous projections. This creates every incentive to pass budget resolutions each year that appear to meet the objectives under specified economic and interest-rate assumptions, but that then routinely are shown ex post to fail to do so. And indeed, unspecified cuts, "magic asterisks," hyperthyroid economic performances, and mysterious drops in the interest rate litter the budget documents, executive and congressional, of recent years.

An irony of these defects is that, taken together, they render each other relatively innocuous from an economic policy standpoint. Budget balancing may be a foolish objective, but under a rolling multiyear target system it need never be achieved: Draconian measures enacted in one year and scheduled to take effect in three years can be offset one way or another in two years, and after all the commotion, nothing in the end will have happened.

The Gramm–Rudman–Hollings budget-balancing law is thus not a rebellion from, but a natural outgrowth of the budget process. After a period of years, the credibility of the symbolic budget resolution exercise had broken down. Gramm–Rudman momentarily restored it, following the familiar general rules of the budget process, which is what made its acceptance so easy on the part of so many members. The effect is achieved by changing the default settings, so that the track toward budget balance appears to be cast in concrete, and only affirmative action (by both houses, subject to veto) can forestall the automatic expenditure cuts built into the law. At the same time

Gramm–Rudman eliminated the rolling nature of the target: Errors in one year are not forgiven in the next.

But what Congress says it will do, however toughly, and what it will ultimately find itself obliged to do are two different things. The elevation of accounting objectives over economic goals is in Gramm–Rudman carried to its reductio ad absurdum: If economic conditions weaken and the deficit widens, the automatic expenditure reductions increase, with effects that would worsen economic outcomes for the sake of accounting objectives. Only outright recession, through a provision inserted at the last minute, will cause the operation of the statute to be suspended. But long before such a point is reached, Congress will assuredly move to avert the consequences of Gramm–Rudman programmed into present law.

Gramm–Rudman thus provides a canonical example of time horizon mismatch: between the effective dates of the changes it makes and the effective range of foresight (the 1986 election) of the legislators voting on it. Gramm–Rudman, not a leadership effort, appealed because it appeared simple. It passed because to support it offered real political benefits in the very short run – the appearance of toughness – while setting up policy changes that were deferred, with minor exceptions, until 1987 or later. Such changes – $70 billion-odd in mandatory spending cuts for fiscal year 1987 – were effectively imaginary to the legislator enacting them. Nor do they plausibly have major real economic effects (such as on financial market expectations and long-term interest rates) since any rational investor analyzing the choices likely to face the Hundredth Congress must face the possibility that the simplest action will be to defer the effective date of the cuts.

Monetary oversight and monetary-fiscal coordination

The 1978 Federal Reserve Act amendments, enacted as part of the Humphrey–Hawkins Full Employment and Balanced Growth Act, specify that the Federal Reserve announce target "ranges of growth" of major monetary aggregates for the year immediately ahead (fourth-quarter over fourth-quarter basis), in a way thought to be consistent with the expected real growth rate of the economy, the expected inflation rate, and the expected rate of unemployment, all within the same one-year time period.[10] Here is another procedural design for the discussion of economic policy issues.

Monetarists and others have criticized the form of the Humphrey–Hawkins monetary targeting procedure for its one-year character, and particularly for the way the procedure allows base drift: Deviations above or below the range in any given year are incorporated into the base for the succeeding year, so that even an unchanging nominal target from one year to the next is potentially consistent with monetary aggregates following a random walk.[11] But this is to miss the procedure's essential political virtue, which is that the monetary targets lie within the time horizons of the politicians to whom they are presented. That being so, the potential exists for rallying political energy, albeit on rare occasion, to a substantive discussion of the monetary issue, one in which future promises cannot substitute freely for current action.

An example of the effective use of the monetary oversight procedure occurred in 1982, when a clear tension emerged between the general policy of the Federal Reserve respecting the nominal values of its annual monetary targets, which was to reduce the announced growth rates more or less steadily in each successive reporting period, and the needs of the economy as perceived by nearly everybody including, so far as one could tell, the Federal Reserve itself. The tension occurred because of tight money and consequent negative drift in 1981, so the nominal M1B growth target of 2.5 to 5.5 percent announced for 1982 would, if adhered to, have implied a cumulative annual average M1 growth rate of only 3.1 percent over the full biennium, 1981–2.

Whether the Federal Reserve truly intended to follow the course it stipulated in early 1982 may be debated, but the relatively short time horizon over which it was required to stipulate its plans did mean that the policy issues could be clearly posed. On March 1 the Joint Economic Committee issued its annual report, stating in the "Democratic Views":

> Given the realized M1B growth of 2.2 percent in 1981, even achievement of the upper third of the Federal Reserve's 1982 range, which the Administration supports, would mean an average monetary expansion over the two-year period 1980:IV to 1982:IV of only 3.3 to 3.6 per cent – far less than the Administration's own early 1981 mandate to the Federal Reserve and far too low to finance any significant economic recovery. . . . The 1982 targets thus send a clear and unwelcome signal that the policies of the Administration and the Federal Reserve may not permit significant recovery for the interest-sensitive sectors of the economy this year. (JEC 1982, pp. 78–79)[12]

Thus the reporting procedures set terms on which a basic debate over monetary policy could be (and was) carried out for the rest of the year; without those procedures, implying acknowledgment by the Federal Reserve of the legitimacy of one-year planning and oversight, a substantive as distinct from symbolic debate would not have occurred.

As the preceding discussion suggests, monetary policy oversight benefits from a rational structure but suffers from a lack of concerted political interest, whereas with budget matters it is just the reverse. One might wish to ask about the prospects for coordinated discussion of the two.

Monetary-fiscal policy coordination has a limited history and dim future in Congress for a basic institutional reason: committee structure and jurisdictions. Monetary policy oversight falls under the Banking committees of the House and Senate; fiscal policy oversight falls to the committees on the budget.

Again, the events of 1982 illustrate the difficulty such procedural matters pose for coherent debate. The recession and interest rates of that year, as described above, seemed strongly to justify an easing of monetary policy, while at the same time the rising federal deficit, then crossing the $100 billion mark for the first time, together with the still vivid memories of inflation, restrained the hands of those who might have been tempted to argue for an all-out demand expansion. Under the leadership of its chairman, Henry Reuss, the Joint Economic Committee Democratic caucus called for a coordinated shift in the monetary-fiscal policy mix, involving deferral of the elements of the individual tax cuts scheduled to take effect in 1983, as well as repeal of tax indexation, in return for an immediate relaxation of the Federal Reserve's monetary targets.

The problems arose in attempting to get the committees of legislative jurisdiction, Budget and Banking, to look at the two aspects of the JEC recommendation as a unified whole. Staffs on the Budget committees were reluctant to take up the monetary recommendation, on the ground that such action would infringe on Banking Committee jurisdiction. Staffs on the Banking committees were also reluctant to take it up, since without concurrent budget action, a call for dramatic monetary easing might betray a willingness to risk inflation, while the Banking Committee had no credible brief for speaking on budget matters. Eventually, an ad hoc solution was reached, relying on Reuss's personal prestige with his colleagues on the Banking Committee to pave the way for the introduction of general language on monetary policy directly into the budget resolution. The final language, merely requesting that the Federal Reserve "reevaluate" its monetary targets as the budget resolution took effect, was drafted by staff to Senator Domenici, accepted by Senator Moynihan on the Senate floor, and identical language was then adopted by the House, putting the precedent beyond the reach of a conference committee. There is some reason to think that these rumblings played a small role in alerting the Federal Reserve to the danger that Congress might act more seriously if, in mid-1982, it had not abandoned its monetary targets.

Unfortunately, the innovation of a direct congressional statement on monetary matters in the budget resolution did not take hold. When, in 1983 and 1984, the Senate Banking Committee resisted the gift of its jurisdiction on this matter, efforts to incorporate monetary language into the budget resolution had to be abandoned.

Lessons for economists

In political economy, healthy conversation is a matter of healthy formulas. Legislative procedures matter. Even where they are designed with administrative criteria in mind, they can and do strongly influence what can plausibly be said by a legislature on economic matters. Institutions tend to serve the purposes they were designed to serve and adapt poorly to auxiliary purposes. The decline of the Keynesian sense of responsibility for the macroeconomy has meant a deemphasizing of aspects of institutional design aimed at achieving economic objectives, which is why the budget and Gramm–Rudman processes contribute nothing to those goals. Should the sense of responsibility return, institutions could be designed that serve it.

How then does the economist contribute most usefully to the political debate over economic issues? In general, by being aware of the political structure and addressing arguments where interest and formal and informal codes suggest action is possible or likely. That is, economic argument should be sensitive to its audience.

Sensitivity to audience, in a political environment, means sensitivity to the institutional framework. Economists should work to distinguish between recommendations that can be implemented within established procedures, those that are hampered because they operate against the procedural grain, and those requiring procedural, institutional, or constitutional innovation – "regime changes." Where there exists a choice between two paths to the same goal, one requiring regime changes and the others not, economists should be sensitive to the far greater political ease of the latter.

A particular feature of institutional design that cuts across issue areas is the time horizon over which the procedure directs attention. Long and symbolic time horizons foster bad legislative practice. They invite illusory actions, taken for their short-term political appeal, and a "sufficient unto the day" attitude toward problems created for subsequent Congresses on substantive policy issues. Coherent debate occurs most readily when a legislator can expect to revisit the consequences of his actions before the voters next pass on his mandate. Since short political payback periods are a constitutional fact of life, it makes sense to think through procedural designs that discourage the substitution of imaginary future for current real action.

Economists tend to think, for their own professional reasons, quite easily in terms of decisions taken in the present with streams of benefits and costs stretching out over the long term. But it is no good asking most legislators to act so as to maximize the esteem in which they will be held in retirement. Within the legislative branch, only a few actors, albeit disproportionately powerful, are in position to take the long view – generally, the leadership in the House. Efforts to use procedures, such as the budget process, to coax the others to think this way are inherently futile. A Congress cannot bind a future Congress. Congress as a whole must generally do its work in the near term, and can only address long-term issues as part of packages that provide adequate near-term political cover for the majority that needs it.

In their general political presentations, addressed to the rank-and-file, economists should specify and stress the immediate and continuing costs of bad policies and the benefits of good ones, the immediate steps that should be taken, and the immediate benefits that should be foreseen. But this process has its limits: Economists lose credibility when they predict dire imminent consequences that do not occur, as they have done repeatedly with respect to the budget deficit.

In addressing the leadership, in contrast, economists should properly take the longer view. Persuading the permanent legislative leadership of the merits of an economic strategy is the sine qua non of having one over the long term. Arguably, to put this point from the conservative perspective, it was Reagan's failure to defeat the House leadership in the 1982 midterm elections that kept the reflexive Keynesianism of the postwar period in power. And here, it may be noted, complexity is no disadvantage. Complexity aids the leadership, as any student of tax politics knows, since legislative time is a scarce resource. An issue's complexity is the one thing that helps assure that, once agreement is reached in one Congress, matters will not be altered casually in later years.

How then does one mediate between – and assure the consistency of – long-term and short-term objectives – the problem that advocates of constitutional amendments for every purpose so persistently pose? My answer is less legalistic than theirs: It is to strengthen yet further the institutional elements in both houses that already take the long view, giving them greater resources with which to trade in the time-dependent political market I have described.[13]

In the House, where long-term perspectives exist, the critical need is for a leadership body capable of integrating the different elements of economic policy into a single platform and imposing that unity on the diverse jurisdictions of budget, banking, appropriations, and ways and means. This would be a relatively achievable matter if the leadership put its mind to it. In the Senate, given the procedural anarchy of the place, the task is altogether greater. Perhaps the best solution would be constitutional reform – if constitutional reform there must be – that simply reduced the Senate's legislative powers in comparison with those of the House.

Life in the short-period is controversial, but it is the only kind of life our political system is set up to lead. Attempts to change that by removing the levers of economic responsibility from politics might alter the economic results. But they would certainly yield poor political results and a system of government in which those whom we elect do not truly govern. On the other hand, we can improve political performance by giving those with the appropriate perspective stronger procedural control and by removing incentives to the others to play in the sandlots of purely symbolic action. In this way a closer harmony between the rhetoric of economics and the grammar of political economy can perhaps be achieved.

Notes

1. Superficial evidence for this statement is in (or not in) McCloskey's book, where this aspect of economic rhetoric is not explicitly treated.
2. By Mancur Olson, in my presence, at a reception for French Finance Minister Jacques Delors in the atrium of the International Monetary Fund, near the top of the stairs, on or about August 7, 1981. I faithfully refrained from repeating this story until after Murray left office.
3. In the words of recently defeated Texas Governor Mark White.
4. This is true even if their party is not in control of the redistricting process. Where (as in Indiana in 1980) Republicans control the redistricting process, they will typically group as many Democratic voters into a single district as they can manage, so as to create a small number of safe Democratic seats and a larger number of Republican or contestable ones.
5. As the late Gillis Long, then the second-ranking member of the House Rules Committee, said to me in private conversation anticipating his own fate, "Many members have gone to their graves waiting for Claude Pepper to go to his."
6. One cannot deny that certain individual Senators operate with very large ambitions and long horizons. The difference is that the institutional means for amplifying the power of such behavior in the Senate is extremely weak.
7. This knowledge was not, in the final analysis, entirely safe. In July of 1982 Senator Roger Jepsen, a man who was then vice-chairman of the Joint Economic Committee but who cannot be supposed to have been thinking independently on the matter, wrote the *New York Times* to warn of the inflationary consequences of relaxing the monetary targets at that time. The Federal Reserve ignored his advice, but the letter, unearthed at a critical moment two years later, made a modest contribution to Jepsen's defeat for reelection.
8. Candor compels me to confess to having drafted this passage.
9. Professor Robert Eisner's recent work (Eisner and Pieper 1984; Eisner 1986) reintegrating budget and economic decision making.
10. Building this modest framework for accountability required years of patient effort, beginning with the passage of H. Con. Res. 133 in 1975. H. Con. Res. 133 required quarterly reports on monetary growth ranges from the Federal Reserve but structured the reporting framework so as to make possible quarterly base drift, while not requiring consistency between money growth targets and economic projections. At the first day-long hearing under H. Con. Res. 133 in the House in 1975, Democratic members pressured Federal Reserve Chairman Burns to pro-

duce projections for real growth, inflation, and unemployment consistent with his announced targets. After declining repeatedly, Burns finally acceded to giving his "personal view" on these matters, which the committee proceeded to interpret as an official view. This continued to be the practice until Burns was replaced by the more cooperative G. William Miller. With the passage of Humphrey–Hawkins in 1978, the Federal Reserve became required by law to present consistent growth, unemployment, and inflation forecasts, but until late 1982 these took the form of "the range of views" of individual Open Market Committee members. Dissatisfied, JEC Chairman Henry Reuss pressed Chairman Volcker to deliver an official collective forecast, and in December 1982 Volcker acquiesced. Since then, the Federal Reserve has presented such a forecast, although it is still referred to as only the "central tendency" of FOMC views.

11. Despite this, the Humphrey–Hawkins procedures have generally enjoyed Monetarist support, and indeed they are partly a Monetarist creation. My late Banking Committee and JEC colleague, the Monetarist Robert Weintraub, had a keen sense for the design of politically workable procedure, which is not shared by all of his academic coreligionists.

12. Candor again compels . . .

13. Political process designers, for their part, can improve the receptivity of Congress to short-run economic argument by focusing decisions on the issues of the palpable present day. Regime changes should also be considered that shorten adjustment lags in the economic system to policy changes, so that the benefits of changing policy settings can be reaped within the political lifetime of the politicians taking responsibility. See my "Price Stabilization: A Proposal" in JEC (1985) for an example. Milton Friedman (1985), Robert E. Lucas (1981), Axel Leijonhufvud (1985), and others are associated with proposals for a different kind of regime change, involving constitutional amendments to limit taxation and spending or to fix the growth rate of the money supply or the size of the monetary base. These proposals are quite the opposite of those discussed here, as they involve taking authority to influence economic outcomes away from the legislature, vesting it instead in the courts. It is fair to say that so long as legislators believe the public will hold them responsible for economic outcomes, such proposals will remain moot.

References

Eisner, Robert. 1986. *How Real Is the Federal Deficit*. New York: The Free Press of Macmillan.

Eisner, Robert, and Paul J. Pieper. 1984. "A New View of the Federal Debt and Budget Deficits." *American Economic Review* 74(1):11–29.

Friedman, Milton. 1985. Presidential Address to the Western Economics Association, July 2, Anaheim, California.

Joint Economic Committee. 1982. *Joint Economic Report*. Washington, D.C.: Government Printing Office.

————. 1985. *Monetarism, Inflation and the Federal Reserve.* Washington, D.C.: Government Printing Office.

Leijonhufvud, Axel. 1985. "What Would Keynes Have Thought of Rational Expectations." in *Keynes and the Modern World,* edited by David Worswick and James Trevithick, New York: Cambridge University Press. 179–205.

Lucas, Robert E. 1981. "Tobin and Monetarism: A Review Article." *Journal of Economic Literature* 19 (June):558–67.

McCloskey, Donald N. 1985. *The Rhetoric of Economics.* Madison: University of Wisconsin Press.

CHAPTER 15

The rhetoric of economics as viewed by a student of politics

Robert O. Keohane

Before speaking about economists, let me distinguish two varieties of that clan. In what follows I am *not* referring to certain select categories of economists whose members do carry on conversations with political scientists: (1) Marxist political economists, (2) most European policy-oriented economists, (3) many and perhaps most economic historians, including Donald McCloskey and Charles Kindleberger, (4) organization theorists following the research program of Herbert Simon, (5) a few highly creative economists who are brilliant commentators (and rhetoricians) about politics (Albert Hirschman, Mancur Olson, Thomas Schelling, for example), and (6) *some* policy-oriented mainstream U.S. economists who are aware of the importance of politics for example, Jeff Sachs. I *am* talking about mainstream U.S. economists whom I encounter at meetings called by economists, on trade, international monetary coordination, or the like. At such meetings it is these economists who usually dominate the conversation.

But what goes on between them and students of politics – political *scientists* in McCloskey's sense (1985, p. 54) of "disciplined inquiry"? (Until I read McCloskey's book I shied away from using the term *political science*, associating science with the attainment of certainty. I thank him for allowing me to use the term with a straight face again.) Political scientists who study the politics of economic policy are highly receptive to economics as a way of thinking about problems – what Joe Kalt called the "marginalist view of the world." We know that we need to understand some economics, and we respect the rigor of economic thought. Furthermore, unlike journalists we do not personalize issues; on the contrary, we differentiated our product from that of journalists largely on the basis of our claim that we can describe and interpret basic forces operating in politics, and that we can therefore explain more of what happens than can observers who dwell too much on the actions of individual leaders. But despite our receptivity to economics, there is little real conversation. Most mainstream economists do not converse with other social scientists; they *preach* to them. And they do so in two ways:

1. By instructing us about the form of explanation that we should use: that is, deductive accounts, beginning with individual interests and the struc-

ture of constraints, using the axiom of rationality to derive equilibrium behavior and outcomes.
2. By prescribing social and political (as well as economic) policies to us, allegedly on the basis of economic analysis.

In their preaching, economists use all five devices that McCloskey attributes to Samuelson: appeals to mathematical virtuosity, authority, relaxation of assumptions, hypothetical toy economies, and analogy.

But from an explanatory standpoint the most powerful appeal is to the beauty and elegance of models using the rationality assumption. This appeal is persuasive to many political scientists because of the apparent applicability of such models to strategic bargaining issues. Competitive equilibrium metaphors are not persuasive to us, but rationality assumptions are. The game theory metaphor not only seems to work for oligopoly theory but for arms control and economic summitry. So to examine both the strengths and limitations of economists' rhetoric when deployed toward political scientists, we need to focus on the concept of rationality. As we will see, this is a double-sided concept.

From a prescriptive standpoint, the economist's appeal is to the value of efficiency at best, and to the metaphor of "natural" and "artificial" at worst. I believe that this appeal is less persuasive to political scientists, who are adept at seeing self-interest behind the claims of those who profess to be telling us what is best for us.

Rationality and explanation

Economists' proselytizing on behalf of the rationality assumption has had salutary effects in political science – or at least so it seems to political scientists like myself who are sympathetic to the use of rational choice axioms. We are no longer as likely as before to hear "explanations" on grounds of an alleged "irrationality" of actors, inferred from the fact that bad outcomes result. The recourse to irrationality or stupidity as an explanatory principle is no longer an acceptable way to rule out further inquiry. We now suspect, with economists, that actors with money or power at stake calculate quite carefully – perhaps politicians are even shrewder than political scientists! ("If you're so smart, why aren't you powerful?") Books have appeared, such as *The Intelligence of Democracy* and *The Rational Peasant* (Lindbloom 1965; Popkin 1979). A whole cottage industry has grown up dedicated to exploring the implications of the assumption that warmongers, revolutionaries, and advocates of international organization are not the starry-eyed fanatics or idealists that they have sometimes been thought, but rather, coldly rational beings. I suspect that most contemporary students of international relations, for instance, are highly suspicious of the notion that Qaddafi is irrational.

What this means is that some political science really has become applied economics and is better for it – except, perhaps, that some of its practitioners, as befits recent converts, seem to have an even less self-conscious view of the rhetorical nature of their enterprise than do their economist teachers, and therefore have difficulty carrying on conversations with the rest of us.

The notion of rationality thus appropriated is doubled-edged, however. In their more casual moments, some economists have fallen into the bad habit of "explaining" national economic policies on the grounds that politicians are too stupid to follow good economic policies. Surely the assumption of rationality makes this account look too glib, and suggests that these economists should be looking to political scientists to provide some evidence about interests and institutions that would account for outcomes that otherwise seem anomalous. Robert Bates (1981), for instance, has shown that the supposedly "irrational" economic policies of African governments – compelling farmers to sell at low fixed prices to the state, but providing seed, farm machinery, and the like at subsidized rates – are quite rational. One only has to understand their real purpose – gaining political influence, in the cities and with *selected* farmers who support the ruling party.

The problem with economists' preaching about rationality is not, however, that they do not always practice what they preach. That will be cured by criticism – from economists or from political scientists, like Bates, who have learned to think like economists. The problem is that reliance on technical means-ends rationality permits only a partial notion of what the political scientist's task is:

1. Political scientists engage in quite a bit of description. Some of this is fairly straightforward political history, not pretentious but useful to policy economists as well as other observers. Some is what Clifford Geertz (1973) has called "thick description," providing an intelligible account of the meaning of people's lives, in terms accessible to people from outside their culture, that does not do violence to the self-perceptions of the people in the culture being studied. "Thick description" requires making sense of overlapping and contrasting interpretations from different perspectives – and may involve sorting through lies as well as silences.
2. But more than this, political scientists try to give some account of preferences. We do not believe that "there is no accounting for tastes." To some extent, we rely on reason to help us sort out reasons for our preferences; we can evaluate ends in rational terms, as well as comparing means. Indeed, it may be hard to tell what is an end and what is a means, since ends

are embedded in larger hierarchies of value, which are likely to be only partially consistent. As McCloskey points out (1985: 66–67), we care about the kinds of tastes we have, and political scientists as well as sociologists and anthropologists care about how societies select the kinds of tastes that they do. And this is obviously not just a rational process of choice, taking place in present time; it is a profoundly historical process. This does not mean that there were not reasons for the choices, but it does suggest that those reasons were dependent on the context, which was partly the result of conjunctures of events. The institutions through which interests are expressed, and which shape those interests, are, in Paul David's (1985) words, "path-dependent."

So we have to account for the *process* by which preferences are shaped. We cannot be satisfied by the easy answer of showing that the preferences we have could be justified rationally. Such an argument is circular unless interests, or actors' utility functions, are defined independently of the observed preferences. Many social systems could be justified rationally given post hoc specification of appropriate values. (This is what was wrong with structural-functionalism, in which the is became the ought.) Friedman's peculiar methodology has always been unpersuasive to political scientists, immersed as we are in the "pleasures of the process," to quote the title of a book of poems by James March. We have too few cases and too many confounding variables to be able to sort out causality at all without resorting to what Alexander George (1979) has called "process-tracing": Seeing whether a plausible argument about outcomes *also* is consistent about what we can discover about process.

For instance, we may assume that states behaved in a given international episode as unitary rational actors, bargaining with each other in familiar game theoretic ways. We may therefore interpret outcomes as equilibria of particular games. But this is not sufficient for explanation. We also have to ask whether independent evidence supports our assumptions about the interests and payoff functions involved in the games. And does the political process support the assumption of unitary actors following canons of rationality? If the actors are organizations, which often have difficulty behaving rationally, how closely do their real decision-making processes mimic rational calculation?

Concern with process, I think, unites economic historians with political scientists, and is perhaps one reason why we have an easier time talking to economic historians, and learning from their work, than we do with macroeconomists or general equilibrium theorists.

So the preaching of economists about how to explain both dazzles and disillusions us. Many of us have been dazzled, and I think we have learned a lot by casting this reflected light, being the moon to the economists' sun. But eventually we become aware of the limitations of the approach, particularly its failure to consider culture, institutions, the sources of preferences, and historical process. Then the preaching seems too narrow, even a little bit like Savanarola, burning the books he didn't like. We don't burn the economist, but lacking a conversation, we may stop listening.

I draw only the modest conclusion from these observations that greater modesty in economists' rhetoric would be appreciated by other social scientists. We appreciate Schumpeter's remark about the boundaries of economics:

> When we succeed in finding a definite causal relationship between two phenomena, our problem is solved if the one which plays the "causal" role is non-economic. We have then accomplished what we, as economists, are capable of in the case in question, and we must give place to other disciplines. (Schumpeter 1934: 4–5)

Prescription: The theology of policy science

When a political scientist turns to the rhetoric of economics as a "policy science," the gaps in communication become even greater. Sometimes when I read economists' attempts to give policy advice, I feel as if I have wandered by mistake into the Council of Constance (1414–17), which sought acrimoniously to restore unity to the Church and extirpate heresy. (It condemned John Hus but did not achieve the other goals.)

Political science has become a highly positive and skeptical form of inquiry, devoted less to prescription than to description and attempts at explanation. But when economists talk to noneconomists they often behave as if they were on a crucial normative mission: to save the world from folly. This is what I have called elsewhere (Keohane 1978), to emphasize the theological parallel, "neo-orthodox economics." Its essence lies in its rhetorical reliance on unexamined and implicit social and political theories. The most common symptom of this theological derangement is to regard the price system of capitalism as "natural" and deviations from it as "unnatural" or "artificial."

Consider, for instance, the rhetoric of a famous report issued by the Organization of Economic Cooperation and Development (OECD) nine years ago. The chief metaphor of the "McCracken Report" was that of a "narrow path to growth," suggesting analogies with the narrow path to heaven in traditional Christian theology (McCracken et al. 1977: 189–90). This report offered a naive form of natural law theory to supports its conclusions:

> The benefits [of price and incomes policies] obtained in terms of any improvement in the trade-off between inflation and high levels of

employment are outweighed by the costs in terms of the distortions introduced into the economy and the diversion of existing social and political institutions *from their natural functions.* (McCracken et al. 1977: 218, emphasis added)

Unfortunately for the cause of black social scientific humor but fortunately for the reputations of the report's authors, this theory of the "natural functions" of contemporary social and political institutions is not further elaborated in the report.

The McCracken Report also illustrates a common tendency among some policy economists to move without sufficient reflection from positive to normative statements. As I wrote some time ago in a review of this document:

> The unstated premises in [the report's] transitions from positive to normative statements is the contention that democratic politics must adjust to capitalist economics rather than vice versa. Capitalism has its own imperatives, according to the report; these cannot be fundamentally altered by political decree. Furthermore, the report assumes that capitalism must be retained. Given the assertion and the assumption, it is a short step to the conclusion that democracy must conform to capitalism – particularly if one has not undertaken an analysis of the political constraints under which modern democratic governments labor. When this conclusion takes on the status of doctrine, and its proponents preach to governments about the "narrow path" to the Heaven of full employment with price stability, policy-oriented economics – whether Keynesian or monetarist – comes to resemble traditional theology. It becomes "neo-orthodox." (Keohane 1978: 119)

Conclusions

The rhetoric of economists inhibits conversation between economists and other social scientists. Much of the rhetoric is obnoxious because it seems designed to assert superiority or to justify unreflective normative positions rather than to persuade through the use of reason. I recommend three changes:

1. *More understanding* that the task of students of politics or other social scientists is not merely one of transplanting economic methods to other subjects – however effective that may be for some limited, well-bounded problems.
2. *Greater awareness* of the perils of leaping from a conclusion about economic models to a conclusion about desirable policies in complex situa-

tions, especially if one has not taken into account the constraints faced by the political system.
3. *Greater modesty,* which is, after all, the condition for holding a conversation in the first place.

References

Bates, Robert H. 1981. *Markets and States in Tropical Africa: The Political Basis of Agricultural Policies.* Berkeley: University of California Press, 1981.

David, Paul. 1985. "Clio and the Economics of QUERTY." *American Economic Review,* Papers and Proceedings (May).

Geertz, Clifford. 1973. *The Interpretation of Cultures.* New York, Basic Books, Ch. 1.

George, Alexander L. 1979. "Case Studies and Theory Development: The Method of Structured, Focused Comparison." In *Diplomacy: New Approaches in History, Theory and Policy,* edited by Paul Gorden Lauren. New York: Free Press.

Keohane, Robert O. 1978. "Economics, Inflation and the Role of the State: Political Implications of the McCracken Report." *World Politics* (October: 108–29.

Lindblom, Charles E. 1965. *The Intelligence of Democracy.* New York: Free Press.

McCloskey, Donald N. 1985. *The Rhetoric of Economics.* Madison: University of Wisconsin Press.

McCracken, Paul, Guido Carli, Herbert Giersch, et al. 1977. *Towards Full Employment and Price Stability.* Paris: Organization for Economic Cooperation and Development.

Popkin, Samuel L. 1979. *The Rational Peasant: The Political Economy of Rural Society in Vietnam.* Berkeley: University of California Press.

Schumpeter, Joseph. 1946. *The Theory of Economic Development: An Inquiry into Profits, Capital, Credit, Interest and the Business Cycle,* translated by Redvers Opie. Cambridge, Mass.: Harvard University Press.

CHAPTER 16

"Yellow rain" and "supply-side economics": Some rhetoric that failed

David Warsh

Much of the difficulty of covering economics for newspapers stems from the fact that serious conversations about economics are carried on at so many different levels of sophistication. In this respect economic doctrines are rather like religious convictions: Everybody has them, but a lot of folks didn't get them from the priest. After all, economic decisions are the very fabric of everyday life, full of every conceivable "could" and "should"; cab drivers and business people and schoolteachers all have opinions about the way the world works. Then there is a very considerable demimonde, where writers such as myself flourish, seeking to translate, interpret, or persuade; vehicles here include trade books, magazines, newspapers, pamphlets, and, of course, broadcast. But economics also has a province of the most learned discourse among scholars of the subject, and this empyrean realm is populated by rival schools that compete for public attention and support; there is no overarching consensus among them. So how exactly is economics different from religion? or science? or law? or politics? Surely the greatest difficulty in "translating economic discourse" into the language of the daily newspapers is knowing what to make of economic discourse in the first place.

This is a hard enough question on which to form a judgment even without Donald McCloskey, but McCloskey's book, *The Rhetoric of Economics* has raised the question in the most radical fashion. I am certainly prepared to think that economists are not yet very successful scientists, compared to their fellows in biology and the physical sciences; that their field is young, even immature; that their quantitative results and even their most fundamental theorizing needs to be treated with extreme skepticism. But McCloskey goes farther than this. He would persuade me, I think, that economists are not scientists at all, that their collective enterprise is not so deeply anchored in what is "true" and universal as they would have us believe. Economics is above all a phenomenon of language, he says: It is a conversation; it is poetry; it is "a collection of literary forms." Whatever it is, it isn't science, and it doesn't promise the eventual freedom from doubt, the mopping up and filling in and moving on that we associate with science. Not even science can promise that credibly any longer, according to McCloskey.

(I say "I think" because I find McCloskey's playful writing hard to pin down. That is the way he likes it, of course; for him, an ability to wheel and deal among the master tropes is a better way of separating sheep from goats than is a knack for doing linear algebra. Whatever the test, I remain a goat – a "professional layman" in McCloskey's nice phrase.)

Here is McCloskey's view of my predicament: "Influenced by the economist's pretension to scientific status, though properly suspicious of it, the journalist has an uneasy time with economists, quite unlike his relation to a space scientist or historian or other newsworthy scholar."[1] I think McCloskey romanticizes my relations with space scholars and historians – they too have their disagreements, after all – but certainly he is right that I have an uneasy time among economists. What does he recommend to make my life easier? McCloskey tells me to give up my vision of right answers. There is only good talk, he says. He tells me to listen to many sides of every issue, to have an ear for the rhythms of the history of economic thought, to mistrust simple answers that are seemingly complete, to talk English and insist that it be spoken to me, to seek to discover for whom economists are writing, and to remember who it is for whom I am writing. This is pretty much what my editor tells me to do, and it is good advice whatever side of the aisle it comes from. But in some sense, it begs the question. What is the relationship of an economist's science to an astronomer's knowledge? A law professor's learning? A Protestant theologian's dogma?

In the next few pages, I will describe a pair of somewhat parallel problems that have arisen in recent years in the coverage by newspaper reporters of expert communities and outside critics of these communities: biologists and economists, respectively. The hope is that they may cast some light on the situation of journalists in a world where even the scientists are capable of radical self-doubt. I believe that the way in which matters were resolved in the case of the biological conundrum gives some clues as to why things turn out as they usually do in economics.

1

Let me begin, however, by stipulating a little background. Before the philosophers among us think, "You poor child, don't you know that we've given up the search for 'truth'?" let me say that I was a member of that generation of undergraduates raised up on Thomas Kuhn's *The Structure of Scientific Revolutions,* therefore a certain relativism comes (relatively) easily to me. But you can get that from reporting, too, and most of us have acquired a better understanding of the ultimate mutability of even the most (apparently) firmly shared consensus in the past quarter century. Just as no one who has read Kuhn's book will take the claims of science to certainty quite as solemnly as before, no reporter who has worked through the Vietnam War will feel strongly that the last word has been uttered on those tragic events. But reporters, like scientists, have had to come to terms with their doubts. They have discovered that they cannot afford to dissolve in a case of logico-anarchic nerves. They have to get on with it. They have to act as though logical empiricism was as much with us as ever, and hope that the philosophers will eventually come up with some sophisticated rationale for this stance.

My guess is that every reporter who works in the field has some opinion about the deep-down nature of the enterprise of technical, university-based economics and that a little interviewing or self-examination would bring it out. My own conviction is that technical economics is certainly a science, but not yet as successful as many others. Young or not, certainly it is nothing at which to sneeze; two hundred years of disciplined conversation and investigation has created an intellectual structure of depth and beauty. I do not know what economics will do to improve its act (though I have my little ideas, naturally), but I firmly believe that it will go on improving, in fits and starts, for a long time to come. In its immaturity, parts of economics continue to resemble many other intellectual enterprises – politics, law, and literature among them. But the fundamental social organization of economics, along the lines of the sciences, is justified, I believe, for there is no more powerful engine for understanding than speculative exploration of the world over time by the peer-selected research community. In any event, the pattern of specialization in economics and the logic behind it has enormous significance to all who aspire to understand and influence economic policy.

A definition of science that can easily accommodate this view was proposed by Norman Campbell, an English physicist, back in 1922. Science, Campbell said, is simply what everybody can agree on, "the study of those judgements concerning which universal agreement can be obtained." Simple as it sounds (and positivist as it is), the principle is a highly useful rule of thumb for deciding what is and what isn't entitled to claim the mantle. Adopted and expanded on by John Ziman in his admirable little book *Public Knowledge,* this approach through consensus can provide a solid framework for understanding.[2] I recommend it to everyone who thinks about these matters.

For Ziman, the whole point of a scientific conversation is the eventual elimination of uncertainty, at least from the well-trained minds of those who are fully conversant with the facts. Hence the emphasis in science on experiment; if the results can be reproduced by anyone, anywhere, the inferences that may be drawn from it have powerful persuasive effects. Similar is the role of measurement: Numbers are said to speak for themselves, meaning that they are rhetorically forceful. Perhaps the most important characteristic of the scientific attitude is its resolve to explain fully the simplest possible things first; more complicated matters are automatically excluded from consideration because they are impossible to prove. Even the rhetoric of a scientific paper, with its passive voice, its elaborate professions of disinterest, contribute to the overall impression that the results can be trusted because no axe is being ground.

(If proof is at one end of the scale, timeliness and relevance – the great gods of journalism, after accuracy – are at the other. In this sense, the problems of economists covering economics don't have so much to do with translating high-brow discourse into low-brow prose as they do with being in the right place at the right time, with calling the right people, with sensing the axes of disagreement about the interpretation of the unexpected events and illuminating them with timely interviews. Somewhere between science and journalism is the writing of history, which aims to build a story around the names and dates but which doesn't suggest that it is the only possible interpretation.)

By these lights technical economics has all the earmarks of a science. It is organized in university departments, is taught by textbooks, proceeds through publication in refereed journals, is funded mostly through peer review. The "invisible college" is the basic unit of organization, the principal audience for reports of new findings. Other social sciences – sociology, anthropology, and psychology – are organized in this way, but a comparison of the state of economics with these fields underscores the strength of Norman Campbell's approach to science as consensus; it is my impression that economists are far more successful in demarcating their field and agreeing to a few basic approaches to it than are social scientists in other fields. Shared concepts like equilibrium and the quantity theory of money give economists a common standpoint hardly less sturdy than the theory of the heliocentric solar system. I hasten to say that this relatively high degree of discipline hasn't prevented the economists from suffering the ultimate indignity: Statistical and empirical evidence published by others is often simply disregarded by investigators. "If I haven't done the regressions myself, I just don't believe them," is a fairly typical remark.

Thinking of economics as a science is useful not so much because it guarantees that we are getting the right answers from economists (it doesn't) but because it illuminates the way economists work. It follows, for example, that a research economist is, in Thomas Kuhn's metaphor, a man who tries to "elucidate topographical detail on a map whose main outlines are available in advance." He hopes, Kuhn says, "if he is wise enough to recognize the nature of his fields, that he will some day undertake a problem in which the anticipated does not occur, a problem that goes wrong in ways that are suggestive of a fundamental weakness in the paradigm itself."[3] A researcher is someone looking for trouble, in other words, but he doesn't want to find it too often.

Obviously, then, a great deal of interest centers on the tenor of doubt, the quality of skepticism that is bred into the scientist. John Ziman begins his chapter on scientific education in *Public Knowledge* with an illuminating quotation from the English mathematician Isaac Todhunter: "If a student does not believe the statements of his tutor – probably a clergyman of mature knowledge, recognized ability and blameless character – his suspicion is irrational, and manifests a want of the power of appreciating evidence, a want fatal to his success in that branch of science which he is supposed to be cultivating."[4] It isn't any different today, whether in physics or economics or linguistics, I think: as Ziman says, the would-be scientist has to master the consensus of his field before he begins working to change it. This is the quality expected from scientists that Kuhn has called the "essential tension" between being bound to a tradition, knowing it and accepting it, and being able to see problems with it – "anomalies," as Kuhn calls them – when they arise. And because so much of what constitutes "science" is simply the accumulation of knowledge reported in the journals, good science requires men and women who are extraordinarily adept at considering all the possibilities. Richard Feynman, the physicist, describes the ideal of scientific integrity as "a kind of utter honesty, a kind of leaning over backwards. . . . The first principle is that you must not fool yourself and you are the easiest person to fool. So you have to be very careful about that."[5]

It is interesting to reflect that this same configuration of skepticism and background knowledge is what is prized in newspaper reporters. We want someone who "knows the scene," won't be "snowed," who "gets the story," who talks to the relevant players, who gives us sophisticated and slightly tart explanations of why things happen as they do. The difference is that the reporters' background knowledge is at once very much more broad and diffuse than the scientist's understanding of his professional consensus. The reporter acquires it in different ways, from on-the-job experience, rather than from graduate school; and he advances along a somewhat different path, judged by his editors and publishers rather than by his peers.

Having sketched this rough definition of the landscape with which we are dealing, let me proceed to tell my stories. They both have to do with what happens when potentially interesting anomalies turn up on the fringes of science, in that demimonde I mentioned at the very beginning, and when their existence and potential significance is amplified by the press before professional science can make a convincing finding. The first story has to do with allegations of chemical warfare, a far cry, you'll think, from economics. The second one has to do with supply-side economics: the pop version that was represented to the nation in trade books and newspaper articles starting in the late 1970s.

Both these situations are close to the heart of the editorial page of the *Wall*

Street Journal; certainly it is helpful to see the same people dealing with both issues. But the really illuminating aspect of this comparison arises from the fact that one controversy is rooted in what we think of as "hard" science (the science of the mass spectrometer and gas chromatograph), the other in social science. The views back and forth cast some of the differences and some of the similarities into sharp relief, for they are both exercises in persuasion, and in the failure to achieve it.

2

Yellow rain, you'll remember, is the chemical or biological warfare agent that was thought to have been used by the Communists in Southeast Asia against primitive tribesmen in remote locations after the fall of Vietnam. The yellow rain phenomena began as rumors from refugee camps in the late 1970s, then attracted a number of expeditions from concerned Western nations, as press accounts began to appear. There weren't many of these accounts, but they packed a real punch in the late 1970s and early 1980s. Fairly typical is Barry Wain's dispatch, which appeared on the editorial page of the *Wall Street Journal* in September 1981 under the headline, "The Chemical Warfare in Southeast Asia."[6]

Wain described a biplane that zoomed low over a Laotian village, "Unleashing a stream of yellow gas that fell like rain along a one-kilometer strip and formed droplets on the ground." Some 83 of the 473 residents fell over dead, along with the animals; the chickens died first, according to Wain, who took the account from a state department dossier. The agent caused an especially horrible death, with victims drowning in their own blood, he suggested. He concluded forcefully, "While Laos and Vietnam have repeatedly denied using toxic chemicals, it is indisputable that they are using gas, spray or powder against resistance forces, often with fatal effects. There are dozens of documented cases."

Yellow rain attained enormous currency after Secretary of State Alexander Haig, then George Shultz, and finally President Reagan himself publicly accused the Soviets of using biological weapons. It was Haig who first startled the world when, in a speech in Berlin in September 1981, he claimed that the army had identified the agent as tricothecene mycotoxin, a poison produced by a fungus that the Russians, he said, had learned much about during World War II. The speech was widely viewed by scientists as a suggestive but ultimately unpersuasive case; the state department went to work to try to shore it up. A White Paper was released in March, detailing the charges; a National Academy of Science task force was enlisted to study the mycotoxin issue.[7] The government campaign had results; it changed opinions in the early months of 1982. The *Washington Post* editorialized, "It seems to us now . . . that the administration has proven out the Soviet pattern by a standard that reasonable people would accept." *Science* published an article headlined, "Yellow Rain, filling in the gaps: the US case on mycotoxin weapons is persuasive now, although experts still see flaws in the evidence"; the administration had "won over popular opinion," the magazine reported, "but its case still meets skepticism from scientists demanding a more rigorous standard of proof."[8]

This was the situation that prevailed until a Harvard biologist named Matthew Meselson and a group of associates introduced a hypothesis that dramatically changed the debate. Perhaps, they ventured, the yellow rain was showers of bee feces, dropped by swarms of bees on cleansing flights after long periods of hibernation. Virtually all reports had mentioned a yellow substance; many, perhaps most, of the accounts were hazy on the details of its delivery. Government specimens of the mysterious substance were put under light microscopes for the first time. They had been subject to nearly every conceivable sophisticated analysis, but no one had previously looked at them under a magnifier. They turned out to be mostly pollen, the same as might be found in bee feces.

Challenged, the U.S. government, which had never mentioned pollen before, retreated briefly, before coming up with a new hypothesis: It proposed that yellow rain was a fiendishly clever weapon, in which pollen was the carrier for the poisonous mycotoxin. There was no certainty here on either side at this early point, but the damage done to the government case was considerable. Suddenly the community was aware that there was hardly any very substantial evidence of biological warfare, aside from refugee interviews.

Meselson went to work to pin down the bee-feces hypothesis. He experimented, tested, assembled evidence – did all the things he had learned to do in graduate school. Meanwhile evidence tending to cast doubt on the government's charge piled up. Chemical warfare specialists derided the mycotoxin hypothesis because it would take tons of the poison to do the killing, a leading expert said.[9] Autopsies failed to produce compelling evidence; site searches failed to turn up candidates for a delivery system. *Chemical and Engineering News*, the weekly organ of the American Chemical Society, spent twenty-seven pages in early 1984 on a demonstration that the evidence the government had made public was at best "tenuous."[10]

Throughout, however, the state department declined to confront the mounting evidence, and the *Wall Street Journal* editorial writers simply fumed at the skeptics who doubted the government's case: the bee-feces hypothesis was "too ludicrous for discussion," they wrote at one point. Another time, they wrote, "Professor Meselson's . . . crusade begins to look at best like an exercise in windmill-tilting." As the bee-feces hypothesis gained ground, they warned that soon they would have to stop listening to scientists: "[There] is always some new standard of evidence to demand, some new hypothesis yet untested, as the Tobacco Institute has so ably demonstrated. This is an abuse of science against which scientists should guard, or men of affairs will start to wonder whether science can help us when we have to decide important issues of public policy." Finally, at precisely the moment that the tide was turning decisively against them, they simply put their fingers in their ears. "Among men of affairs, the yellow rain debate is closed."[11]

I think that it is fair to say that over the past three years, Matthew Meselson has won the day, quickly and completely, at least among qualified and disinterested scientists who have tuned in to the debate. Virtually everyone who has studied the matter believes that the yellow substance found on rocks and leaves that the government once alleged to be an agent of chemical warfare turned out to be bee droppings. That's not to say that there are not a handful of competent scientists who continue to argue that yellow rain was a sophisticated weapon, but they tend to be those who work for the government, and they have routinely failed to come forth in professional gatherings to defend their findings. An excellent account of the development of the mycotoxin and the bee-feces hypotheses by journalist Peter Pringle is to be found in *Atlantic Monthly* for October 1985.[12] And more or less the last word on the subject was a *Scientific American* article in September 1985.[13] Since then, the controversy's focus has shifted to the failure of other nations' fact-finding authorities to support the U.S. government's claims in the matter; indeed, in May of 1986 the Canadian and British governments released the results of careful studies that demonstrated that naturally occurring tricothecenes – the poison associated with yellow rain for which the Americans had blamed the Soviets – were far more common in Southeast Asia than has been previously believed.

It is important to understand that the Meselson team was careful to say they couldn't prove that biological attacks hadn't happened, but they were increasingly certain about the nature of yellow rain, the only really hard evidence of funny business that the authorities had ever produced. And long before Meselson had nailed down the details, most of the world retreated into sophisticated agnosticism about the reports of chemical or biological warfare in the Indochinese interior. "I think maybe something happened out there," a colonel told me in 1984. "I can't prove it. Clearly it has stopped happening. But I have a hunch they tried something funny back then, and stopped it when they got caught." He could be right. Certainly this is a position that I, as a reporter, find easy to live with. The Soviets can be, and often are, incredibly cruel and ruthless enemies. It is precisely because I know this that I was inclined to take seriously the initial reports of biological warfare in Southeast Asia.

So it is as someone who shares a general concern about the Soviets that I find the *Wall Street Journal*'s continuing position on yellow rain to be deeply disturbing. But there is a world of difference between a knowledgeable skepticism and the "my mind's made up; don't confuse me with the facts" attitude adopted by the editor of the *Wall Street Journal*. Despite the nearly universal skepticism that now prevails among scientists, the paper's editorialists go on reporting their charges as though they were proven fact (as do a few agencies of the U.S. government, including the Bureau of Political and Military Affairs of the State Department). No one on the separately managed news side of the newspaper, as opposed to the editorial page, has successfully reported the dramatic shift of opinion among scientists since the bee-feces hypothesis was first advanced. And in none of this has there been any systematic attempt by the U.S. government to come to grips with the problems of its sloppily made case; there have been no more White Papers from the State Department. Instead, the *Wall Street Journal* editorialists have escalated their claims. In 1984 they energetically argued that the Soviet Union was engaged in a determined research program using genetic engineering to develop a new generation of deadly biological weapons[14]: "[It] would appear that the Soviet Union is well into one of the most massive, and perhaps most dangerous, abuses of science ever conceived by the mind of man."[15]

It may be so, but I'm not going to believe what I hear from the *Wall Street Journal*. They have demonstrated a deep disinterest in the facts of this technical matter, and the result has been a classic erosion of credibility – and not just the newspaper's credibility. Today, many U.S. claims about the ruthlessness of its enemies, from charges of bombs disguised as toys in Afghanistan to Nicaraguan involvement in drug traffic, are being called into question. In Stockholm, for example, where intrusions by Russian submarines into Swedish waters had been for a time an issue capable of commanding widespread agreement, one influential group is now circulating a film whose very premise is radical doubt. Under the credits, it shows Winnie the Pooh tracking the Heffalump – following his own footsteps around a tree.

3

The situation with respect to supply-side economics is infinitely more complicated, and its history won't be written for many years to come.[16] Still, it is possible to put a structure on it; not surprisingly, it doesn't look all that different from the saga of yellow rain.

The amorphous series of political events that we now describe as "the tax revolt" built throughout the 1970s, in Europe as well as America. Never mind, for the moment, technical economics. Quite apart from politics, a great number of disparate strands of analysis emerged during this period in what I have called the demimonde, each alleging deleterious economic effects of taxation, and it is difficult to imagine now the novelty with which each new bit of argument burst on the scene. The Turner, Jackson, and Wilkinson book entitled *Do Trade Unions Cause Inflation?;* the Robert Bacon and Walter Eltis series in the *London Times;* the Daniel Bell article on Schumpeter's "tax state" in *The Public Interest;* Warren Brookes's columns in the *Boston Herald,* John Hotson's book on stagflation: These are some of the voices that made the most distinct impression on me. There were many others, including the grassroots organizers of ballot initiatives such as Proposition 13 in California and Proposition 2 in Massachusetts. But nowhere was there a more vocal or influential group of analysts than those assembled under Robert Bartley and George Melloan on the editorial page of the *Wall Street Journal,* including Jude Wanniski, Irving Kristol, James Adams, and Paul Craig Roberts.

Indeed, for sheer impact, probably nothing came close to Wanniski's 1977 article in *The Public Interest,* later incorporated in *The Way the World Works.* All of the elements of what later came to be known as supply-side economics are here: the reliance on professional authority (it is intimated that Robert Mundell and Arthur Laffer are collectively "a new Keynes"), the simple, powerful rhetorical device (the Laffer Curve, drawn on a napkin), the relatively extravagant claims for the effects of changing marginal tax rates as an incentive to work (tax shelters would vanish and economic activity boom). It remained mainly for the publication of George Gilder's *Wealth and Poverty;* the famous "Dunkirk memo" from David Stockman and Lewis Lehrman, calling for emergency measures in the days just after the election of Ronald Reagan in 1980; for the rosy Claremont Institute forecasts in connection with the first Reagan administration budget; and the implication of Ibn Khaldoun in the analysis for supply-side economics to be complete.

It is importance to recognize that all the while, a parallel movement was taking place in technical economics at a substantially more sophisticated level. Again, it is hard to sort out the strands: Certainly the 1973 oil price shock had a great deal to do with making economists look at the determinants of aggregate supply, and some serious people believe that technical supply-side economics was in fact invented at a Brookings Conference in 1974 by Robert Gordon (in which case Mundell's advocacy of tight money/loose fiscal policy as an antidote to stagflation at Bologna in 1970 is presumably a case of "premature discovery," like Alfred Wegener venturing the continental drift hypothesis fifty years before the experts were ready for it).

Indeed, economists all along the line were taking a considerable leap forward in technique during the 1970s. Martin Feldstein in public finance and Dale Jorgenson in capital theory, to name two of the most prominent, were awakening their colleagues to the possibilities that there was something more to economics than overall monetary and fiscal policies. The deregulation movement was gathering force. So was the "public choice" school. By December 1977 Lawrence Klein (who was no tax protester) began his presidential address to the American Economic Association on "The Supply Side," saying, "It is worth considering whether a new basic model should guide our thinking about the performance of the economy as a whole."[17]

These parallel movements, each pitched to a very different level of discourse, gave rise to some pretty funny conversations among persons ostensibly serving the same gods. Jude Wanniski wrote *The Way the World Works* at that citadel of traditional Republicanism, the American Enterprise Institute, for example. George Gilder often found himself in rooms full of graybeards. It was no good to protest that both movements were dedicated to a rediscovery of the virtues of *The Wealth of Nations,* to clearing away governmental impediments to individual action (as indeed they were); the standards of proof, to say nothing of the social systems of the two groups of analysts, were so completely at odds as to ensure nearly total war, rhetorically speaking. The battle lines were drawn early on. George Bush's "voodoo economics" was an early signal; Herbert Stein's "punk supply-sidism" was a choice example of the rhetoric of this debate. William Greider's account for *Atlantic Monthly* of his conversations with David Stockman over a period of many months in 1981 was surely the most important document in this contest; when the Reagan administration's budget chief disavowed his belief in the more glowing promises of the tax-cutters, the authority of the dissidents collapsed.

How much did the press have to do with the diffusion of these "supply-side" ideas? Rather little, I would say, at least if we are talking about the national press. It is simply not possible to accuse the *Washington Post* or the *New York Times* or even the news columns of the *Wall Street Journal* of having led the tax revolt. True, the big eastern newspapers were instrumental in debunking the more extravagant claims of the supply-siders, after the fact, but aside from journalists like Warren Brookes and Tom Bethell, who worked around the edges of the pack, I find it difficult to think of a single mainstream reporter who was associated with covering the tax revolt with the same degree of sympathy that, say, William Serrin covers labor issues for the *New York Times* today.

In the end, I would say that the supply-siders lost credibility with the press for many of the same reasons that the investigators of yellow rain failed to persuade the media. They tended to "go over the heads" of the professional community, directly to the public, but failed utterly to prove their charges in the arena that mattered most, the professional. The yellow rain activists accused the Soviets and their allies of making widespread use of chemical or biological agents; the supply-siders averred that it was reasonable to cut taxes without cutting spending and not suffer any dire effects in the form of deficits. In most cases, the advocates refused to respond or to change their views when challenged. They made no pretense of trying to attain that "leaning-over-backwards" honesty described by Richard Feynman as the first principle of scientific investigation.

The supply-siders picked their battles poorly. In some cases, they exhibited bad manners. Anybody who has followed Craig Roberts's columns in *Business Week* over the years is familiar with his tiresome tone to the effect that "I and only I have the secret"; never mind that what he has to say is often extremely interesting. In other cases, they simply repeated the pieties they had uttered a couple of years before without seeking to rejoin economists' responses to them, which led to devastating rejections, such as Robert Solow's curt dismissal of George Gilder's book *The Spirit of Enterprise* in *The New Republic* (there is a big literature on entrepreneurs, but Gilder hasn't read it, Solow said in effect). In still other cases supply-siders plugged into the debate by hiring economists to work with them and became part of the professional debate. Indeed, I suppose that the collaboration of Jude Wanniski and his associate Alan Reynolds has set a relatively good example to those who want to remain in the conversation. But my impression is that Wanniski and Reynolds have been lackadaisical controversialists in the technical sphere; most of their enthusiasm is reserved for the policy arena, where they continue to be highly effective.

When I drew this parallel between yellow rain and supply-side economics for the first time in 1984, I wrote, "Extravagant claims have been made, facile remedies have been offered, and repeated so insistently, in the face of so many troublesome facts, that the boys who cried Nirvana have suffered the same fate as boys who have cried wolf – indeed, in this case, they happen to be the same fellows." Very little has happened to make me change my mind, including Alan Reynolds's assertion that among the mainstream "there is a panicky political impulse to fix things that are not broken and ruin things that were almost fixed." For my money, the supply-siders lost their credibility when they chose not to deal intellectually or politically with the most important consequence of the tax act of 1981, meaning the enormous federal deficits that ensued. They lost their respectability when they attempted to deny any credit for the recovery to the foes who pushed through four tax increases in five years. Today there is little evidence that the supply-siders were right, and much evidence that they were wrong.

Mind you, there is no question at all, at least in my mind, that the conventional wisdom among economists was often wrong during the 1970s and 1980s, in ways that make you wonder how much they really know. First there was inflation, which couldn't possibly come down – until it did. Then there was the anemic, sputtering, lopsided recovery that soon broadened out into the longest sustained expansion since World War II. Then there were the twin deficits, trade and the budget, that extended as far as the eye could see, problems whose significance remains hotly debated. But all these failures are within the range of what I think of as being normal for technical economics, matters of timing and degree. As with, say, oil prices, economists may not have been very precise about the performance of the macroeconomy, but they got the broad outlines right.

An important point is that most reporters didn't climb on the supply-side bandwagon, any more than they were persuaded, except momentarily, by the government's analysis of yellow rain. They retreated into pretty much the same sophisticated agnosticism that I described in connection with the charge of chemical warfare. In their contempt for the consensus, in their unwillingness to debate, in their readiness forever to escalate their calls for a new nostrum (I think of the agitation for a return to the gold standard), supply-side economists excluded themselves from further serious consideration, at least in the main ring of the policy circus. Instead of being regarded as the repository of still-promising new ideas, supply-side economics has been assigned, permanently, I expect, to the fringe.

I chose supply-side economics to contrast with the episode of yellow rain because, in each case, advocates got themselves taken very seriously. But I could have taken critical legal studies or the Marxism associated with the University of Massachusetts at Amherst and the New School of Social Research in New York or some of the more extreme forms of monetarism associated with the universities of Rochester and Chicago. These are all movements that have failed to find their way into the mainstream; they linger on the outside. They are not quite what we mean when we talk of quacks or cranks; they are too social for that. They might even be right. But to the extent that they decline to confront their twilight status and instead seek to attract converts from outside economics and allied professions, they are fooling mainly the easiest targets: themselves.

4

What light do these episodes shed on the questions that were asked back at the beginning? We are back at McCloskey's formulation of the uneasy relationship between journalists and economists. What is a reporter to do, confronted by economists with competing claims, each armed with elaborate significance tests? What is he to do when faced with conferences like this one, where the very significance of significance tests is questioned? Here are some lessons that I suggest can be drawn, highly tentatively, from these two cases.

1. There is nothing essentially incommensurable about scientific rhetoric and the rhetoric of the demimonde. That is, the conversation can go either way, but only with the greatest difficulty. It is by no means certain that new insights won't occasionally originate outside economics, or at least on its fringe; indeed, there is some reason to believe that chance occasionally favors the less-well-prepared mind. But in fairly short order, all claims to superior wisdom must be submitted to the community of scientists for testing, and their collective judgment must be accepted and not derogated, for they do the best that they can. Clever insights, like those of Alfred Wegener about the drift of continents across the surface of the earth, might be resisted for a time, but they are not lost; even Henry George is having a vogue these days in economics, because land-use taxes are so attractive to city planners. What is essential is that in all circumstances the two communities keep talking, seeking to persuade one another, modifying claims in the light of what becomes known. The kind of I-can't-hear-you-I've-got-my fingers-in-my-ears behavior exhibited by the editorial page of the *Wall Street Journal* is the death of conversation.

2. Some rhetoric is better than other rhetoric, but the superiority of a particular mode varies with the circumstances. Models are always better than folksongs for purposes of arguing with experts, and quantifiable arguments are almost always better than unquantifiable ones, but well-modulated English language sentences are better than models for appealing to broad audiences, as, for instance, when talking economics to those outside the discipline.

3. Some sciences are more successful than others at achieving powerful consensus. Biology, for example, is far better than economics; economics is better than psychology. Why? Well, the first thing an outsider notices is that economics is not very good at the kind of relentless thin-slicing that is characteristic of the hard sciences. I recently watched Gerard M. Edelman, a distinguished biologist, attend what he said was his first-ever "scholarly" meeting. What struck him, he remarked several times, was the enormous complexity of the material under discussion. The talk was of a sort that would never be heard at a meeting of scientists, he said. It was far too ambitious in scope.

Why should economics continually fail to tear the seamless web of its subject matter? Why doesn't it mop up one small area of disagreement and then move on to the next? Well, in some sense, it does. The foundations of microeconomics and of portions of public finance have been universally agreed upon for decades. But such "reliable economic knowledge" is very difficult to apply to the human world, and you hear all kinds of reasons advanced to explain this difficulty. They range from the observation that the human condition is constantly changing in response to new knowledge to the flat assertion that the economists got it right the first time and the rest of the world is just too stupid to be persuaded. Another view, which I will merely mention, is that the field has achieved a kind of premature closure and so denies itself the tools it needs to cope. The situation in economics may bear some relation to seventeenth-century chemistry: Despite superficial controversy, there is deep-down agreement – about an interpretation that is ultimately not very fruitful.

My faith is that, even if economics is caught in a box of sorts, it will sooner or later break out, just as chemistry did, and move on to a broader, fuller understanding of the social world. Donald McCloskey, if I understand him, draws just the opposite conclusion: We may move on, but it won't necessarily be to something better. Even science isn't really "science," he says, and mathematicians themselves don't prove their theorems once and for all: They merely satisfy their interlocutors in a conversation.

To put it bluntly, in my role as "professional layman," I just don't buy this. Scientific proof, not robust conversation, is the better metaphor of economic scholarship, at least among economists. Proof allows the audience a role, too, but its rules are infinitely more demanding than those of plain old good talk, and ultimately, they yield greater satisfactions. It has been a long time since I wrote a proof or performed an experiment, but I recall rather clearly (and I hope not romantically) the exhilaration that accompanies the demonstration that "this and only this" is the right answer and will be for the rest of time (at least in this dispensation). I believe that economists already enjoy these small but breathtaking satisfactions to a considerable extent, and my hope, as a citizen and beneficiary of their science, is that the frequency and depth of the experience of discovery will continue to increase, perhaps even by leaps and bounds. Meanwhile, I must admit that the word "conversation" finds its way more and more frequently into my descriptions of what it is that economists do – a sop either to McCloskey or to my conviction that economists still have a way to go in their studies before they are entitled to cloak themselves in the rhetoric of science.

In any case, all involved will owe a debt of gratitude to Donald Mc-Closkey. He has made a powerful critique of scientism that is convincing across a broad front. More good economists will speak English and think clearly as a result. If we decline to throw the baby out with the bathwater, we owe him on that count, too. Somewhere in the vicinity of the five-hundredth anniversary of its founding, the fundamental truth of science is still what Roger Bacon said it was at the beginning: "Truth emerges more readily from error than from confusion."

Notes

1. Donald N. McCloskey, *The Rhetoric of Economics* (Madison; University of Wisconsin Press, 1985), 180.
2. John Ziman, *Public Knowledge* (New York: Cambridge University Press: 1968).
3. Thomas Kuhn, *The Essential Tension* (Chicago: University of Chicago Press, 1977), 235.
4. Ziman, *Public Knowledge,* 63.
5. Richard P. Feynman, *"Surely You're Joking, Mr. Feynman!"* (New York: Norton, 1986).
6. Barry Wain, "The Chemical Warfare in Southeast Asia," *Wall Street Journal,* September 24, 1981.
7. Alexander M. Haig, Jr., "Chemical Warfare in Southeast Asia," Special Report No. 98, March 22, 1982; George P. Schultz, "Chemical Warfare in Southeast Asia and Afghanistan: An Update," Special Report No. 104, November 1982; Committee on Protection Against Mycotoxins, "Protection Against Mycotoxins," Washington, D.C.: National Academy Press, 1983.
8. Eliot Marshall, "Yellow Rain, Filling in the Gaps," *Science* 217 (July 2, 1983).
9. Sol Harmatz, *Washington Post National Weekly,* March 12, 1983.
10. Lois R. Ember, "Yellow Rain," *Chemical and Engineering News,* January 9, 1984.
11. "Science and Windmills" (editorial), *Wall Street Journal,* January 15, 1984; "None of Your Bees Wax" (editorial), March 30, 1984.
12. Peter Pringle, "Political Science," *Atlantic Monthly* (October 1985).
13. Thomas D. Seeley, Joan W. Nowicke, Matthew Meselson, et al., "Yellow Rain," *Scientific American,* September 1985. For a more personal account, see an interview with Matthew Meselson in *Arms Control Today,* September 1986. See also "Yellow Rain Evidence Slowly Whittled Away," *Science* 233 (July 4, 1986), and Philip J. Hilts, "Doubt Cast on Soviet Use of Toxins," *Washington Post,* May 29, 1987.
14. William Kucewicz, "Beyond 'Yellow Rain': The Threat of Soviet Genetic Engineering," six-part series in *Wall Street Journal.* "Soviets Search for Eerie New Weapons," April 23, 1984; "The Soviet Science of Snake Venom," April 26, 1984; "Surveying the Lethal Literature," April 27, 1984; "Lead Scientist in a Scourge Search," May 1, 1988; "Accident Prone and Asking for Calamity," May 3, 1984; "The Gates Slam Shut on a Microbiologist," May 8, 1984; "A Non-stop Russian response to World War I," May 10 1984; "When Arms Control Falls Short," May 18, 1984.
15. "The Conscience of Science" (editorial), *Wall Street Journal,* May 3, 1984.
16. For a more complete account of the supply-side movement than the sketch offered here, including citations, see the chapter on the evolution of supply-side doctrines in David Warsh, *Lindbeck's Limit* (New York: Viking, forthcoming 1989).
17. Lawrence Klein, "The Supply Side," *American Economic Review* (March 1978).

PART V

Economic rhetoric:
Its rhetoric and its consequences

CHAPTER 17

Negotiating a new conversation about economics

Arjo Klamer

We all know that, with a few exceptions, conferences are serious activities and play a critical role in our intellectual lives. But we do not necessarily know what that role is. Consequently our defense against criticism and parody is weak.

During this particular conference several people mentioned to me David Lodge's *Small World*. It was easy to understand why: The book makes fun of the world of literary critics, the very same world in which we as economists are getting interested, and especially of its conferences. "The modern conference," Lodge writes in the warm-up to his story, "resembles the modern pilgrimage of medieval Christendom in that it allows the participants to indulge themselves in all the pleasures and diversions of travel while appearing to be austerely bent on self-improvement."

But David Lodge's *Small World* is fiction, its characters are literary (although rumors have it that Stanley Fish, who is the author of Chapter 3 in this book, stood model for Professor Zapp), and its descriptions of conferences are a caricature. Conferences are not as ludicrous as Lodge makes them out to be; not many will experience them as "long hours of compulsory sociability" and end up with "the familiar conference syndrome of bad breath, coated tongue, and persistent headache, that came from smoking, drinking and talking."

So if Lodge's book, entertaining as it may be, misses the mark, what, then, are the reasons for attending conferences like this one?

The following interpretation of the conference proceedings will give a clue. In addition it will show how the proceedings amplified the themes of the new conversation as described in the first chapter by McCloskey and me; why their written representations are partly misleading, how the informal discussions brought out greater resistance to and confusion about the new conversation than the published papers indicate, how the new conversation appears to offer the best hints as to why such confusion occurs, *and* how the conference discussions have affected the new conversation.[1]

What the conference was meant to be

In the grant proposal to the National Endowment for the Humanities McCloskey, Solow, and I wrote:

> This conference will 1) stimulate interest among rhetoricians, literary critics, semioticians and philosophers for economic discourse as a text; 2) generate further interest among economists for this inquiry; 3) and bring together economists, other social scientists, humanists, economic journalists and politicians to explore the characteristics of economic rhetoric. The result should be a clearer understanding of what economists do and what we can expect from them.[2]

Accordingly, we hoped that an interdisciplinary setting would serve our objective, which was to engage economists in a discussion on their rhetoric. Several referees of the grant proposal for the National Science Foundation criticized the absence of economic methodologists who are critical of the rhetorical approach. We wanted in this conference, however, to emphasize the dialogue with practicing economists, economic journalists, and economists who are operating in the political arena.[3]

Economic rhetoric in the papers

In the opening paper McCloskey and I attempted to steer the conference away from the "old conversation" of conventional methodology to a "new conversation" that explores the discursive practice in economics. We tried to spell out the consequences of viewing economics as a form of rhetoric or an exercise in persuasion, and to anticipate the questions and criticisms that usually come our way. The conference papers published in this volume express some criticisms and reservations but generally support our proposals and take the new conversation further. The following themes emerge.

The epistemological question

The new conversation is an invitation to go beyond positivism, the epistemological position to which economists and their methodologists have been wedded during the past three decades or so. Bicchieri, a philosopher of science, makes this seem an invitation almost not worth stating. "Positivism is dead; we all agree," she proclaims at the beginning of her chapter. She refers to the loss of faith in a logic of induction, empirical verification of scientific theories, or even the possibility of strict falsification. As Bicchieri indicates, with the death of positivism the certainty with which we used to separate the objective from the subjective, the positive from the normative, facts from values, and the logic from the process of discovery is gone. The epistemological *foundation* that we once attributed to them has collapsed. There are no definite epistemological standards, such as consistency and correspondence with the facts, by which we can establish the truth and henceforth the objectivity or positivity, of a particular proposition.

The philosophical death of positivism notwithstanding, economists often seem to argue as if positivism were still alive. At least that is the claim by Wolff and Resnick in their chapter. They perceive within the Marxist tradition the continuing influence of empiricist and essentialist epistemologies that produce, according to them, deterministic and reductionistic theories. Their writing, including the essay in this volume, can be interpreted as an attempt to exorcise all traces of foundationalist beliefs and to avoid any such deterministic, essentialistic, or reductionistic form of reasoning.

Wolff and Resnick focus on the Marxist tradition, but their observations could be pertinent to economic discourse in general. Like Evelyn Waugh's Julia of *Brideshead Revisited,* who has abandoned the Catholic faith but cannot forsake Catholic mores, economists may have lost their faith in positivism – although many may actually have not gone that far – but still live by its prescriptions. Without hesitation, they keep drawing the same old distinctions, relegating final authority to the "facts" and "logic." Even in this volume we detect the legacies of positivism when Solow evokes the facticity of Emerson Hall. Keohane distinguishes positive from normative economics, and Warsh puts the natural sciences on a pedestal, alluding to their irrefutable proofs and experiments.

Naturally, it is perfectly acceptable to argue that Emerson Hall is a better "fact" than a poltergeist or, for that matter, the measured rate of inflation. Likewise, it is possible to argue on behalf of economic "science" in opposition to staring in a crystal ball. I myself would do so. Yet – and here Stanley Fish waves with his finger in the air to emphasize the point – there is *no* epistemological argument that awards science or a fact priority status by natural right. There is no authoritative standard (such as a series of "facts") that can settle in any definite way the relative merits of writing down formulas versus staring into the crystal ball. Each of the mentioned arguments is just that: arguments, that is, statements that can be disputed and may need further argumentation. There is no final criterion that ends all discussion.

And so what? Fish challenges anyone who is willing to follow the argument thus far. He himself believes that no consequences follow for what he does as a literary critic: "[My] epistemology, which I was rehearsing so blithely

and liberally to the theoreticians on Monday, is irrelevant to what I see and
say about [*Paradise Lost*] on Tuesday.'' But the chapters that follow his seem
to belie the assertion.

The interpretation of economics

A major consequence of the antifoundationalist position turns out to
be a reinterpretation of what it is that economists do. The logical structure of
economic theories, narrowly logical criteria of appraisal, the main objects of
study in conventional methodology, are subsumed in a more comprehensive
interpretive framework; logical expressions and ''facts'' are only two of the
many rhetorical devices that characterize economic discourse. Within the new
conversation, as an interpretation of what economists do, we explore the non-
logical factors that operate in economic discourse, analyze the production of
meanings, and search for principles, values, and argumentative strategies that
enable and constrain the furthering of discourse. Michel Foucault (1972),
using economic terms, expresses this project as follows:

> To analyze a discursive formation is to weigh the ''value'' of state-
> ments, a value that is not defined by their truth, that is not gauged
> by a secret content, but which characterizes their place, their capac-
> ity for circulation and exchange, their possibility of transformation,
> not only in the economy of discourse but more generally in the ad-
> ministration of scarce resources. (p. 125)

We can interpret the chapters by Mirowski, Weintraub, Denton, Goodwin
and Hartmann and Folbre as contributions to this reinterpretation of economics as a discursive or rhetorical practice. Each of these chapters brings out
new insights into specific episodes and aspects of neoclassical economics.
Weintraub, for example, ventures to deal with a question of meaning, a question that has no place in conventional economic methodology.[4] He analyzes
how we can distinguish two discursive practices through the different meanings they produce of the concept ''equilibrium.'' Denton shows the peculiarities of the rhetorical practice in econometrics and Mirowski analyzes the
impact of physical analogies in economic reasoning. Hartmann and Folbre
discuss the neoclassical treatment of the family as the location where the
principle of self-interest mysteriously ceases to operate, and expose the ideological implications and analytical contradictions that result.

Whereas these chapters look into economic texts and in particular into their
language, Coats advocates a furthering of the inquiry into the social realm. In
accordance with his reasoning, standards by which economists argue are the
products of social processes. For example, we might interpret certain do's
and don't's in economic discourse as the result of the academization of that

discourse.[5] There does not appear to be a serious theoretical opposition be-tween the sociological framework that Coats champions and the linguistic interpretations that dominate in the other chapters. Admittedly, sociological research will take us away from the economic texts into seminar rooms, ref-eree reports, information on social networks, graduate programs, and so on, but this research too will compel us to achieve discourse. After all, what else is a social convention but a discursive practice congealed?

The terms *practice* and *process,* which appear many times in the preceding paragraphs, contain a first hint as to the role of conferences in economic discourse. The new conversation prods us to let loose of the conventional distinction between the product and the process of economic reasoning or, similarly, between the logic and process of economic discovery. Discovery and validation occur in a continuous process, with scientific articles being mere stills taken from a movie. Studying the articles without seeing and ex-periencing the process will not enable one to understand what is going on and, more importantly, how to participate. The informal setting of a conference provides a condensed experience of the process of (economic) argumentation.

I will later return to this theme; in the meantime it behooves me to point out that if there is indeed more to a discourse than can be learned from its written form, then reading the written proceedings of this conference and the written interpretation thereof is only a partial representation of what went on.

Rhetorical devices in economic discourse

Being accustomed to slice the logical structures from economic dis-course, we still have much to learn about the complex compositions of argu-ments, analogies, enthymemes (incomplete syllogisms), stories, and other rhetorical devices that make up actual economic discourse. Several essays contribute to this learning. Clower's chapter, for example, expose the stories that physicists tell. Implicit is an argument a fortiori: If physicists tell stories, then we should not be surprised that economists do. His essay is significant not only on this account, but also because it predates the work on rhetoric of economics by more than ten years.

Denton's discussion of argumentative strategies in econometrics is not rhe-torical in the sense that it exploits rhetorical concepts. It could, however, be interpreted as a deconstruction of econometric discourse, exposing its hiatuses and inconsistencies.

An important theme that emerges in the essays is the role of metaphors and their kin, analogies, in economic discourse. McCloskey has gone a long way in pointing out the ubiquity of metaphors in economics; Goodwin in his con-tribution to this volume takes up the suggestion to direct our attention to the change in the metaphors economists use when they switch from the academic to the political arena. Bicchieri and Mirowski further the argument. Bicchieri makes a theoretical argument for the cognitive significance of scientific metaphors, and Mirowski makes mainly an empirical argument, pointing out the dominant presence of the natural science in economics through the use of physical analogies and suggestive labels and titles. Their arguments bring out new questions. We are, namely, asked to wonder how metaphors facilitate and constrain economic discourse, and which meanings they make possible and which ones they exclude.

That metaphors matter and are more than ornament is also illustrated by reactions to the metaphors in the new conversation. "Conversation," "argument," "rhetoric," "discourse," and "interpretation," as terms to characterize the activities of economists, are metaphors that produce particular meanings, that is, connections with other things we know, with phrases that pop up in our mind, with things we have read. Those meanings are not necessarily positive; Solow, for example, is bothered by the very suggestion that economics is "like a conversation." It sounds too permissive to him. In the context of the new conversation the use of these metaphors is intentional; They change the perspective on what economists do and produce new meanings. The intended references are to the writings of people like Ludwig Wittgenstein, Richard Rorty, Michel Foucault, Thomas Kuhn, Chaim Perelman, and Jürgen Habermas. But as long as people associate "conversation" with what usually happens in the drawing room, "rhetoric" with "mere rhetoric," "argument" with war, and "metaphor" with ornament, we are in for difficult times.[6]

Differences

Several of the essays in the volume entertain the possibility that economic discourse consists of incommensurable discursive practices. Such possibility is usually not entertained in the conventional conversation about economics: There, themes of unity, identity, and continuity prevail. The conventional argument represses historical, cultural, and personal varieties in favor of one or another universal structure; to demonstrate continuity, Adam Smith is preferably depicted as Milton Friedman or Robert Lucas wearing a wig, and the desire for unity, the preeminent feature of a mature science, readily prompts a playing down of disagreements among economists. In contrast, the new conversation stimulates the consideration of a difference, discontinuity, and disagreement.[7]

Difference is the theme in Weintraub's chapter, which can be read as a study of the different meanings that the concept "equilibrium" assumes in economics. The implication is that there are different discursive practices. Hartmann and Folbre try to legitimize an economic argumentation that is different from conventional neoclassical reasoning: In their world altruistic and selfish motives operate in both places to which they are commonly confined in conventional economics, namely altruistic motives to family economics and selfish motives to market economics.

The theme of differences also plays in several of the other essays. Keohane, Goodwin, Galbraith, and to a lesser extent Warsh deal with the phenomenon of different audiences or interpretive communities. They all perceive the transformation of academic discourse when it is taken out of the community of academic economists and placed in the midst of politicians, board members of foundations, political scientists, and the public. I have already mentioned Goodwin's observation of the switch from mechanical to biological metaphors when economists venture into the public domain. Galbraith notes that "economists [in congressional hearings] leave the special languages of their profession at home." The reason for this is, according to him, that in the situation of the politician the rhetoric of economists fails to make sense: Its terms are unintelligible; moreover, their interests differ from those of academic economists. Keohane takes a similar approach in his attempt to disentangle economic from political (academic) discourse. Like Galbraith, Keohane claims differences for his discourse that render the generic neoclassical model at least partially inadequate. Finally, Warsh compares two argumentative strategies, namely, the one followed by *Wall Street Journal* editors and the other by the scientist.

These studies of differences within and without economic discourse evoke further questions. For example, to what extent can one mode of discourse be translated into another without loss of meaning? Do these cases truly represent incommensurability (cf. Thomas Kuhn)? My tentative answers are affirmative: Incommensurability expresses itself in the emotional and cognitive problems that people experience when they move from one discursive practice to another. Incommensurability points at structural communication problems. Incommensurability may also be the cause of the problems experienced during the conference.

Consequences

What are the consequences of one discursive activity for another? Fish sprung the question when he asserted that nothing follows from the rhetorical perspective or from statements, such as that "all economic conversations are rhetorical" and "metaphors matter." This is the type of question that can engender confusion and embarrassment in almost any situation. We only need to ask, after listening to whatever people have to say, "What is the big deal?" or more politely, "What you say is interesting, but what difference does it make?" to make anyone, from the poet to a politician, and certainly an academic economist, flutter. Socrates might have shrugged his shoulders, but in this modern age we feel compelled to respond; There must be an external purpose to what we say; it must do some good.

The question had certainly an impact on the conference participants. It inspired the title of this volume and the concluding essay by McCloskey. A few remarks will suffice here.

As I have remarked earlier, the essays bespeak the consequences of the new conversation for the interpretation of economics as a discipline. But what are the consequences for the discipline? Does the new conversation call the discipline into question or does it affirm the status quo?

According to several authors in this volume, the main consequences are moral with only minor consequences for the practice of economics as such. Keohane, for example, concludes that economists could be more modest, and Denton hopes that awareness of their rhetorical practice will spur econometricians to search for better methods. These implied consequences are in line with those envisioned in the introductory chapter.

Others, however, use their rhetorical interpretation as an argument for change. To Wolff and Resnick the consequence of their epistemological critique of Marxism is a Marxist economics that is nondeterministic, nonessentialistic, and nonreductionistic. Mirowski exploits the analysis of physical analogies in physics to persuade the reader that something is wrong in neoclassical economics. Folbre and Hartmann follow a similar strategy, suggesting an economics that incorporates both selfish and altruistic motives in the analysis of both market and intrafamily behavior. In all these cases the hegemony of a particular discursive practice is called into question.

These responses notwithstanding, the question stands. As much as we can claim for our thoughts, we do not know how they affect the thoughts of others and the actions of anyone, including ourselves. Fish may be right when he suggests that specific consequences for economic discourse do not *necessarily* follow from the new conversation. Nevertheless, it is conceivable that the moral and interpretive implications will alter argumentative strategies in neoclassical and Marxist discourse. McCloskey has thus far maintained that no such consequence follows for neoclassical economics, but as Mirowski says, there appears to be a cognitive dissonance between his neoclassical portrayal of human behavior and the portrayal that emerges in his writing on the rhetoric of economics. Who knows what consequences such a tension will produce?

Further negotiation

The conference proceedings matter. Let me give a personal example to illustrate (and to introduce the next step in the interpretation).

While writing this interpretation I have become painfully aware of short-comings in "rhetoric" and "conversation" as metaphors for what we do. The image of the rhetor appears to pit the speaker as a sole individual against the others who are the audience. Such an image negates the goings back and forth, the dialogues, the interactions, poor as they often may be, that take place. These interactions are certainly part of the associative network that the metaphor "conversation" engenders, but here the associations take us to the other extreme of the communicative possibilities as they allude to an intimacy and familiarity that only rarely occurs in our world. In view of our differences and the resulting communication problems, genuine conversation with all partners participating more or less equally is rare. It occurred to me that the interactions during the conference resembled a negotiation: We were negoti-ating our positions more than anything else. It seems to me now that "nego-tiation" is a better metaphor than "rhetoric" or "conversation." Persuasion is part of the negotiation, but in the academic community persuasion cannot be too blatant lest one be dismissed. At times conversation, the most pleasant form of negotiation, is possible, but at other times, certainly with someone like Fish in the room, argumentation with complete abandon is the medium for negotiation. Negotiations can result in some kind of compromise; they also can break down.

So we negotiated. Some of the negotiations come through in the essays. For example, McCloskey and I had claimed there is no such thing as an Archimedean point from which we can appraise all candidates for truth, but Fish pointed out, correctly I think, that we, by being in a particular (discur-sive) situation, necessarily assume an Archimedean point from which we judge other situations. (But, again, it matters that we deny such a point any absolute status.)

Solow asks to negotiate when he wonders whether the new conversation is "Going Too Far." He objects in his commentary to the "conversation" met-aphor and does not see why we would not award priority status to certain facts. His comments could be interpreted as the reactions of someone who maintains a commitment to the positivistic perspective, or simply someone who reads anarchy and relativism into the new conversation. But, and now I negotiate quite openly, there is also a possibility that Solow tells us that *we have not yet gone far enough*. His discomfort may namely be attributed to the lack of a fully developed interpretive framework in the new conversation. We have identified metaphors, arguments, and other rhetorical devices in eco-nomic discourse, all of which is fine, but the question is, now what? We could ask ourselves how, for example, the inquiry into cognitive processes would fit, how we can connect with sociological and anthropological research, and where rhetoric and hermeneutics could merge. I would agree with such im-plications of Solow's comments.

Heilbroner asserts that McCloskey does not go far enough. Part of his argument is that McCloskey leaves the ideological content of neoclassical economics untouched. On this I side with Heilbroner, and Mirowski, Folbre, and Hartmann, who make a similar argument. But this is no argument against the new conversation as such: Mirowski, Folbre, and Hartmann show how we can unpack "ideological" aspects of neoclassical economics through a rhetorical analysis. The other part of Heilbroner's argument is that McCloskey's rhetorical approach only deals with stylistic issues, not with substance. Here I object. As McCloskey and I argue in the opening chapter, our understanding of economic discourse will improve if we think of style as substance. In that case we will consider metaphors, the use of mathematics, poetic phrases, and so on as part of our argumentative strategies. (We can, of course, reach the conclusion that certain elements of an argumentative strategy are superfluous, vague, or misleading, but it is misleading to call such elements "stylistic.")

From written to spoken discourse

Up till now the interpretation produces a favorable picture of the new conversation. The authors in the volume, with the possible exception of David Warsh, virtually overrule the rhetorician Stanley Fish through their endorsement of the rhetorical perspective on economics.

However, the interpretation is based on the written records of the conference. And those records are only a partial representation of the events. Even though several authors revised their essays after the conference, in a few cases quite thoroughly, the essays do not really respond to the discussions. McCloskey's is an exception as it was written in reaction to Fish's provocation, illustrating the toughness of the negotiations.[8]

And indeed the informal discussions were often unsatisfactory. I (it is difficult to speak for others on this) was left with the strong impression that several of the participants may not have understood what the new conversation is all about and certainly were not persuaded by it.

For example, the following statements came up time and again:

- "This stuff [that is, the new conversation] is interesting, but I am bothered by the fact that they throw out the question."
- "This is a dangerous line: If they [McCloskey and Klamer] are right, then Hitler could be right."
- "The rhetorical position implies that we should let a thousand flowers bloom."

All these statements amount to the identification of the antifoundationalist position, which is implicit in the new conversation, with "relativism" and Feyerabend's world, where allegedly "anything goes."

We argued that the new conversation does not imply a relativistic position. Any discourse or conversation necessarily embodies standards, but no standard earns its place by natural right or, for that matter, by verdict of the philosopher. We can only meaningfully operate within a particular discursive situation the standards that constrain our "rationality" or "good sense." Fish's phrase is that "we can never not be in a situation." On the fear of relativism he writes "while relativism is a position one can entertain, it is not a position one can occupy" (1980: 319) For better or worse, we are always wedded to an interpretive community.

These difficulties could be the symptoms of an incommensurability between the "old," conventional notions of what economics is, and the new perspective. The metaphors of "rhetoric," "conversation," "discourse," and "argument" may produce too many negative meanings for those familiar with the introductions to textbooks. Some may resist because they still fail to perceive a fully developed alternative. Whatever the reason, the communication problem seems real.

It behooves me to point out that the preceding paragraphs are informed by the heuristics of the new conversation. Some of the books that one reads within that conversation call attention to the role of *spoken* discourse in science.[9] It appears that spoken discourse can generate a different sense of what people think. That suggests a further argument in support of conferences.

Some time ago Socrates told Phaedrus that spoken discourse is to be preferred over written discourse (as we know thanks to Plato's writings). Writing, Socrates said, "is a recipe not for memory, but for reminder. . . . [Written words] seem to talk to you as though they were intelligent, but if you ask them anything about what they say, from a desire to be instructed, they go on telling you the same thing forever" (Plato 1961: 520–1). Socrates refers here to the dialogue as only possible in the oral situation such as is provided by a conference. In a short span of time we learn a lot because we can query the spoken text simply by checking with the speaker.

A conference as an occasion for talk is furthermore important because it provides an opportunity to "perform" our discourse. We learn to memorize and appropriate the tacit rules that separate the permissible from the impermissible, the persuasive from the unpersuasive.

Conversations with Economists (Klamer 1983) intended to show how spoken discourse adds crucial insights into the way a discourse proceeds. Economists tend to alter their rhetoric when they speak rather than write about their ideas. Recently various sociological studies have analyzed the difference between spoken and written accounts to learn more about the formation of scientific discourse (see note 9). Laboratory talk deviates from the written article in the sense that it is more personal and political. Its stories are different, too. For example, whereas in writing scientists emphasize continuity and agreement and the role of facts in the process of discovery, when they talk about their work they more readily refer to change, to strong and unresolvable disagreement with colleagues, and to the importance of the "gut" feeling in discoveries. In writing scientists present a formal and rational picture of their discourse. In talk they tell personalized stories in which excitement, persuasion, frustration, and commitment feature prominently. The very same appears to be happening in economics. This conference was a good example.

Someone who knows economics mainly through its written accounts would have been likely taken aback by what he or she heard during the conference. At least my students were. What follows are a series of comments they picked up from the discussions and conversations.

"[. .] was fun." "That may be so, but he did not make much sense to me. Frankly, I thought it was hogwash." "That guy was incredible: He had the economists in the palm of his hands." "[. .] clearly made an impression. I had not heard his talk, but I quickly learned all about it as people kept on referring to what he had said."

"[. .] is a true Renaissance scholar, a rare phenomenon in economics." "He seemed terrible defensive." "He is bullying us, and that annoys me a great deal."

"Does [. .] have an axe to grind?" "Those two made terrible sexist remarks; no, they did not impress me at all."

"How can he talk about rhetoric if he doesn't even speak English well? "I think, and I don't mind if you tell [. .] this, for I'm a great admirer of his, that he's struck a vein none too rich nor too deep."

"The journalists were interesting." "The journalists had no clue; I cannot believe that they are so hostile to all this."

"Fish may think that polemics is war; I think that war is hell, and polemics is a pain in the ass."

"The set up of this conference was antithetical to its very subject. In place of conversation we had the usual ex cathedra pronouncements by authorities and comments on those authoritative pronouncements with virtually no time allowed for the conversations we were there to analyze or celebrate." [To a journalist] "You completely ignore the ideological context in which your sources operate." "I would pay attention to Marxists if they had a product. But they don't."

The mores of the profession preclude the mentioning of names and the reporting of the more personal statements. After all, the prevalent rhetorical strategy is devised to maintain a facade of neutrality and to keep feelings of excitement, frustration, and anger and personal disputes within the profession. This strategy befits the modern age that sets great store by the separation of the public sphere, where rationality rules, and the personal sphere, where we can be angry, inspired, troubled, and loving. Accordingly, the common reaction of economists when confronted with the personalized and politicized language in their spoken discourse is to wave it off as having no bearing on their scientific arguments. All the gossip, all the personal opinions, all the passions that fill our conversations are denied significance.

At this point we have to acquit ourselves by lack of evidence. But the suspicion does not disappear. Could it be that through this personalized language we reveal values and standards, that we use the spoken discourse to negotiate what is permissible and what is not in a direct way that is not possible in written discourse? Could it be that through personal encounters, as they are stimulated in conference meetings, we socialize to increase the coherence of our community and thus of our discourse? Could it be that it is easier to understand the writings of someone we know and, still better, someone we like?

The sociologists and anthropologists to whom I have referred earlier would argue that the personalized spoken discourse is an integral part of scientific discourse. In the case of this conference the spoken discourse brings out more tension, more disagreement than the written discourse.

A manifesto

The shortest summary of the conference is contained in the following dialogue between two Wellesley custodians who helped out with the logistics:

"Do you know what they are talking about?"
"No, do you?"
"No, but I think that that is what they are talking about."

In other words, the conference was an exchange on the communication problem in economics, its discussions produced a discourse on discourse and the overall attempt to create clarity on rhetorical practice in economics was itself thwarted by tensions in rhetorical practices of the participants.

Through the discussions I have come to recognize that those of us who are eager to advance the new conversation may overlook the contributions of conventional methodology. The investigation of the logic of economic theories *is* important and we may not need to deny the realism of scientific objects.

But like many of the authors in this volume, I reaffirm the desire to expand the possibilities for inquiry through new questions and new concepts. We do not want to be restricted to the dissection and minute analysis of logical propositions; we want to engage in a discourse that ventures to interpret the economic discipline as a discursive activity and explores its rules of formation and its premises. These papers and these discussions are an expression of the desire to connect with intellectual traditions long ignored and disparaged within economics, to recapture the richness of history and the variety of cultures in which we operate, to redefine economists as intellectuals who do not recoil from self-imposed boundaries.

Accordingly, we want to open the border of economic discourse. Yes, we have reasons to worry about the negative effects, about the possibility that we lose the sense of a discipline and will wander around without a shared direction. But then the eagerness to invite new initiative depends on the assessment of need. Does economics need new stimulus? Do economists need to reconsider their place in the intellectual *and* the public realm?

Economics as a science is experiencing its heyday. Enrollments in economics programs have reached historic heights. Yet, as in so many instances before – the fruit of historical knowledge! – an empire at the pinnacle of its powers is prone to complacency. It would be a pity if it overlooked the forces gathering around its walls.

Notes

1. One consequence is this essay, and particularly the voice in which I have tried to write it. After writing the first version I realized, with the reactions during the conference in mind, that confrontation and provocation may be counterproductive at this time. Robert Fisher and Maria Elena Campbell helped me a great deal in this. They, together with Michel Grimaud, Donald McCloskey, and Robert Solow made many useful comments on earlier drafts.

   In addition I owe thanks to the students in the seminar on the Art of Economic Persuasion.
2. The formulation in the proposal for the National Science Foundation was slightly different.
3. In December of the previous year (1985) McCloskey and I had discussed the topic of economic rhetoric at a conference for economic methodologists. At this conference we wanted to stimulate a dialogue with economic theorists, as well as economic journalists, philosophers, and other social scientists. The proceedings of this conference are in Neil deMarchi and Wim Driehuis (eds.), *The Popperian Legacy in Economics* (Cambridge: Cambridge University Press, forthcoming).
4. The question does not appear in two collections of essays in conventional economic methodology. Cf. Bruce Caldwell (ed.), *Appraisal and Criticism in Economics*

(London: Allen & Unwin, 1984); Daniel Hausman (ed.), *Philosophy and Economics* (Cambridge: Cambridge University Press, 1984).

5. Although not mentioned as such by Coats, the claim that academic and scientific standards are socially produced begs the legitimation question that is central in the writings of Habermas. If the philosopher cannot provide a justification of science in general and scientific theories in particular, who can? I think that Coats directs us in the right way. In order to understand the privileged position of neoclassical economics since the early part of this century we need to consider the institutional environment in which the economics discipline came to flourish; we may look beyond the institutions of academia and consider the general culture and political environment that made this type of economics possible.

6. Fish says that he likes the "argument is war" metaphor. I myself, in an attempt to teach argumentation, discovered that the very association of argument with war can make for unproductive debates. At least, my students felt terrible. They were thinking in terms of who won and who lost, of beating their opponents or surrendering to them. As Lakoff and Johnson (1980) say, argument can also be thought of as a building – we construct an argument and give it support – or as a container – it has no content – or as a journey – an argument can cover a lot of terrain and we can explore the arguments. The students in my seminar liked the last associations much better. The debates improved noticeably. Apparently, metaphors do matter.

7. McCloskey has thus far emphasized agreement among economists and the unity between economics and disciplines like history and poetry. So there is disagreement within the new conversation.

8. Unfortunately, space constraints forced us to leave out the official comments on the papers. The loss of the recordings of the discussions because of technical problems hampered the interpretation that now follows.

   Space and other constraints also forced us to leave out several other presentations made during the conference. See the conference program in the appendix.

9. Such as G. Nigel Gilbert and Michael Mulkay, *Opening Pandora's Box* (Cambridge: Cambridge University Press, 1984).

Further references

Fish, Stanley. 1980. *Is There a Text in This Class: The Authority of Interpretive Communities.* Cambridge, Mass.: Harvard University Press.

Foucault, Michel. 1974. *Archeology of Knowledge,* translated by A. M. Sheridan Smith. New York: Pantheon Books.

Klamer, Arjo. 1983. *Conversations with Economists.* Totowa: Rowman and Allenheld.

Lakoff, George, and Mark Johnson. 1980. *Metaphors We Live By.* Chicago: University of Chicago Press.

Lodge, David. 1984. *Small World.* London: Penguin Books.

Plato. 1961. *The Collected Dialogues,* edited by Edith Hamilton and Huntington Cairns. Princeton: Princeton University Press.

CHAPTER 18

The consequences of rhetoric

Donald N. McCloskey

The Last Word suggests a rhetoric of "bringing the conversation to a conclusion." A conclusion would be too ambitious here. After all, aside from the trickle of anticipations by Robert Clower, Albert Hirschman, Mark Perlman, and a few others it has only been a while that economists have thought about words like rhetoric, conversation, and the social structure of scientific discourse. We are just beginning an economic criticism, as in "literary criticism," giving new readings of economics and maybe of the economy, too. A handful of people have tried to write criticism, some in this book. But the arbitrage between economics and the rest of the culture has only just begun.

So wait and see. At present it would be premature for advocates of the rhetorical approach to erect Conclusions for all time. Likewise, it would be premature for those who now consider themselves as its opponents – we live in hope they will realize soon that they are its natural allies – to throttle the infant in its cradle. Their rhetoric has been "Show me now sixty full and finished pieces of literary criticism of economics, or I won't take it seriously." We can show them six or ten or maybe twenty, and daily we produce more. Each day another economist sees that economics deserves a richer technique of reading than a three-by-five-card philosophy of science. It dawns on us that that those people in English and linguistics and communication studies cannot really all be idiots unworthy of attention. The ex-idiots' subject is reading and writing, in mathematics or in prose, of a sort that economists and watchers of economists do habitually if unselfconsciously on the job. We begin to grasp what a literary criticism of economics could mean. But it's early days yet, as I said. For the real test, the proof of the pudding, you'll have to wait.

Instead, I want to try to respond here to the best of all questions one can ask about anything: "So What?" Some of the chapters in this volume ask the question more or less explicitly; the question was the most common one at the conference itself, if sometimes only suggested by a tone of voice. An economist locked in converse with other economists can well ask why he should be made to lend an ear to another group of talkers, such as ancient rhetoricians and modern literary critics. Mathematics in the 1940s had the same problem in economics: Why should I listen to this stuff? So What?

Note that I am only trying to "respond to" the question, not answer it once and for all. Let us have a conversation. Question and response; you may well be right; I see what you mean. But note also, that "So What?" is a question about what is significant to economists, what it means to human beings, what matters to us. It will matter to us, not to God or Nature or Analytic Statements. As the "rhetoric of inquiry" in other fields has pointed out recently, the question of what matters can be answered only by attending to the conversation of the scholars who decide; it is not given an answer in God's rules of method or a table of Student's *t* (Nelson, Megill, and McCloskey 1987). Look therefore at the conversation.

The "So What?" comes from two sides. On the one side, some economists are puzzled by claims that economics is rhetorical or that economists tell stories. Since they are not much acquainted with the humanities, or even sorry that they aren't, they do not see how much claims are freighted. The word *metaphor* calls to their minds fancy writing, not models. The word *story* calls to mind fairy tales, not equilibrium. The word *authority* calls to mind the IRS, not scientific tradition. They do not see how the words of the humanities could fit a science like economics.

On the other side, many of the humanists, such as our Stanley Fish, do not see how it could matter if the words did apply. (The title "humanists," by the way, makes them uncomfortable, because it seems pretentiously parallel with "scientists," and it is equivocal with a party name inside literary studies, as Democrat is with democrat. But let it stand.) The humanists have heard all this before. So What Else Is New? They do not appreciate how unsettling it is for someone educated in modernist science to realize suddenly that argument is more than syllogism. The humanists thought everyone knew that and cannot believe that what they teach at low wages to sophomores is useful here. They cannot believe that the argumentativeness and literariness and figurativeness of economics has not been discounted already. They are like the bankers in a *New Yorker* cartoon gazing out of a War-of-the-Worlds scene: "I suppose," says one with a look of resignation, "that the market has discounted *this*, too."

Two unpersuasive answers, though true

At the highest and noblest level a scientist is a truth teller (small *t*, mind you), so it cannot be irrelevant to say truly that economic science uses metaphors and stories and other devices of rhetoric. The first answer to the question why it matters, in other words, is that economics, dammit, *is* rhetorical.

Unfortunately, the answer is not very helpful unless one is already prepared to see the devices of rhetoric as significant. After all, economics uses the Roman alphabet, too, but no one says that economics would be a lot different if it were written in the Arabic alphabet (now, if it were written *in Arabic* that would be another story). The alphabet is not significant: Changing to another alphabet would not matter, at least to us. Similarly, someone who is outside the word-culture, or who anyway believes fondly that he is, resists the idea that words matter. Rhetoric is just a surface ornament, right?

The problem with responding to such resistance to the significance of words is that you need to be raised up to take things as significant. The attribution of significance is a human habit, limited by nature but not forced by it. Someone unacquainted with the culture of baseball will see episodes of meaningless rushing about in a context of meaningless standing around. Someone acquainted with it, who takes the meaning, sees a shift of the infield for a pull hitter, a hard chance to deep shortstop, and a sweetly turned double play.

Therefore the most general argument from truth telling is not persuasive to the audience addressed. It is rhetorically ineffective, the central teaching of rhetoric being that speech is addressed to an audience. The "simple truth" (as we see it) that economics is rhetorical may be accepted as "true" in some weak sense, but not in the strong sense of "true and, by God, significant." Klamer and I discovered this at the conference. The conference contained mostly people working in another tradition than the humanistic. (Although it must be admitted that Klamer and I have come to our humanistic learning a bit late, in my own case after forty and after Iowa. Our lack of believable claims to expertise in such stuff is another complication in our rhetorical task.) It was hard for the audience at the conference to agree to our changing in the subject. Changing the subject is always hard, because the audience must accept that the new subject is on its face significant. And that is a matter of intellectual culture.

To come down a turret or two from the peaks of plain truth, then, one can argue alternatively yet equally grandly that a literary approach to economics will bring economics back into the conversation of mankind. By showing that economics works in ways that poems and novels work we show economics to be humanistic as well as scientific, part of the rest of the conversation. But you see the problem. The argument is again unpersuasive to much of the audience, the much that sneers at the very word *humanistic*. Surely, they say as their lips curl in contempt, the purpose of all this wearisome mathematics is precisely to get away from the imprecise, touchie-feelie, value-laden, and, yes, let it be said, feminine world of words and to get over into the solid, masculine world of science.

A place to stand

All right, let's be harshly practical, then. A low-brow answer to the question "So What?" is this: A literary, humanistic, rhetorical approach to economics provides the economist with a place to stand outside the field. We need it, and think so, as we demonstrate in our frequent appeals to fancied rules of epistemology or scientific method. ("All macroeconomics must be grounded in microeconomics"; "Survey research cannot yield truthful results"; "Economics will only become scientific when it becomes experimental.") We economists cannot see what we are doing from inside economics itself.

"Well," the modernist will reply, "in finding places from which to look at economics, why not stick at least with the old familiar lookouts in epistemology and philosophy of science?" I have already answered the question at length elsewhere, heaping scorn on the Received View, so the argument here will stick to a modest and pragmatic point (cf. McCloskey 1988a, where it is given at greater length). The point is that the humanistic half of our feast, a theory of reading and writing now two and a half millenia from its beginnings, is thicker in the eating than the thin little philosophies of epistemology and scientific method permitted to a modernist. That is one theme in the papers here. The rhetorical tradition is thick and rich and nourishing. It sustains the life of the mind better. It gives us more true things to say about economic science, more analogies to draw on, more insights into why we agree or disagree. An uncriticized science is not worth having. As a place from which to articulate an economic criticism, humanism works better than modernism.

To put the point another way, a rhetorical approach to economics fits better with being human. This is not to say that the method of science is inhuman. The problem is that it is only one tiny part of being human. (The defenders of modernism at this stage leap up and shout, "Aha! Yes, it is the *scientific* part of being human." They exhibit again their strange nationalism about a border between Science and other things. When asked why the border is desirable, they will start talking politics. Their political arguments are not very good. The political argument for modernism is that we must be closed minded to protect ourselves from the unscientific, as we must adopt police-state methods to compete with police states. But democratic values would seem to be defended best by open-minded pragmatism and good rhetoric. It seems unlikely that they are best defended by chanting some philosopher's notion of scientific method and lynching the spoonbenders and psychoanalysts. In any case, the philosophical border patrol, jack-booted and bureaucratized, has not succeeded. The philosophical distinction between scientific and other thinking has proven to be self-contradictory and lacking in point. Sociologists and historians of science have found nothing corresponding to the distinction in the lives of actual scientists.)

Rhetoric fits a life in science better. It seems so in my own life. A rhetorical look at economics, for instance, fits the human love of stories. The stories in *The Worldly Philosophers* entranced many a sophomore like me, solving sweetly the problem of an economics without a past, an economics inaccessible to outsiders and unpersuasive to insiders. Even high theory speaks with such a story, an intellectual adventure yarn in which D. Ricardo's and A. Smith's verbal insights are rendered wonderfully exact and portentous by P. Sraffa or F. Hahn.

Rhetoric, again, gives a way to understand the persuasive power of diagrams in economics, their metaphors and symmetries, which I came like so many others to admire passionately in my second year. For the same esthetic reasons I came in my third or fourth year to admire the mathematics. Its beauty is its truth, or it had better be. A thin little philosophy of alleged prediction – although it, too, had its esthetic attractions to a graduate student – cannot account for our scientific convictions.

Rhetoric provides a place to stand from which to admire and criticize radically different metaphors of economic life, such as the Marxist metaphor of class struggle, which I admired as an undergraduate, or the institutionalist metaphor of human geography, which I fell naturally into as an early graduate student, or, at length discovering the truth in my third year at Harvard, the Chicago School metaphor of tough little monads rushing about in search of rents. Rhetoric, therefore, allows human politics to matter, in an open and self-critical spirit. At present we allow it only secretly. Here is an answer to Heilbroner's argument that rhetoric is about style, not political substance. Woolf, Resnick, Hartmann, and Folbre find rhetoric useful for a politics that is not mine.

The antirhetorical split of fact from value in the modernism I espoused as a graduate student had the advantage of allowing specialized work on one metaphor. (Incidentally, when specialization is wheeled out as an argument for academic narrowness, everyone forgets, as a graduate student would be likely to and did, that the point of specialization is to achieve in the end wider exchange for other goods.) The specialization allowed many an economist-in-training to believe that his values did not figure in his science. It allowed the economist to make the traverse from socialist to libertarian without noticing the role that the learning of economics itself had played in the traverse.

Rhetoric also makes for understanding between different styles of thought, such as economics and history, the one metaphorical, the other storytelling. I experienced this, too, as an economist speaking to historians and as a nineteenth-century liberal speaking to twentieth-century liberals. The tolerance in rhetoric is not the thoughtless pluralism forced on the modernist by his lack of a way of debating values – "Heh, man; you have your opinion; I have mine. Let's leave it at that." It is principled pluralism, insisting that people defend their values openly. It is not apolitical. Rhetoric is a theory of democratic pluralism and of general education in a free society. That is no news. Rhetoric was the handmaiden of freedom in the Greek assemblies, the Roman law courts, and latterly the parliaments of Europe. It was the education of the West from Socrates to Francis Bacon.

The good of having economists educated to see their field from the outside will be certain improvements in the practice of economic argument. To the sneer that learning rhetoric "isn't economics" one can only point out that most of what economists do is reading. It would be like saying that learning mathematics "isn't economics," and then expect the economist denied mathematical sophistication to read and write well in mathematical theory. Economists at present misread. The humanities constitute a theory of reading, and a way of improving the readings. Humanistic criticism in other fields, such as literature and painting, does not so much change the practice of the artists as create an audience of sophisticated readers. Economists who could see that Becker's theory of the family depends on the aptness of certain metaphors or that Keynes's theory of the business cycle depends on the reader filling in certain blanks with his own stories would be better scientists and more cautious advocates. A better reader of Jane Austen or of Joan Robinson has critical understanding.

An audience of better readers of economics would demand the writers to be better, too. The derived demand for courses on writing would at last force the graduate schools to do their job of teaching people to write. Sweet prospects open up: of economic writing without the table-of-contents paragraphs ("The organization of this paper is as follows") and without the acronyms weighing down the reader's memory ("The coefficient on DMWITSCI is significant at the 0.05 level and the coefficient on FAKESCHL at the 0.01 level").

But more than literary style is at stake. The substance of economic scholarship depends on how well we argue with each other. Economists cannot be honest about their arguments if they cannot see what they are. Economists write badly because their audience is not their colleagues in labor economics or trade theory across the hall: Unlike most historians, they barely read their colleagues' work in other fields, even for cases of promotion, and depend instead on the candidate's reputation among his fellow specialists. This makes for quick and voluminous but shallow and fashion-ridden science. Rhetorical self-awareness is a substitute for critical reading by colleagues in different fields.

Style and substance in economic argument

And the substance of economic scholarship will be changed. That's another argument, besides the blessed place to stand. "Aha," says the modernist, "he's finally gotten to the substance, after all the maundering about style." To which comes the reply: Get serious. The distinction between style and substance has burrowed like a worm deep into our culture, and even people who recognize its sophomoric character can barely keep it out of their speech, yet it has few merits. It is all style and no substance. Consider. What is the distinction of style and substance in ice skating or still-life painting or economic analysis? Is one accomplished in the substance of skiing, stripped of mere style, if one rolls down the hill or falls every ten feet? By style we mean properly the details of substance. God dwells in the details. Style is not a frosting added to a substantial cake. The cake itself has style, as when whipped egg whites produce angel food. The "substance" of a cake is not the list of basic ingredients. It is the style in which they are combined. Talking about the style of modern economics, therefore, does not forsake the substance.

All right, all right, get to it, then. If economists pay more attention to their style and recognize their rhetoric, how will economics change?

The question should make an economist uncomfortable. To answer it is to claim prescience – pre-science, knowing before one knows. The methodologies do this. They say that they know what will make for good economics, an economics of this or that sort, and they say they know it before it is known. Wait a minute. An economist should ask, "If you're so smart why aren't you rich?" (McCloskey 1988b). Still, if they turn out better than predictions of interest rates or of the Dow-Jones average I'll be surprised, and for the same economic reasons.

The chief way that a rhetorical economics would differ from the present economics, to repeat, is that it would face the arguments. An economics that does not recognize its own rhetoric can avoid facing the arguments of opponents indefinitely. That is how things have gone so far. Unrhetorical economics claims to "test" its "hypotheses" by confronting "the facts" and scrutinizing "the theory." That this is not a persuasive description of economic discourse may be inferred from one decisive observation: Economists go on disagreeing violently about the degree of competition in American markets, the degree of dependence on international markets, the closeness of fit of rational models to ordinary people, and twenty other things.

As I said at the beginning, the question of what arguments should count in settling such disagreements – a variant of the question "So What?" – is about what is significant to economists, what matters to them. It matters to *us*, not to God. We have no way to get outside our own human conversations and get into the mind of God in order to tell whether such and such an argument is True. We only have ourselves to argue with, showing to each other whatever numbers and symmetries and metaphors we agree should matter. In the absence of rhetorical self-consciousness – the rough-and-tumble of seminars or the conversations of coauthors can often produce such self-consciousness without explicit education – we have low argumentative standards. (Take note: the "lack of standards" so often attributed to an antiepistemological approach is on the other foot.) The ignorance of rhetoric leaves economists unable to confront doubts, really confront them. Run another regression that no one else believes. Deduce another consequence that no one else is persuaded by. Adduce another institutional fact that no one else sees as relevant.

For instance, it would be hard for a rhetorically sophisticated economist to go on speaking of macroeconomics in a closed economy. A rhetorical approach would show most of macroeconomics to be misled. Rhetoric notes that economic theory is a way of speaking, convenient to human purposes, not a report on the mind of God. We speak about the openness of, say, Iowa to the prices and interest rates of the rest of the world, and would not think of building a closed model of the Iowa economy. The price of soybeans and the wage of well-motivated and well-educated workers is determined in the world economy, not in Iowa. Iowa is open. But by the same standards of speaking we would not think of the American economy as closed. (That the point is routinely mixed up with the small-country assumption is testimony to the rhetorical muddle. It does not in fact matter whether America bulks large or small in the world; what matters is whether its price for wheat is connected with that of India.) A rhetorically alert economist can see that there is no standard for the openness or closedness of an economy beyond what definition we choose to give the words. God will not tell us what He has in mind for a standard of openness. We human economists have to decide. And when we decide for one economy (Iowa's, say), we have implicitly decided for economies as open as our standard.

It is suddenly common in the late 1980s to talk about one world economy. It's about time. Since the eighteenth century the American economy has been as open in some respects as Iowa is today. To say that we are *now* in a single world economy is a little behind the times. We have been in the world economy for some centuries now. (The real theory of international trade assumes without comment that prices are arbitraged internationally; the financial theory, mysteriously, does not.) The United States is located between the Atlantic and Pacific oceans, not on Mars.

Why should it matter? So what? Well, to put it sharply, the models of the money supply or the aggregate demand that have depended on an economy being closed have been mistaken, all this time. They have to be fitted all over

again. Throw away all the previous work. Because we were not paying attention to our standards of argument, we economists have blown it. Entirely.
Modern macroeconomics is erroneous. The econometrics is misspecified and
therefore biased. The theorizing is misinformed and therefore irrelevant. The
models of Friedman, Tobin, Lucas, or the other admirable closed-economy
thinkers may or may not work for the world considered as one. That remains
to be seen and is the relevant question. But the theories would hold for the
American economy in isolation only if it were reasonable to locate America
outside the world. Only in that case would American prices and interest rates
be determined by largely American phenomena, as the theories that we teach
our students say. By ignoring the rhetorical character of science and the human persuasion on which it turns, leaving the argument to proofs and tests,
godlike but unpersuasive, the economists have wasted their time.

The point is a general one, applying to many of the differences that separate economists. Take perfect competition (please). The Chicago School believes that perfect competition, near enough, characterizes the American
economy. Everyone else says perfect competition is ''unrealistic.'' Perhaps
what Milton Friedman was groping for in his famous dismissal of talk about
realism was a rhetorical standard. What mattered, he was saying in a pragmatic way, was how a proposition was used, its human use in argument, not
God's Truth. This is surely right. We can't go on hurling insults at each other
about the ''realism'' of our opponents' assumptions. We should come to agree
on some particular, human rhetorical standard by which the quarrel can yield
progress. The ability to predict might be one such standard, though we have
found that a lot hinges on what ''ability to predict'' means. For all the dominance of it as a rhetorical standard since the 1950s it has not ended many
arguments in economics.

But Friedman's rhetorical suggestion got mixed up in positivism, with its
supposition that ''good prediction,'' like ''empirical observation'' or ''economic theory,'' is a simple thing that any child can detect. Positivism begs
the main scientific issue. The main issue is the *adequacy* of the ''prediction''
(more likely, in economics, a postdiction), an adequacy to be determined by
standards of human speech. A prediction is not good or bad all by itself,
without the intrusion of human standards of good or bad. An R-squared of
0.90 is adequately ''good'' for some human purposes, rotten for others. It
would probably be good enough as a correlation between national incomes
for the purpose of justifying the notion of an international business cycle, but
it would probably be too low in a correlation of exchange rates for the purpose
of making money on the exchanges. Scientific explanation is a human purpose, not that glimpse into the mind of God that holy men since Plato have
been seeking in their caves. We humans decide the purposes of the phrase

"perfect competition." R-squares are nice but not enough. We need to join the argument. "What do you mean by 'perfect competition'? What standard would you accept as showing it to be usefully true? All right, let us go together and settle the matter." If economists would recognize this and stop thinking that irrelevant *t*-statistics or high-sounding "good predictions" will answer their questions free of human intervention, they would come to grips with each others' arguments.

A trial at law requires a pragmatic decision. The trial cannot go on forever or just stop without decision when the lawyers get tenure. The two sides must agree to a standard of evidence that puts a strain on them, enough strain to separate the winner from the loser. The positivist philosopher will claim that using such a rhetorical, forensic approach to science would not have standards. But he is wrong. On the contrary, the standards of "consistent theory" or "good prediction" presently in use are low, to the point of scientific fraud. They are six-inch hurdles over which the economist leaps with a show of athletic effort. A nonrhetorical economics has low argumentative standards.

The standard of a rhetorical economics would be higher, fully thirty inches: the standard, namely, of persuading readers honestly. Consider this. Is it more difficult for a Chicago economist to produce still another regression "consistent with the hypothesis" of peasant rationality or, on the other hand, to produce a set of arguments, drawn from all the evidence he can find and his audience thinks relevant, that can actually persuade an economist from Yale?

The claim that rhetoric has "no standards" is supported by an equivocation between "empirical" and "empiricism." No one in his or her right mind opposes "empirical work," so long as the phrase is understood as consulting the phenomena. It really would be antiscientific madness for an economic historian like me to suddenly begin advocating the closing down of libraries. Not just mad, but evil. Let it be said, then, that no one who wishes economists to become more self-conscious about their arguments is against empirical work – especially genuine empirical work, going beyond fitting hyperplanes through data culled from the *Economic Report of the President*.

Yet a rhetorical approach to economics does oppose the narrowing of science associated especially with British "empiric*ist*" philosophy since Hume. Empiricism in the form in which it has affected the philosophical thinking of scientists would reduce all argument to first-order predicate logic and all observation to controlled experiment. In this form it has had a bad effect on a lot of sciences. Take a look at psychology some day – or much of economics. In a search for godlike certainty the evidence has been narrowed to a rump unpersuasive to anyone. The result is a lowering of standards, the six-inch hurdles mentioned above. So it does not justify the narrowness of empiri*cism* to appeal to the undoubted virtue of the broadly empiri*cal*. Empirical work would be better, not worse, in a rhetorically self-conscious economics. The work is already better in fields, such as urban economics or economic history, that take seriously their responsibility to persuade an audience with facticity.

A rhetorical economics would be tougher and more cumulative. This sounds paradoxical, but only because the method of science is accustomed to sneering at human argument. Yet arguments are not arbitrary. They get settled if they get joined. Most arguments in economics have not been joined, at least by the standard met daily in courts of law or in most domestic squabbles. Economics since the War has been mostly noncumulative. What do we know about international trade that we did not know in 1965? Oh, really? What large issue in economics since 1940 has been settled by an econometric finding? I said "large issue." Why has economic history, where arguments are open and broad-based, made cumulative progress since 1960, and labor economics, similarly catholic in its arguments, since 1970? What argument about the economic world has general equilibrium theory advanced since 1950? A rhetorically sophisticated economics would get down to work. Economics would begin to look more like evolutionary biology, the identical twin to economics raised separately. Economics would be better if it took the arguments more seriously, by seeing them.

What will not change

On the other hand, some alleged consequences of rhetoric do not seem plausible. The openness of rhetoric gives voice to minority opinions, as may be seen in some of the chapters here. To this extent rhetoric is hostile to the mainstream, if the mainstream can hold its dominance only by erecting big dams to stop the flow of alternative arguments. That's good. But rhetoric is not hostile to the mainstream. Rhetorical alertness can be used to force the dominant groups to face up to institutionalism or Marxism or feminism or Austrianism, as they should, but nothing inside the rhetoric itself implies one or the other view.

Or so I claim. Philip Mirowski among others accuses me of "inconsistency" for advocating a rhetorical view of economics along with a Chicago neoclassical view of the economy. He wants to argue that a rhetorical approach must overturn neoclassical economics. I don't think so, at least if the word *neoclassical* is not used ahistorically. If it is narrowed to mean "the view dominant in the United States c. 1980 that economics is to be identified with fourth-rate applied mathematics," then I suppose rhetoric will at least show that the mathematics is feeble. Mirowski is probably right to attack the physics analogy, and is certainly right that rhetorical thinking can be used to open the analogy for scrutiny. But if neoclassical economics means the tradition of Marshall in economics, which in my neck of the woods means people like Theodore Schultz, Margaret Reid, Milton Friedman, Harry Johnson, Robert Fogel, and Gary Becker, then I doubt it. There is nothing inconsistent in using mathematics when it seems useful, historical example when it seems useful, thought experiment when it seems useful, to argue a case. The people I mention, and others of Chicago past, have done just this.

The attacks from various quarters on neoclassical economics seem to depend on a misapprehension of its core. A notion that important social forces arise out of self-interested behavior and that these forces are hedged about by entry and competition is plausible on its face and perfectly healthy as a program in economics. Along with some parallel and very different programs, it has been going strong since the eighteenth century. It explains many of the social facts we wish to explain, from the rise of real wages since 1840 to the difficulties of big bankers in the 1980s. I sometimes wonder if the critics of neoclassicism know what they are talking about, literally. They seem to identify neoclassical economics with Paul Samuelson's youthful enthusiasm for identifying economics with constrained maximization, embodied now in dozens of intermediate and graduate texts. I wonder if the critics have read enough real price theory from the hands of the masters, such as Armen Alchian or Ronald Coase. I wonder if they could handle the end-chapter questions in *Economic Theory, Price Theory, The Theory of Price,* or *The Applied Theory of Price.* But anyway, the rhetorical program is consistent with the genuinely neoclassical. Rhetoric is consistent with any number of beliefs about the economy.

A final calming of fears

The response in seminars and writings to the discussion of rhetoric in economics has been revealingly bimodal. The working stiffs among economists nod their heads and say, "Why, sure, of course, come to think of it, we *do* argue in more ways than fit the official scientific method. Hmm. That's interesting." Since they have no stake in a philosophical reading of economics, the proposal to give it an anthropological or literary reading does not especially alarm them. They focus on the reports from the field in Klamer's *Conversations with Economists* or the *explications des textes* in *The Rhetoric of Economics.* The philosophical prefaces to these do not stir them.

The economists with an interest in philosophical methodology, however, read differently. For them the philosophical discussion of positivism, modernism, behaviorism, and the like is what matters, not the concrete examples that fill most of the books. They misread the philosophy, construing it as "against standards" or "nihilist" or "deconstructionist'," in favor of "anything goes."

It was notable at the conference that the people with worked-out theories of economic discourse – the methodologists and the economic journalists – had the hardest time understanding what a rhetoric of economics could mean. The worked-out theories obstructed their ability to see that rhetoric is richly socio-logical as description and mildly liberal as policy. That is, they could not see that rhetorical analysis is what they have always done, if unconsciously.

But I do not want to leave the impression that the only difference between the rhetoricians and some of the methodologists is misunderstanding. True, there is a lot of that, as some of the methodologists are beginning to see. Yet philosophical disagreements remain. The primary one is what divided Plato from Aristotle and after them much of the intellectual world, namely, the transcendental absolute as against the social character of truth. For 2500 years the followers of Plato have been trying to find a way to vault out of human society into a higher realm of forms, to find a procedure for deciding whether a proposition is True or False in the eyes of God. Meanwhile the rest of us have been making decisions in human terms, sentencing people to death, resolving to mount an expedition to Syracuse, concluding that the multiplier on government spending is greater than 1.0. We have made the decisions on many grounds, good and bad, but grounds richer than the philosophical ac-counts of science.

The rhetoricians of economics are accused sometimes of being "trendy." If the charge is meant to suggest that we came to our ideas by looking around in Paris for What's New, it is biographically false and rhetorically unfair. Klamer's experience in journalism and the history of thought and mine in radical politics and economic history led us naturally to wonder about speech communities. Being shouted at and sneered at, as Wolff, Resnick, Folbre, Hartmann, Lavoie, Mirowski, and Galbraith can also testify, is a practical education in rhetoric.

If the charge of being "trendy" means merely that we have noticed lots of other people doing rhetoric and wonder dimly whether we should join, then it is true and fair. Every two weeks or so I find another part of the intellectual community – military history last week, mathematical logic this – that has discovered the rhetorical character of human speech. They do not all use the word. But they see the breadth of human argument, the limit of formulas for thinking, the way that words matter to the conclusions drawn, the conversa-tions in politics and the politics in conversations. They have learned that speech has designs on us, and that it is better to know the designs outright.

It is, when all is said, something like growing up. Perhaps the time has come for economics to grow up, too.

Works cited

McCloskey, D. N. 1988a. "Thick and Thin Methodologies in the History of Economic Thought." In *The Popperian Legacy in Economics, and Beyond: A Symposium in Honor of J. J. Klant,* edited by N. DeMarchi and W. Dreihuis. Cambridge: Cambridge University Press.

McCloskey, D. N. 1988b. "If You're So Smart: Economics and the Limits of Criticism." *The American Scholar* (Summer).

Nelson, John, Allan Megill, and Donald McCloskey, eds. 1987. *The Rhetoric of the Human Sciences.* Madison: University of Wisconsin Press.

Appendix: Other contributors and participants

The volume is a selection of the papers presented at the conference. Other presentations were:

Frank Hahn (Economics, Cambridge University): "On Some Common Mistakes in Economic Theorizing."

Robert W. Clower (Economics, University of South Carolina): "Keynes and the Classicals Revisited."

Gordon Winston: Comments on the papers by Hahn, Clower, and Folbre and Hartmann.

John Nelson (Political Science, University of Iowa): Comments on the papers by Hahn, Clower, and Folbre and Hartmann.

Zvi Griliches (Economics, Harvard University): Comments on paper by Denton.

Axel Leyonhufvud (Economics, UCLA): Comments on papers by Weintraub and Mirowski.

Donald Lavoie (Economics, George Mason University): Comments on papers by Bicchieri, Coats, and Wolff and Resnick.

"Economic Rhetoric and the General Public": A panel discussion among David Warsh, Craufurd Goodwin (see their chapters in volume), Joe Kalt (Economics, Harvard University), Karen Arenson (the *New York Times)*, and Robert Samuelson *(Newsweek).*

"Economic Rhetoric in the Political Arena": A panel discussion among Galbraith, Keohane (see their papers in this volume), and Jeffrey Sachs (Economics, Harvard University).

Other participants in the conference were:

Thomas Bayard (Ford Foundation)
Sheila Biddle (Ford Foundation)
Bruce Caldwell (Economics, UNC Greensboro)
David Colander (Economics, Middlebury College)
Colin Day (Cambridge University Press)
Neil de Marchi (Economics, Duke University).
Stephen Graubard (Daedalus)

Charles Kindleberger (Economics, Brandeis University)
J. J. Klant (Economics, University of Amsterdam)
Meir Kohn (Economics, Dartmouth College)
Students in the seminar on "The Art of Economic Persuasion" (Wellesley
   College)

Index